Pirating and Publishing

The Book Trade in the Age of Enlightenment

ROBERT DARNTON

OXFORD
UNIVERSITY PRESS

OXFORD
UNIVERSITY PRESS

Oxford University Press is a department of the University of Oxford. It furthers
the University's objective of excellence in research, scholarship, and education
by publishing worldwide. Oxford is a registered trade mark of Oxford University
Press in the UK and certain other countries.

Published in the United States of America by Oxford University Press
198 Madison Avenue, New York, NY 10016, United States of America.

© Oxford Univesity Press 2021

Library of Congress Cataloging-in-Publication Data
Names: Darnton, Robert, author.
Title: Pirating and publishing : the book trade in the age of Enlightenment /
by Robert Darnton.
Description: New York, NY : Oxford University Press, [2021] |
Includes bibliographical references and index.
Identifiers: LCCN 2020022939 (print) | LCCN 2020022940 (ebook) |
ISBN 9780195144529 (hardback) | ISBN 9780197529737 (epub)
Subjects: LCSH: Book industries and trade—France—History—18th century. |
Publishers and publishing—Government policy—France—History—
18th century. | Literature publishing—France—History—18th century. |
Authors and publishing—France—History—18th century. |
French imprints—Publishing—Foreign countries—History—18th century. |
Société typographique de Neuchâtel—History—18th century. |
Book industries and trade—Europe—History—18th century. |
Enlightenment—France.
Classification: LCC Z305 .D344 2021 (print) |
LCC Z305 (ebook) | DDC 381/.45002094409033—dc23
LC record available at https://lccn.loc.gov/2020022939
LC ebook record available at https://lccn.loc.gov/2020022940

DOI: 10.1093/oso/9780195144529.001.0001

1 3 5 7 9 8 6 4 2

Printed by Sheridan Books, Inc., United States of America

Contents

———◆———

Introduction

"ALL OF THE KNOWN universe is governed solely by books," Voltaire asserted, looking back at the end of his life on the battles he had fought against prejudice, ignorance, and injustice.[1] The Enlightenment as a whole was driven by the power of books. Yet under the Ancien Régime, the book trade was encumbered by conditions that would seem impossible today. There was no liberty of the press or copyright; there were no royalties or returns; and there was no limited liability. There were virtually no authors who lived from their pens and very few banks. There was also very little money—none, in fact, that took the form of paper bills guaranteed as legal specie by the state. How could books become such a force under such conditions?

This book is meant to explain their power by showing how the publishing industry operated.[2] It explores the ways that publishers behaved—their modes of thought and their strategies for translating intellectual capital into commercial value. Of course, the power of books lay primarily in their contents: the crack of Voltaire's wit, the grip of Rousseau's passion, the audacity of Diderot's thought experiments have rightly won recognition at the heart of literary history. But that history has not taken adequate account of the middlemen who brought literature to readers. Publishers played a decisive role at the juncture where literary, political, and economic history flowed into one another.

Historians generally date the emergence of the publisher as distinct from the bookseller and printer to some time in the first half of the nineteenth century.[3] In fact, publishers proliferated during the last years of the Ancien Régime in France and in much of Western Europe. Yet the concept of publisher and related ideas, such as intellectual property and piracy, remained ambiguous.

According to its most basic meaning, "to publish" is "to make public."[4] It could be argued, therefore, that publishers have existed ever since anyone spread the word about anything. Yet the term "publisher" (*éditeur* in French) did not come into general use until the nineteenth century.[5] Although, as will be shown, professionals within the book trade began to use the word in the 1770s, "bookseller" (*libraire*) generally prevailed.[6] The entry for "éditeur" in Diderot's *Encyclopédie* referred to the older notion of someone who prepared copy for printing—a usage that is closer to "editor" than to "publisher" in English.

When it came to pirating (*contrefaçon*), the *Encyclopédie* entered contested territory.[7] It explained that the noun referred to the reprinting of a book "to the prejudice of the person who possesses it by virtue of the property ceded to him by the author, a property made public and authentic by the privilege of the king or equivalent letters from the [royal] Seal." Pirating therefore raised the issue of intellectual property, and the *Encyclopédie* adopted a position taken by the booksellers' guild of Paris—namely, that the author had an absolute right of ownership to his text, a right of property equivalent to the ownership of land, and that he could transfer it unimpaired to a bookseller who produced it for sale.[8] A privilege for a book merely confirmed a preexisting right that was a matter of justice, not of the king's will—an assertion that the Crown rejected. The *Encyclopédie* entry on the verb "contrefaire" conveyed the same notion of absolute property, but then discussed the activity of pirates in a way that undermined it: "But . . . there is a real dishonor attached to this illicit commerce, because it breaks the most respectable connections in society, the confidence and good will in commerce. This damage and dishonor take place only within a country subjected to a common authority, because in relations between one foreigner and another usage seems to have authorized this injustice." In practice, therefore, piracy appeared to be a matter of social convention rather than normative standards; it conveyed dishonor. And although it violated a general principle of justice, it "seemed" to be legitimate if it took place outside the jurisdiction of a state where the original publication had occurred. Tied up in contradictions and inconsistencies, the uncertain, innovative concept of intellectual property did not provide an effective weapon against the practice of piracy.

Kant dealt with this knotty problem when he discussed the rights of authors in *The Metaphysics of Morals* (1797). Four years earlier, he had published the famous essay that began with a question, "What is Enlightenment?" This time, he asked a related question, "What is a book?" The answer led directly to the issue of piracy. Kant did not consider the composition of a book as the creation of property. Instead, he understood a book to be the expression of an author's thoughts as he exercised them in writing through the power of free speech. By giving a bookseller a "mandate" to sell a book that he had created, an author made the bookseller an agent who could speak to the public on his behalf, not a property owner. A pirate violated that right of agency. He stole the publisher's profits and therefore committed an action "forbidden as a matter of right," but he did not infringe a natural right of property.[9] This argument did not become absorbed in debates about copyright, but it illustrates the ambiguity inherent in the way books were understood at a time when piracy played a key part in the exchange of ideas.

Although pirates weren't philosophers and most likely did not read Kant, they could make use of the concept of a book as an expression of ideas rather than an item of property. By multiplying the number of books, they could argue, they contributed to the circulation of ideas; and by diffusing the works of the *philosophes*, they promoted Enlightenment. One pro-Enlightenment pirate, Fortuné Barthélemy de Félice, who churned out *contrefaçons* from Yverdon, Switzerland, made precisely that argument: "But I envisage books from a more noble viewpoint [than the view of them as articles of commerce], because I believe that good books do not belong to booksellers but rather to humanity, which needs to be enlightened and developed according to virtue. . . . Any bookseller or printer who by means of *contrefaçons* spreads good books more abundantly and rapidly, deserves well of humanity."[10]

Everyone understood that in practice literary property did not extend beyond the borders of individual countries, but no one could do anything to resolve that difficulty. In an attempt to solve the problem of piracy, a proposal to ban *contrefaçons* on an international scale had been submitted during the diplomatic deliberations connected with the Peace of Aix-la-Chapelle of 1748.[11] It got nowhere. The problem went beyond the lack of a universal copyright agreement. Books, authorship, publishing, pirating—all such concepts remained fluid and unfixed in early modern Europe.

The general ambiguity did not prevent a vast pirating industry from developing alongside the legal trade in publishing. On the contrary, while authorized publishers produced high-quality books for a wealthy elite, the pirates flourished, pursuing profits in the downscale sector of the market where a growing public clamored for inexpensive books. The opposition between the two modes of publishing resulted in large part from a conflict between Parisian and provincial booksellers. Thanks to the centralizing policies of the state, the Parisian Guild of booksellers and printers gained a dominant position in the trade by the end of the seventeenth century. Guild members monopolized book *privilèges* (the functional equivalent of copyrights; see the section "Technical Note: Terminology, Institutions, and Practices" for an explanation of this term and related others) and nearly destroyed publishing in the provinces, except in the case of certain genres such as local works, liturgical tracts, and popular chapbooks. By 1777, when it issued a set of largely ineffectual reforms, the state showed more sympathy for provincial publishers and booksellers. But the provincials remained hostile to the Parisians, and throughout the eighteenth century they increasingly drew supplies from publishing houses that produced French books from strategic locations outside France's borders in what I have called a Fertile Crescent. From Amsterdam to Brussels, through the Rhineland, across Switzerland, and down to Avignon, which was papal territory in the eighteenth century, publishers pirated everything that could be sold with any success in France.

The foreign houses also produced everything that could not get past censors employed by the French government. With notable exceptions such as the *Encyclopédie*, nearly all the works of the French Enlightenment were printed abroad, smuggled across the border, and distributed through an underground trade that extended everywhere in the kingdom. The Enlightenment was in large part a campaign to spread light—that is, to diffuse ideas, not merely to create them. French books produced in publishing houses outside France embodied the Enlightenment. By conveying its ideas across borders, they made it a force that pervaded the Ancien Régime. Yet the books of the *philosophes* occupied only a small portion of the market. Thanks to inexpensive paper and labor, as well as the avoidance of payment to authors, pirated books were much cheaper than works produced with *privilèges* in Paris. Therefore, a natural alliance grew between the foreign publishers and the provincial booksellers. It functioned so effectively that at least half the trade books—as opposed to chapbooks, devotional tracts, and ephemera—sold in France between 1750 and 1789 were pirated. That estimate is based on long study of all the available documents, and I admit I cannot prove it; but I doubt that anyone would question the importance of investigating the pirating industry, both in itself, because little is known about it, and for what it reveals about the opening up of literary culture to a broad public.

Far from being a peripheral aspect of sociocultural history, therefore, piracy deserves a place at its center.[12] By 1750 a boom in piracy was undermining the traditional mode of publishing in France. Pirates operated outside the law, or at least the French law. In a few provincial centers like Lyon and Rouen, booksellers secretly produced and marketed pirated books, but for the most part, they imported them from the numerous publishing houses beyond France's borders. The foreign publishers sometimes ran into trouble with local authorities, who could be as tough as the French when they discovered atheistic and seditious tracts, even those intended exclusively for export. But the sovereigns of city states, principalities, and autonomous municipalities like Geneva, Neuchâtel, Bouillon, Maastricht, and Amsterdam welcomed the economic benefit from pirate publishing, and in an age without international copyright there was nothing illegal about reprinting a French book outside France.

On the whole, the foreign publishers operated under few constraints other than the marketplace. They sought to satisfy demand with a willingness to take risks that made the publishers living off *privilèges* in Paris look like *rentiers*. Of course, as will be shown, some Parisians speculated on risky enterprises, and some foreign publishers avoided the most hazardous sectors of the trade. But most pirates raided markets with a spirit of audacious entrepreneurship. Although they were often solid bourgeois in their hometowns, they pursued profits with an uninhibited appetite for what Max Weber identified as booty capitalism,[13] whose character has not been fully understood, because its operations have not been studied up close, owing to a lack of source materials. This book tells the inside story of pirate publishing and takes its inspiration from Balzac as well as Weber. Balzac's *Illusions perdues* captures the scramble for prestige and profit among people in the book trade in the early nineteenth century. Publishers, booksellers, and authors inhabited an equally vivid world in the Age of Enlightenment, and their lives are worth recounting, not only for what they reveal about eighteenth-century culture, but also in themselves. They have a fascination of their own as stories within a *comédie humaine* peculiar to the Ancien Régime.

Although limited to the trade in France and neighboring regions, this book refers occasionally to England and Germany, where the same issues were handled in different ways.[14] The first chapters survey the history of publishing and the nature of the book trade in Paris, complex subjects that involve a great deal more than state power and corporatism. The human element added to the complexity, especially among the pirates, who appeared as patricians in some places and as rogues in others. Later chapters describe their biographies and businesses, following trails that lead from one dossier to another in the manuscript sources. Because the trails frequently crossed, it is possible to follow the formation of networks and to detect patterns in a general system of production and distribution.

The last chapters concentrate on the activities of one publisher, the Société typographique de Neuchâtel (STN), because it offers the richest material. The archives of the STN are the only papers of an eighteenth-century publishing house that have survived almost intact and are vast enough (about 50,000 letters) to reveal the inside story of pirate publishing and of publishing in general. Of course, they have a built-in bias, and I have tried to make allowances for the STN's particular character. Fortunately, many persons with intriguing dossiers in Neuchâtel also appear in the archives of the Bastille, the papers of the Parisian Guild, reports of the Parisian police, bankruptcy records, and various archives of the French administration.

Having worked through this material for more than fifty years, I hope to do justice to its richness. Although this book brings my research to an end, it does not pretend to reach anything comparable to a bottom line, for history is bottomless, and in this work I only hope to sound its depths.

Technical Note: Terminology, Institutions, and Practices

If any word can convey the richness and complexity of France's social order under the Ancien Régime, it is privilege. The term comes from the Latin meaning "private law." It characterized rights restricted to one person or group and denied to others. Although the nobility and clergy were known as privileged orders, they were not the only ones to enjoy privileges. Virtually everyone, including artisans in guilds and peasants in "pays de franc-salé" (areas that paid relatively low salt taxes), participated in the system of privileges. The notion of a general law, which fell equally on everyone, was alien to the nature of the Ancien Régime, a hierarchical society in which it was assumed that people were unequal and that inequality was ordained by God and built into the order of nature. Enlightenment philosophers, Rousseau in particular, contested the legitimacy of privileges, and the French Revolution destroyed them; but privilege was the cement that held institutions together in what the revolutionaries recognized in retrospect to have constituted a regime.

Privilege existed in three distinct ways in the book trade. First and above all, it inhered in books themselves, at least in the legal sector of the trade. Book *privilèges* were granted by the king, announced on the title pages of books, and printed in full length in their texts. To obtain a privilege, an author— or, more often, the bookseller to whom he had sold the manuscript—had to submit the text to the director of the book trade, who would assign it to a censor. If the censor approved it, he would notify the director, who would also approve it and pass the dossier on for a final approval by the Keeper of the Seals in the Royal Chancellery. Once it had cleared this last hurdle, a privilege would be issued in the name of the king. Its text, the *privilège* in the strict sense of the term, was addressed by the king to the officials in his courts and took the form of a decree, ending with the standard phrase "for such is our pleasure." To take legal effect, it had to be registered—that is, copied into a register kept by the Parisian booksellers' Guild. It was granted to a bookseller, who then enjoyed the exclusive right to produce and sell the book, usually for a certain number of years, although the right could be extended as a *continuation*, and booksellers frequently claimed that they owned it indefinitely.

In making this claim, they treated the *privilège* as a form of property. They often sold shares in it and willed it, as if it were a physical object, to their heirs. However, the Crown maintained that book *privilèges* derived from the grace of the king and could be limited or revoked according to the king's will. This concept of *privilège* differed considerably from the notion of copyright. To be sure, the first copyright law, the Statute of Anne passed by Parliament in 1710, was contested throughout the eighteenth century in English courts, but it belonged to a different conceptual universe from that of the French edicts on *privilèges*—as did the Danish copyright act of 1741, the first on the Continent. In order to emphasize its peculiar character, the French version of *privilège* will appear in italics throughout this book.

Second, the booksellers were privileged individuals. In conformity with royal regulations, they had to undergo an apprenticeship to a master, to fulfill various requirements, including an examination, and to be received in a guild. The system allowed for a few exceptions. It permitted a limited number of peddlers to hawk books; it tolerated *bouquinistes* who operated stalls in privileged areas (*lieux privilégiés*) such as the Palais-Royal in Paris; and it sold licenses (*brevets de libraire*) to some dealers in the provinces. In principle, however, no one could sell books who had not been admitted as a master in a guild. In 1781 there were 148 master booksellers and printers in the Parisian Guild. They included thirty-six widows who inherited masterships after the deaths of their husbands and often were tough and canny businesswomen.

Third, the guilds were privileged corporations. Not only did they have the exclusive right to engage in the book trade, but they also enjoyed certain tax exemptions and ran their own affairs by electing officers (*syndics* and *adjoints*) and holding meetings in the manner of other corporate bodies. They also had police powers such as the right to inspect book imports, bookshops, and printing shops. These responsibilities were executed by their governing body known as a *chambre syndicale*, a term that was also used to designate the physical setting in which book inspections and other business took place. In 1777 the Crown established twenty *chambres syndicales*, which covered all of France, each with its own area of jurisdiction. As explained in Chapters 1 and 2, the Parisian Guild, or Communauté des libraires et des imprimeurs de Paris, dominated the book trade throughout the kingdom and frequently came into conflict with the provincial guilds. To make its identity clear, it will be referred to in the following pages as the Guild with an uppercase "G."

The book trade was administered by a division of the chancellery known as the Direction de la librairie (referred to henceforth as the Direction). Under the guidance of a *directeur général*, it oversaw censorship and the granting of *privilèges*, the activities of *chambres syndicales*, and all conflicts within the trade. It also cooperated with book-trade inspectors attached to the municipal police. One of its main responsibilities was to repress the trade in pirated books, which were usually known as *contrefaçons*. But the Direction was understaffed, and it frequently had little idea of what was going on outside Paris.

The Direction cooperated with the police in the attempt to repress books that were forbidden because they offended religion, the state, morality, or the reputation of high-ranking individuals. In the jargon of the book trade, these extremely illegal works were known as *livres philosophiques*, although the police usually called them *mauvais livres* or, occasionally, *marrons*. French terms of these sorts will be retained and printed in italics (even when they are quotations) in order to get across the specificity of eighteenth-century practices, but I have tried to keep the use of French to a minimum and have done all the translating myself. The original quotations, given at greater length along with fuller descriptions of some technical aspects of the book trade, can be consulted in the French version of this book, published by Gallimard in a translation by Jean-François Sené.

One technicality that should be mentioned at the outset is the practice among publishers of swapping books. When they completed an edition, they frequently exchanged a large part of it, sometimes as much as half, for the equivalent value in books taken from the stock of an allied publisher. In this way, they reduced the risk of not selling all of their own edition and they increased the variety of their own stock. Exchanges were usually measured in sheets (*feuilles*) and recorded in special accounts. The sheet was the basic unit of production. Publishers calculated costs and profits in terms of sheets, and they normally shipped books in bales made up of unbound sheets. Binding was generally handled by consumers or retail booksellers.

Finally, it is important to have a clear idea of money and its value under the Ancien Régime. As explained in the final chapter, the working classes commonly dealt in coins made of copper such as *oboles* and *liards*. At the level of merchants, business was conducted in "account money" (*monnaie de compte*) consisting of livres, sous, and deniers: 12 deniers to the sou, 20 sous to the livre. The effective value of money can be calculated in different ways. Although its price varied, an ordinary, four-pound loaf of bread, which was the mainstay of a worker's daily diet, usually cost 8 sous. A skilled artisan generally made 30–50 sous a day, a semiskilled worker 20 sous, and an indigent laborer as little as 10 sous. Book prices varied enormously, but they often came to about 30 sous for an octavo volume of 200 pages. Payment from the retailer to the publisher took the form of bills of exchange (*lettres de change* or, more loosely, *effets*), which became due at the date specified on the bill. They could be negotiated at any time, although at a discount rate that could be very unfavorable to the holder. The key unit to keep in mind while following transactions is the *livre*, which as a rule of thumb can be thought of as the equivalent of a day's work for most urban laborers. It will be abbreviated as L. following a sum of money—e.g., "Rigaud of Montpellier paid 200 L. for a bale of books"—in order to avoid confusion with the French *livre* for book.

PART 1

PUBLISHING

1

The Rules of the Game

WHEN THE PRINTED WORD first appeared in France in 1470, the state did not know what to make of it. The authorities simply left the oversight of printing presses to the University of Paris, just as they had entrusted the university to supervise the work of scribes and booksellers throughout the Middle Ages. Although manuscript books could be turned out rapidly through an assembly-line kind of copying known as the pecia system, their production and sale remained confined for the most part to the Latin Quarter and a small public of customers, most of them students. In the sixteenth century, however, printing became an explosive force fueled by the spread of Protestantism. The monarchy reacted at first by attempting to extinguish it. On January 13, 1535, Francis I decreed that anyone who printed anything would be hanged. That policy did not work. Nor did a series of repressive measures adopted during the religious wars and the civic unrest that shook the kingdom until Louis XIV consolidated power in the second half of the seventeenth century. By 1700, the state had developed an elaborate mechanism to control printing and the book trade. From then until the Revolution, it issued edicts and ordinances of all kinds, at least 3,000 of them, in an effort to contain the power of the press, while the demand for books kept expanding, and printers and booksellers did their best to satisfy it. Yet the administration of the book trade in the eighteenth century cannot be reduced to the opposition of an authoritarian regime on the one hand and the book professionals on the other, nor can it be understood merely by studying the texts of edicts. Seen from the inside, it is a story of lobbying, string pulling, influence peddling, and power brokering—that is, politics of a kind peculiar to the Ancien Régime.[1]

The politicking took place out of sight, within a branch of the government known as the Direction de la librairie (henceforth the Direction). The word *bureaucrate* began to be used in the mid-eighteenth century, at a time when red tape—or *paperasse*, as it then was called—began to accumulate everywhere in the corridors of power. Paper piled up in such profusion in the

Direction that it can overwhelm anyone who ventures into the collections at the Bibliothèque nationale de France (henceforth BnF), where much of it has survived. Occasionally, however, a phrase leaps off the page. Here is a passage of prose-poetry buried incongruously in one of the memos. It is by Denis Diderot:[2] "What property can possibly belong to a man, if a work of his spirit, the unique fruit of his education, of his studies, his vigils, his time, his research, his observations, if his finest hours, the most beautiful moments of his life, if his own thoughts, the sentiments of his heart, the most precious portion of his self, that which does not perish, that which immortalizes him, does not belong to him?"

Diderot was discussing what is known today as intellectual property. His eloquence, so similar to that of John Milton in *Areopagitica*,[3] Milton's appeal for unlicensed publishing in 1664, reinforced an argument to loosen restrictions on the freedom of the press, yet it was buried and lost under the weight of the main business that occupied men in power at that time: not the creativity of authors—they counted for little—but the contending interests of booksellers and the attempts of the state to accommodate them while defending interests of its own. In fact, the purpose of Diderot's memoir was to support his publisher, André-François Le Breton, and the Parisian booksellers' Guild in a campaign to maintain their monopoly of book *privilèges*. In 1764 the new head of the Book Trade Administration, Antoine de Sartine, entertained ideas of undercutting the monopoly by limiting the duration of privileges. That would be outrageous, Diderot argued. By creating a text, an author acquired an unlimited right of property to the work of his imagination; and in purchasing the text, a publisher assumed an equally absolute right to that property. To be sure, the publisher had to have the text approved by a censor and then had to purchase a *privilège*, steps that gave him an exclusive right to sell the book, provided it had been registered by the Guild. But those formalities merely confirmed a preexisting right derived from the act of creation.

When the Guild submitted Diderot's memoir to the Direction, it left off his name, deleted the personal passages, and bowdlerized the argument so thoroughly as to eliminate any suggestion of sympathy for the freedom of the press (in his correspondence Diderot later referred to the memoir as a work on "la liberté de la presse.")[4] Despite the editing, the administrators in the Direction knew exactly what was going on, as we can tell by following the paper trail through the bureaucracy. Diderot had written the original memoir in the form of a letter to Sartine, whom he knew personally. Sartine received the Guild's reworked version of the letter and passed it on to Joseph d'Hémery, a veteran police inspector assigned to oversee the book trade. D'Hémery, who also knew Diderot and had years of experience in dealing with the Guild, submitted it to François Marin, the general secretary in the Direction. Marin then drew up a memo that refuted Diderot's argument by exposing it as an attempt to defend the Guild's domination of the trade. A comparison of the original and the doctored version of Diderot's memoir confirms that reading. Having gained a monopoly of most *privilèges*, the members of the Guild wanted them to be recognized by the state as a permanent kind of property, and they could not find a more eloquent spokesman for their cause than the archetypical *philosophe*.[5]

Diderot as a propagandist in a lobbying operation? The notion is bound to offend anyone who reveres him as the embodiment of the Enlightenment's spirit of free inquiry. Yet he was a man of his time, and nothing could be more typical of the ways of doing business under the Ancien Régime than petitioning the Crown for special advantage. From the perspective of the state, a book *privilège* was nothing more than a favor bestowed by the king. As Marin put it, "Privileges are only temporary *grâces,* very different from the possession of a house or of a plot of land."[6] *Grâce* or property? The question came to a head in a series of edicts issued by the Crown on August 30, 1777, which created a new general code to regulate publishing and bookselling—and used the term "droit d'auteur" (copyright) for the first time in an official document. The notion itself had a long history, however, and it was only one of many issues that the Direction attempted to sort out while accumulating *paperasse.*

When booksellers and printers began to emerge as a professional group in the sixteenth century, they remained within the jurisdiction of the University of Paris, whose main concern was still to prevent deviations from religious dogma by guaranteeing the accuracy of manuscript copies. With the advent of printing and Protestantism, this function evolved into the exercise of censorship—too important, from the viewpoint of the state, to be left entirely to professors in the Sorbonne. In 1566 the Ordonnance of Moulin, issued in the midst of France's bloody religious wars, shifted the control of publishing to the state by requiring that books receive *privilèges* sealed by the great seal of the Royal Chancellor or his substitute, the Keeper of the Seals. Meanwhile, the number of booksellers and printers expanded, although they remained formally members (*suppôts*) of the university. This status meant that unlike other trade groups, booksellers and printers did not acquire a corporate existence until the seventeenth century. On June 16, 1618, the Crown, which was consolidating its power under the Bourbons, created the Guild with statutes that spelled out its privileges, organization, and functions. The printing, selling, and binding of books was restricted to Guild members, who remained connected in principle to the university (they had to pass pro forma examinations proving their ability to read Latin and decipher Greek; the binders eventually formed a separate corporation) but became subordinate to the chancellor's office.

The Bourbons built the monarchy into an absolutist state, and in the process increased the power of the Guild and their own authority over it. Edicts of 1643, 1665, and 1686 laid down precise quality standards for paper and printing along with strict rules governing access to masterships and internal governance, all of them attuned to the spirit of Colbertism (the French variety of mercantilism named for the minister of finance under Louis XIV). Some were designed by Jean-Baptiste Colbert himself. The printing and selling of books was restricted to Guild members, who were also given the power to enforce their monopoly by policing the trade. The Guild's *syndics* and their deputies (*adjoints*) were to regularly inspect all printing and book shops and also all shipments of books that arrived from outside the city. In doing so, they served their own interests as well as the state, because they were to confiscate pirated as well as prohibited books. In 1667 Louis XIV imposed a powerful police organization on Paris, and it, too, enforced restrictions on the book industry. A succession of special inspectors of the book trade oversaw all printing and bookselling, dispatched a great many deviants to the Bastille, and even raided shops in faraway provinces. *Privilège* remained the basic principle of the system. Only Guild members could own *privilèges*, and they did not become legally effective until they were entered in a register kept by the Guild.

This general organization was imposed on the rest of France by other edicts over the course of the seventeenth century. Publishing had flourished in the provinces, especially in Lyon and Rouen, during the sixteenth century, and a few provincial printing-bookselling houses maintained large businesses for the next hundred years, producing books with the authorization of local officials. But they could not resist the combined power of the Crown and the Guild. In principle, they could acquire *privilèges*, but the traffic in them was increasingly limited to Paris, not only through the process of registration but also through commercial transactions, because the members of the Paris Guild limited the sale of *privilèges* to fellow Guild members, acquired them

in closed auctions, and divided them into portions (some as small as $\frac{1}{48}$),
which they also sold, used as dowries, and willed to their heirs in the expectation that they were a form of property that would last forever. At the same
time, the state reduced the number of presses throughout the kingdom and
even in Paris itself. The edict of August 1686, which provided the first general
code for the book trade, limited the number of printing shops in Paris to
thirty-six. A second code, issued on February 28, 1723, and extended to the
entire kingdom on March 24, 1744, brought all of these elements together
into a full-fledged regime for governing the production and sale of books.
Seen from the perspective of Versailles, the Crown and the Guild had combined to bring the printed word under control.[7]

Reality, of course, was different, though it is difficult to know what actually took place in towns across the kingdom. The best source of information is the archives of the Direction, and the best starting point for studying
them is the Code of 1723. It prescribed the organization of the Paris Guild in
enormous detail, along with rules concerning type, paper, presses, shipping,
apprenticeships, and all the activities of printers and booksellers. Yet when
it came to *privilèges*, the Code merely described established procedures: to
be published, a text had to receive the written approbation of a censor and
be sanctioned by the office of the chancellor; the approbation and *privilège*
had to be entered in the register of the Guild; and once registered, the work
could be printed and sold only by the Guild member who had acquired the
privilège. The Code did not define the nature of *privilèges* or specify how
long they would last. Nor did it mention authors, to say nothing of their
rights. Instead, its entire emphasis fell on the "rights, liberties, immunities,
prerogatives and privileges" of the Parisian Guild. In reiterating the prohibition of piracy, it set severe penalties for unauthorized reprints of books
with *privilèges* or "*continuations de privilèges*." The vagueness of the phrasing
left open the possibility that *continuations* could go on indefinitely, as Guild
members maintained. Although earlier legislation had required considerable augmentation of a text for its *privilège* to be continued, the Parisian
booksellers had ignored that requirement and had even claimed exclusive
rights to works that had long been in the public domain. By 1723 it seemed
that the Parisian Guild had gained a monopoly over most French literature.[8]

The publication of the Code of 1723 therefore touched off a polemic,
which for the first time made *privilèges* and vested interests a matter of public
debate. The case against the hegemony of the Parisian Guild was argued in
a pamphlet, *Mémoire sur les vexations qu'exercent les libraires et imprimeurs*

de Paris (1725), by Pierre-Jacques Blondel, a cleric with a deep knowledge of the publishing industry, and the case in favor of the Guild took the form of a legal memoir addressed to the Keeper of the Seals and written by a prominent lawyer, Louis d'Héricourt.

Blondel heaped scorn on the master printers and booksellers—a feckless lot, he argued, who combined ignorance, incompetence, and greed in an outrageous monopoly, which they exercised by influence over state policy. Far from reforming the book trade, the latest code merely reinforced its abuses—and Blondel gave many examples of them, naming names and exposing profit gouging with damning precision. Yet he did not challenge the basic principles of the system—censorship, corporatism, or the concept of the *privilège* itself. Far from advocating freedom of thought in the manner of the Enlightenment, he evoked a world of classical scholarship and religious writing from a century earlier. The most original aspect of his argument was its defense of the interests of authors. They did the true work of creation, he argued, while the booksellers creamed off the profits from their labor. Blondel's stress on the creativity of authors came close to making a case for intellectual property but did not quite get there.[9]

D'Héricourt, by contrast, offered a full-fledged argument in favor of the "droits des auteurs," though only as a way to justify the unlimited property rights of the Parisian booksellers against the incursions from provincial dealers. By writing texts, he claimed, authors gained a right to them that was every bit as absolute as the kind of property acquired in the purchase of a house or a plot of land, and the sale of those texts transmitted the same rights to booksellers.[10] *Privilèges* expired, he admitted, but that did not release the texts into the public domain, where they could be reprinted by anyone, because the property right existed independently of a royal *privilège*, which merely confirmed it. This argument reduced the king's authority over literary property to a "happy impotence"; it confirmed the monopoly of the Parisian Guild; and it condemned the "odious conduct" of the provincial booksellers in opposition to the law-abiding behavior of the Parisians.[11] D'Héricourt outdid Blondel in asserting the property rights of authors while advocating the opposite cause—namely, the economic monopoly of the Guild. Either way, the issue appeared as a contest of vested interests, which pitted Paris against the provinces, rather than as an elevated debate over state policy.

The state, still an absolute monarchy, did not appreciate "impotence" as a way of characterizing its authority. The Keeper of the Seals, Fleuriau d'Armenonville, was so outraged by the Guild's pamphlet that he forced its *syndic* and deputies to resign, and the printer who produced it fled from Paris in order to escape imprisonment in the Bastille.[12] Yet, in a manner typical of the Ancien Régime, the general issues remained unresolved while all the parties went about their business as they had always done, gaining whatever leverage they could whenever they could. The Code of 1723, extended to the entire kingdom in 1744, continued to determine the norms of the book trade, tested and stretched in one direction or another as conflicts occurred during the mid-century years.

The best-known incidents evoked sympathies attached to three authors from the seventeenth century, which was coming to be known in retrospect as "le grand siècle": Thomas Corneille, Jean de La Fontaine, and François Fénelon. Voltaire's *Le Siècle de Louis XIV*, published in 1751, spread the notion that the Sun King's reign was a golden age, when French civilization reached its highest point, thanks in large part to the greatness of its writers. Unfortunately, some of the writers' descendants had fallen on hard times during the subsequent reign. Had they been able to collect income from the continued sales of their ancestors' works, they would have been rescued from penury, but the *privilèges* remained in the hands of the booksellers. Voltaire rescued a descendant of Corneille (not in a direct line, as he originally believed, nor absolutely penniless, as he liked to proclaim) by producing a new edition of Corneille's works (heavily annotated and therefore eligible for a fresh *privilège*) in 1764 and turning the proceeds over to her, with much fanfare about the nation's duty to honor the memory of its greatest authors. The *privilège* to the works of La Fontaine had been sold and resold to several booksellers, but the King's Council ignored those transactions by awarding a fifteen-year *privilège* to his impoverished granddaughters in 1761. Faced with a threat to its basic source of income, the officers of the Guild then smothered the affair by buying the new *privilège* and turning the money from the sale over to the granddaughters. In the case of Fénelon's works, the King's Council decreed in 1771 that the original *privilège* could not be continued without the consent of his heirs, but after a long, legal battle the courts upheld the claims of the booksellers, leaving the issue of *continuations* unresolved but tilted in favor of indefinite renewal. Meanwhile, however, an obscure but intrepid author, Pierre-Joseph Luneau de Boisgermain, dared to produce a newly annotated edition of Racine and to sell it himself, even though he was not a member of the Guild. The Guild protested against this obvious violation of the Code of 1723, but in 1770 the King's Council ruled in favor of Boisgermain.[13]

Although these cases indicated a growing inclination of the authorities to favor authors, they had little cumulative effect and left many questions dangling: Did authors possess rights to their works? Did the rights of booksellers derive from *privilèges* granted by the Crown? Did *privilèges* last indefinitely? And could the virtual monopoly of *privilèges* by members of the Parisian Guild justify the virtual exclusion of provincial booksellers from the publishing industry? While the rules that governed the industry remained as obscure as they had been a century earlier, booksellers and printers continued with business as usual—and business boomed. The middle decades were the best of the century for France as a whole. Harvests returned record surpluses, the economy expanded, the population grew, consumption flourished, and literacy rates increased—all indicators pointed to the emergence of a society freed from much of the misery that had weighed it down a century earlier. Of course, ignorance and poverty persisted on an appalling scale, and economic historians disagree about the incidence and the extent of the improved conditions. But overall, France entered a phase of growth that contrasted substantially to the famine, pestilence, and war that had ravaged the population during "le grand siècle."[14]

While the first stirrings of a consumer society certainly stimulated the book trade, they did not produce anything like the general reading public that emerged in the mid-nineteenth century.[15] Nonetheless, in place of the small elite that had bought devotional tracts and Latin classics in the age of Louis XIV, a heterogeneous public of readers, mainly from the professional classes, clergy, and nobility, now spent several dozen livres a year on an increasingly wide variety of books. The popular new genres included the works of fiction and philosophy that eventually came to be identified with the Enlightenment. In fact, the most important works of the *philosophes* appeared in print during the mid-century years—from Montesquieu's *De l'esprit des lois* (1748), Diderot's *Lettre sur les aveugles* (1749), and Rousseau's *Discours sur les sciences et les arts* (1750) to Rousseau's *Contrat social* (1762), his *Émile* (1762) and Voltaire's *Candide* (1759), his *Traité sur la tolérance* (1763), and his *Dictionnaire philosophique* (1764). This succession of philosophical works was framed at either end by Diderot's *Encyclopédie*, whose first volume appeared in 1751 and whose last volume of text (volume 17; the last of the ten volumes of plates came out in 1772) was published in 1765.

In retrospect, the publications of those astonishingly creative years, from 1748 to 1765, left such a mark on French culture that the entire century came to be known as the Age of Enlightenment. At the time, however, the public's attention concentrated on other things—Jansenism (an austere variety of Catholicism condemned as heretical by the papacy); the affairs of the parlements (law courts that often opposed royal edicts, although they were not representative bodies comparable to the British Parliament); court intrigues (the rise and fall of factions and royal mistresses, notably Mme de Pompadour); the victories of the maréchal de Saxe during the War of the Austrian Succession (1740–1748); the loss of an overseas empire during the Seven Years' War (1756–1763); and the dissolution of the Jesuits (1764). Was Voltaire better known to Parisians than "le Grand Thomas," a theatrical tooth puller who operated on the Pont Neuf? Probably, but it would be wrong to assume that France devoted most of its attention to the *philosophes*. Their works occupied a relatively small sector of the literary marketplace before 1765, when the Enlightenment entered a new phase, one marked more by popularization than creation. The reading public consumed devotional booklets, sermons, travel memoirs, histories, medical tracts, treatises on natural history, self-help manuals, and all sorts of literature, from chapbooks to the classics, some in Latin, many in translation.

All these books were published with *privilèges* owned by members of the Parisian Guild, and nearly all were pirated. Pirating was an inevitable response to the monopoly of the Guild and the constraints on publishing imposed by the state. Having lost the trade war with the Parisians in the previous century, the provincial booksellers fell back on the illegal but lucrative commerce in *contrefaçons*. Some of them, especially in Lyon and Rouen, produced their own pirated editions, but most relied on imports from abroad. Foreign publishers of French books had proliferated since the sixteenth century, when Amsterdam and Geneva provided Protestant works to Huguenots within France. This trade grew into a major industry with the increased persecution of Huguenots culminating in the revocation of the Edict of Nantes in 1685, which outlawed Protestantism in France and deprived Protestants of civic rights. The flood of Huguenot refugees in the late seventeenth century included printers and booksellers, who joined their predecessors or set up shops of their own across France's borders. By 1750, France was surrounded to the north and east by a string of publishing houses, extending from Amsterdam to Geneva and down to Avignon, the papal enclave in southeastern Provence. Along with Protestant tracts, these publishers produced everything that could not pass the censorship within the kingdom, including most of the works of the *philosophes*. Some of the publishers—notably Marc-Michel Rey in Amsterdam, Jean-François Bassompierre in Liège,

Pierre Rousseau in Bouillon, and Gabriel Cramer in Geneva—developed special lines in Enlightenment literature. Some—certainly Rey and Pierre Rousseau—embraced Enlightenment as a cause, one that represented tolerance and reason in opposition to persecution and bigotry, although the lack of documentation makes it difficult to estimate the degree of their engagement. But whatever their private convictions might have been, publishers were businessmen, and their business was to satisfy the growing demand for books—books of all kinds, not just the few that posterity has selected in histories of French literature.[16]

The rise in demand could not be satisfied within the book-trade structure inherited from the seventeenth century. By 1750, an enlarged reading public was eager to purchase a wide variety of literature at the lowest possible prices. Books produced in Paris cost far more than those published abroad. Parisian publishers usually had to buy a manuscript from the author and to print it according to quality standards set by royal edicts. The foreign publishers could reprint books that had already proven their ability to sell. They paid far less for paper and labor, and they could eliminate what they called *luxe typographique*—that is, wide margins, airy spacing between letters and lines, the use of fresh fonts of type, illustrations, notes, and appendices. Only rarely did the pirates attempt to counterfeit (*contrefaire*) an original edition by reproducing it exactly, and they did not hesitate to cut a text or even add to it if they thought the changes would increase their profit. They represented a new element in publishing history: the production of downmarket books for a mass-market public. To do so, of course, they had to get their books across the border and into bookshops everywhere in France. That could be a complex and costly undertaking. But the foreign publishers came to rely on provincial booksellers who had been relegated to the margins of the industry by the monopolists of Paris. By the middle of the eighteenth century, the dominant trend in publishing had shifted from a Paris-centered luxury trade to a broad national market based on collaboration between foreign pirates and provincial retailers.

This argument requires nuancing, as will be clear in what follows, but it conforms to the view of the official in charge of the book trade, Chrétien Guillaume de Lamoignon de Malesherbes, who was director of the book trade during those crucial years, from 1750 to 1763. In 1759, at the request of the Dauphin, heir to the throne of Louis XV, Malesherbes wrote five confidential *Mémoires sur la librairie*. Although he could hardly advocate overthrowing regulations that had governed the trade for at least a century, he argued that the system had become radically dysfunctional. The standards and procedures for granting *privilèges* were so rigid that they excluded a vast amount of current literature. In fact, as he later argued in his *Mémoire sur la liberté de la presse*, a person who read nothing but books that carried *privilèges* would "be a century behind" in keeping up with intellectual life. As a way to offset the inflexibility of the official system, Malesherbes advocated the use of "tacit permissions," a regulatory loophole that went back to 1709 and that made it possible to publish a book without a *privilège*. To receive a tacit permission, a book had to be approved by a censor, but the approval remained secret and the title page usually indicated that it had been printed outside France, even if the printing had occurred in Paris. Should the content offend someone in authority, such as a bishop, a powerful magistrate in the Parlement of Paris, or an influential courtier, the book could be discretely withdrawn from the market, and the Crown would not have been compromised. Under Malesherbes, the use of tacit permissions increased enormously—from an average of fourteen a year to seventy-nine, nearly 30 percent of all books authorized during his period as directeur de la librairie.[17]

The Malesherbes administration has rightly been celebrated as a critical period to the survival of the Enlightenment. Only twenty-seven when he took charge of the book trade, Malesherbes sympathized with many of the new ideas advocated by the *philosophes*. On several occasions, he intervened to protect them. The most famous occurred in 1759, when it seemed that everyone in power, from the pope to the Parlement of Paris, the King's Council, the Sorbonne, and many influential members of the clergy, especially among the Jesuits, was determined to destroy the *Encyclopédie*. Following the publication of volume 7, the King's Council revoked its *privilège*, and Malesherbes secretly warned Diderot that the police were about to descend on his study and seize his papers. Desperate to save his working materials, Diderot asked where he could store them, and Malesherbes obliged by taking them into his own residence, where, he assured Diderot, no one would think to look for them.[18] Although the story has been told so often that it has taken on the proportions of myth, Malesherbes certainly provided enough cover for Diderot to continue work and for the last ten volumes of text to appear in Paris under the false address of Neuchâtel in 1765. But the decisive factors probably were political and economic. By having the *privilège* revoked, Malesherbes prevented the Parlement of Paris from interfering with the Crown's authority over the book trade. And he saved the publishers of the

Encyclopédie, a consortium led by André-François Le Breton, from losing a fortune. Le Breton was one of the few great entrepreneurs in the Parisian Guild, and the *Encyclopédie* as an enterprise, one that changed hands and went through many editions, produced millions of livres in profits—the most, its backers believed, that any book had earned in the entire history of French publishing.

Despite his connections with the *philosophes*, Malesherbes can hardly be considered a fifth-column agent of the Enlightenment. As the son of Chancellor Guillaume de Lamoignon de Blancmesnil, the supreme head of France's judicial system, he was a loyal servant of the state. While functioning as director of the book trade, he succeeded his father as premier président de la Cour des aides, which adjudicated tax cases. Taxes probably occupied him more than books. In fact, his knowledge of the book trade apparently was limited. He relied on a tiny staff and did not correspond regularly with the *chambres syndicales* of the provincial guilds that supposedly regulated the trade outside of Paris. His main concern was not merely to free publishing from some of the constraints of censorship but also to make it economically more viable. He detested the "odious monopoly"[19] of the Parisian Guild, and he deplored the shift of printing to presses outside France, a move that drained capital from the kingdom and promoted the sale of pirated editions, especially in the provinces, which had suffered so badly from the dominance of Paris. Despite the best of intentions, however, Malesherbes failed to transform the system. He left it in 1763 pretty much as he had found it in 1750.

When Malesherbes's successor, Antoine Raymond Gabriel de Sartine, took over the Direction in 1763, it was clear that the state needed to reform the abuses and inequities of the publishing industry. Sartine prepared the way for a new general code of the book trade by organizing a vast survey of all the printing shops and book businesses in the kingdom. Royal *intendants* and their subordinates (*subdélégués*, usually non-paid local officials) filled out forms with detailed reports about presses, type fonts, employees, genres of books on sale, estimated value of the stock, reputation of the booksellers, and the extent of the trade in their area. Although the state had collected similar data earlier, notably in 1701, never before had it accumulated so much information about an industry that by now had become a powerful force, despite its subjection to an archaic code of regulations.[20]

The lobbying to influence the future code gathered momentum from the moment Sartine arrived. Diderot's memoir, or the expurgated version of it submitted by the Guild in 1764, was the first salvo in the new battle to determine the government's policy. As mentioned earlier, the officials in the Direction received it skeptically, because they recognized the vested interest behind it. But they had other factors to take into consideration, above all the problem of piracy. Provincial booksellers had relied increasingly on *contrefaçons* during the first half of the century, while the Parisian publishers extended their monopoly of *privilèges* and the demand for inexpensive books kept growing.

An incident a few years earlier, in 1752, dramatically revealed that these factors—demand and piracy—had upset the book market.[21] In September, the officers of the Paris Guild got wind of an underground trade in *contrefaçons* being conducted in Paris by a binder turned peddler named Louis-Vincent Ratillon. They dispatched the police to raid the stockrooms where he stored his books and confiscated ninety-seven bundles of pirated works, along with all of his accounts and correspondence. Ratillon was sent to the Bastille, where he revealed the names of his suppliers, and the police eventually uncovered a network of booksellers who dealt heavily in pirated works, extending from Paris to Versailles, Rouen, Dijon, Amiens, and Blois. One of them, Robert Machuel of Rouen, printed *contrefaçons* on his own presses. The others drew their stock from him and from foreign publishers, both in Flanders and in Avignon, which, as noted, was then a papal territory. Further raids in Rouen indicated that the trade in *contrefaçons* extended to "nearly all the cities of the kingdom," according to the police reports.[22] Compared with earlier police action, this discovery was an important breakthrough in the attempts of the Parisians to stifle illegal competition.

The Guild officers followed it up with petitions for stronger measures to extirpate all piracy, which, they claimed, had badly damaged their trade. Most of the implicated provincial dealers received harsh punishment—fines, imprisonment, and in the case of Robert Machuel expulsion from the profession. Yet some of the provincials seemed unrepentant. François Desventes of Dijon, who paid a fine of 500 L., said in his defense that the high wholesale prices charged by the Guild had forced him to seek cheaper sources of supply and to pursue a downmarket strategy—namely, to lower his prices and to serve a broad range of customers, thereby increasing the consumption of books and benefiting the public.[23]

While urging the Direction to suppress piracy more effectively, the Guild then took action on its own. In June 1754 its members voted to tax themselves at an annual rate of 50 L. apiece in order to create a fund to finance inspections and raids of provincial bookshops. Soon afterward,

Michel-Antoine David, a deputy *syndic* of the Guild (and also one of the publishers of the *Encyclopédie*), set off for the south of France on a mission, financed by the fund, to destroy the piracy trade linked to the book fair in Beaucaire, just outside Avignon. Although the general Code of 1723 authorized the Guild officers to police the trade in Paris, it did not empower them to inspect bookshops throughout the kingdom. But David received clearance from the chancellery and cooperation from the local intendant. On July 22, he engineered a raid on the book fair, which resulted in the confiscation of about eighty different *contrefaçons*—not a great haul, he admitted, because it included only a few copies per title. Further detective work led to the conclusion that the Beaucaire fair had ceased to be the main outlet for the pirated works printed in Avignon. Most of them, estimated by David's informants to be worth more than 200,000 L. a year, were sold by swarms of peddlers, who bought their stock directly from the Avignonnais publishers and flogged it everywhere in southern France. In a report on his mission, David claimed that the trade could be stopped only by rigorous inspections along all the routes that led out of Avignon. The Guild adopted his recommendations in a memoir submitted to the Direction in September, and it continued to stress them in subsequent lobbying. Privileged books could not compete with pirated books on an open market, it argued. The foreign publishers, whether in Avignon or elsewhere, took advantage of much cheaper production costs and did not have to purchase original manuscripts. The only answer to the problem of piracy was tougher policing.[24]

The provincial booksellers did not see things that way. Although they did not defend piracy, they contested the Parisians' notion of *privilège*; and suppression, as they described it in their own memoirs and petitions, amounted to little more than an abuse of power by the Parisian Guild. In May 1761, Jean-Baptiste Garnier, one of the most powerful booksellers in Paris, organized a raid on the business of Jean-Marie Bruyset, one of the wealthiest and most respectable bookseller-printers in Lyon. Garnier sent his wife and an aide to oversee the operation. They enlisted a police inspector with a squad of agents to surround Bruyset's house, bookshop, printing shop, and two warehouses; to close off all the entrances and exits; and to search the premises for a putative *contrefaçon* of a religious tract, *Traité de la confiance en Dieu*. Garnier had acquired a six-year *privilège* for the book in 1752. Considering that the *privilège* had expired, Bruyset had reprinted it, and in an indignant protest to the Direction he defended his right to do so. At stake, he insisted, was a question of principle: did *privilèges* continue indefinitely, or did books fall in the public domain after a prescribed number of years? According to Bruyset, Garnier had not only taken an untenable stand on the general issue, but he had also resorted to an outrageous use of force. A crowd of 300 had gathered from all over Lyon to watch the police swarm over his property. Rumors then spread that Bruyset was being forced into bankruptcy; his creditors threatened to cut off funds; and his competitors had gained an unfair advantage, because his confidential accounts and correspondence had been exposed to the public gaze. He had suffered an injury to his reputation, honor, and credit; and he wanted to collect damages: 20,000 L. along with the return of fourteen supposedly pirated copies of *Traité de la confiance en Dieu*, which were all the police had found.[25]

The damage was compounded, in Bruyset's eyes, by a related case in which several Parisian booksellers had accused him of pirating a *Dictionnaire portatif des cas de conscience*. They collectively owned a *privilège* for it that was due to expire in 1762, but the book had been out of print for four years. Bruyset had reprinted a revised version of an Avignon edition, and he had done so with the permission of the Direction. Far from having suffered any loss, he argued in another petition to the Direction, the Parisians merely wanted to assert their domination over the provincial booksellers—in fact, to reduce the provincials to "a shameful slavery." In protesting against this oppression, he claimed to express the general view of the "provincial booksellers who do not want to be humiliated and reduced to the vile function of pedlars for the booksellers of the capital."[26]

The archives do not reveal how this quarrel was resolved, but they contain plenty of evidence about increased quarreling during the years following Sartine's arrival in 1763, while the Parisian and provincial booksellers argued their cases within the French bureaucracy.[27] Everyone in the trade knew that a new code was being prepared, and everyone wanted to influence it in favor of his own interests. In 1769, another member of the Bruyset dynasty in Lyon, Pierre Bruyset-Ponthus, submitted a "Mémoire sur les contrefaçons" to the Direction de la librairie, a document arguing that the commerce in pirated books had become so extensive that it now was a fundamental ingredient throughout the provincial trade. Any attempt to eradicate it suddenly and by force, as the Parisians advocated, would ruin most provincial booksellers. In setting policy, therefore, the Direction should take account of economic realities. It should tolerate piracy in the short run and eliminate it gradually by winning the support of officers in the provincial guilds and concentrating on the repression of their competitors, the illegal peddlers.[28]

The Parisians replied by taking action. In 1773 and 1775, they organized more raids on Lyonnais bookshops just as they had done in 1761. Having received authorization from the lieutenant general of police, Widow Desaint, one of the toughest of the many widows in the Guild and a formidable publisher in her own right, sent some agents to search the shops of Regnault and Duplain in Lyon in August 1773. They came up with so few *contrefaçons* that she herself led another search in November, accompanied by a large squadron of bailiffs and police agents. According to a protest sent by the Lyonnais, the printing shops and warehouses of Regnault, Duplain, Barret, Grabit and other Lyonnais dealers were surrounded, closed to prevent anyone from entering or exiting, and rigorously searched from two o'clock in the afternoon until three in the morning on November 2–3. Although thirty-two persons ransacked all the premises, they found little incriminating evidence, the Lyonnais claimed. One printing shop was caught running off copies of a work whose *privilège* belonged to Widow Desaint, but the *privilège* had been prolonged by two or three *continuations,* making it illegitimate in the eyes of the Lyonnais. They therefore protested with more petitions, supported by their colleagues in Rouen, Toulouse, Marseille, and Nîmes, in 1774.

Meanwhile, the Parisians sent counter-petitions, and Widow Desaint exacted an order from the Paris police to conduct yet a third raid. She hired spies to keep the Lyon shops under surveillance until October 1775, when she struck again, this time with a large force of police agents led by two of her Parisian allies, Didot the younger and Fournier. Again they surrounded the shops and warehouses of several Lyonnais printer-booksellers, searched everything, including even the pockets of the booksellers, went through private papers, and yet again failed to find a single *contrefaçon*. More protests came from the Lyonnais, supported by their allies in other cities, who by now were convinced that the Parisians intended to destroy the independence of all provincial booksellers and to take over their trade, reducing them to the role of distributors of the overpriced works produced in Paris.[29]

The battle over *privilèges* was exacerbated by another economic issue, which generated an equally intense round of lobbying—namely, a tax on paper and an import duty on books.[30] These measures cut to the heart of the publishing industry, and they affected different sectors of it in different ways. Although various kinds of stamp duties on paper had existed in several European countries since the 1620s, royal edicts, including the general Code of 1723, had exempted French books from taxation. Yet the need for fresh sources of revenue increased along with the disastrous deficit created by the Seven Years' War (1756–1763) between France and England.[31] When faced with the same fiscal pressure, Britain had tried to impose a stamp tax on paper in the American colonies in 1765, and the result was the first great explosion of protest against British rule. Although conditions were less combustible in France, a tax on paper was certain to arouse strong protests. However, the French parlements, which had provided the main opposition to taxation, were reorganized and stripped of their political power by a series of measures beginning in December 1770 by Chancellor René-Nicolas-Charles-Augustin de Maupeou, the minister at the head of the judicial system. This coup cleared the way for a reform of the state's' finances by abbé Joseph Marie Terray, controller general of finances, and one of the first new measures was a tax on paper promulgated on March 1, 1771, at the height of the political agitation.[32]

Paper represented at least half the production costs of books, depending on the size of the press run and the quality of the material. The tax came to 20 sous per ream (a ream contained 500 sheets), and in January 1782 it was increased by a surtax, making it 30 sous per ream. In practice, as the booksellers calculated, the taxation meant that a ream of good "papier d'Auvergne" commonly cost 11 L., as opposed to a comparable ream that the foreign publishers could procure for 8 L. Moreover, exports of French paper paid no tax at all. Therefore, the government imposed a heavy burden on French publishers and at the same time put them at a disadvantage relative to their foreign competitors, who already benefited from cheaper production costs and of course paid nothing for the manuscript when they pirated a book. To enforce these measures, the government announced that it would create new teams of agents who would collect the tax and inspect printing shops and bookshops, levying heavy penalties for infractions.[33]

Word of the proposed tax had leaked to the members of the Paris Guild before its publication, and they responded with vehement protests both to the chancellor and to the controller general of finances. All Europe now read French, they emphasized; French books were in great demand, and as instruments of French culture, they should continue to be protected by the government. Yet the paper tax would drive the publishing industry outside the kingdom, decimating all the trades that had grown up around it and producing far too little in revenue to offset the loss to the general economy, a loss that would come to at least 10 million L. a year.[34] The Guild elaborated on this argument in a protest submitted soon after the publication of the edict of March 1. The tax, they objected, would cover all printed documents, even ephemera; it would apply retroactively to books already in stock; it would be impossibly cumbersome to collect; and while stimulating a boom in foreign publishing, it would produce "the total ruin of printers and booksellers and the destruction of the book trade throughout the kingdom."[35]

The Guild's protest resonated with all the other agitation against the Maupeou-Terray policies. According to a current news sheet, a "torrent" of pamphlets attacked the paper tax as well as other measures.[36] On September 11, 1771, the government responded with another decree, which in principle would redress the balance in favor of the French publishers while providing still more income: a duty of 60 L. per hundredweight on all imports of French and Latin books.[37] Far from welcoming this decree, however, the Guild objected that it would consummate the ruin of their industry. They wanted to destroy pirate publishing, not to cease all trade with foreign publishers. That trade depended in large part on exchanges—that is, on swapping portions of their own editions against an assortment of equal value from the stock of foreign houses. By raising the cost of imports, the tariff would decimate the exchange trade and, along with it, all exports of books, for the French could not expect foreign publishers to buy their books if the duty made the foreigners' editions prohibitively expensive. Worse, the duty would actually stimulate the production of *contrefaçons* outside France. Unable to procure French books by exchanges, the foreign houses would simply reprint them and take over the market for French publications in the rest of Europe.[38]

In the face of these protests, the government began to backtrack. On November 24, 1771, it reduced the import duty to 20 L. per hundredweight. Two years later, it acknowledged that the reduction had not been enough to restore the foreign trade and cut the duty to 6 L. 10 sous.[39] Finally, on April 23, 1775, it eliminated the duty altogether. By that time, Louis XVI had succeeded to the throne; he had dismissed the ministers of Louis XV and had appointed Anne Robert Jacques Turgot as controller general of finances. As part of his effort to liberalize the conditions of trade, Turgot restored the traditional exemption of books from tariffs. Unlike the earlier edicts, which had justified the duty as a way to protect French printing, the text of the edict of 1775 emphasized that "the book trade deserves special protection, considering its utility for letters and public instruction."[40] Yet the government never withdrew the lucrative tax on paper. The Guild was still protesting it in the cahiers that it submitted before the election to the Estates General in 1788, on the eve of the Revolution.[41]

For four years, between 1771 and 1775, the state had issued edict after edict, and the booksellers had replied with "memorandums upon memorandums," protesting every move.[42] The measure that created the most damage, according to the material piled up in the Direction, was the paper tax of March 1, 1771: "It is since then that the Swiss, realizing that they could sell our books at 50 percent less than what we charge, have pillaged and ravaged our trade," wrote a disgruntled bookseller.[43] To be sure, he added, the disparity in production costs had favored the Swiss long before the disastrous tax. "The Swiss pirate everything—good books, bad books, large and small works, everything has become their prey."[44] The provincial booksellers also deplored the paper tax, though they benefited from the economic advantages that it gave to their foreign suppliers, and they avoided the subject of piracy in their protests. While damaging the book trade in general, therefore, the government's taxes and tariffs exacerbated the conflict between the provincials and the Parisians.

There was a larger dimension to this conflict, because the opposition between guild monopolies and open markets existed everywhere in Europe, notably in Britain.[45] The Stationers' Company in London dominated the English book trade in the same way that the Parisian Guild did in France, and it maintained its supremacy by using many of the same tactics and arguments. Although the Statute of Anne, passed by Parliament in 1710 and named for the queen, subjected earlier notions of literary property to the new concept of copyright, the Londoners construed copyright exactly as the Parisians interpreted *privilège*—to be an unlimited kind of property derived from the creative labor of an author. The statute of 1710 restricted the publishers' "rights to copy"—that is, the exclusive right to reproduce and sell texts—to fourteen years, renewable once. But the members of the Stationers' Company, backed by the ablest lawyers in England, claimed that according to natural rights inherent in the Common Law, they enjoyed perpetual ownership of the texts they had purchased from authors. While the lawyers fought over the legal principles in a long series of cases, the Londoners tried to enforce their rights over recalcitrant booksellers in the rest of the country. They even engaged "riding officers" to raid bookshops that sold cheap reprints published in Scotland and Ireland. In February 1774 the issue was resolved by a decision in the House of Lords, which acted as the highest court of appeal, in the case of *Donaldson v. Becket*. Far from being perpetual, copyright was limited to fourteen years, renewable once; books that had fallen in the public domain could be reprinted and sold in an open market.

When news of the decision in *Donaldson v. Becket* reached Lyon, the local publishers rejoiced. Benoît Duplain, the *syndic* of the Lyonnais guild, wrote to a Parisian correspondent that the French should take inspiration from the English example. Booksellers in all the provincial cities should join forces to block the attempt of the Parisians to take over the public domain and make *privilèges* last forever by means of *continuations*. The Lyonnais *chambre syndicale* hired a lawyer to bring their case to the Conseil du Roi in a formal petition, which they printed and circulated among their allies. The petition recounted all their grievances, stressing the "scandalous confiscations" of the raids in Lyon. Although it conceded that in principle authors had an exclusive right to income from their creation, it insisted that they could not transfer any such right to a publisher by selling their work. Above all, it stressed the economic aspect to the dispute. The reading public had expanded dramatically during the course of the last fifty years, it explained, and these new consumers wanted cheaper books. Yet the Guild kept production low and prices high by exploiting its monopoly on *privilèges*. In consequence, many booksellers and printers had set up businesses across France's borders, where they produced cheap books in order to satisfy the demand inside the kingdom. They often sold *contrefaçons* in France for 20–30 sous (1 to 1½ L.), whereas the Parisian editions cost 3–4 L. The Parisians maintained their monopoly by privileged access to the seat of power, where the royal administration had given them favorable treatment ever since the trade wars of the seventeenth century. But now at last the time had come for the Crown to hear the protests from the provinces, to organize the book trade on an equitable basis, and to begin by abolishing all *continuations* of *privilèges*, except in cases in which at least a quarter of the text was new.[46]

This petition had no immediate effect, because on May 10, 1774, a few weeks after it was printed, Louis XV died. Current affairs were suspended during the long process of redistributing power through a new set of ministers at the beginning of Louis XVI's reign. With the nomination of Turgot as controller general of finances in August 1774, new, liberal policies threatened to undermine the corporate order of French manufacturing and commerce. The Guild was one of the few corporations exempted from Turgot's suppression of most Parisian guilds in March 1776, two months before he was forced out of office. But it had been targeted for reform since 1763, when Sartine took over the Direction. He had not yet completed the preparations for a new code of the book trade by 1774 when he was promoted to the position of naval minister, and plans remained in abeyance until July 1776, when

François-Claude-Michel-Benoît Le Camus de Néville was named director. Under his impetus the code was finally published in six edicts issued on August 30, 1777.

During the reshuffling of the ministries, the Lyonnais booksellers continued to lobby, coordinating their efforts with their colleagues in Rouen, Toulouse, Marseille, and Nîmes. On October 15, 1776, they submitted a joint *Mémoire . . . concernant les privilèges en librairie*, which expanded the arguments they had made two years earlier into a book-length (118 printed pages) jeremiad about everything they had suffered since the beginning of the century. Because it represents the culmination of their efforts to defend themselves against the domination of the Guild and to reshape the fundamental conditions of publishing and the book trade, it is worth considering in some detail.

The *Mémoire* directly attacked the position of the Guild on privileges, including the argument about intellectual property that had been developed (anonymously) by Diderot. Whatever "génie" an author had invested in a text, the *Mémoire* claimed, he sacrificed all property rights to it once he had sold it to a bookseller, and the bookseller's ownership derived entirely from the *privilège* accorded by the Crown. Nothing in the royal edicts, which it reviewed in detail, justified the notion of *privilège* as a permanent kind of property—not even the general Code of 1723, which the *Mémoire* disparaged as jumble of measures cobbled together from a draft produced by the Guild to further its own interests. The sovereign granted *privilèges* for a limited time, and attempts to extend them as *continuations* (unless the text had been augmented by at least a third) violated the basic principles that had regulated the book trade since the first days of printing. The provincial booksellers had reiterated this argument for years, but in the *Mémoire* of 1776 it took on a new tone—bitter, angry, deeply imbued with a sense of injustice, and even political in its rhetoric. The provincials recounted the raids on their shops as if they were battles in a commercial war that was intended to annihilate them. They described their situation as "beaten down, debased, nearly destroyed under the weight of the most revolting and unrelenting oppression." In defending their cause, they spoke up for "equality and liberty."[47]

The *Mémoire* supported this appeal to principles with an economic argument supplemented by acid comments on the mores that distinguished Parisian from provincial publishers. The Parisians, it claimed had no spirit of enterprise. They simply lived off their *privilèges*. Of course, the trade in Paris was a complex affair, composed of many different participants, they conceded. It included 220 booksellers and printers, of whom 120 were actively engaged in selling books. Of these, at least half limited their business to the secondhand trade, rare books, and services connected with the sale of libraries. The remaining 60 dealt in "the ordinary book trade," but this commerce was dominated by twelve to sixteen houses, which ran monopolies extending throughout the kingdom. This small elite of "literary despots" undercut competition from the lesser booksellers in Paris, using various maneuvers such as closing off information exchanged in commercial correspondence, and they led the campaign to destroy the *contrefaçon* trade in the provinces. Not that they were active as businessmen. They lazed about in their homes, enjoyed the pleasures of the city, and lived extravagantly by milking their monopoly.

In contrast, according to the *Mémoire*, the provincial booksellers worked day and night, "seeking out, creating businesses, profiting from the smallest operations as well as the largest enterprises, neglecting nothing, reaping everything, combining thrift and frugality with the love of their profession and responsibility to its demands." Frustrated by persecution at the hands of the Parisians, the most enterprising provincials had moved their businesses across the border and made fortunes by supplying the rest of Europe with French books and by flooding France with cheap editions, many of them *contrefaçons*. The demand for literature had grown enormously, the *Mémoire* emphasized, and yet the Parisian publishers refused to take advantage of it, preferring to seek profits in their traditional manner, by maintaining high prices and restricting the number of copies produced. The state supported them by reducing the number of printers and refusing all reforms of the book trade. As a result, the foreign publishers could sell their books at half the prices charged by the Parisians, and the French economy had failed to profit from the expansion of a vital industry. The opposition between the Parisians and the provincials had reached such a state, the *Mémoire* concluded, that the problem to be solved was not simply the accumulation of *contrefaçons* in the provincial bookshops but the structure of the trade itself. The new code for the *librairie* should renounce the monopolistic measures of the past and redefine the rules of the game so that everyone could profit equally from them.[48]

The code promulgated in the form of six edicts on August 30, 1777, addressed many of these arguments, although it did so in such a way as to open up more debate and to leave everyone dissatisfied. By this time, the government had begun to show some concern for the public reaction to its measures, and royal edicts often contained preambles, which explained their purpose, instead of simply announcing the will of the Crown. The edicts of 1777 used language that contrasted markedly with earlier decrees on the book trade. Whereas the Code of 1723 echoed the Colbertist legislation of the seventeenth century and emphasized maintaining high standards of quality as opposed to "the greed for profit,"[49] the new code proclaimed the Crown's intention to "increase commercial activity." It condemned monopoly, praised "competition," favored "speculations" that would benefit the public by lowering prices, and promoted measures that would "put an end to the rivalry that divides the Parisian from the provincial book trade." It also announced its intention to favor authors by granting them the right to sell their own works and even to commission booksellers to market their books for them. In fact, for the first time in a royal edict, it used the phrase "*droit des auteurs*" (roughly, copyright), although it did not endorse the concept of literary property advocated by the Guild.[50]

The six edicts covered so many aspects of printing and the book trade that they should be identified separately.

The first edict subjected all journeymen to strict control by requiring them to register, for a fee of 30 sous (somewhat less than the wages for a day's work), in the nearest *chambre syndicale*, which would issue a parchment work permit (*cartouche*) that they had to produce whenever they changed employment. The master of the shop they left would sign it, certifying his consent, and they would have to submit it for registration in the *chambre syndicale* of the shop that they joined.

The second edict required the Parisian *chambre syndicale* to hold two public auctions each year for the sale of booksellers' stock, *privilèges*, and portions of *privilèges*. Auctions previously had been closed affairs, which made it possible for the Parisians to monopolize most *privilèges*. By opening them to provincial booksellers, the edict sought to encourage the publishing industry outside Paris.

The third edict strengthened the requirements for accession to masterships.

The fourth edict reinforced the policing of the book trade by eliminating guilds in three cities where the commerce was relatively inactive (Limoges, Rennes, and Vitry) and creating new ones in five cities (Besançon, Caen, Poitier, Strasbourg, and Nancy) located at important nodal points in the trade. Among their duties, the officers in the guilds would inspect all book shipments and confiscate forbidden and pirated books. They would be accompanied by special police inspectors, who also would be empowered to inspect the local bookshops and printing shops.

The fifth edict limited the duration of *privilèges* to the life of the author, and it also provided that the bookseller who had bought the *privilège* would possess it for at least ten years. It abolished all *continuations* of *privilèges* unless the text of the book had been increased by at least a quarter. It required booksellers to submit documentation (*titres*) to Néville to prove their ownership of *privilèges*; and if Néville found the documents to be valid, it held out the possibility of a further "last and definitive *privilège*," but it decisively rejected the notion that *privilèges* were permanent.

The sixth edict legalized all the pirated books in all the bookshops in France, provided that certain procedures were followed. The booksellers were to declare the *contrefaçons* they had in stock within an allotted time period (usually two months after the edict was registered in the nearest guild), get the title pages stamped by an officer of their guild, and have the stamps signed by the local *inspecteur de la librairie*. They could then sell the stamped books as freely as books protected by *privilèges*. Once this special amnesty had expired, all *contrefaçons*, whether old or new, would be confiscated. The owner of a *privilège* could, with the permission of an inspector, search through a bookshop where he suspected a *contrefaçon* of his book was in stock. If he found one, he could have it confiscated and collect damages. If he did not, the bookseller could collect damages from him.

Although nearly every detail of the code touched off disputes, the last two edicts aroused the greatest controversy. On the subject of *privilèges*, the fifth edict reaffirmed the Crown's long-standing position: "His Majesty has recognized that a *privilège* in the book trade is a grace founded in justice." As authors deserved compensation for their work, they and their heirs could enjoy *privilèges* permanently. But to permit booksellers to profit from the *continuations* of *privilèges* beyond the legal limit "would be to convert the enjoyment of a grace into a property by right." Even when one bookseller earned a *continuation* by increasing the size of a text by the required one quarter, others would be free to reprint the old version. The edict therefore created an enormous public domain, one that included most of the literature from the past and was open to provincial and Parisian publishers. Provincial booksellers also would be able to purchase *privilèges* or portions of *privilèges* at the biannual auctions, which previously had been closed to them. While correcting the 1723 Code's bias against the provincials, the new code was certain to arouse fierce opposition by the Parisians.

The sixth edict looked equally offensive from the perspective of the Guild. In one fell swoop, the Crown legitimized the products of an underground activity that it had been trying to suppress for decades; and at the same time it acknowledged the extent to which piracy had permeated the provincial book trade. While aligning its policy with economic realities, the edict implicitly admitted the state's inability to enforce the law that had previously existed, because it could not possibly impound a large proportion of the stock of booksellers everywhere in the kingdom; and even if it were capable of raiding bookshops on such a scale, in doing so it would inflict such losses as to ruin the entire trade. The Parisians saw themselves as the victims of this retroactive reworking of past law, and they had little confidence that the new law would prevent pirating in the future. The edict claimed that the disappearance of the Guild's monopoly of *privilèges*, which had been the root cause of the trade in *contrefaçons*, would be enough to make piracy disappear, provided that adequate police measures were adopted.

Taken together, the six edicts were intended to open up the book trade and adjust its governing code to the conditions of an expanding commercial economy. Yet, like much legislation from the Ancien Régime, the new code contained contradictory elements, some archaic and others forward looking. It treated books as goods to be freely exchanged on a market, but it insisted that their legal status derived from the grace of the king—a notion far removed from the modern concept of copyright. And while encouraging competition, it subjected printing and the book trade more thoroughly than ever to the guild structure inherited from the seventeenth century. Despite their inconsistencies, however, the edicts indicated a fundamental shift in government policy. They redressed the balance of earlier legislation, which had favored the hegemony of the Guild, and they showed that after fifty years of protest the provincial booksellers had finally made themselves heard.

Information about the edicts did not circulate widely until early October 1777. From that point on, the controversies can be followed in two sources: the diary of Siméon-Prosper Hardy, a retired bookseller and former *adjoint* (deputy *syndic*) of the Guild, and the *Mémoires secrets pour servir à l'histoire de la république des lettres en France*, a gossipy account of current events compiled by two well-connected, minor men of letters, Mathieu-François Pidansat de Mairobert and Bathélemy-François-Joseph Moufle d'Angerville. Both sources provide a minute, day-by-day account of events that interested the Paris public, and despite their ideological differences (Hardy was a Jansenist and supporter of the Parlement of Paris; Mairobert and Moufle d'Angerville sympathized with the *philosophes*), both have the same bias—in favor of the Guild, as opposed to the director of the book trade, Le Camus de Néville, and the provincial booksellers.[51]

On October 23, at the order of the lieutenant general of police, the *chambre syndicale* of the Guild entered the six edicts in its official register, an act that made them effective in its area of jurisdiction. By requiring registration in this manner, the government avoided submitting them to the Parlement of Paris, which could have obstructed their execution, as it often did when faced with edicts concerning general issues such as taxation. The Parisian booksellers immediately raised a great hue and cry, protesting that they had been dispossessed of their most valuable property and that the book trade would be ruined.[52] On October 30, four of the most influential widows from the Parisian Guild, including Widow Desaint, outfitted in formal mourning attire, brought the protest before the court in Fontainebleau. Their dress signaled the view held by Guild members such as Hardy that the edicts had been "the death blow" for the book trade.[53] Offended by this public demonstration, the Keeper of the Seals, Armand Thomas Hue de Miromesnil, received them coldly and warned them not to publish their petition, because the government would not permit any discussion of the edicts to circulate in print.

Miromesnil had been responsible for overseeing the book trade in Normandy when he had served as premier president of the Parlement of Rouen from 1757 to 1774. In that capacity, he developed some sympathy for the attempts of the local booksellers and printers to resist the domination of the Parisian Guild.[54] When he became Keeper of the Seals in 1774, he acquired authority over the trade throughout the kingdom. He appointed Néville, a fellow Norman, to head the Direction in 1776, and together they opposed every effort of the Guild to eviscerate the edicts of May 1777. Néville was only twenty-eight at the time. Although he continued the reformist policies of his predecessors, Malesherbes and Sartine, he was vulnerable to accusations of youthful ambition and abuses of power. Satirical verse began to circulate under the cloak, mocking his commoner origins and disparaging Miromensil as well. Hardy saw the satire as a campaign to undermine them in the shifting politics of the court and eagerly jotted down every rumor about their impending disgrace.

But they stood firm. On November 9, 1777, a deputation from the Guild presented Miromesnil with a memoir, drawn up by a lawyer, requesting the withdrawal of the edicts. The rector of the university expressed his support of the booksellers in their formal capacity as members (*suppôts*) of the university. A larger group of widows sent another protest, duly signed by a lawyer and printed, despite the prohibition against publications. Members of the Guild met in several "general assemblies" in their *chambre syndicale*. On December 14 they voted to present yet another petition to Miromesnil, who rejected it and warned them that he would not be moved, despite all their protests. They persevered nonetheless, working with lawyers on *consult-ations* that called for revisions to the edicts, but by the end of the year all legal channels seemed to be blocked, except one—an appeal over Miromesnil's head to the Conseil du Roi, the supreme consultative body that could render justice on matters that the king reserved for himself.[55]

While their masters continued with these legal maneuvers, the workers in the printing shops threatened to strike. The restrictions imposed on them by the edicts amounted to virtual slavery, they objected, because it bound them to their employers and prevented them from changing jobs as they pleased. They hired a lawyer of their own to protest to Miromesnil and reportedly threatened to kill any journeyman who complied with the edict by regis-tering with the *chambre syndicale* and accepting a work permit. By January 1778, however, several workers had registered, and the resistance had begun to crumble, partly in response to the intervention of the lieutenant general of police, Jean-Charles-Pierre Lenoir, who cooperated with the masters to calm the situation. In the end, perhaps through the influence of Lenoir, the requirement for the work permit was not enforced.[56]

Having reasserted control of the printing shops, the officers of the Guild began to resist on their own by refusing to stamp any *contrefaçons* from bookshops within the jurisdiction of the Paris *chambre syndicale*. Guillaume Debure, a *syndic* of the Guild, was summoned to stamp the books in the stock of the booksellers in Versailles. Despite threats from Miromesnil, he refused and was imprisoned in the Bastille on January 23, 1778. This incident produced a general outcry about the abuse of power. The Guild celebrated Debure as a hero and a martyr. His wife and her mother, Widow Barrois, one of the most militant of the book-seller widows, visited him in his cell, attracting sympathy and stirring up "fermentation" among the general public. The Guild sent a deputation to Versailles, requesting Debure's liberty and dispensation from the re-quirement to stamp books within its area of authority. At first, Miromesnil refused to make any concessions. But on January 29 Debure was released and the government announced that it would delegate the stamping to the book trade inspectors rather than forcing it on the officers of the Guild.

Although the evidence is unclear, it seems that little if any stamping occurred within the Parisian area.[57]

The nature of *privilèges* was a more sensitive matter. By arguing for the absolute character of literary property on the part of authors, the Guild hoped to prevail in its claim that the purchase of a *privilège* by a bookseller gave him an equally permanent right to sell a book. If the authors themselves backed that claim, the Guild might persuade the government to change its policy, and therefore it sought support from the Académie française. The Academy debated the issue on February 7 and 23, 1778. It failed to reach a consensus, although most of its members took the view that booksellers should have only limited *privilèges*. In the end, the Academy refused to pronounce and merely requested that the Crown clarify a provision in the edict that seemed to allow authors to maintain their *privilèges* permanently while hiring printers and booksellers to produce and market their works. Miromesnil replied obligingly that the intention of the edict was to favor authors and indeed to protect them against "the greed of the booksellers." Taking the Academy's request as an endorsement of the new code, he arranged for the promulgation of a supplementary edict on July 30, 1778. It reaffirmed the edicts of 1777 and made explicit the right of authors to contract out the production and marketing of their works without losing their perpetual *privilèges*.[58]

While defending their view of literary property in theory, the Parisian booksellers faced a concrete dilemma. The fifth edict required them to submit proof of their ownership of *privilèges* to Néville within two months. If they refused to do so, their *privilèges* would be ineligible for renewal and any bookseller could then reprint the books that had fallen into the public domain. In the eyes of the Parisians, this provision retroactively deprived them of their property rights and destroyed the legal basis of their businesses. According to the edict, the indefinite continuation of *privilèges* had created a monopoly for the Parisians and had caused the provincials to fall back on the trade in *contrefaçons*. Limited *privilèges*, open to all, would give the provincial dealers a stake in repressing piracy, it maintained, and everyone in the trade would benefit, "because a limited but certain enjoyment is preferable to an indefinite but illusory enjoyment." The Parisian booksellers therefore faced a painful decision: Would they submit their *titres* to Néville?

Hardy followed their behavior carefully in his journal. Some booksellers, he noted on January 10, 1778, had submitted documentation in the hope of having their *privilèges* confirmed. Although Miromesnil told deputations from the Guild that he would not swerve from his determination to enforce the edicts, he extended the deadline for the submission of *titres* until January 31. After that date, he warned, all booksellers would be free to print works whose *privilèges* were deemed to have expired. More Guild members then capitulated, though others continued to resist for several months, particularly after Néville began to refuse renewals for standard works, asserting that "classic books belong to everyone." One steady seller, a Latin-French dictionary known as the *Dictionnaire de Boudot*, had gone through seventeen editions since the seventeenth century, but the fact that it remained in print did not stop the Direction from pronouncing that it had entered the public domain. Even booksellers who had submitted their *titres* to the Direction found that many *privilèges* were not renewed. One bookseller declared 534 *privilèges* only to learn that 490 of them had expired and that the remainder would receive new *privilèges* limited to forty years. By the end of 1778, Hardy acknowledged that the Guild had lost the battle to retain permanent *privilèges*, because of the "cowardly treason of too large a number of its members."[59]

Legal action remained the only recourse for the Guild. Having given up on direct appeals to Miromesnil, it hoped to prevail in its appeal to the Conseil du Roi, an appeal that took the form of a *Requête au roi* prepared by a lawyer named Cochu. The members of the Guild discussed the *Requête* at a meeting in the *chambre syndicale* on January 12, 1778, and submitted it on January 14. Despite the prohibition of publishing anything related to the edicts, a printed version of the *Requête* was circulating in early February, and therefore it became the centerpiece of the Guild's case, both in public and within the confines of the chancellery, against the new code. Although it attracted a great deal of attention, the *Requête* added little to the general debate. In fact, it lifted much of its argument from a pamphlet that had attacked the edicts, *Lettre à un ami sur les arrêts du conseil du 30 août 1777*, and the argument, in any case, was already familiar: as the edicts acknowledged, authors enjoyed a full, unlimited right of property in the works of their creation, and that right, the Guild claimed, remained intact when an author transferred it to a bookseller. Far from creating a right of property, *privilèges* merely confirmed it. Property was a "natural right," which kings were obliged to defend—and also were in "a happy impotence" to violate. That phrase, taken from d'Héricourt's memoir of 1725, sounded like a provocation, and so did the *Requête*'s discussion of *contrefaçons*. Piracy was theft, it argued; therefore, by legalizing *contrefaçons*, the Crown was rewarding robbery. Moreover, the edicts were obviously biased, because they were based on petitions from the provincial booksellers. If the Conseil du roi failed to revoke them, it would become complicit in "the complete ruin of the entire body of booksellers and printers in Paris."[60]

Whether or not the Conseil considered the *Requête*, the Crown never responded to it. Faced with this silence, the Guild fell back on a last gambit: it attempted to get the Parlement of Paris to intervene on its behalf. The Parlement had no authority to do so, because, as mentioned, the edicts were royal orders (*arrêts du conseil*), not laws (*lettres patentes*) that required registration by the Parlement and that could be blocked, at least temporarily, if the Parlement objected to them by issuing remonstrances. To open a passage to the Parlement, Widow Desaint arranged a suit in the Châtelet (inferior) court with one of her authors, Alexis-Jean-Pierre Paucton, who had sold her the rights to his *Métrologie ou Traité des mesures, poids et monnaies de l'antiquité et d'aujourd'hui* for the considerable sum of 1,200 L. The contract had been signed before the registration of the six edicts in the Paris *chambre syndicale*, and Paucton had not yet collected the money owed to him. While he demanded full payment, Widow Desaint refused, on the grounds that the edicts had retroactively reduced the value of the *privilège*. On August 11, 1778, the Châtelet ruled that the original contract remained valid and that Widow Desaint continued to possess a permanent *privilège*, despite the restrictions of the new code. The case was appealed to the Parlement, which confirmed the Châtelet's decision on February 10, 1779, although it declined to pronounce on the general validity of the six edicts.[61]

The opposition to the edicts within the Parlement was then being led by Jean-Jacques Duval d'Eprémesnil, one of the most outspoken magistrates and a radical opponent of many government measures (in 1787 he would be among the first to demand the convocation of the Estates-General in 1787, thereby opening a way to the Revolution). In a powerful speech on April 23, 1779, he challenged the Parlement to fulfill what he described as its responsibility to be the champion of the oppressed and the defender of citizens' rights. He invoked the Paucton case along with others and added a note of pathos by quoting from a memoir by Charles-Guillaume Leclerc, a Parisian bookseller who testified to the damage that the edicts would inflict on an "unfortunate head of a family." He had a wife and five children, Leclerc wrote. Their livelihood depended entirely on fifty-six *privilèges*, all he had in the world. If the state stripped him of this patrimony, they would be reduced to destitution; and when he contemplated that fate, his only consolation was the thought that nine of his other children had died in infancy and therefore were beyond the harm that would be inflicted on the family. Leclerc had published an anonymous open letter to Néville four months earlier, arguing that the edicts were illegal, because they violated the basic right of property. They were nothing more than an act of force, "the height of barbarism," which Néville used to extend his power and line his pocket, because he illegally appropriated the fees charged to booksellers for getting their *privilèges* approved.

D'Eprémesnil did not go that far in his own indictment of the government's policy, but he went over all the protests against the edicts and submitted a set of memoirs, petitions, and guild resolutions for the Parlement to consider in investigating the affair. A full investigation was required, he insisted, although the basic issue was simple. The Parlement should reaffirm the right to literary property, which derived from the labor of authors, not from the grace of the king. Royal *privilèges* protected this fundamental right, but they did not determine its nature, which remained unchanged when authors sold their property to booksellers.[62]

The Parlement responded by directing the state attorneys (the *gens du roi* who represented the Crown in parlementary cases) to study d'Eprémesnil's argument and the accompanying documentation and to report back on July 2. Antoine-Louis Séguier, premier *avocat général du roi*, did not come up with the report until August 10, fully two years after the edicts were first announced, but then he covered so much ground that he had to stretch his oration over three sessions. He put the issues in perspective with historical reflections that went back to the invention of writing, surveyed royal policy since the invention of printing, and discussed the polemics surrounding the 1777 edicts in such detail that the printed version of his speech ran to eighty-one pages. It was actually published by the Guild, even though Séguier, as the king's representative, was supposed to defend royal policy. He did in the end conclude in favor of the edicts, as his role required; but the conclusion read as a non sequitur, for he presented the arguments against them so sympathetically that his harangue was received as an endorsement of the Guild's position.[63]

The Parlement then named a committee to study the issues further. Hoping that at last the tide had turned, the Guild sent deputations to key magistrates, urging them to take a stand against the edicts. Lobbying behind the scenes turned out to be difficult, however. When the Guild's *syndic*, Auguste-Martin Lottin, called on the Parlement's powerful first president, Étienne-François d'Aligre, who had close ties to Miromesnil, he learned that that there was little support within the Parlement for open opposition to the government. D'Aligre finally agreed to name the committee on January 24, 1780, but it rarely met. On July 25, 1780, it recommended sending some "représentations"—informal protests—to Miromesnil with the understanding that, if they failed to produce a satisfactory reply, it would consider making formal "remonstrances." Nothing happened for the next two years. Draft remonstrances had been drawn up by December 1782, and they were scheduled to be read before a session of the Parlement in January 1784. But nothing ever came of them.

Although Néville left the Direction to become intendant in Pau in 1784, his successors refused to withdraw the edicts. The Guild made a final appeal to Miromesnil in 1787, a decade after they were announced: "Ruined, annihilated by the six edicts of August 30, 1777, it dares to supplicate that you reactivate the Code of 1723." Miromesnil ignored this petition, the last in a long line of *mémoires*, *requêtes*, and *représentations* submitted to the state, and the Code of 1777 continued in effect until the Revolution.[64]

Such were the rules of the game. To find out how the game was played, it is necessary to look more closely into the social composition of the Guild and then to investigate the character of its enemies outside France's borders.

2

The Landscape in Paris

PARIS WAS THE CAPITAL of the eighteenth century. Everywhere in Europe the elite read French. Parisian writers set the tone in literature as much as couturiers did in clothes, and Parisian publishers benefited from the dense concentration of authors as well as access to censors and protectors in the royal administration. Yet the publishers lacked the capacity to satisfy literary demand, because the book industry remained enclosed within the narrow confines of the Guild.

The best way to gain a place in this small world was to be born into it. And to be born a male. If you were a woman, the only way in was to marry a master or a journeyman destined for a mastership. Then, if you outlived your husband, you could take over his business as a widow, and you might even select a new husband from a journeyman of your choice. Widows inherited the use of their husbands' *qualité*, or professional standing, and they occupied a prominent position within the Guild, as indicated by their special treatment in publications such as the annual *Tableau des libraires et des imprimeurs* and the *Almanach de la librairie*.[1] Marriages sometimes followed a pattern: older master/younger wife, older widow/younger journeyman. Sentiment might have played some part in the selection process, but the key elements were family connections and professional advancement.

Boys rose through the ranks in the prescribed order, from apprentice to journeyman and master. Sons of masters enjoyed dispensation from the requirements at the first stages—four years as an apprentice and at least three as a journeyman. Therefore, they often jumped into masterships at an early age—if one was available. As mentioned in the previous chapter, the government limited the number of master printers in Paris to thirty-six and held it down by restricting apprenticeships. No restrictions were placed on the number of master booksellers, which came to 146 plus thirty-six widows in Paris in 1781. But the entry price was high: 1,000 L., reduced to 600 L. for the sons of masters and the husbands of masters' daughters. Moreover, a young man could not simply buy his way into the Guild, even if he came from a long line of masters. He had to have an adequate knowledge of Latin and an ability to decipher Greek letters, as verified by a certificate from the rector of the University of Paris, to whom he had to be formally presented by an officer of the Guild—that is, a *syndic* or one of his four deputies (*adjoints*). To be admitted as a master the aspirant also was required to prove his knowledge of the book trade or of printing techniques during a two-hour examination before a jury of masters, including the Guild officers. If he passed, he also had to provide evidence of good morals and adherence to Catholicism before another jury of four more masters. Certificates of success in these examinations would be presented to the lieutenant general of police, who would forward them with his approval to the Keeper of the Seals, who in turn would clear the way for the aspirant to be named a master by an edict of the King's Council, as required by the edicts of 1777. All this examining and certifying may have been little more than a formality in the case of favored sons, but it served to keep outsiders outside.[2]

Insiders also had to conform to elaborate regulations. The Code established in 1723 consolidated requirements that went back for many decades, especially to seventeenth-century mercantilist policies, which reinforced corporate monopolies and imposed quality controls. Although the Code originally applied only to the Parisian region, it was extended to the rest of the kingdom in 1744, and it laid down the rules governing printing and bookselling for most of the eighteenth century. Seen at a distance of three centuries, the Code looks like legislation at its most baroque. It regulated every aspect of the trade—for example: the thickness of typefaces (three *l*s and three *i*s must exactly equal one *m*); the location of shops (they could not extend in the Latin Quarter beyond the Jacobin monastery on the rue Saint Jacques); the examinations for masterships (they had to last two hours, and the candidate had to receive at least two-thirds of the votes of the nine examiners, who must have been masters for at least ten years); and the protocol of Guild assemblies (the *syndics* must have preferred seats in meetings at the *chambre syndicale* according to the dates of their election; their *adjoints* must be seated after them in the same hierarchical order; and ordinary members would be fined 50 L. if they spoke ill of their officers).

The profusion of detail demonstrated the state's attempt to bring the printed word under its control by adopting measures of the kind that it had used a century earlier, above all by reinforcing the monopoly of the Guild. In 1686, when the Crown limited the number of master printers to thirty-six, it sought to reduce the ranks of printers by more than half. Although the thinning took place slowly through the closing of apprenticeships and the retirement of masters, printing had become a tightly restricted monopoly by the mid-eighteenth century.[3] The Code of 1723 did not set a limit on the number of booksellers, but it placed so many obstacles in the way of access to masterships that it restricted the trade to a privileged elite.

Of course, everyday practices might have had only a remote relation to the standards set by royal decrees. In fact, the decrees can be read against the grain, as symptoms of behavior that had become so widespread that the state intervened to repress it. For example, the provision of a fine for insulting a *syndic* could be taken as an indication that plenty of insulting took place and that the deference to hierarchy fell short of what the Crown intended.

How oligarchic was the trade in eighteenth-century Paris? Fortunately, it is possible to answer that question, because the Crown did not merely publish decrees; it also developed an extensive police force, which kept everything under close surveillance. On January 1, 1749, Joseph d'Hémery, a particularly conscientious *inspecteur de la librairie*, began to compile a survey of every printer and bookseller in Paris. His reports, completed for the most part by 1753, cover 261 masters. For a basis for his research, he used a contemporary *Liste chronologique des libraires et imprimeurs* published by the Guild, which includes 257 names (193 masters and sixty-four widows). D'Hémery's survey therefore represents the entire population of professionals involved in the trade. It also was systematic. D'Hémery used printed forms with standard rubrics—name, age, place of birth, description, address, and *histoire*—which a secretary filled out by hand, using information that the inspector had accumulated as he made his rounds. Although less complete than a similar survey of authors, which d'Hémery compiled at the same time, the reports make it possible to determine each person's position within the trade and, to some extent, the surrounding society. Taken as a whole, the files can be seen as a series of snapshots, which form a composite tableau of the landscape inhabited by the booksellers and printers in mid-eighteenth century Paris.[4]

The files do not provide an unmediated view of their subject, because they reflect d'Hémery's professional concerns, above all his responsibility to repress the circulation of forbidden books. He focused on everything that he considered *suspect*. The word recurs constantly, accompanied by nuances when applied to individual booksellers: "not suspect" (Denis Mouchet); "a little suspect" (Antoine-Chrétien Boudet); "very suspect" (the wife of Léonard-Marie Morel); and "one of the most suspect" (Laurent Durand). At the other extreme, he favored the term *honnête*, meaning upright and law abiding: "*honnête homme*" (Bernard Brunet); "*honnête homme* who is not at all suspect" (François Debure); "very much an *honnête homme* who is not suspect" (Pierre Guillyn).

Suspicion, as d'Hémery understood it, was attached to booksellers who dealt in illegal books, known by the police as *marrons* (literally, chestnuts, a term also applied in the colonies to fugitive slaves), whether they attacked religion, the state, morality, or the reputation of public personages. Thus Jean-Augustin Grangé was "one of the most suspect and incorrigible booksellers," who specialized in "very naughty books." D'Hémery was fully informed about the origins of the *Encyclopédie*, as one can see from his report on André-François Le Breton: "He is closely connected with Diderot and d'Alembert and consequently is the main printer of the *Encyclopédie*." But he did not pay a great deal of attention to the works of the Enlightenment. The ideological threat that occupied him most was Jansenism, the extreme Augustinian strain of Catholicism that had been declared heretical by the papacy and that aroused enormous controversy during the mid-century years. Thus the reports on François Babuty who had been sent to the Bastille several times for his Jansenist connections, and Philippe-Nicolas Lottin, who "hosts meetings every evening of the priests of that sect."

Yet d'Hémery did not detect widespread ideological danger among booksellers and printers. In fact, he paid special attention to their professional qualities, expressing admiration for those who had mastered technical difficulties and ran their businesses well. D'Hémery understood the art of printing and the commerce of bookselling thoroughly enough to assess the shops he inspected. He gave high marks to Jacques Chardon, who ran "a good printing shop," and he scorned the widow of Jacques-François Grou for maintaining "one of the very worst printing shops, which turns out many works of no consequence." D'Hémery also attributed great importance to the personal qualities of the masters. Jacques-François Mérigot, he noted, "neglects his profession," dealt in *drogues* (books of poor quality), and had fallen into bankruptcy. Christophe-Jean-François Ballard was born into a family of prosperous bookseller-printers but did not take advantage of his inheritance: "He is a lazy man, greatly lacking in genius." By contrast, Rombault Davidts, a shop assistant who had married the widow of his master, was "a very *honnête* lad who knows the trade and will amount to something."

D'Hémery knew most, perhaps all, the printers and booksellers in Paris. As he described them in the reports, which were intended for his own use and not for his superiors, they made up a rich and varied world of their own. He sketched their traits in few words, frank and free of sentimentality. Thus Jean-Louis Genneau was "an animal and a drunkard"; Jean-Baptiste-Claude Bauche "a horse without any manners or education"; and Charles de Poilly "a big bullock lacking in wit." If they had successive run-ins with the police, he added enough notes under the rubric *histoire* for one to follow the unfolding of a career. The most elaborate report concerned Jacques Clousier, who first appeared as "an *honnête homme*, who however sells only *drogues* permitted by the police." Although he had inherited the business from his father and had married another bookseller's daughter, who brought him a dowry of 6,000 L., Clousier accumulated more debts than he could cover by the sale of the books he published. He had to declare bankruptcy in 1749 and accept an agreement to pay off his creditors over a period of six years. While struggling to keep up his business, he speculated on a libertine novel, *Les Sonnetes ou Mémoires de monsieur le marquis D**** by Jean-Baptiste Guiard de Servigné. The manuscript cost only 300 L., and the edition, printed at 1,500 copies, raised the possibility of filling part of the hole in Clousier's finances. But Guiard de Servigné was arrested. Clousier then tried to save his own skin by confessing to the lieutenant general of police, who agreed to let him off without punishment, provided that he turn over the entire edition. In fact, Clousier kept back 300 copies to sell secretly (*sous le manteau*, or under the cloak). The police discovered this maneuver, and Clousier fled, leaving his business to his son. His daughter had run off earlier with a troupe of actors in Lille. The last d'Hémery heard, Clousier had joined her and was scratching out a living as a prompter (*souffleur*) in the troupe.

No other report contained so much picaresque detail. Most were short, prosaic, and, in many cases, positive, indicating admiration for successful masters who worked hard and got ahead in life. D'Hémery mentioned several dynasties whose founders had arrived in Paris (figuratively) "in wooden shoes." They broke into the trade by marrying widows of masters and then worked their way up through the ranks. Although firmly fixed within a corporate structure, the world of the book professionals was therefore in constant flux, mainly because of economic forces. Membership in the guild conveyed a *qualité*, or *état*,—that is, an official status, marked by the exclusive right to sell or print books—but it did not guarantee an income. While some masters made fortunes, others mismanaged their affairs and fell on such hard times that they had to give up their shops and hire themselves out to other masters. D'Hémery noted a half-dozen cases of masters who took jobs in stockrooms and printing shops, working alongside ordinary journeymen. Yet they retained their *qualité*, a matter of social importance and economic value. D'Hémery observed that the widow of Étienne Hochereau had married him "only in order to have a *qualité*," and he recounted the sadder story of Jean-Pierre Auclou: "He is wretched and poor, old and infirm, and quit working. But then he married a woman known as la Grande Javotte, who was a peddlar and only married him to have a *qualité*. Since then she has had a stand at the quai de Gesres, and she peddles everything that is illegal. She is a disreputable subject, who enrages her husband and often fights with him." Unlike the official peddlers—limited to 120 who displayed their privileged status by wearing copper badges—la Grande Javotte had no right to hawk books. Once she had married a master—impoverished, aged, and decrepit as he was—she crossed the line that separated the shadowy dealers from those who possessed a *qualité*.

Seen from the outside, the Guild might appear to be a homogeneous body of masters distinguished by their common *qualité*. But d'Hémery knew it from the inside, and in his reports he noted that its members occupied different strata, depending on their wealth, connections, and ancestry. Although several dynasties dominated the Guild at the top, it also contained a large number of *pauvres diables* who struggled to survive in the bottom ranks. D'Hémery paid special attention to the poorest masters, because they were most likely to *maronner*—that is, to deal in the illegal sector, where the risks and profits were greatest. They included *bouquinistes* who operated from stalls in the Palais de Justice, on the Quai des Augustins, and at other designated locations. On rare occasions, a down-at-the-heel bookseller tried to strike it rich by illicit publishing. Thus Charles Robustel, "a very bad subject, who sells the raciest stuff and even undertakes to have it printed." Booksellers' widows, if they did not marry an enterprising journeyman, easily sank into indigence. The toughest fought off bankruptcy by selling sex books and other forbidden works under the cloak. Widows also existed at the top of the hierarchy, where they commanded a great deal of respect, but those at the bottom had no escape from destitution. D'Hémery wrote off Widow Belley with one sentence: "She is a poor devil who has no bread." He did not go into much detail when he reported on masters in the middle range of the profession, for they did not require much attention by the police.

Masters in the upper ranks occupied a prominent place in the reports, because they exercised power as *syndics* and *adjoints*, and they dominated the trade throughout the kingdom. It was at this level that d'Hémery identified the interlocking links of an oligarchy. Pierre Prault, for example, stood out as a wealthy patriarch. By marrying the daughter of Guillaume Saugrain, whose line of masters went back to 1518, he gained access to masterships in both printing and bookselling. He acquired the monopoly of publishing all decrees of the King's Council and ordonnances of the General Tax Farm, which brought in a steady income, supplemented by a variety of legal books. His printing shop contained nine presses and a workforce of twenty-one journeymen plus two *alloués* (workers who had not gone through apprenticeships). His wife gave birth to seventeen children, of whom four sons became master booksellers and a daughter married into another ancient dynasty, the Le Clercs. The Le Clerc couple then had a son who became a bookseller and a daughter who married a bookseller. Meanwhile, Pierre-Prault's eldest son succeeded his father and became an *adjoint* of the Guild. A protégé of the comte de Clermont, he acquired the valuable office of *imprimeur du roi* and published administrative decrees along with various works of fiction and plays, all of them legal. He had three sons, all of whom became booksellers.

To follow the intermarriages among the masters is to watch the oligarchy extend its dominion. Not only did sons succeed fathers, but they also often married the daughters of other masters. Sons-in-law inherited masterships after marrying daughters, and journeymen acquired them by marrying widows. D'Hémery assumed that matrimony was a means of developing a career, rather than an affectionate bond. Jacques Rollin, for example, took over his father's bookselling business and expanded it by marrying into the wealthy and well-connected Delespine family of printer-booksellers, but he did not shower much sentiment on his wife: "He prefers cooks to her." Moreover, family strategies were subject to the brutal demographic conditions of the Ancien Régime. Pierre-Augustin Paulus-Du-Mesnil married the daughter of one bookseller; then, after she died, he married the daughter of another, who was the widow of a third. Philippe-Nicolas Lottin, scion of a long line of booksellers and printers, married the daughter of Pierre-Augustin Le Mercier, from another long line. They had fourteen children, of whom seven lived to adulthood. Two of their sons became booksellers, and two daughters married booksellers. The oldest son married into the illustrious Hérissant line of booksellers and printers and had seven children, of whom three survived to an adult age. A daughter married a bookseller, and a son became a *syndic* of the guild and one of the best-known printer-booksellers in the kingdom. (He taught the art of typography to the future King Louis XVI.)

For their part, the Hérissants followed a similar trajectory. Claude-Jean-Baptiste, the son of a bookseller, married the widow of his bookseller cousin, Jean Hérissant; made a fortune by publishing liturgical works; and left the business to his son, who had three daughters, two of whom married brothers in the distinguished Barrois family of printer-booksellers.

D'Hémery's reports covered many dynasties—the Barbou, Gaudouin, Ganeau, d'Houry, Knapen, Lamesle, Le Gras, Nyon, Saugrain, and Simon, among others. Their lines expanded vertically, from father to son, and horizontally, through networks of relatives and collaborators. Along the way, they accumulated wealth and offices, including monopolies for the printing and sale of periodicals, administrative ordonnances, and liturgical works. The most prominent of them, André-François Le Breton, built a fortune from the *privilège* for the *Almanach royal*, which he inherited from his maternal grandfather of the powerful d'Houry family. He acquired several positions that brought in lucrative commissions: *premier libraire et imprimeur ordinaire du Roi*, printer to the cathedral chapter of Notre Dame, and *imprimeur ordinaire de l'ordre de Malte*. Within the Guild he exercised great influence, first as an *adjoint*, then as a *syndic*. D'Hémery described him as an *honnête homme*, who ran his business well, although he speculated on some illegal works. His greatest speculation, the *Encyclopédie*, was a joint enterprise, which he published with three other wealthy masters, Antoine-Claude Briasson, Michel-Antoine David, and Laurent Durand, who also served as officers in the guild and had powerful relatives scattered throughout the trade. Although the *Encyclopédie* was condemned for its unorthodox content in 1759, it represented such a gigantic investment that, as mentioned, Malesherbes secretly permitted Diderot to continue editing it. Just before its last ten volumes appeared under the false imprint of Neuchâtel in 1765, and just after he had corrected the final proofs in 1764, Diderot discovered to his horror that Le Breton had surreptitiously cut the most audacious passages behind his back. This perfidy wounded him more than anything else that he had suffered during his hard life in Grub Street,[5] but for Le Breton it protected an investment of hundreds of thousands of livres, which could go down the drain had the authorities decided to suppress the last volumes.

It would be wrong, therefore, to consider Le Breton as a partisan of the Enlightenment. He seized an opportunity when he saw it. True, he had published some Enlightenment tracts, and his associates, especially Laurent Durand, took even greater risks. (Durand published several works by Diderot and *De l'esprit* by Helvétius, which passed the censorship but was condemned and burned in 1759.) D'Hémery noted their tendency to speculate occasionally on illegal works, but he did not take it very seriously. They were wealthy and well connected and held the highest offices of the Guild. What set Le Breton apart from the other patriarchs of the Guild was his entrepreneurial spirit. Instead of relying on conventional steady sellers, as they did, he took risks, though only up to a point, relying on his income from the *Almanach royal* and sinecures to prevent insolvency.[6] More typical among the professional elite were Jean-François Josse, *libraire-imprimeur de Sa Majesté la reine d'Espagne;* Pierre-Alexandre Le Prieur, *imprimeur-libraire ordinaire du roi;* and Pierre-Jean Mariette, *imprimeur du lieutenant général de police.* All three accumulated large fortunes, rose to become *adjoints* in the Guild, and retired from the trade by purchasing the office of *secrétaire du roi*—that is, nobility.

If we stand back from individual details and attempt to take in the entire landscape in mid-eighteenth century Paris, it seems clear that a wealthy, endogamous oligarchy dominated the Guild and the publishing industry in general. The patriarchs had a strong sense of their standing. One of them, Auguste-Martin Lottin, published a treatise in 1789 that purported to trace family lines since the introduction of printing in 1470. He claimed that twenty-seven families (notably his own) had supplied Guild members for the last 100 to 200 years and that they should be proud of it, because "if any names are destined to endure forever, it is those of booksellers and printers."[7] Despite its monopoly of the trade, however, the Guild had not hardened into an ossified hierarchy. Although its wealthiest members from the oldest families remained firmly established at its highest level, masters rose and fell within its middle ranks; and at the bottom, professionals of certified *qualité* struggled desperately to survive—often by selling illegal literature that had little or no place in the commerce of those at the top.

As a police inspector, d'Hémery developed a sharp eye for *marrons*, but his reports contain little information about the ordinary literature printed and sold by the members of the Guild. To form an idea of all the books being produced at a particular time, it is necessary to consult another document, which also serves as a snapshot of the publishing industry. According to the Code of 1723, the *syndic* and *adjoints* of the Guild were required to conduct regular inspections of all the printing shops in Paris. The best of the surviving records of their inspections comes from May 1769. For seven days, they went through every printing shop and noted everything that was then in press. Using a standard printed form, which compelled them to be systematic, they

entered the name and address of each master printer, the number of presses
and workers in the shop, the title of each book being printed (and also all the
casual jobs known as *ouvrages de ville*), and the name of the bookseller who
had commissioned the work—that is the publisher, whether a "bookseller"
or a "bookseller-printer" (a bookseller who was also a master printer).[8]

The inspections show how significant publishing had become as an industry in Paris. The reports covered 37 printing shops with 297 presses and
a workforce of 850 (789 journeymen and 61 non-guild *alloués*). At that time
191 books were being printed, along with a great deal of job printing for
administrative offices, the lottery, the police, and the church. All but nineteen of the books had received *privilèges*. The remaining nineteen books had
received *permissions tacites*, meaning they had been approved by a censor
but carried no indication of their legal status. As already explained, the government had used *permissions tacites* as a loophole to permit an increasing
number of books to circulate without official sanction.[9] That only 9 percent
of the books being printed in May 1769 belonged to this category suggests
that the members of the Guild did not stray far from the standard legal
pathway of publishing. The nineteen semiofficial books were mainly novels
and works related to public affairs—for example, Rousseau's *La Nouvelle
Héloïse*, then being reprinted by Widow Duchesne; *Lettres athéniennes*, an
epistolary novel by Claude-Prosper Jolyot de Crébillon; *Les Amours de Lucile
et de Doligny*, a sentimental romance by Jean Tesson de Laguerrie; a translation of John Dickinson's *Letters from a Farmer in Pennsylvania*; a tract by
a member of the Parlement d'Aix-en-Provence on the French claim to the
Comtat Venaissin; and *Les Économiques*, a physiocratic treatise by the marquis de Mirabeau. None of these works, not even *La Nouvelle Héloïse*, openly
challenged the established authorities, but the state did not want to give them
its official imprimatur.

The other 172 titles, which did carry a royal stamp of approval, covered
a broad range of subjects. They can be grouped together and classified according to Table 2.1:

Religious books, which constituted the largest number of texts then being
printed, included a great many liturgical works (breviaries, missals, books of
hours), several moral treatises and devotional tracts, but no formal theology.
History, along with related subjects such as biography, geography, and travel,
came next in importance. It occupied many presses, because it included
multi-volume works, such as *Histoire générale de la France*, eight volumes,
by the abbé Paul-François Velly; *Histoire générale de l'Amérique*, fourteen

Table 2.1 Subjects of books being printed in Paris, May 1769

Religion	42
History	24
Biography	3
Memoirs	1
Geography	1
Travel	5
Economics and current affairs	3
Law	7
Military affairs	4
Science	22, including
Medicine	11
Botany	3
Mathematics	1
Mechanical arts	4
Classics	13
Philosophy	2
Belles-lettres	8
Fiction	6
Theater	9
Collected works	3
Dictionaries and grammar	7
Music	2
General reference	4
Miscellaneous	6
Unidentified	15

volumes, by the Dominican Antoine Touron; and *Histoire universelle sacrée et profane*, eighteen volumes, by Jacques Hardion. These works had a strong religious component, especially in the case of Touron, who celebrated the role of the Catholic Church in Latin America, and Hardion, who served as librarian to the king and tutor to the children of Louis XV. The inspectors also noted that a volume of writings by Jacques-Benigne Bossuet, bishop of Meaux and court preacher to Louis XIV, was in press. Although they did not describe its contents, it might well have included Bossuet's *Discours sur l'histoire universelle*, his sermons, or other works in which he argued for the divine right of kings. The category of scientific books included both standard treatises, like Pierre-Joseph Macquer's *Éléments de chimie théorique*; and popular works such as *Amusements magnétiques*, attributed to Edmé-Gilles Guyot; along with many medical tracts, e.g., *Précis dematière médicale* by Gabriel-François Venel, a prolific contributor to the *Encyclopédie*. French translations of the classics were being printed in large numbers, especially in the much-esteemed shop of Joseph-Gérard Barbou, where works of Virgil, Quintilian, and Titus Livius were in press. Among works of fiction, novels were not so prevalent in 1769 as they would be in later centuries. *La Nouvelle Héloîse*, a huge bestseller, was an exception, less typical of what was being printed than *Lettres de Milady Juliette Catesby* by the popular author of sentimental romances, Marie-Jeanne Laboras de Mézières, known as Mme Riccoboni. The printing shops were turning out large numbers of plays, whether as anthologies (*Différentes Pièces de théâtre*) or as editions of collected works (Racine and Molière). Equally important were works in the category of belles-lettres—that is, essays on literature and anthologies, such as *Le Portefeuille d'un homme de goût* by the indefatigable compiler, Joseph de La Porte. Finally, the presses were producing all sorts of reference works, dictionaries, and books on grammar, including the great *Grammaire de Port Royal*.

Because it took several months to print a book, this sketch, minimal as it is, provides a good indication of the output of literature during one year at the center of the French publishing industry. To be sure, it is a sample taken from a thin slice of time. But one conclusion seems clear: in 1769 the printing shops of Paris produced texts that conformed closely to the values of the church and state.[10] Far from challenging orthodox ideas, all the books had received the approval of royal censors, and many of them conveyed a culture steeped in traditional religion, classical learning, and classics from the "the great century" of Louis XIV. Forbidden books certainly circulated "under the cloak." D'Hémery made it his business to hunt them down, and he noted that some secret presses existed and some established booksellers occasionally dealt in *marrons*. Yet most illegal literature was published outside Paris, especially in the printing shops located across France's borders. Judging from the inspection of printing shops, we can see that Parisian publishers kept to the safest channels of the trade, where they could market standard works protected by *privilèges*.

The most active publishers occupied a particular place within the Parisian landscape. Many of them clustered around the rue Saint-Jacques and the rue des Mathurins in shops set off by wrought-iron signs, which extended over the street and occasionally, when worn and rusted, fell on pedestrians: hence the order in 1761 to "shave" Paris of its overhanging signs and to replace them with signs painted on the facades of the shops.[11] The reports show that only a small minority of the booksellers in Paris—29 of 211—had commissioned the printing of the books that were in press in May 1769.[12] They belonged to families that were interlocked by marriages, apprenticeships, and joint enterprises. Jean Desaint, for example, did business in the manner of a modern publisher, because he did not have a printing shop of his own, and he had commissioned nine works, which were being printed in five different shops. Two bookseller-printers from the Hérissant dynasty operated on a grander scale. Jean-Thomas Hérissant, an *adjoint* and later a *syndic* of the Guild, ran one of the largest printing shops in Paris. Located on the rue Saint-Jacques at the sign "À Saint Paul," it had eleven presses and employed forty-five workers. In 1769 he was printing twelve books: ten for other booksellers, one for himself (an edition of the Bible), and another religious work, *Le Code matrimonial*, for Claude-Jean-Baptiste Hérissant, a relative. The latter's printing shop, nearby on the rue neuve Notre-Dame at the sign "Aux Trois Vertus," was almost as large (nine presses), and it was producing four works, which included Jean-Claude-Baptiste's edition of an eight-volume *Chronologie historique-militaire* by an administrator in the War Ministry named Pinard.

While commissioning editions and printing them for one another, the elite of masters frequently collaborated on joint enterprises. These included nineteen works being produced by a "Compagnie"—evidently the Compagnie des libraires associés, a group of booksellers who jointly owned *privilèges* and portions of *privilèges*. Although its history is difficult to determine, its name appears on title pages going back to the seventeenth century.[13] The Compagnie books in press in 1769 were primarily religious works (breviaries, a moral tract, a book of canon law, a treatise on the Bible) along with steady sellers such as the works of Virgil and Racine.

Having examined the activities of booksellers and printers as they appear in these two sets of documents—the files of inspector d'Hémery and the reports of the Guild examiners—we can draw some general conclusions.[14] The Guild's formal monopoly of the publishing industry, guaranteed by the Code of 1723, was exercised in practice by a small oligarchy. Bound together by family ties and professional connections, this elite of a few dozen masters dominated the trade by concentrating on the production of standard books within a wide variety of genres, especially in the fields of religion, history, classics, medicine, law, and belles-lettres. All of these works had been approved by censors; many of them had gone through several earlier editions; and they probably brought in steady profits at little risk. The 300 or so presses of Paris manned by about 850 workers produced little else, except ephemera and *ouvrages de ville*. Yet the conservative character of the industry did not exclude innovation. The legal loophole of *permissions tacites* made it possible for original works like *La Nouvelle Héloïse* to be printed in edition after edition. Le Breton, a Guild *syndic* and one of its most eminent members, masterminded the publication of the *Encyclopédie* and even published Diderot's audacious *Lettre sur les aveugles*, although he based his trade on his monopoly of the *Almanach royal*, and d'Hémery gave him a favorable report.

By contrast, d'Hémery had nothing good to say about a few publishers like Jean-Augustin Grangé, who speculated on forbidden books. But they were rare exceptions. *Marronage* existed among booksellers rather than publishers, and most of those underground retailers occupied places in the lower ranks of the trade. The inspectors' reports show that the presses of Paris turned out conventional, legal literature and that the publishers who commissioned it belonged to an exclusive elite.

3

The Fertile Crescent

BOOKS DON'T RESPECT BORDERS. They cannot be contained, either within states, or religions, or cultures, or any barrier meant to close off communication. They do not even burn easily, as public hangmen learned from centuries of trying to set them on fire—not that persecution can be taken as an indication of a book's progressive character. Books purvey something of everything, the vulgar as well as the refined, scattering ideas and emotions in all directions. Diderot put it well in his memorandum to Sartine, who became director of the Book Trade Administration in 1763: "Station, Monsieur, soldiers all around your borders; arm them with bayonets to repel all the dangerous books that may appear, and these books—if you will excuse the expression—will slip between their legs, leap over their heads, and arrive among us."[1]

As Diderot knew from experience, French books penetrated France from everywhere around her borders in the eighteenth century.[2] A Fertile Crescent of publishing houses extended from Amsterdam to Brussels, through the Rhineland, into Switzerland, and down to Avignon, which then was papal territory. At a time when French had replaced Latin as a lingua franca, Europeans everywhere read French books,[3] and by 1750 most of those books were produced by foreign publishers. The following chapters will show how this industry operated, concentrating on Switzerland. Before examining its inner workings, however, we need to study the general topography of French publishing outside France.

As this map shows, publishers produced French books in large numbers from certain strongholds—in Holland, from Amsterdam, The Hague, and Maastricht; in Switzerland, from Geneva, Lausanne, and Neuchâtel; and from autonomous principalities such as Bouillon, Liège, and Neuwied. Each house developed its own network of customers in France. Most of them also supplied booksellers scattered throughout Europe, and some concentrated on markets in Germany. In addition to these large-scale publishers,

MAP 1   Publishers and booksellers in the Fertile Crescent.

who usually owned printing shops as well as bookstores, many also participated in the cross-border trade, whether as retailers, *entrepôt* keepers, or smugglers. Moreover, the Fertile Crescent shaded off into France itself, because French booksellers close to the border often collaborated with the foreign publishers. Not only did they funnel shipments into the kingdom, but they also sometimes invested in joint editions—and, when they could get away with it, produced *contrefaçons* of their own. There were a great many of them. The *Almanach de la librairie* of 1781 listed forty booksellers and printers in Rouen, twelve in Lille, twelve in Metz, twelve in Strasbourg, sixteen in Besançon, and forty-three in Lyon, a great center for piracy.[4] To the south, publishers in the papal enclave of Avignon turned out enormous quantities of *contrefaçons*. Far from being exhaustive, therefore, the map gives only a minimal picture of the cross-border trade.

The books followed routes carved out by centuries of religious war as well as commercial exchange. Protestantism, especially in its Calvinist form, was a religion of the book, and religious texts poured out of the Protestant bastions, Geneva and Amsterdam. In 1526 the Sorbonne banned the publishing of Bibles in the vernacular. In 1550, the renowned French printer Robert Estienne joined Calvin in Geneva and began producing Bibles in French. From then until the French Revolution, Swiss presses supplied French Huguenots with an endless stream of Bibles, psalters, and other religious books, all of them diffused through underground networks. In 1585, Antwerp, one of the greatest capitals of publishing during the Renaissance, fell to Spanish troops, and many of its Protestant printers and booksellers fled to Amsterdam, which soon eclipsed its rival to the south. For the next 200 years, Switzerland and France attracted wave after wave of French refugees, many of them book professionals. Although the persecution of Huguenots declined in France after the religious wars (1562–1598), it resumed again under Louis XIV and culminated in the revocation of the Edict of Nantes (1685). More Huguenots fled from France, reinforcing the publishing industry and its underground system of distribution. The Protestant "International" had lost much of its militancy by the middle of the eighteenth century, when the publishing houses outside of France began to produce the works of the *philosophes*. Yet the books of the Enlightenment circulated through the clandestine channels established by their Protestant predecessors. Genevan Bibles with their Calvinist commentaries continued to be illegal, although they were increasingly tolerated in the 1770s and 1780s during inspections of shipments in the *chambres syndicales*. Swiss publishers in particular maintained close contact with Huguenots in France, who helped recruit customers and collect bills. The publishers shipped Bibles and psalters with the works of Voltaire and d'Holbach in the same bales.

Far from being uniformly Protestant and enlightened, however, the publishing houses developed in different ways, because they took root within different environments—in duchies, principalities, independent city states, and fragments of the Holy Roman Empire. Although Amsterdam and Geneva retained semblances of republican self-rule, they had hardened into aristocratic oligarchies by 1750. Many of the other political bodies were Catholic, and they favored several varieties of Catholicism. Cologne, for example, was an independent state within the Holy Roman Empire, while the archbishopric of Cologne was a separate entity ruled by the Bavarian Wittelsbach dynasty. The absentee archbishop was more willing to tolerate publishing than were the city officials, who were dominated by the local clergy and a militant papal nuncio. A Parisian adventurer turned publisher named Louis-François Mettra set up shop in Münz, which was under the archbishop's jurisdiction, just outside the city walls. In 1785 he moved to Neuwied, where the local princeling was still more permissive. After establishing a large printing shop and adopting the imposing name of Société typographique de Neuwied, Mettra turned out large quantities of pirated and banned books, including his own journal, the *Correspondance littéraire secrète*, a printed version of a manuscript news-sheet.[5]

Favorable political conditions also helped publishing flourish in Liège, an ecclesiastical principality, which became one of the greatest centers of piracy in the 1760s and 1770s.[6] The Counter-Reformation had reinforced the power of the clergy throughout much of the area that is now Belgium, but the Habsburgs, who retained sovereignty in the Austrian Netherlands, ruled with a light hand, first under Maria Theresa (1740–1780), then under Joseph II (1780–1790). Joseph's edict of toleration (October 13, 1781) created a great deal of freedom for the book trade as well as for non-Catholic religions. In Liège authority was exercised at the height of the pirating boom by a prince-bishop (*prince-évêque*, a prelate who exercised secular sovereignty), François-Charles de Velbruck, who gained a posthumous reputation as a "clerical enlightened despot." He enjoyed the pleasures of the flesh, reputedly belonged to a Masonic lodge, embraced progressive ideas, and welcomed the stimulus that printing provided for Liège's lethargic economy. With his encouragement, four publishers—Jean-François Bassompierre, Clément Plomteux, Denis de Boubers, and Jean-Jacques Tutot—reprinted the works of all the major *philosophes* and everything else that would sell. Liège at its prime had fifteen printing shops with a total of fifteen presses, according to one report.[7]

The city's notoriety came up whenever piracy was discussed—in Diderot's *Lettre sur le commerce de la librairie*, for example.[8] The pirates prided themselves on their success, as the popular writer and *philosophe* Jean-François Marmontel learned when he met Bassompierre on his way back from a trip to Spa. To his amazement, the publisher looked him up in his inn, congratulated him on writing bestsellers, and boasted about having made a great deal of money by reprinting them. When Marmontel protested that this practice amounted to "stealing the fruit of my labor," Bassompierre replied that French *privilèges* did not extend to Liège, which was a "free country." "We have a right to print everything that is good: that is our trade." He then invited Marmontel to his house for dinner: "You will see one of the most handsome printing shops of Europe, and you will be pleased with the way your works are produced in it."[9]

Bassompierre's firm thrived throughout the second half of the eighteenth century. He had pirated books since the 1740s. His son, also named Jean-François, joined him in 1757 and continued after his father's death in 1777. Plomteux operated on an even grander scale. He bought shares in international consortiums that speculated on the *Encyclopédie* and the *Encyclopédie méthodique*. He published a thirty-two-volume edition of Voltaire's works and the first edition of the complete works of Helvétius. Not only did he lead the rush to reprint Raynal's *Histoire philosophique*, a great bestseller, but he also befriended Raynal and sheltered him when the *philosophe* fled France after the condemnation of his book in 1781.[10] Having become an intimate advisor to Bishop Velbruck, Plomteux had no worries about publishing Enlightenment works. He owned the "Vaux-Hall," or gambling facility, nearby in Spa, which also was a great center for selling illicit literature, and in 1787 he was elected as a top official (*bourgmestre*) of Liège. Everything suggests that he belonged to the most active and influential elite of the city.

Yet one should not exaggerate the liberty enjoyed by the publishers in Liège or anywhere else in the Fertile Crescent. Every state, down to the smallest principality, had censorship of one kind or other. In Liège it was exercised—subject to the authority of the prince-bishop and the prime minister of his Privy Council—by the powerful canons of the cathedral, who did their best to enforce strict orthodoxy. Demazeau, a Liégeois publisher with a large business in France, complained that he was "increasingly tormented by our censors . . . so hungry to promote the welfare of the church" and that their "ecclesiastical bile" forced him to rely on smuggling to conduct his trade.[11] Velbruck's reign from 1772 to 1784 brought what one chronicler called "the golden age of piracy"[12] to a climax in Liège, but his successors, like his predecessors, had little sympathy for independent publishers and none at all for the Enlightenment. Insofar as they permitted the book industry to exist, it was for its contribution to the local economy.

In 1755, a minor playwright turned journalist named Pierre Rousseau moved to Liège in order to publish a periodical that would promote the cause of the *philosophes*, as proclaimed by its title, *Journal encyclopédique*.[13] The prince-bishop at that time, Jean Théodore de Bavière, resided in Munich and left the administration of the principality to his prime minister, Maximilien Henri de Horion. Horion, who embraced the ideas of the Enlightenment, exempted Rousseau from formal censorship and kept the canons at bay. For two years the journal gained subscribers and prestige. Rousseau supplemented it by pirating books from his press. But Horion died in May 1759. The canons mounted an offensive, mobilizing theologians in Louvain, papal nuncios in Cologne and Brussels, and lobbyists in Brussels and Munich. Rousseau left for Brussels, hoping to transfer his business to a less hostile environment, but Prince Kaunitz, Maria Theresa's chancellor in Vienna, refused to grant permission. By the end of the year, it looked as though the *Journal encyclopédique* would succumb to the combined powers of the Church and the Habsburg state.

It was saved in January 1760, when Charles Godefroy de La Tour d'Auvergne, the absentee sovereign of the tiny Duchy of Bouillon, offered Rousseau a refuge. The duke had no love for the Enlightenment, but he hated Liège, a hostile mini-power sixty-two miles to the north, and he welcomed the opportunity to improve the economy of Bouillon, a poor city of 3,000 souls close to the French border. Although he submitted to a nominal censorship, Rousseau was left free to develop the *Journal encyclopédique* and two other journals. They succeeded so well that he created a separate publishing company, the Société typographique de Bouillon. From 1767 until Rousseau's death in 1785, it turned out about 200 books, most of them *contrefaçons* aimed at the French market just across the border. He kept a large work force busy at six presses, made a fortune, and established himself as a peer of the most famous publishers of the Enlightenment, notably Marc-Michel Rey, his friend and ally in Amsterdam. Although it nearly went bankrupt in the 1780s when Rousseau had withdrawn into semiretirement in Paris, the Société typographique seemed to suggest a simple business model for enterprising publishers: set up shop outside France, find out what the French want to read, and flood the kingdom with cheap reprints.

In practice, however, businesses had to overcome all sorts of obstacles, and they required astute management. The experience of the de Boubers brothers illustrates how spectacularly things could go wrong as well as right. There were at least three brothers—the sources are ambiguous—all born in Lille, all determined to make their fortune in the borderland of the book trade.[14] The oldest, Henri-François, became a successful printer in Saint-Omer forty-two miles west-northwest of Lille. His younger brother Denis joined him as an apprentice and then set up shop on his own. In 1759 Denis was caught publishing *Thérèse philosophe* and other pornographic books, fined 3,000 L., and banished from France. He emigrated to Liège, where he started all over again. This time Denis began with religious tracts and added illegal works as his business grew. In 1766 he acquired the rights of a bourgeois. He sold so many *contrefaçons* in France that he acquired an outlet in Dunkirk, which he used to stock his shipments and those of his allies throughout the international trade. By 1772, when the reign of Velbruck began, he had gained a place alongside Bassompierre and Plomteux at the top of Liège's publishing industry.

The career of the third and youngest brother, Jean-Louis de Boubers, followed the same pattern but ended in disaster. In 1764 he, too, was banished from France for trafficking in forbidden books. He took refuge with his brother in Liège and four years later managed to establish himself as a printer and type founder in Brussels. Soon he was pirating books on a large scale. He had them smuggled across the border and stored in the Dunkirk branch of the business, which he shared with his brother. Working four or five presses, he published a handsome, quarto edition of Jean-Jacques Rousseau's complete works along with cheaper *contrefaçons*. By the mid-1770s Jean-Louis had gained a reputation as the most prominent printer-bookseller of the city.[15]

On a business trip to Switzerland in the autumn of 1770, Boubers arrived in Neuchâtel with a proposition.[16] He had learned that the STN planned to counter-pirate his pirated edition of Paul-François Velly's *Histoire de France*. If it would abandon that project, he would give it 125 cut-rate copies in exchange for books in its stock, and he also would make a deal to produce d'Holbach's atheistic *Système de la nature*, which then was the hottest book on the market but nearly impossible to procure. Boubers would provide a copy for the STN to reprint and he would commit himself to purchase a large portion of its edition—500 copies of a press run of 2,000. Although the STN fulfilled its part of the bargain and shipped the 500 copies in March 1771, Boubers refused to pay for them except in the form of an exchange restricted to more copies of his Velly. Threats and recriminations filled the mail between Neuchâtel and Brussels for the next four years. In the end, the STN recovered most of the 1,480 L. Boubers owed, but wrote him off as a "shifty character of bad faith."[17]

This episode was but one of many that occupied Boubers in the 1770s. After Jean-Jacques Rousseau's death on July 2, 1778, Boubers procured letters that Rousseau had written to his first mistress, Mme de Warens. They went into volume 8 of Boubers's supposedly complete edition of Rousseau's works, which he planned to expand by pirating the material to be printed by the Société typographique de Genève. The Genevan publishers were authorized by the guardians of Rousseau's manuscripts to produce a definitive, posthumous edition, which would provide an income for Thérèse Levasseur, Rousseau's widow. Other publishers, including the STN, were plotting to pirate the Genevan edition, and Boubers considered joining forces with them.[18] In the end, however, he attacked the Genevans on his own, trying to win subscribers with some audacious false advertising in the *Gazette de Leyde* and other periodicals. He pretended to possess the bulk of the manuscripts, but he eventually backed down when the Genevans, speaking in the name of Mme Levasseur, refuted his claim. Meanwhile, he speculated on other enterprises and accumulated a growing burden of debt. In December 1782, he had nearly completed a ten-volume reprint of Raynal's *Histoire philosophique*. Before he could run off the last copies, however, his creditors and the police descended on his shop. He managed to escape, and, though he avoided debtors' prison, he was ruined. According to a report that the STN received from a Brussels bookseller, Boubers had absconded with the plates to Raynal's *Histoire philosophique* and left a debt of more than 300,000 L., "the biggest bankruptcy that is conceivable in the book trade."[19] That is the last trace of him that can be found in the archives.

The fate of other publishers in Brussels is less apparent. Although most of the population spoke Flemish, the city became increasingly Frenchified during the eighteenth century, thanks in large measure to the influence of prince Charles of Lorraine, the governor general of the Austrian Netherlands from 1744 to 1780. He and the Habsburg minister plenipotentiary, Charles de Cobenzl, favored progressive policies, and they tolerated the activities of

Jean-Louis de Boubers, although they failed to protect Pierre Rousseau when he attempted to move the *Journal encyclopédique* to Brussels. The city had twenty printers and eleven booksellers in 1781, but there is little evidence that they speculated heavily in publishing.[20] Four of them show up in the archives of the STN. According to its local informant, the most reputable were Dujardin and Lemaire.[21] Although they indicated a willingness to order books from Neuchâtel, the STN never did any business with them. Instead, it was drawn into relations with two more marginal dealers, Delahaye & Compagnie and de Villebon & Compagnie. Delahaye traded heavily in *livres philosophiques* and offered to provide new publications for the STN to pirate, but did not publish original works. Although the company's three directors kept on the alert for French agents and spies, they were arrested on February 19, 1785, for dealing in illegal literature. One of them was released, and he attributed their imprisonment to *menées sourdes*—machinations—of their commercial rivals.[22] Their stock, which he evaluated at 90,000 L., was sold off by their creditors. The STN's agent failed to collect a debt of 1,409 L. and considered the firm permanently ruined.[23] Villebon drew supplies from the great publishing centers of the region, but he also had books printed, and he developed a large list of his own, which included many prohibited works. While on a trip to Ostend in 1782, he was seized by the police and carried off to the Bastille. Released after four months of imprisonment, he resumed his business and apparently kept it going until the Revolution.[24]

No other publishing houses in Belgian territory participated heavily in the French book trade. Antwerp had lost its dominant position at the end of the sixteenth century and by the end of the seventeenth century had been eclipsed by the thriving centers of publishing to the north: Amsterdam, Rotterdam, Leiden, and The Hague. The Netherlands became an economic superpower after gaining independence from Spain at the end of the Eighty Years' War (1568–1648).[25] Printers and booksellers shared in the general prosperity, benefiting from the country's exceptional financial institutions, commercial networks, and transportation facilities. Reinforced by Huguenot refugees, they published many books in French; and as mastery of the French language became increasingly widespread, they continued to dominate much of the international book trade well into the eighteenth century. The tolerant atmosphere in The Netherlands made it possible for them to produce books that would never be allowed in other countries—not that the Dutch practiced freedom of the press: the Estates of Holland condemned Rousseau's *Émile* and *Contrat social* in 1762 and his *Lettres écrites de la montagne* in 1765.

Conditions varied throughout the highly autonomous towns and provinces in The Netherlands. An aristocratic elite of "Regents" controlled much of urban life, arousing resentment among burghers who agitated for democratic reforms. Political tensions increased during the second half of the eighteenth century and erupted in a rebellion in 1785, when the "Patriot" radicals attempted to seize power. They were put down in 1787 by William V, Prince of Orange and Stadholder (chief magistrate), who controlled the military and summoned troops from Prussia to help him restore the Dutch version of the Ancien Régime. By this time, the "Golden Age" of the Netherlands was a distant memory. Although the Amsterdam bourse continued to dominate international finance, the Dutch merchant fleet had been eclipsed by the English and French (in the late seventeenth century it had far more ships than the two of them combined), and the entire economy had sunk into decline. Dominance in the publishing industry shifted to Switzerland in the mid-century years. Yet the Dutch and Swiss spheres of influence were never entirely separate. Three great publishers stood out among the many in the Netherlands who dealt in French books at the height of the Enlightenment: Marc-Michel Rey in Amsterdam, Pierre-Frédéric Gosse in The Hague, and Jean-Edmé Dufour in Maastricht.[26] All had strong Swiss connections. Rey was born in Geneva and trained in Lausanne. The Gosse family had deep Genevan roots, and Dufour became the closest Dutch ally of the Société typographique de Neuchâtel.

Marc-Michel Rey is celebrated as the most important publisher of the Enlightenment—and rightly so: he produced the original editions of many works by the *philosophes* and reprinted still more.[27] Unlike Voltaire's principal publisher, Gabriel Cramer, who belonged to the sophisticated Genevan elite, Rey was not an intellectual. The son of poor Huguenot refugees, he had little schooling and was apprenticed to a bookseller in Lausanne in 1737 at the age of seventeen. Although he established his own business in Amsterdam in 1744 and continued it until his death in 1780, he never mastered Dutch. He concentrated on the trade in French books, as did others in Amsterdam such as the firms of Changuion, Néaulme, and Arkstée et Markus. Rey's relations with Rousseau have received the most attention from scholars, thanks to the material available in R. A. Leigh's edition of Rousseau's correspondence. Leigh and others describe Rey as a businessman, fiercely intent on making money, yet they emphasize the ties of mutual affection that bound the publisher to the philosopher.[28] Rey paid Rousseau reasonable fees for his manuscripts, and he financed a pension for Thérèse

Levasseur. The payments seem modest in retrospect: 2,161 L. for *La Nouvelle Héloise*, one of the greatest bestsellers of the century, and one that brought Rey 10,000 L. within a year and went through more than a dozen editions, most of them pirated. The letters exchanged between the two show that Rey admired Rousseau "with a dog-like devotion,"[29] believed in his ideas, made allowances for his psychological instability, and never wavered in supporting him. He asked Rousseau to serve as godfather to one of his daughters, and Rousseau took the responsibility seriously.

By 1765, the demand for Rousseau's works had reached such heights that even some Parisian publishers tried to cash in on it, despite the danger of dealing in illegal books. Pierre Guy, who ran the Parisian house of Veuve Duchesne, tried to recruit Arkstée in a plot to pirate Rey's original editions of *Du contrat social* and *Lettre à Christophe de Beaumont*. Although supposedly bound to secrecy, Arkstée informed Rey, because he did not want to alienate a colleague and he also felt bound by an informal version of copyright among Dutch publishers: if one of them published a book and kept it in print, the others respected his exclusive right to sell it. Armed with this information, Rey protested to Guy, and Guy eventually commissioned him to do the printing—that is, to pirate his own publications. As he knew that they would be pirated in any case, Rey preferred to cream off the profits with an early *contrefaçon* that he would produce himself.[30] This episode and others like it occurred fairly often in the publishing industry and illustrate the scramble to profit from books that sold well.

Rey made a fortune, thanks in large part to his skill at carving out a niche for publishing the most illegal works of the *philosophes*. He produced many books by Voltaire, often behind the back of Cramer and with Voltaire's connivance. In 1764 and 1765 he did editions of the *Dictionnaire philosophique* and *L'Évangile de la raison*, which were both condemned to be burned by the Estates of Holland—much to Voltaire's delight, because bonfires increased demand. Rey published the first editions of most of the works written by d'Holbach and others in his circle of radical freethinkers. The manuscripts arrived in Amsterdam through a clandestine network, and Rey managed to print and distribute them under the cover of anonymity. Although he never realized his plan to publish the works of Diderot, he brought so much of the Enlightenment into print that he can come across as a propagandist and fellow traveler of the *philosophes*. Yet he remained a member in good standing of the Protestant Walloon church in Amsterdam, and he published an edition of the Bible, a translation of sermons by John Tillotson (an archbishop of

Canterbury in the seventeenth century), and other religious works, possibly including a *Liturgie pour les Protestants de France.*[31] Most of the books that Rey pirated—and he pirated on a large scale—were inoffensive to the Dutch and French authorities. Among the 2,685 titles in his sales catalogue of 1754, the biggest category (18.6 percent) was devoted to standard works on religion.[32] Did ideology drive his business? Probably not. Although he certainly sympathized with the *philosophes*, Rousseau above all, Rey seems to have been guided by an astute sense of what would sell. His mastery of the market led him to become the most eminent publisher of the Enlightenment.

Gosse and Dufour also took a businesslike approach to publishing. Although little is known about their careers, their correspondence with the STN shows that they made decisions according to what today would be called market research. Gosse warned the STN against pirating anything that would not appeal to general readers, as will be explained in the following chapter. He eagerly snapped up the works of Voltaire, although he grumbled about Voltaire's habit of tinkering with old texts to pass them off as new. Yet he excluded the most radical books from his trade. Dufour did not. He published plenty of highly illegal literature and was particularly eager to procure the seditious and pornographic works of Mirabeau. In fact, the two Dutch houses did business in a different manner, determined in large part by their geopolitical situation. Located close to the stadholder's offices in The Hague, Gosse enjoyed a position as the official bookseller to the court. He derived a steady income from publishing one of the largest French-language journals, the *Gazette de la Haye*, and he did an enormous wholesale business. In return for large orders, the STN gave him the exclusive right to market its books in The Netherlands and the British Isles. The kind of literature he favored can be appreciated from his order for *Lettres du comte Algarotti sur la Russie: Contenant l'état du commerce, de la marine, des revenus & des forces de cet empire* (1770) by the diplomat and polymath Francesco Algarotti. It could sell pretty well, he remarked, "and so we will take 400 copies."[33] Few booksellers tossed off such a large order so casually, without even bargaining for a discount. Gosse did not swap his own publications with those of the STN, because the distance between The Hague and Neuchâtel made the shipping costs too heavy. He paid in solid bills of exchange and retired in 1774, leaving a prosperous business to his son. By that time he had mellowed. His son and the STN quarreled bitterly over an order for the STN's *Description des arts et métiers*, and then made peace. The father welcomed their reconciliation with a letter that gives a glimpse of a publisher looking back on a successful career: "For my part, having arrived at a quite advanced age, I am more interested in peace and quiet than in business and making money, but that will not prevent me, for as long as the All Powerful accords me health and strength, to take true pleasure in being useful to you in every way I can."[34]

Whether Dufour held such pious sentiments seems unlikely. He published a first edition of an atheistic work, *Vrai Sens du système de la nature*, and a four-volume edition of Helvétius's *Oeuvres complètes*, which included a reprint of d'Holbach's *Système de la nature*.[35] A Parisian trained in the printing shop of Bassompierre in Liège, he set up his own publishing house in 1766 in Maastricht, far from the great cities on the west coast of the Netherlands. Maastricht had developed its own variety of toleration, having been governed by dual sovereigns, the prince-bishop of Liège and the duke of Brabant, in the Middle Ages and subjected to both Protestant and Catholic rule during the era of religious wars. Tucked away in the southernmost province of the Dutch Republic, it enjoyed great autonomy during the eighteenth century. It had two administrations under two bourgmestres, one for Catholics and one for Protestants. Taking full advantage of the leeway created by the awkward institutional machinery, Dufour published new works and pirated old ones on a large scale. He acquired a partner in 1775 and attracted several financial backers. By the end of 1776 he had expanded his shop to include six presses. After visiting him in September 1779, Abram Bosset de Luze, one of the STN's directors, called him "the scourge of the publishers in Holland, since he is capable of undercutting them with our editions as well as his own."[36]

As Bosset's remarks suggest, Dufour provided a bridge between publishers in Switzerland and Holland. Unlike Rey and Gosse, he dealt heavily in exchanges, minimizing the transport costs from Neuchâtel on a route that led through Basel and Nymegen. He sent a standing order for the STN to send as swaps twenty-five copies of all its *nouveautés* (editions of the most recent books).[37] For its part, the STN declared itself delighted to deal with "a house as distinguished as yours."[38] In fact, the two houses were quite similar. Both relied primarily on pirating. Dufour's catalogues, which he issued at the beginning of each year, contained the same variety of books as the STN's, and in the first catalogue he received from the STN, he found six works that he already had in stock. Sometimes they pirated the same book. In 1787 Dufour learned that the STN planned to reprint the nine-volume *Éléments d'histoire générale ancienne et moderne* by Claude-François-Xavier Millot. Having already begun to produce it himself, he sent off a warning that the competition would hurt their relations and damage their profits.[39]

To preserve peace, he offered to abandon his edition, and in the end neither house published the book, probably because the market had been sated with a Parisian edition. Both publishers produced editions of William Robertson's four-volume *Histoire de l'Amérique* in 1778 at the height of the interest in the new American republic. Having commissioned a translation, Dufour considered his edition an original work and objected when the STN pirated it, all the more so as it claimed to have corrected errors and to have done a superior printing job.

Despite such occasional friction and hard bargaining over the terms of exchanges, the two houses became close allies. In 1776, when he began to trade heavily with the STN, Dufour sent a list of thirty works that he had printed and was willing to swap for works of the STN. They included a wide variety of *contrefaçons* of legal books and several *livres philosophiques*, including a good deal of off-color literature such as *L'Art de péter* (*The Art of Farting*) and *Parapilla*, "a libertine poem [printed] from the manuscript."[40] In other letters he indicated that he had produced similar books "from manuscript." He also printed a pamphlet for Simon-Nicolas-Henri Linguet, a famous polemicist who set up headquarters in Maastricht for a while in 1776. For the most part, however, Dufour pirated current works that sold well on the legal market. They included sentimental novels such as *Cécilia, ou mémoires d'une héritière* (*Cécilia, or Memoirs of an Heiress*) along with the spicier novellas of Crébillon fils. Among his more weighty *contrefaçons* were the works of Beaumarchais and four editions of Raynal's *Histoire philosophique*. Dufour had no bookshop in Maastricht. He operated as a printer-wholesaler, supplying a large network of retailers and other wholesalers. As he also developed an exchange trade with Dutch publishers in the great coastal cities, a good number of Swiss books were funneled through him to the eastern Netherlands as well as to Belgian territories and France.

Dufour's business occupied a pivotal, middle ground at a time when the publishing of French books shifted from The Netherlands to Switzerland. Printing was 25 percent cheaper in Switzerland,[41] yet the production of French books continued to occupy publishers in many Dutch cities well into the eighteenth century. Rotterdam ceased to be a great center after the abatement in the flood of Huguenot refugees, which had included outstanding printers (Abraham Acher and Henri Desbordes) as well as authors (Pierre Bayle and Pierre Jurieu). But Amsterdam retained several houses that specialized in French books—Changuion, Néaulme, and Arkstée et Markus in addition to Rey. In Leiden a long line of publishers produced more academic works, continuing the tradition established by the house of Elsevier in the seventeenth century.[42] By 1780, however, publishing, along with many other industries, suffered from the conflict between the Orangists and the Patriots, a conflict that brought the country close to civil war.[43]

STN's Bosset had an opportunity to observe all the variations in the publishing industry during a three-month tour through the Rhineland and the Low Countries in the summer of 1779. He set out to explore possibilities of collaboration and marketing in the rich book country that extended from Basel to Amsterdam and back from Brussels and Liège to Neuchâtel.[44] With the exception of Dufour, situated so close to Belgian territory, the Dutch received him coldly. In Amsterdam, he visited all the major publishers, and all treated him as a dangerous competitor. They told him frankly that they would not trade with the STN and did not want to have anything to do with its cheap *contrefaçons*. On the contrary, they planned to league together so as to favor their own original editions. As befitted a colleague and a fellow Swiss, Rey invited Bosset to dinner. They covered the current topics of shoptalk in the book trade—projects to publish the posthumous works of Rousseau and rival editions of the *Encyclopédie*—but Rey did not disguise his hostility to the STN.[45] In the end, Bosset concluded that the STN could not do business in Holland. It was hostile territory.[46]

As Bosset remarked, publishers in the Low Countries and Switzerland pirated the same books. Because the Swiss could print them at a lower cost, they had come to dominate the market for *contrefaçons* and did not trade extensively with the Dutch. The distance between the two countries, as well as the disparities in production expenses, made the exchange trade unfeasible. Therefore, the Swiss swapped books and formed alliances among themselves, while the Dutch also banded together. Competition produced rivalries as well as cooperation within each camp, and at the summit of the international trade a few houses joined forces in large enterprises. Cramer cooperated with Rey in arranging editions of Voltaire and Rousseau, and the STN aligned itself with Plomteux in speculations on the *Encyclopédie*, while Panckoucke in Paris pulled strings and plotted with everyone. International consortiums, which required multiple investors, were exceptional, however. Few publishers could afford to risk capital on them, and only a few concentrated on the equally risky business of producing original works. Most based their businesses on pirating.

In deciding what to pirate, the publishers drew on the same source of supply—that is, the market place in France, which provided the copy and generated reports about steady sellers as well as *nouveautés* that promised to sell. Although the pirates competed with one another in the race to get their editions on the market, they exchanged so many of their books among themselves that they carried very similar stock. They often printed the same books, and therefore the catalogues of the Swiss, Belgian, and Dutch houses contain a large number of the same titles.[47] Pierre-Frédéric Gosse noted that many of the books that the STN proposed to him were already available in other editions, and he was unhappy to find that some of them had been pirated from editions of his own.[48] Daniel Jean Changuion of Amsterdam also discovered to his surprise that several of his books appeared in the STN's catalogues.[49] The STN itself learned from its customers that they had purchased copies of its own editions from other publishers.[50] Thanks to the exchange system, there was so much fluidity on the supply side that a common corpus of titles, a kind of floating general stock, was available to many pirate publishers. The *sociétés typographiques* of Neuchâtel and Lausanne swapped books so intensively that, as a dealer in Leipzig remarked, their catalogues were virtually the same.[51] The sameness in this kind of publishing is suggested by the term *société typographique* itself. There were *sociétés typographiques* in Neuchâtel, Bern, Lausanne, Yverdon, Saarbrucken, Liège, Bouillon, Neuwied, Brussels, Cologne, Kehl, and even London, where a good deal of pirating of French books took place. Of course, the adoption of the name does not prove that a publisher specialized in *contrefaçons*, although that was usually the case. At a minimum, however, it indicates the spread of French publishing houses around the border of France.

Indeed, the publishers had France surrounded. Although they produced French books for dealers everywhere in Europe, they aimed their output primarily at the French market; and if one adds Avignon to their number, it looks as though they had the capacity to flood it.[52] There is no statistical measure of the proliferation of *contrefaçons*, but all the evidence indicates that it was enormous. According to the vast survey of the book trade conducted by the Direction de la librairie in 1764, great quantities of *contrefaçons* existed everywhere. Intendants and their subordinates in Lyon, Toulouse, Montpellier, Besançon, and other provincial capitals reported that cheap pirated books had conquered the local markets. Miromesnil, who at that time was responsible for overseeing the trade in Rouen, wrote that the expensive price of privileged books from Paris had forced provincial retailers to rely totally on supplies from pirates: "Most provincial booksellers carry only pirated books."[53] An earlier report from Lyon concluded bluntly, "The trade of our booksellers is based entirely on pirated books."[54]

The key edict of the six promulgated on August 30, 1777, treated piracy as the greatest problem to be solved in reorganizing publishing and the book trade. As explained in the previous chapter, the edict acknowledged that pirated books formed such a large part of the stock in provincial book stores that they could not be confiscated without ruining a great many booksellers, and therefore it legitimized all *contrefaçons* currently held everywhere in France, provided they were stamped in the guilds' *chambres syndicales*. Although records of only eight of the twenty *chambres syndicales* have survived (they do not include the largest, Lyon and Rouen, and members of the Parisian *chambre syndicale* generally refused to comply), they show that the stamping took place on a gigantic scale: 387,000 volumes from 118 bookshops were stamped, and they came from approximately 2,450 different editions.[55]

The debate surrounding the reform of 1777 illustrates the crucial importance of piracy for the book industry. Whether they supported or opposed the edict, booksellers agreed that *contrefaçons* dominated the provincial trade. Jean-Baptiste-Antoine Suard emphasized that, among the supporters, pirated books accounted for more than the total value of all the legal books produced in Paris. He estimated that 6 million *contrefaçons* existed in the stock of French booksellers and that 30 million had been produced in the last twenty years—a number that exceeded the population of France. Every provincial bookshop stocked them, he wrote. They were printed by more than 200 presses "located along the borders of France, in Geneva, Lausanne, Yverdon, etc." The Swiss could pirate a book for 30 to 40 percent less than the Parisians, he asserted. The same work was sometimes printed in ten different places and snapped up at bargain prices everywhere in France. "To put it frankly, everything has been pirated, large works as well as small; nothing has been respected." So many *contrefaçons* existed that the government could not possibly impound them. Its only course was to legitimize the current stock and take new measures to prevent more from arriving from abroad.[56]

Like the partisans of the edict, the Parisian publishers emphasized the omnipresence of pirated books. "Any book that has the slightest success is instantly pirated," they argued in one of their appeals to the Conseil du roi. "That is the fate of every good book," wrote one of their pamphleteers. The pirates were "real brigands who have flooded France with *contrefaçons*," wrote another. Yet the Parisians drew the opposite conclusion from the provincials while citing the same kind of evidence. Instead of stamping out the trade in *contrefaçons*, they insisted, the government was legalizing it—at least in respect to the enormous number of pirated books currently in stock. This misguided policy would bring a windfall to the provincial booksellers, but in the long run it would produce an economic disaster for everyone.[57]

The Parisians had pounded away at this argument for many years in their lobbying with the government. In a memoir published in 1759, nearly twenty years before the 1777 edicts, they complained, "There is not one of our books that has not been pirated if it has had the slightest success."[58] In 1763 Pierre Guy—the director of the Duchesne publishing house who engineered the pirated edition of Rousseau in Amsterdam—submitted a memoire to the Direction. The foreign pirates, he wrote, had turned the book trade into "the most atrocious brigandage, unlimited in its license." They carried off hundreds of thousands of livres every year by raiding the French market.[59] Four years later, Guy found himself in the Bastille, locked up for cooperating with the very pirates he had denounced. In another memoir, probably written this time to ingratiate himself with the police and to win his release, he described the operations of the illegal trade from the perspective of an insider. The book trade, he wrote, "is nothing more than piracy. . . . Those people turn out editions the way our masons make buildings, by the yard."[60]

This theme reappeared in many other memoires, petitions, and confidential reports. Although the Parisian and provincial booksellers advocated contrary solutions to the problem of piracy, they agreed about its cause. For half a century, the publishing boom in the Fertile Crescent had inundated France with cheap books. It had transformed the book trade. A Lyonnais dealer stated in a matter-of-fact way an assumption that everyone took to be self-evident: "Dealing in pirated books has become a necessity in the book trade."[61]

Although the French authorities failed to stop the flood, they certainly tried, not only by the edicts of August 30, 1777, but also in later measures; and they scored some significant successes. Their efforts—in border patrols, inspection of shipments, and raids on book stores—affected the publishing industry throughout the Fertile Crescent. Fortunately, enough documentation survives for one to assess the effects during the final years of the Ancien Régime. The story goes back to the sixth of the 1777 edicts, which required that all pirated books be stamped in *chambres syndicales*.

The STN's correspondence shows that booksellers throughout the kingdom rushed to submit their *contrefaçons* for stamping—and understandably so, because by complying with the edict they legalized a large portion of their stock. Sometimes they sent urgent orders for new supplies from Neuchâtel so that they could increase their holdings of pirated books before the deadline for the stamping elapsed. Although labor intensive and cumbersome, the stamping certainly provided a windfall for the provincial trade, and the edict's provision for preventing the resumption of pirating added nothing to the measures that had failed so egregiously to repress piracy before 1777.[62] In fact, the new code provided no incentives for the provincial booksellers to abandon a trade that had proven to be so profitable. Nothing prevented them from resuming business as usual—and they did. The foreign publishers continued to produce cheap *contrefaçons*, and the provincial dealers continued to order them.

The trade did indeed decline for a few months while the booksellers assessed the threat to their businesses, and its resumption varied from place to place. In a few cities, such as Rouen and Dijon, the reorganized *chambres syndicales* enforced the edicts severely enough to inflict severe damage on the commerce with foreign publishers. Machuel, the largest bookseller in Rouen, complained bitterly to the STN, "You, Messieurs, are in a free country, not subject to changes [in government policy]; and no doubt your liberty consists in printing everything you want. Things are very different here. Ever since the edicts of August 30, 1777, and everything that followed them, . . . the provincial trade has been crushed, and it won't recover from this upheaval for a long time."[63]

By 1780, however, the STN had resumed shipping *contrefaçons* to most of its customers in provincial France. In Marseille, Jean Mossy, the principal bookseller of the city, sent the following report on June 29, 1779: "I have had to get my pirated books stamped. In fact, I am in the middle of this operation. The book inspector is constantly at my place: you can imagine that this is hardly a good time [for business]. But this kind of interruption in our trade is too great to continue for long." Soon afterward, he was ordering *contrefaçons* as usual. In Bordeaux Antoine Laporte, the city's top bookseller, became *syndic* when the local guild was reorganized in accordance with the edicts, and he used his authority to protect the STN's shipments of pirated works. In Besançon, the main bookseller, Charles-Antoine Charmet, became the *syndic* of the new *chambre syndicale* and also intervened to help with the STN's shipments while he was continuing with his own orders for *contrefaçons*. In Lyon, Jacques Revol, the STN's shipping agent and smuggler, steered its pirated works through the *chambre syndicale* and forwarded them to its customers throughout the kingdom. As an attempt to eradicate the trade in *contrefaçons*, the Code of 1777 was a failure.

However, the government succeeded in a final effort to stop the flood of books from the Fertile Crescent before the whole system came crashing down in 1789. On June 12, 1783, France's foreign minister Charles Gravier, comte de Vergennes, issued an order to the Ferme générale, the tax-collecting agency that policed France's borders, requiring that all imports of books be sent for inspection to the Parisian *chambre syndicale*, no matter what their destination. A shipment from Neuchâtel to Marseille (or from Brussels to Bordeaux or from Avignon to Nancy) would therefore have to take a ruinously expensive detour to Paris, and it would be subjected to inspection by the commercial enemies of the foreign publishers. According to past practice and previous regulations, book imports were to be sent from border stations to the *chambre syndicale* in the nearest *ville d'entrée* for inspection and then would be forwarded to the customers who ordered them. As the key nodal points in the distribution network, the provincial *chambres syndicales* regulated the flow of the import trade. Vergennes's order eliminated that function. It was a highly unusual measure, because the book trade fell under the authority of the Direction de la librairie located within the chancellery, not the foreign office.

Vergennes, the most powerful minister in the government, had his reasons for asserting his authority in this unprecedented manner. He had become appalled at the profusion of seditious libels, which made the monarchy look like a despotism and often slandered grandees in Versailles.[64] Unlike *contrefaçons*, these hard-core forbidden books were produced by only a few foreign publishers, usually marginal entrepreneurs who were willing to take great risks in pursuit of high profits. One of the STN's original partners, Samuel Fauche, who established his own business after a quarrel with the other partners in 1772, often speculated in this sector of the trade. He published Mirabeau's *Essai sur le despotisme* in 1775 but then fell out with his son and son-in-law, who set up their own company, Fauche fils aîné, Favre et Witel, and published Mirabeau's later works, both political (*Des lettres de cachet et des prisons d'État*, 1782) and pornographic (*Errotika biblion*, 1783 and *Le Libertin de qualité*, 1783).

In February 1783 the Parisian inspector of the book trade, Joseph d'Hémery, learned that these works, along with Linguet's equally illegal *Mémoires sur la Bastille*, were being produced in Neuchâtel. He informed Néville, Lenoir, and Vergennes. At Vergennes's instigation, the French ambassador in Soleure persuaded the Conseil d'État in Neuchâtel to investigate. It turned up nothing, but the inspector of the book trade in Lyon had sources who informed him about the printing operations in Neuchâtel, and the authorities in Besançon were put on the alert. In May they confiscated seven bales of forbidden works that had been shipped from Neuchâtel by Fauche fils aîné, Favre et Witel and had cleared the border near Pontarlier without difficulty. Armed with this information, Vergennes sent a letter to the directors of the Ferme générale to complain about the negligence of their agents in Pontarlier, and a few days later he followed it up with his order of June 12, 1783.[65]

Vergennes made the purpose of his order clear: it would stifle "the vast number of libels printed in foreign countries."[66] Instead of being inspected in provincial *chambres syndicales*, which were notoriously complicit with foreign publishers, book imports now had to make the long journey to Paris and undergo inspection by the lieutenant general of police and officers of the Parisian *chambre syndicale*, who were still seething with resentment about the favorable treatment of the provincial booksellers in the edicts of 1777.

Soon after Vergennes issued his order, the Paris police arrested Jacques Mallet, an agent of Fauche fils aîné, Favre et Witel who was marketing their books in France. Confined to a cell in the Bastille and desperate to be released, he confessed everything and wrote a long report, which described every aspect of their operation. This information confirmed Vergennes in his inclination to make the order of June 12, 1783, permanent and thereby to establish a strict policy for controlling the importation of all books from all locations along France's borders.[67]

Protests poured in from the provinces. The booksellers in Rouen shot off an immediate warning that the order would ruin their business. The same complaint was repeated in letters from the *chambre syndicale* of Lille and various booksellers in French Flanders. The booksellers in Lyon, led by Jean-André Périsse-Duluc and Jean-Marie Bruyset, lobbied desperately to get the order withdrawn. Writing as *syndic* of the Lyon guild, Périsse warned that the order had forced all his colleagues to suspend business. The extra transport costs were so expensive, except of course for shipments to Paris, that they often exceeded the value of the merchandise itself. The order had brought book imports to a halt, inflicting particular damage on Lyon's role as an intermediary in the commerce between northern Europe and the Mediterranean countries. Exports also suffered, because they depended on the exchange trade, and no foreign bookseller would swap books with the French if he could not get his own books into France. Instead of ordering books from Lyon, the foreign booksellers were now certain to pirate them and thereby dominate the trade in French books throughout the rest of Europe.

Moreover, Périsse claimed, Vergennes's order would fail to achieve its purpose, because forbidden books did not pass through Lyon's *chambre syndicale*. They entered France through underground channels employed by professional smugglers. Therefore, while killing the legal trade, the order would not prevent the diffusion of the very works it was meant to suppress. Périsse elaborated on this argument with a long account of how smuggling actually operated, taking care to exculpate his colleagues at every point. The memoir by Bruyset made the same points and put them in the context of all the ills that the provincial trade had suffered for the last dozen years. Vergennes's order reinforced the advantages of the Parisian booksellers, Bruyset stressed, because unlike their provincial rivals they paid no additional transport costs. Once again, on June 12, 1783, the French government had reset the basic conditions of the book trade in a way that reinforced the hegemony of Paris.[68]

Despite the protests, Vergennes's order was never rescinded, and it transformed the policing of the foreign book trade. After several attempts to find a way around it, many of the best customers of the STN—Racine in Rouen, Waroquier in Soissons, Poinçot in Versailles, Cazin in Reims, Grabit in Lyon—stopped ordering books. In Marseille, Mossy, who had shrugged off the threat of the 1777 edicts, fell back on the route over the Alps to Turin and Nice in late 1783, but the cost and delays made it unfeasible, and he ceased doing business with the STN in 1786. With help from smugglers, the STN managed to get a few bales to its closest and most trusted customer, Widow Charmet in Besançon. She heard that some other Swiss publishers had resumed shipments to France after 1785. But when the STN made inquiries in Geneva and Lausanne, it learned that that the French market remained blocked, and its shipping agents confirmed that information. Some smuggling ventures succeeded, but they never opened up regular trade of the kind that had prevailed before 1783, when the Swiss publishers had relied on allies in the provincial *chambres syndicales*, along with agents who knew how to steer shipments past inspections in most provincial cities.

Although Vergennes's order made the route from Neuchâtel to Pontarlier especially dangerous, owing to the shipments confiscated from Fauche fils aîné, Favre et Witel, it applied to all the publishing houses that encircled France. How badly it affected imports from Amsterdam, Brussels, and the

Rhineland cannot be determined. But all the information that reached the STN—from other publishers and shipping agents as well as French booksellers—indicated that the French-Swiss border remained closed to all shipments except those sent under seal for inspection in Paris. In December 1787, a report from Dijon confirmed that Vergennes's order was still active and still stifling the trade with foreign publishers.[69]

Although Vergennes had made it clear that his purpose was to prevent the importation of seditious books, his order of June 12, 1783, did far more than the edicts of 1777 to suppress piracy. It closed off the French market to the foreign publishers who had flooded it with cheap *contrefaçons* for the last thirty years. By that time the book trade had already gone into a decline, so it would be wrong to attribute all the difficulties of the book market to the intervention of Vergennes. In fact, the profusion of pirated books had contributed to the downturn, according to the best-informed booksellers like Cazin of Reims. He stopped ordering shipments from the STN as soon as he learned of Vergennes's order and remarked in a letter of July 27, 1784, "The rage for pirating and for multiplying the [pirated] editions makes this commerce extremely uncertain and is ruining the book trade in all of Europe."

Above all, Vergennes's order showed the determination of the French government to reassert its control of the book trade. It did so, just as it had done a hundred years earlier, by reinforcing the police power of the Parisian Guild. Seen in the context of all the lobbying and politicking that had taken place since 1750, Vergennes's order was the culmination of a deep-seated struggle between the provincial and Parisian booksellers. It can be counted as a defeat for the provincials, yet it was not much of a victory for the Parisians, because they, too, suffered from the general slump. In the end, therefore, all of them lost.

Although Vergennes's order damaged the publishing industry throughout the Fertile Crescent, it arrived too late to eliminate the *contrefaçons* that had piled up in booksellers' stock rooms everywhere in France. Piracy permeated the French book industry, that is clear. But how exactly did it operate? The documentation, particularly from the STN archives, is rich enough to provide an answer.

PART 2

PIRATING

4

How to Pirate a Book

IT LOOKS AS EASY as shooting fish in a barrel. Take a book that is selling well, reprint it, package it, market it, and ship it out, then haul in the profit. Moreover, in most cases it was perfectly legal. A pirate in Holland or Switzerland could reprint a book published in France without breaking the law, because no international copyright existed. Of course, the French publishers protested. Their correspondence abounds in expressions like "pirate," "corsaire," and "bandit." Yet most pirates were respectable businessmen, and they went about their business by following what one of the directors of the Société typographique de Neuchâtel called "calculation, a demonstrative science."[1] How they made their calculations is a question worth pursuing, for it goes to the heart of publishing under the Ancien Régime. The archives of the STN provide an answer to that question.

The STN was founded in 1769 in the Swiss principality of Neuchâtel by four local notables who sought to tap the demand for French books by reprinting those that they judged would sell best, both in France and throughout Europe. Frédéric-Samuel Ostervald, the leader of the enterprise, was a prominent figure in Neuchâtel's politics and a man of letters, but he had no experience of publishing. Nor did his associates. They set up a printing shop in the summer of 1769, and then faced a question: What should they select to reprint from the vast output of French books?

In order to cope with this question, Ostervald consulted a few leading booksellers, some of whom he already knew and others he got to know by handling the STN's commercial correspondence. The most significant of his advisors was Pierre-Frédéric Gosse, Junior, a bookseller in The Hague, who ran one of the largest businesses in the Low Countries and, after thirty years of experience, had acquired a profound knowledge of the book trade everywhere in Europe, especially in France. Gosse sent the STN orders as well as counsel. In return, it furnished him with books at a reduced price and with an exclusive arrangement for their sale in his region (provided that he bought enough copies).

The letters between Ostervald and Gosse turned into a correspondence course in the art of piracy. In his first requests for advice, Ostervald adopted a deferential tone. "The agreeable obligation we have assumed, with your permission, to inform you not only of what we are doing but also of the projects that we are considering, and the high regard we have of your wise counsel. . . ." Ostervald went on to ask Gosse's opinion of a *Treatise on Wool-Bearing Animals*, currently available in quarto format with illustrations. He would reduce the format to an octavo or duodecimo; eliminate the illustrations, "since they are hardly necessary for things that everyone sees every day"; and cut the price.[2] The commercial calculation can be distinguished easily behind the flowery language. Ostervald was not proposing a work by a Voltaire or a Rousseau but rather a quite ordinary and practical sort of book, the kind that seemed likely to sell in a particular sector of the public and that would be relatively cheap. As already explained, pirates often undersold original editions by eliminating what they called *luxe typographique*, and they minimized risks by persuading favorite clients to make large advance orders at special discounts. Gosse sometimes ordered 100, 500, or even 1,000 copies at a time. He had purchased three-quarters of the *Encyclopédie* that the Italian man of letters, Fortunato Bartolomeo de Felice (later known as Barthélemy de Félice) was printing in Yverdon, at the other end of the Lake of Neuchâtel, at a run of 2,500 copies. But Gosse had no interest in the *Treatise on Wool-Bearing Animals*. "We don't believe that, by its nature, it will sell very well," he replied. However, he was tempted by another book that Ostervald proposed at the same time: J.-B. Suard's translation of the *History of Charles V* by William Robertson, which "will certainly be an excellent enterprise."[3]

The exchange jumped in this way from one kind of book to another, covering the entire spectrum of the literature that was being published in French. In a series of letters sent to Gosse in March 1770, Ostervald requested advice about seven works that the STN was considering: a popular scientific manual on inoculation; a translation of *Sermons for Young Women* by James Fordyce; a history of Spanish poetry by Louis Joseph Velasquez; a treatise on jurisprudence by Emmerich de Vatel; and two literary anthologies—"a collection of all French dramatists from Corneille to our day" and *Amusements for Social Gatherings*, which was "another collection of all the best moral and philosophical tales, chosen with impeccable taste."[4]

Gosse considered them one after the other and delivered his verdicts in a blunt, businesslike manner. He would not order any more books about inoculation: the market was saturated with them. Fordyce's sermons struck him as "a good seller," so he sent an advance order for 250 copies. He refused to consider the book about Spanish poetry, because he had never heard of it and never bought a *chat en poche* (a pig in a poke). Vatel's treatise, though excellent, did not suit him for reasons peculiar to the Dutch trade: "Since the booksellers of Leiden, by printing the first edition, have acquired what we here call the right of copy (*droit de copie*), and not the *privilège*, and since we in the Dutch book trade religiously respect this right of copy among ourselves, I cannot sell it in this country." Although *droit de copie*, a trade convention, was not the same thing as copyright, the Dutch occupied a position closer to the English, who had benefited from a copyright law since 1710, than to the French in the spectrum of concepts about intellectual property. As to the two anthologies, Gosse advised against them, because a volume of moral tales had just been published in Liège and collections of plays had not been selling well. "You certainly can employ your presses better on something else."[5]

Information clearly was crucial in developing a publishing strategy. Ostervald needed to know what editions had been published, how well they had sold, and whether the demand was adequate in certain genres. Gosse's letters contained so much crucial information that they determined Ostervald's publishing decisions. The STN abandoned all the projects he had mentioned, except Fordyce's sermons, which it decided to pirate, because Gosse's endorsement and his advance order of 250 copies tipped the balance in favor of an edition. Meanwhile, Ostervald continued to fire off requests for more professional counseling. What did Gosse think of Abbé Chapt's *Travels in Siberia*, a book "that is likely to please everyone" and that could be reduced economically from four to two volumes by cutting esoteric details?[6] Gosse showed no interest, so Ostervald tried again with some sales talk about Chapt's "curious and original description of both Siberia and Kamstchatka and of the customs of the Russians." He was sure that given the current interest in Russia, it would sell like hot cakes.[7] Gosse finally replied, rather reluctantly, that the book was indeed excellent but that he could not order it, because Marc-Michel Rey had recently published it in Amsterdam, and he was an ally of Rey's. Once again, Dutch solidarity thwarted Swiss publishing, but Ostervald had plenty of other projects:

What would Gosse say to a *Dictionary of Animals*?
"No" was the answer. "We strongly advise you against this enterprise."[8]
A *Description of Swiss Glaciers*?
No. "It is an interesting work, but it isn't selling well these days."[9]

A refutation of d'Holbach's notorious *System of Nature* by Jean de Castillon?

Gosse had imported the Berlin edition, which had sold badly; and he did not want any more, because "we judge according to our sales." Furthermore, "the people who buy those kinds of books couldn't care less about refutations."[10]

Bougainville's *Voyage around the World*?

Gosse pronounced it "a very good, an excellent enterprise," but would commit himself only to an advance order of fifty copies, because, he noted sourly, "the book trade is doing so badly everywhere these days."[11]

A *History of Field Marshall Saxe* and a *Supplement to the "Roman comique," or Life of Jean Monnet, Director of Acting Troupes*?

No, and no again. "Those are books that nowadays sell only for a short time after their first publication. We don't want to fill our stockrooms with them."[12]

It may seem that Gosse was a crusty nay-sayer. But he speculated heavily on books he thought would actually sell. The difficulty existed on Ostervald's side of the exchange. He had enough experience as a writer and reader to know his way around the Republic of Letters, but he knew little about publishing. He admitted as much in a letter written after his first eighteen months at the head of the STN: "Perhaps we still are only apprentices."[13] It took years of practice to master the complexities of the publishing industry. Gosse, one of the most respected masters in Europe, spoke about it in a strictly commercial manner: "Today, Monsieur, it is absolutely necessary to conform to current taste, to the taste of the public, in one's business. Men of learning often get that wrong. A bookseller with a large trade is far better than a scholar at assessing the public's taste."[14]

The main lesson that Ostervald learned from Gosse was the complexity of piracy as a business. Far from simply selecting a book that looked like a good read, a publisher had to gather information from many sources and to weigh many factors, including the existence of previous editions, the likelihood of new ones, putative sales records, commercial alliances, shifts in the tastes of the public, and the general economic outlook. In addition to these challenges, the STN also had to solve production problems. During the first two years of its operations, it lacked adequate fonts of type, a well-disciplined work force, and an effective foreman in its printing shop. Its directors had not yet learned to defend themselves against the endless tricks of the paper suppliers, nor had they mastered the craft of French-style book design. And worst of all, they did not yet know how to coordinate all their activities in such a way as to get their books to their customers on time—that is, before the publication of other editions put out by other pirates.

Time was the most important factor in the pirating business, time and information. In a world without effective copyright, there was an open war on any book that promised to sell, especially in France. Pirates raced to the French market with reprints turned out from printing shops along the Fertile Crescent. In fact, the only thing that held them back was the competition among themselves, for they undercut one another as fiercely as they slashed into the profits of the Guild. But with adequate information and good enough timing, they could make a killing. Thanks to their cut-throat tactics and cut-rate books, they provided the most dynamic element in the French book trade.

The best way to understand their practices is to follow the ups and downs of a single speculation. The STN's edition of Voltaire's *Questions sur l'Encyclopédie* offers a good case study, which can be examined in detail through the correspondence between Ostervald and Gosse.[15] The *Questions* was Voltaire's last great work and the biggest enterprise—nine volumes in-octavo—undertaken by the STN in its first years. When he first announced it to Gosse, in March 1770, Ostervald indicated that he planned to put out an original edition printed from a manuscript to be furnished by Voltaire himself. Gosse replied with a letter that, unlike the others already cited, fairly quivered with enthusiasm. Here is an eighteenth-century book dealer contemplating the prospect of a sure-fire bestseller: "It is an enterprise of solid gold . . . I will tell you right away that we commit ourselves to taking a large number. . . . Certainly, Monsieur, as you say, this work will contain all kinds of things that are new, curious, and extraordinarily powerful, and it will be snapped up at any price as soon as it appears. . . . There are prohibitions to be feared, and one will not be able to sell the book openly, but that will only make it sell faster and better. . . . The [STN] is sure to make a great coup."[16]

This book obviously did not belong to the same category as treatises on wooly animals and Swiss glaciers. The race to make a fortune from it, however, turned out to be far less straightforward than Gosse had anticipated. He soon learned that Ostervald was not proposing an original edition but a pirated version of the original that Gabriel Cramer, Voltaire's main publisher, was producing in Geneva. Hoping to snare Gosse's business before Cramer got to him, Ostervald had avoided any reference to the Genevan side of the affair when he first dangled it in front of Gosse. But he was not entirely disingenuous. Early in March 1770, Ostervald had gone to Ferney in search of copy. Voltaire was happy to oblige, because by then he no longer cared about making money from his pen. After more than fifty years of experience with publishers, he knew every trick in their trade; he also had learned to put the tricks to use for a higher cause: the diffusion of Enlightenment, the campaign to *écraser l'infâme*. He therefore agreed to supply Ostervald with a copy of Cramer's proofs, corrected and expanded, provided that everything took place behind Cramer's back. Voltaire was happy, that is, to pirate himself. It was a way to multiply copies. Besides, he knew that the *Questions* would be pirated anyway. By cooperating with the STN, he could control that process, while touching up the text with additional audacities that he also could disavow. And to top it all, he proposed that the STN publish an expanded edition of his complete works in forty octavo volumes.[17]

The details of this arrangement were revealed, little by little, in Ostervald's letters to Gosse. At first, Ostervald emphasized the need for advice about the new edition of the works, which was to be made from revised versions of Voltaire's published texts and "scattered pieces" from his manuscripts. Gosse had expressed amazement at Voltaire's energy, and Ostervald answered, "You are absolutely right, Monsieur, to be surprised that a man of letters, at the age of 77, can still work 12 hours and more each day, in his bed, with a concentration, a presence of mind, and a tone of admirable gaiety, writing, chatting, and dictating all at the same time, surrounded by books and papers. It goes beyond the powers of ordinary mortals, and one has to have seen it to believe it."[18]

If such a sight could quicken the pulse of a publisher, it did not inspire much enthusiasm on the part of the bookseller. Gosse had already come across so many editions of Voltaire's supposedly complete works that the prospect of another one made him groan, "When will it ever end?" Cramer had not yet completed his edition in Geneva, and François Grasset had just begun a new one in Lausanne. More editions might appear, claiming to be still more complete. Gosse's advice was this: "Take everything he wants to give you for a new edition of all his works, but be prudent and don't begin that edition until after his death. . . . [Then] you will pull off the best enterprise ever undertaken in the book trade, and most certainly we will be able to buy a very large number from you."[19]

Gosse wasn't alone. Booksellers often distrusted Voltaire, because by modifying his texts and multiplying the editions, he alienated their customers. No one wanted to pay good money for a slightly new version of a book that one had already bought. And some booksellers had become disenchanted with his endless variations on the same themes. As Jean-Marie Bruyset wrote to the STN from Lyon, "I will tell you frankly that almost all the works produced by that author for the last six to seven years are roughly the same dish served up with different sauces."[20] By 1770, the entire book trade was waiting impatiently for the death of the great man who had caused them so much grief by tinkering with his texts. But he kept them waiting for another eight years, tinkering till the end.

Ostervald followed Gosse's advice and concentrated on producing the *Questions sur l'Encyclopédie*. Before his compositors started setting type, he asked how many copies Gosse would order in advance—a consideration that could determine the press run. Five hundred, came the reply. Only five hundred? Ostervald sounded disappointed, but he entered the order immediately in the ledger called *Livre des commissions* and wrote in August that he soon expected to receive the first volume "corrected by the author." The STN's edition would appear on the heels of Cramer's and would be "far superior to it." As evidence of the STN's ability to be quick off the mark, Ostervald announced that he had just received the two sheets of proof for the essay in the *Questions* on God: "Starting tomorrow, these two sheets will be in press, and you will get some of the first copies. It will serve as a sample of the paper and the type in our edition, and it can be sold separately as a pamphlet."[21]

Despite Ostervald's efforts to make his sales talk sound attractive, it revealed that he had misled Gosse about a fundamental fact: the STN was publishing a pirated edition. Gosse shot back an indignant reply: "We were firmly persuaded that you would print this work from the manuscript. Now things look completely different. Cramer will get to the market first. It is absolutely crucial that you rush everything so that your edition arrives soon after his. If you fail to do so, it will be like serving the mustard after the dinner."[22] Nevertheless, Gosse did not cancel his order—perhaps because the STN edition cost much less than Cramer's: 1 sou per sheet or 23 sous 6 deniers for volume 1 as opposed to the 35 sous charged by Cramer.

Ostervald sent a reassuring answer. The STN could print as fast as Cramer and had the advantage of working on a text "reviewed, corrected, and augmented by the author, who has made fairly extensive changes on our copy." Moreover, Cramer was said to have sold his entire edition to distributors in Paris—and "what is one edition more or less of a work of this kind from the pen of the most famous writer of our century?"[23]

Meanwhile, Ostervald turned to problems on the production side of the enterprise. The *Questions* was one of the first major books undertaken by the printing shop in Neuchâtel, and the flow of work soon got caught in snags: paper did not arrive on time; workers quit in order to take jobs with better conditions in Lausanne and Geneva; and the foreman failed to co-ordinate operations effectively. Moreover, when the STN finally completed volume 1, after thirteen weeks of hard labor, it ran into difficulties with distribution. It shipped off Gosse's five hundred copies in two large bales on December 9, 1770, instructing its agent in Basel, Luc Preiswerck, to forward them down the Rhine. The Rhine offered an excellent route to The Hague, despite its expensive tolls. But Gosse's books had not reached him six weeks later, when volumes 2 through 3 of Cramer's edition were already being sold in the shops of other Dutch dealers.

Gosse was furious. He thought he'd been had;[24] and as to the pamphlet version of "God," it left him unimpressed. "As this brochure contains only two sheets, it will soon be pirated by some young booksellers in this country."[25] Thus pirating took place at several levels. Beneath the large enterprises sold on an international scale, smaller works were pirated by smaller publishers for local markets. There were *contrefaçons* of *contrefaçons*.

It may seem misleading to speak of a pirated edition in the case of the *Questions*, because Cramer did not purchase the text from Voltaire and he possessed no legal right to reproduce it. In fact, the consistory of Geneva would censor him for the book's impieties in March 1772, while Voltaire dismissed the pirating with witticisms such as the following burlesque edict issued from Ferney: "It is hereby permitted to any bookseller to print my silliness, be it true or false, at his risk, peril, and profit."[26] Yet Voltaire felt morally committed to his publisher and refused to offend him by collaborating openly with the pirates. He even urged Cramer to fight back against them: "You won't be pirated if you take the right measures, and you can put a notice in Volume II that will discredit the pirated editions."[27] In fact, Cramer knew very well that his *Questions* would be pirated. He merely sought to cream off the demand with a first edition by beating the pirates to the market. That is why the delay in the STN's shipments aroused such fury in Gosse.

Ostervald fended off Gosse's complaints with various excuses, while complaining with equal vehemence to Preiswerck about the shipping; for the bales with volume 1 still had not arrived in The Hague by the beginning of March, nearly three months after their departure from Neuchâtel. By then, at least, the printing shop was functioning quite well, and Ostervald began to speak of his pirating with a certain pride: "We are firmly resolved on the one hand to make our reprints the equal, as far as possible, of the originals . . . and, on the other, to organize our operations in such a way that our books will always be finished at the prescribed and agreed time—something that frequent desertions of workers occasionally prevented us from accomplishing in previous times."[28]

In the spring of 1771, thanks to new arrangements with shipping agents, boatsmen, and wagon drivers, the shipments went better, not only down the Rhine but also over the Jura Mountains to Lyon, where five hundred copies of the first three volumes arrived in June.[29]

But as soon as the distribution problems were solved, a new calamity struck the production side: the copy stopped arriving. In order to fight back against the pirates, who threatened to attack him from Lausanne, Amsterdam, and Berlin, as well as from Neuchâtel, Cramer decided to release several volumes at once, thereby gaining time to market his edition while his competitors were printing theirs. He therefore held back volumes 1 and 2 until he had finished volume 3 and then sent them all at once to his customers—wholesale or retail booksellers—who were able to offer them for sale long before their competitors.

This tactic actually threatened the other pirates more than the STN, because it drew its copy directly from Ferney in the form of duplicate proofs. Ostervald had been introduced into the household by Elie Bertrand, a confident of Voltaire and an uncle of Jean-Elie Bertrand, Ostervald's son-in-law, who was also a co-director of the STN. Family relations and friendships played a crucial part in the functioning of the supply line, especially at its source, because everyone close to Voltaire—his niece, Marie-Louise Denis; his companion, Père Antoine Adam; and his secretaries, Jean-Louis Wagnière and Joseph-Marie Durey de Morsan—became caught up in the intrigues of the publishers. Ferney was a factory of diabolical literature. But its machinery required lubrication and careful maintenance. While the master churned out copy, the staff handled relations with various sectors of the book trade. In the case of the *Questions*, Voltaire had agreed to add some "corrections and additions" to Cramer's proofs and then looked the other way while his secretaries forwarded them to Neuchâtel. But Ostervald could not resist the temptation to reveal this arrangement while marketing his edition. He boasted openly about it in a circular letter that he mailed to the favorite customers of the STN in September 1770. The news spread rapidly through the grapevine of the book trade and soon reached Cramer in Geneva. He complained to

Voltaire; Voltaire disavowed all complicity with Neuchâtel; and the flow of copy suddenly stopped.[30]

In consternation, Ostervald fired off letter after letter to Ferney—first to Voltaire, who did not reply; then to Wagnière, who agreed to continue his services as a middleman in return for a dozen free sets of the *Questions*; to Durey de Morsan, who functioned as a kind of domestic spy; and to Mme Denis, who liked the Neuchâtelois better than the Genevans but did not dare lobby too aggressively with her uncle.[31] Although Voltaire knew full well about the machinations all around him, he pretended to ignore them while pursuing interests of his own. He wanted better service from Cramer, who had neglected the printing of the *Questions* and had fallen behind in his edition of Voltaire's complete works in order to concentrate on a new edition of the *Encyclopédie*. Voltaire was a hard taskmaster when it came to typography. He pummeled Cramer with complaints about the foreman of his printing shop, "the fat Swiss," and found so many errors in the first three volumes of the *Questions* that he wrote, "*New edition* carefully purged of the typographical mistakes that abound throughout the others" at the top of the proof of volume 4 and permitted Wagnière to send it to Neuchâtel.[32]

The STN therefore resumed its printing and did its best to cope with the complaints that it received from Gosse, whose letters contained nothing but lamentations about delays, poor sales, and even the text itself, because in spite of Ostervald's assurances, he found no significant differences between the Neuchâtel and the Genevan editions.[33] When the copy for volume 8 arrived, Ostervald assured him that they had almost reached the end and bragged about a manuscript note to the article on superstition that did not exist in Cramer's text. Gosse was not impressed: "We are distressed to learn that M. de Voltaire did not complete the *Questions* at volume eight and that there will be a ninth volume. This book is becoming a burden, and up to now, Messieurs, it is selling very badly, because we still have more than 450 copies in our warehouse."[34]

The sour tone that now prevailed in Gosse's correspondence did not in fact result from the sales of the *Questions*. He had become disgusted with the book trade in general, and in May 1772 he announced that he would retire. "The book trade is in such a sad state, the sale of good works is so miserable, that we no longer know what to do. The good books frequently remain in our storerooms, and the paltry ones find customers."[35] The *Questions* belonged in his estimation to the category of the good, but it was not the bestseller he had expected. "This work, even though it is by the great Voltaire, hardly sells at all,"[36] he concluded in one of his last letters to the STN. He closed his account and turned his business over to his son, Pierre-Frédéric, in December 1773.

No bookseller commanded a perfect view of the literary marketplace. Although Gosse knew it as well as anyone, his judgment seemed to have clouded over in his old age. His son threw himself into the business with fresh energy and optimism. Pierre-Frédéric soon sold off all their copies of the *Questions* and ordered more: six in February 1775, six in March, and thirty in May. So the demand for the book had not dried up, despite the jeremiads of Gosse père; and the general trade in pirated works continued to hold up, although, as will be demonstrated later, it soon would fall into a period of crisis.

5

Portraits of Pirates

THE FOREIGN PUBLISHERS DENOUNCED as *corsaires* by the Parisians appear in a different light when seen from within their home environments. In most cases, they were obscure figures, the kind who rarely rate a sentence, if anything at all, in history books. Fortunately, however, some of them have large dossiers in the archives of the STN. A few even wrote books in addition to business letters. Compiling all the evidence makes it possible to sketch portraits of them, both as individuals with peculiarities of their own and as professionals playing a crucial role in the production of literature. Taken together, the biographical and business stories provide an overview of pirating as it was practiced in three major hubs: Neuchâtel, Lausanne, and Geneva.

Frédéric-Samuel Ostervald and Abram Bosset de Luze

The best place to begin is with the STN itself and the senior of its three directors at the height of its activity in the 1770s, Frédéric-Samuel Ostervald. Far from being a buccaneer, he was a pillar of society in Neuchâtel, which then was the capital of an autonomous Swiss principality under the sovereignty of the King of Prussia.[1] Ostervald came from a distinguished family that had been ennobled in the seventeenth century, and after marrying a young lady from a wealthy Protestant family in Rouen, he occupied a prominent place in the upper ranks of Neuchâtel society. He lived in a townhouse with a garden near the Lac de Neuchâtel, possessed vineyards outside the city, and drove about in an expensive carriage.[2] He frequented the finest company in an exclusive club known as the Société du Jardin. He helped found a reading society and directed the local Collège, or boarding school, where he occasionally taught classes in arithmetic and geography (one of his students may have been Jean-Paul Marat, the future revolutionary). Meanwhile, he rose steadily through the town's political institutions: the Grand Conseil

(1746), the Petit Conseil (1751), and the executive body of the town councils known as Les Quatre-Ministraux (1757). He was named chief executive officer within that body: Maître Bourgeois en Chef, a powerful position, which qualified him to receive the more honorific post of Banneret in 1762.

The baroque institutions and grandiloquent titles were typical of the urban polities scattered through Europe in the eighteenth century. Beneath their colorful facades, towns were often torn by ideological struggle and conflicting interests. Two issues disturbed the peace of Neuchâtel in the 1760s, at the height of Ostervald's career as a politician. The first concerned a controversy about hellfire. Ferdinand-Olivier Petitpierre, a Calvinist pastor with modern ideas in the nearby city of La-Chaux-de-Fonds, which was part of the principality of Neuchâtel and Valangin, raised a hornets' nest by preaching that the damned would not suffer punishment eternally, because endless torment could not be reconciled with the Christian notion of a beneficent God. The official body of clergy in the principality, known as the Vénérable Classe des Pasteurs, reacted to this heresy by expelling Petitpierre from his church. Strange as it may seem in light of a later quarrel over the STN's publication of an atheistic treatise, *Système de la nature*, Ostervald backed the pastors. He did not endorse the concept of eternal damnation, nor did he deny the right of individuals to hold their own beliefs, but he insisted on the importance of religious orthodoxy and the power of the Vénérable Classe as essential parts of the principality's political system: "Among well-governed peoples, religion is essentially an affair of the state."[3] Ostervald defended the interests of the bourgeoisie for the same reasons during the second controversy, a fierce debate over a proposal to reorganize the system of collecting taxes in a way that would infringe the privileges of the bourgeois elite. In this case, too, Ostervald took up a position for privilege and tradition, the opposite of what might have been expected from a partisan of Enlightenment.

To understand Ostervald's role as a politician, we can consult a treatise that he never published, *Devoirs généraux et particuliers du Maître Bourgeois en Chef pendant sa préfecture*. He wrote it as a confidential guide to the highest political office that he occupied, Maître Bourgeois en Chef, which made him head of the municipal bourgeoisie. As in many parts of Western Europe at that time, the term "bourgeois" had an aristocratic ring to it, indicating privileges restricted to an urban elite, among them the exclusive right to participate in the city's political life. The manuscript treatise provides an explanation of this position. In it, Ostervald went over the functions of the Maître Bourgeois en Chef in minute detail: the proper measures to inspect forests and regulate the distribution of wood; to enforce restrictions on the kegs of wine allowed into the city from particular vineyards; to expel women from other towns who got pregnant outside marriage; to register declarations of ownership in butcheries before permitting the slaughter of a steer; and so on with extensive notes on "the measures taken to ensure their conservation by our respectable ancestors."[4]

This was the stuff of which politics was made under the Ancien Régime. Ostervald expounded it in the conventional language of his time and also wrote elaborate accounts of civic ceremonies in which privileges were acted out—the passing of keys and seals from one Maître Bourgeois to another, the order in processions, the precedence in the deliberations of assemblies, the proper way to receive petitions and conduct audiences, the roles of all municipal officers, down to the livery of the chasse-gueux (policemen who dealt with beggars). Having described the sets and costumes, he then provided instructions on how to manipulate the system from behind the scenes. The Maître Bourgeois en Chef should arrange the agendas of meetings so that the items he wanted to pass would be discussed at the most opportune time. He should plan when to postpone a proposal and when to rush it through. And above all, he should know how to keep crucial deliberations secret, "a matter of the greatest importance for the good of the bourgeoisie."[5] In short, Ostervald combined a concern for tradition and privilege with a Machiavellian sense of how to manage the levers of power in order to get things done.

He abandoned politics for publishing in 1769. Then he ran the STN in ways that recalled his program for administering the city. He calculated strategy, enmeshed it in rhetoric, embroiled himself in secret plots, and played the game in a patrician manner, not merely to make money, although he had a healthy appetite for profits, but for the sake of the game itself. There might seem to be a contradiction at the heart of it all, because Ostervald defended the principle of privilege as a politician and violated it as a publisher. But of course, he infringed the *privilèges* of publishers located far from Neuchâtel. If that was piracy, he was a very patrician pirate.

Ostervald was fifty-six, when, along with two other partners, he founded the STN in 1769. That age made him old by the standards of the Ancien Régime, though he still had twenty-six years of active life ahead of him; and as the effective head of the STN's trio of directors, he intervened vigorously in all of its affairs. Every day he wrote up to a dozen letters, calculated the pros and cons of publishing new books, plotted sales campaigns, supervised the staff, and dealt with crises that constantly cried out for attention. He confessed his "well-proven ignorance" of finance,[6] which he left to a businessman, Abram Bosset de Luze, who joined the STN as a partner in 1777; and he probably did not spend much time in the stockrooms and the printing shop, which was the domain of Jean-Elie Bertrand, his son-in-law and the third partner. But he directed every other aspect of the business, teaching it to himself along the way.

Ostervald went into publishing as a gentleman amateur. He picked up some of the tricks of the trade from Samuel Fauche, a Neuchâtel bookseller who had helped found the STN in 1769 and left it after a quarrel in 1772, in order to continue business on his own. A scrappy, feisty entrepreneur, Fauche knew the book trade inside out. He had begun as an apprentice to a bookseller in nearby Morat in 1746, had worked as a binder in François Grasset's bookshop in Lausanne, and had run his own business in Neuchâtel since 1753. In March 1772, before his break with the STN, he accompanied Ostervald on a business trip to Lyon. As fellow travelers, they made an odd pair—Ostervald, the patrician man of letters taking lessons from Fauche, a man of the people. Ostervald's diary and his letters show him learning how to explore smuggling routes, inspect bookshops, and get a feel for the market. He was delighted to make the acquaintance of a former innkeeper in Lyon's suburb of Croix Rousse, who seemed capable of getting anything past the *chambre syndicale*. However, he found the Lyonnais booksellers "despicable," "curiously haughty," and financially unsound.[7]

The superior accent suggests Ostervald's approach to publishing. He concentrated on its literary and diplomatic side—that is, the intrigues that went into speculations on important editions. On his way back from Lyons, he stopped off for dinner with Voltaire in Ferney. "We were very well received in Parnassus," he reported. "But we left with nothing more than a sprinkling of holy water [i.e. no new manuscript to print.] However, something is being prepared there that could suit us."[8] In the end, as already recounted, he persuaded Voltaire to collaborate behind the back of Gabriel Cramer on the STN's reprint of his *Questions sur l'Encyclopédie*. Ostervald also devoted a great deal of his diplomatic skill to negotiations for new works by Rousseau. Soon after the foundation of the STN, he tried to extract some copy from Pierre-Alexandre Du Peyrou, Rousseau's host and the keeper of his manuscripts in Neuchâtel. He returned empty handed but full of projects for a future coup involving Rousseau, to whom Du Peyrou would write, testifying to the "ease and safety" with which his work would be produced. "He will be invited to come back and live in our vicinity, and his response will be communicated to us."[9]

Nothing came of this plan, or of Ostervald's other grand projects, except for a series of speculations on the *Encyclopédie*. But he loved to concoct them and to savor their possibilities while talking shop with publishers and writers. Ostervald was a man of letters himself, and he had no inhibitions about courting famous authors. Not only did he know Voltaire and Rousseau, but at one time or other, he also negotiated with d'Alembert, Condorcet, Beaumarchais, Mably, Raynal, Suard, Morellet, Marmontel, and Naigeon— that is, the best-known writers of his time. In trying to get them to publish with the STN, he frequently stressed that his business was run by men of letters who valued literature and would take extra care with the books that came off their presses. Yet the STN never published new works by the *philosophes*. It based its business on piracy.

Ostervald's own writing shows a concern for clarity, rational argument, and well-ordered exposition—that is, qualities that placed him toward the Voltairean end of the literary spectrum. Admittedly, he did not publish much, and he generally kept to local topics. His main work, an account of the topography in the principality of Neuchâtel and Valangin published in 1764, reads like a guidebook, contrasting Swiss liberty favorably with conditions across the Jura Mountains on the French side of the border.[10] He also wrote a textbook about world geography, which was used in the Collège of Neuchâtel and assumed the form of questions and answers. It exhibits a confidently Eurocentric manner (Ostervald ignored Australia, which Dutch explorers had discovered in the seventeenth century, although James Cook did not chart its east coast until 1770.)[11] "*Question*: What is the most famous of the four parts of the earth? *Answer*: It is Europe, although it is the smallest, because it is the most populous, and its inhabitants are the most enlightened and industrious." In describing England, Ostervald deplored the attempts of the Stuarts to establish arbitrary power, and in his section on Turkey he denounced despotism in a manner that evoked Montesquieu. But the book does not have an overtly ideological or religious message, nor does it demonstrate much original thought.

Ostervald's turn of mind is best revealed in his correspondence. A letter from a friend in Paris evoked the "tears of sensitivity" that they had wept during one of Ostervald's visits.[12] Yet tears flowed easily in the late eighteenth century, and Ostervald did not correspond to the contemporary prototype of *l'homme sensible*. His business letters, thousands of them preserved in the thick, folio *copies de lettres* of the STN archives, show him thinking his way through problems without veering off into sentimentality. They give the impression of a shrewd and somewhat disabused man of the world. Insofar as Ostervald had a general view of his experience, he expressed it in a letter to the home office after a hard day of negotiating with publishers and authors during a business trip to Paris: "One must not promise more butter than bread, not believe anything except what one can see, and not count on anything other than what one can grip with four fingers and the thumb."[13]

Abram Bosset de Luze joined the STN as a partner on January 1, 1777, bringing an infusion of fresh capital at a time when it was expanding its activities. He was a wealthy financier and manufacturer (a partner in a calico factory in nearby Cortaillod) with other interests to pursue, so he left most of the daily administration to Ostervald. But he became increasingly intrigued with the business aspects of publishing, and therefore his dossier complements Ostervald's, although it does not contain enough information for one to make more than a rough sketch of his role.

In the spring of 1780 Bosset accompanied Ostervald on a trip to Paris. After Ostervald returned, Bosset remained behind, tending to the STN's affairs as well as his own. His letters to the home office show him pursuing all sorts of possibilities to promote the STN's business. He set up a peddler named Cugnet to sell STN works from a boutique in the Palais-Royal, bargained with Beaumarchais over an octavo edition of Voltaire, tried to get d'Alembert and Marmontel to switch from their Parisian publishers to the STN, and negotiated over future speculations with the most powerful publisher in France, Charles Joseph Panckoucke, whom he considered cunning and devious: "Panckoucke . . . is good neither for roasting nor for boiling."[14] Bosset also had an interest in the literary side of publishing. In fact, he wrote some essays of his own and submitted them for publication in the STN's *Journal helvétique*. He was an avid reader. Among contemporary writers, he preferred Raynal and Louis-Sébastien Mercier, the bestselling author of *Tableau de Paris*, and he detested Rousseau, although for financial reasons he favored speculating on Rousseau's works.[15]

Despite his literary inclinations, Bosset approached publishing as a business. Within the STN he concentrated on finances, "my department."[16] Reputation, he insisted, was crucial to success in commerce, and therefore the STN should never fail to pay its bills on time.[17] He wrote stern letters to Abram David Mercier, the STN's bookkeeper, about the need for greater diligence and rigor in preparing the accounts and producing an annual balance sheet: "As a rule, all accounts must be brought up to date once a week. Here in Paris, the bankers are very strict about that. Their accounts are brought up to date every day by ten o'clock."[18] He worried that the STN was overextending itself. It had too much of its capital tied up in stocks of paper, which usually represented at least half the manufacturing cost of a book, and its press runs were too large. Only an experienced merchant could appreciate the danger of a diminishing cash flow, he insisted. Ostervald might have plenty of great ideas for new editions, but he failed to understand the importance of the bottom line: "The problem is not the difficulty of finding good things to publish, wonderful, marvelous things; no, the sole concern, the unique goal that must absorb all our attention, is, before printing something, to make sure that it will bring in hard cash."[19]

In fact, Bosset was right. As the STN expanded in the 1770s, it did not pay adequate attention to the debit side of its balance sheet. The debts mounted from one account book to another, though their accumulation remained invisible to anyone who contemplated the numbers without adequate expertise in double-entry bookkeeping. The bottom line did not show through clearly until the end of 1783, when the STN had to suspend payments temporarily for lack of cash on hand. This crisis provoked a reorganization of the firm in 1784 under a new group of partners, who kept it alive by a new supply of capital. By then Ostervald had withdrawn into semiretirement, although he continued to collaborate on the correspondence. Bosset was also gone from the scene. His letters in 1780 and 1781 showed that he was chronically ill, and on August 6, 1781, he died.

Jean-Pierre Bérenger and Jean-Pierre Heubach

For Jean-Pierre Bérenger, the road to piracy led not only through literature, as with Ostervald, but also politics. He became a partner of the Société typographique de Lausanne (STL), which closely resembled the STN. Its founder, Jean-Pierre (or Hans Peter) Heubach, was a German who knew his way around the book trade but needed advice when it came to choosing what to pirate. Unlike Ostervald, Bérenger came from the lower classes. At a time when literary careers depended on patronage and pensions, he stood out as a rarity. He was a self-made man of letters.

Born in Geneva in 1737, Bérenger grew up among the segment of the population (roughly 10 percent) known as Natifs, commoners who were excluded from most professions and all political life.[20] His father had a job in the shipping industry, working with mule drivers. Jean-Pierre had little formal schooling, yet he read widely, taught himself history and philosophy, and learned from local scholars such as Firmin Abauzit, a polymath and friend of Rousseau's. Abauzit founded Geneva's library, where Jean-Pierre spent a great deal of time. After a brief apprenticeship to a goldsmith, Bérenger supported himself by writing articles for journals, giving private lessons, and taking on whatever odd jobs came to hand.

He also wrote pamphlets in favor of the Natifs' struggle to gain representation in Geneva's civic life, which was limited to males with the formal status of "citizen"—or "bourgeois," as some were called. Geneva was a microcosm of the social and ideological tensions that ran through all Western Europe during the eighteenth century.[21] A tiny republic of 30,000 inhabitants, it was dominated by an oligarchy of wealthy merchants and aristocrats. They governed through a Petit Conseil composed of twenty-five members who served for life and who left the day-to-day administration to four *syndics* chosen from their ranks. A Conseil des Deux-Cents—Council of the Two Hundred—had some legislative authority and sometimes came into conflict with the Petit Conseil, particularly over matters of taxation, but it exercised little effective power, and it, too, was restricted to an elite: its constituents were limited to Geneva's 3,000 citizens and bourgeois, excluding the 3,800 Natifs, who, as noted, lacked any real political rights, and a larger population of Habitants, menial workers who had none. In the course of ideological conflicts throughout the century, two parties emerged. The Négatifs, identified with the Petit Conseil, opposed all efforts to limit the power of the oligarchy, whereas the Représentants, sometimes supported by the Natifs, agitated to open up civic life.

The tensions threatened to explode in the 1760s, when they were fueled by Geneva's most famous philosopher, Jean-Jacques Rousseau. Writing as a "citoyen de Genève" in his *Lettre à d'Alembert sur les spectacles* (1758), Rousseau broke with his fellow *philosophes* by denouncing a proposal to install a theater in Geneva, a plan backed by d'Alembert and Voltaire, as a threat to the democratic spirit at the heart of the republic. Far from welcoming this manifesto, the Genevan authorities were horrified by Rousseau's account of their political culture. And they were appalled by what he published next, especially *Du Contrat social* (1762) and *Émile* (1762). They condemned both books to be lacerated and burned in front of the Hôtel de Ville by the public hangman in 1763. When their attorney general, Jean-Robert Tronchin, defended the burning of the books in a political tract, *Lettres écrites de la campagne*, Rousseau replied with a defiant defense of democracy, *Lettres écrites de la montagne* (1764), which directly challenged the legitimacy of the Genevan oligarchy. Rousseau renounced his citizenship (he inherited the status of citizen from his father, a watchmaker) even before the Genevan Conseil voted to strip him of it. While he was forced to flee from his refuge near Neuchâtel in Môtiers and later in the Île Saint-Pierre, Geneva's Natifs continued to read his tracts as a program that perfectly fit their demands. Not that they needed *Lettres écrites de la montagne* to make sense of their situation. They had struggled to democratize Geneva for decades, particularly during political crises in the 1730s and 1750s, when they had support from the Représentants.

Bérenger grew up in this atmosphere. By the time he reached adulthood, he had become a passionate Rousseauist. Like many readers of *La Nouvelle Héloïse*, he found that Rousseau touched a chord deep within him, bringing forth "sweet tears."[22] Bérenger became an outspoken ally of the Représentants and a propagandist for the cause of the Natifs. Among the many pamphlets that he wrote, *Mémoire instructif, concernant les natifs* laid out the Natifs' demands for civic rights, and *Le Natif ou lettres de Théodore et d'Annette* reworked the political themes in the form of an epistolary exchange loaded with Rousseauistic sentiment.[23] The Genevan authorities condemned both works to be burned by the public hangman in 1767.

In October 1769, as discontent continued to mount among the Natifs, two *syndics* summoned Bérenger to answer a charge of sedition. When he failed to defend himself satisfactorily, they ordered him to cease from publishing. He then withdrew to the town of Thônex, located close to Geneva. While he remained outside the fray, the agitation grew more heated, and on February 15, 1770, it boiled over. The Natifs staged a small-scale insurrection in which three men were killed. After restoring order, the authorities arrested several Natif leaders, including Bérenger, although he had not been involved in the violence. After keeping him in a military prison for six days, they sent him into exile, without a trial.[24]

Judging from his involvement with the Natifs, we might think that Bérenger embraced a revolutionary version of Rousseauism. In fact, however, he shied away from conflict and preferred literature to politics. According to his friend and fellow Genevan, François D'Yvernois, he was "excessively timid and without the imposing exterior that is necessary for popular success."[25] After leaving Geneva, Bérenger went into publishing.

Of course, he did not walk right into a job. At first, he settled in Lausanne and appealed for help among his literary friends, including Jacques Mallet du Pan, Pierre Samuel du Pont de Nemours, and Ostervald, whom he knew quite well, judging from their correspondence in the STN archives.[26] Bérenger's first letters to Ostervald show him casting about for a career. Should he learn German and put in for a teaching position in Baden? Or would it be better to seek patronage through a contact in Poland, despite the cold? He needed assistance in selling his library, and that would help him finance a pension in the Pays de Vaud, where he could give lessons. On June 4, 1773, he married the daughter of a Genevan furbisher (a finisher of swords and other weapons). Her dowry might have made it possible for him to open the pension in Versoix outside Lausanne. By October 1773 he had two *pensionnaires* under his tutelage, though he mainly used the house as a retreat in which to write. He planned to do a new history of the reign of Philip II in Spain and to turn his love letters to his former fiancée (and now wife) into a novel, "half tender, half political," about his experience in Geneva.

Bérenger's most significant undertaking was a six-volume history of Geneva. Although he did not publish it with the STN, he discussed it at length with Ostervald. He would keep to a moderate tone, he explained, hoping to avoid offending the Genevan government. Above all, he needed to make money from the book.[27] Although he had planned at first to sell the manuscript to a publisher, Genevan friends assured him that he could do better by retaining possession of the edition and marketing it through a Genevan printer by means of subscriptions. They thought he could count on 1,500 sales in Geneva alone. Bérenger opted for the subscription plan and had the manuscript printed either by Jean-Samuel Cailler, a Genevan who often dealt in the underground trade, or by Jacques-Benjamin Téron l'aîné, an even more marginal publisher, whose business rose and fell through speculations separated by bankruptcies and prison sentences.[28] In August 1772 Téron placed a notice in the *Gazette de Berne* to announce that subscriptions for this history by the "famous exiled author" could now be purchased. As a result, he was called before the Genevan Petit Conseil and reprimanded, and the Genevan authorities persuaded their allies in Bern to forbid any further advertising. When the *Histoire de Genève* appeared in January 1773, they promptly burned it. Despite this—or perhaps because of it—the book sold well. By October 1775 Bérenger informed Ostervald that nearly every copy had been bought.

Although Bérenger put this enterprise together, "understanding nothing about trade," as he admitted to Ostervald, he learned a great deal from it. He had dealt with the printers and booksellers in Geneva and Lausanne for years and therefore was no ingénu when he informed Ostervald in March 1775 that he was considering a proposal to join "an enterprise similar to yours." This was the Société typographique de Lausanne, which did indeed resemble the Société typographique de Neuchâtel. Heubach, its founder, had developed a successful business as a bookseller and printer in Lausanne. By 1774, he had published two dozen books and was ready to expand. Hoping to tap the market for pirated works, he enlisted financial backers from Bern and took as principal partner Louis Scanavin, who looked after the printing shop while Heubach handled the commercial affairs. What they lacked and what Bérenger could provide was editorial expertise.

On June 6, 1775, Bérenger informed Ostervald that the two directors of the STL had offered to make him a partner. They had divided their company into five shares based on a capital of 40,000 Swiss livres—roughly 60,000 French livres, a large sum. Heubach possessed two shares and proposed to sell half of another share to Bérenger for 4,000 L. Where Bérenger was able to find this money is unclear. Perhaps it came from his wife's dowry and the sales of the *Histoire de Genève*, or Heubach might have advanced it to him, for they were close friends (in 1782 Heubach became the godfather of Bérenger's son Jean Charles). In any case, Bérenger became a silent partner with a half share in the company and a guaranteed income of 1,400 L. a year for serving "as a man of letters charged in that capacity with doing everything that could be useful for the Société."[29] His main function was to provide advice about which books to pirate. He also corrected proofs, edited and abridged texts, and kept the STL informed about literary matters by drawing on his correspondence with other writers.

Bérenger's role can be understood best by following the STL's relations with the STN, as we will see. But before taking that up, it is worth considering Bérenger's own writings, for they provide an unusual view of a publisher's tastes.

Unlike Ostervald, whose books were incidental to his public career, Bérenger poured his thoughts and feelings into everything he wrote, and he wrote a great deal. The most revealing of his books is *Les Amants républicains ou lettres de Nicias et Cynire* (1782), a political novel that Bérenger adapted from those love letters to his fiancée. Although set in the world of ancient Greece, it clearly evokes the conflicts of contemporary Geneva and continues the argument he had developed in *Le Natif*. Its hero, a dedicated but moderate champion of the common people, is, like Bérenger, driven into exile, and his love for his country is equaled only by his love for his sweetheart, which he declared voluminously in the sort of *sensiblerie* inspired by Rousseau: "I love you, I will always love you; my heart, my blood, my life belong to you; everything I have, everything that I am, my soul, my entire being is yours."[30] The epistolary form of the novel derived from *La Nouvelle Héloïse*, and the political message came straight from *Du Contrat social*. A city republic, like Geneva and ancient Syracuse, would fall into ruin if civic virtue faltered.

Bérenger made his Rousseauism and its relevance to Geneva explicit in *Rousseau justifié envers sa patrie* (1782). He describes how he has pored over Rousseau's works, suffered vicariously through the *philosophe's* misfortunes, and deplored the persecution of him by the Genevan oligarchs. Everything that Rousseau had written, from *La Nouvelle Héloïse* to the *Lettres écrites de la montagne*, served as a lesson to the common people of Geneva. Rousseau's enemies were theirs; he had shown them how to assert their rights and to defend their liberty. Yet the means to that end required restraint, not revolt. Bérenger asserted this philosophy on good authority—from Rousseau himself, who had counseled moderation in letters to the Représentant leaders, which they had made available to Bérenger. By weaving the letters into an account of the injustices inflicted on Rousseau, Bérenger elevated the cause of the Natifs to the high moral ground. He also asserted his own authority—although he remained anonymous—in transmitting the gospel from the prophet and determining its implications, for all of humanity as well as Genevans: "Friends of humanity, it is for you that I produced this work."[31]

Bérenger's six-volume history of Geneva was saturated with these sentiments. Yet he toned down his rhetoric, perhaps because he feared persecution. His other works were anonymous, but the *Histoire de Genève* carried his name on its title page, and he confided to Ostervald that the Genevan authorities might put pressure on Bern (which held sovereignty over Lausanne) to do him harm.[32] Despite its claim to cover Geneva's history from the beginning to the present, four of the six volumes concentrated on the eighteenth century, and the last volume brought the story to a close in 1761. Therefore, Bérenger did not cover the political crisis that led to his exile in 1770 or describe his own involvement in politics. He did, however, identify himself as a supporter of the Natifs and the "party of the people." He claimed that the common people had been deprived of their representation in Geneva's Conseil Général, which went back to 1568 and was the rightful seat of sovereignty. He even used the term *volonté générale* and cited Rousseau's *Discours sur l'économie politique* to justify the right of the people to consent to taxation.

These remarks were overshadowed by appeals for peace and patriotism, as if political conflict could have been overcome by sentiment bathed in "sweet tears." Instead of mentioning the agitation of the 1760s and the repression that had driven him out of the republic, Bérenger gave the narrative a curiously happy ending—a thirty-one-page description of a patriotic festival, which conforms closely to Rousseau's version of the same theme in his *Lettre à d'Alembert*. It offers a blissful spectacle of "citizens joined together, without distinctions of rank or standing, knowing no livery other than that of the fatherland." Political conflict was dissolved in fraternity: "Thousands of souls were fused into one," and "the name of Rousseau was on their lips and in their hearts."[33]

Did Bérenger's passionate Rousseauism determine his activities as a partner in a publishing house? The question concerns the larger issue of assessing ideology and personal bias as factors in publishing, and the short answer to it is no. Judging from his correspondence with Ostervald, Bérenger evaluated books according to their literary qualities and their sales potential, but he did not push works that conformed to his political beliefs. His recommendations, which belonged to the running debate about literature conducted within the Swiss Confédération typographique, were strictly professional. In a letter to Ostervald of December 31, 1779, he remarked, as if it were self-evident, that the publishers had "to do their job, which is to make money."

Jean-Pierre Heubach was above all an entrepreneur.[34] Starting from nearly nothing, he built the Société typographique de Lausanne into a large, successful publishing house, and demonstrated considerable commercial savvy. He was born in Mainbernheim, Bavaria in 1736. Having taken up his father's trade as a binder, he migrated to Lausanne in 1759. By acquiring the status of a bourgeois in nearby Renens, he was able to expand from binding to bookselling. In 1762 he married an older woman with a large dowry: the equivalent of 18,000 French livres. He installed his bookshop and his wife in a grand house in the middle of Lausanne in 1765. Two years later, he applied to Bern for permission to establish a printing shop. At first the authorities refused, and then gave their approval in 1768, when Heubach bought out a local printer and hired a foreman to run the shop. Binding, bookselling, and printing led to publishing. By November 1773 when he founded the STL,

Heubach had published twenty-five books, most of them religious tracts that he sold to Protestants scattered throughout the Pays de Vaud.

In order to finance his expanding operations, Heubach took on and sloughed off partners as circumstances required. His first were the Genevan booksellers Marc Chapuis and Jean-Samuel Cailler. In a printed circular dated July 3, 1770, he announced that he had parted amicably with them and was continuing his firm alone under the trade name Jean Pierre Heubach. He reorganized this business as the STL in November 1773 after attracting some investors in Bern. A printed circular of February 22, 1774, informed booksellers of the new firm's existence. It invited them to suggest works for it to reprint—that is, to pirate—and named Louis Scanavin as Heubach's principal partner. However, Scanavin went bankrupt and fled in June 1775, never to be heard of again. Heubach assured the STN that his business had not suffered from this crisis, and he sent out yet another circular on June 13, 1775, naming Jean-Pierre Duplan as his new partner. It was at this point that Bérenger joined the STL, purchasing half of one of its five shares. The other shareholders eventually included several wealthy and influential Bernese, notably Samuel Kirchberger and Johann Rudolf Tscharner, who also be-came partners in the Société typographique de Berne, the STB. The overlapping partnerships and collaborative editions made the publishing houses of Lausanne and Bern close allies.

Heubach supplied the energy behind this commercial combination. As he put it in a letter of May 7, 1785, he was "almost alone the driving force of production and trade." By that time, his printing shop had grown to include seven presses, and he had bought a country estate valued at 15,000 Swiss livres (about 22,500 French livres).[35] How he arrived at such prosperity is difficult to say. Although he (or his clerks) wrote hundreds of letters to the STN, which did a great deal of business with him, they reveal little about his character, aside from his sharp commercial sense and his rigor when it came to settling accounts. They do suggest that he lacked the literary sophistication of the francophone publishers in Geneva, Brussels, and Liège. Mallet du Pan wrote disparagingly of "that fathead Heubach" in a letter to Ostervald.[36] A few details can be gleaned from sources in Lausanne. Heubach spoke with a heavy German accent, and friends reported that he gave rollicking dinners in his country house. He also had an eye for women—or so it seems from the terms of his will, because he left most of his estate to four daughters that he had from one mistress and to a son by another.[37]

Whatever Heubach's private life might have been, he proved to be a canny businessman, and he needed all the shrewdness he coul muster to survive in the publishing industry of Lausanne. The STN's correspondence with other booksellers shows that the trade in Lausanne took place in an atmosphere of dog eat dog. The two top dogs, Heubach and François Grasset, Lausanne's other large-scale publisher, were locked in a feud. In a letter to the STN, Grasset declared open hatred of Heubach.[38] Heubach reciprocated his feeling, and their hostility reverberated among the smaller publishers in Lausanne. One, Gabriel Décombaz, went into business on his own in July 1775 after working as a clerk for Grasset and marrying the daughter of Grasset's brother, Gabriel, in Geneva. Not having any presses of his own, Décombaz jobbed out the printing of his books; and lacking capital, he sometimes speculated on joint editions produced by others, including two editions of Raynal's *Histoire philosophique*. But he overextended his limited resources and had to suspend payments in March 1784. As often happened in such cases, he entered into negotiations with the body (*masse*) of his creditors, who were led by none other than Heubach. They agreed to let him continue his business so that he could earn enough to pay them back over a period of four years. He was to begin with a long trip through Italy, selling off his stock. Two-thirds of the proceeds would go to the creditors, one-third to his wife, who would run the shop in his absence and supply him with enough money to cover his expenses.

While on the road, according to his version of events, Décombaz discovered that some of the creditors (that is, those under Heubach's direction) had sabotaged the agreement in order to appropriate the stock, which had been evaluated at 45,000 L. He hurried back to Lausanne, entered into a long battle in the courts, and lost. Threatened with imprisonment for debt, he wrote a desperate letter to the STN. He had been betrayed "in the most odious manner possible," he wrote. Pleading as a victim of "guile and bad faith," he begged the STN to hire him as a clerk. It replied that it had no available position. Décombaz then escaped to the French colony of Saint-Domingue (now Haiti), where he established a bookshop with a commercial lending library (*cabinet littéraire*). After Saint-Domingue exploded in the slave revolt of 1791, he escaped again, this time to Philadelphia, where he got a job in a bookstore at Walnut and Fort Streets, a gathering place for French refugees. What became of his wife cannot be determined.[39]

Lausanne's other bookseller-publishers lived in difficult if less dramatic circumstances. Jean Mourer, a former apprentice of Grasset, set up shop in

Lausanne in 1781. He pirated several works, including Linguet's *Mémoires sur la Bastille*, by hiring others to do the printing. Those enterprises led to a falling out with his former master, whom he excoriated as "unredeemably bad." The correspondence does not reveal how they settled their conflict, but it suggests that Mourer managed to stay in business only by operating within Grasset's sphere of influence.[40] François Lacombe, a similar, small-time retailer, published a few works while remaining within Heubach's orbit. He, too, had nothing good to say about the book trade: "I know that most booksellers are insensitive to what is called *honnêteté*."[41]

Judging from these and other dossiers, we can imagine the industry in Lausanne as a force field, charged with conflicts and organized around the opposing poles of the rival publisher-wholesalers, Grasset and Heubach.[42] Heubach did not allude to the surrounding environment in his own letters, which remained terse and businesslike in tone. His role in the STL resembled that of Bosset de Luzes in the STN. They both kept a close watch on the account books, while their literary partner scouted for texts. In fact, the parallel between the Heubach-Bérenger and the Bosset-Ostervald partnerships—allowing for the fact that Heubach was the dominant partner and Bosset was not—suggests an important characteristic of publishing in the late eighteenth century. The printing shop was crucial to both businesses, of course; but Heubach left it in the hands of a foreman (prote), and the STN did the same after the death of Jean-Elie Bertrand in 1779.[43] In each case, the primary role played by the commercial and literary partners illustrates the emergence of publishing as a specialized function, one distinct from printing and bookselling, in the history of books.

Jean-Abram Nouffer

Among the many Genevan publishers who corresponded with the STN, Jean-Abram Nouffer revealed most about the practices of pirating. Nouffer took over the business of the De Tournes house, one of Geneva's oldest and most illustrious publishers, in 1776. This was quite a coup, for Nouffer was only twenty-four years old at the time, and he was not a bourgeois of Geneva—that is, not a member of the oligarchic elite who enjoyed exclusive privileges, including the right to operate bookselling and printing businesses. He came from Morat, a city under the control of Bern, the superpower among the Swiss states. Although his dossier in the STN archives (175 letters) reveals little about his background, he came from a wealthy family.[44] His letters, written in highly polished French, have a cosmopolitan tone, and he seems to have had a thorough knowledge of German and French literature, as could be expected from a well-educated young man from Morat (Murten in German), a bilingual city.

Needing an associate who had full civic rights, Nouffer took as a partner Jean-François Bassompierre, a Genevan who had worked as a clerk for De Tournes and who provided some of the capital for the new firm. In a circular letter of June 12, 1776, "Nouffer et Bassompierre" announced that as a successor to De Tournes, it had a large assortment of books and was eager to enter into exchanges with other publishers—that is, to swap portions of its stock for an equal amount in theirs, calculating the exchanges in sheets. From Neuchâtel Ostervald sent a reply welcoming Nouffer to the business. There was plenty of room for a new firm in the burgeoning trade of the Swiss publishers, he said, "and it is in our interest to make our Swiss products superior to the others by the variety of our works and the correctness of their execution."[45] The STN then agreed to open mutual exchange accounts in which the sheets would be tallied on both sides and the balance paid off at a rate of 9 deniers per sheet when the accounts were squared. Its main condition was that Nouffer should never undersell its books, which it marketed at a standard wholesale price of one sous (12 deniers) per sheet, because that would ruin its own sales among retail book dealers.

The STN's first orders were for highly illegal *livres philosophiques* (which covered all forbidden literature, from pornography to atheistic philosophy): 300 copies of an obscene, anticlerical novel, *Le Monialisme*; 100 copies of *Lettres chinoises*, a satirical work by Jean-Baptiste Boyer de Boyer, marquis d'Argens; 200 *Anecdotes sur Mme la comtesse du Barry*, an off-color political libel by Mathieu-François Pidansat de Mairobert; and 200 copies of Voltaire's *Lettres philosophiques*.

Whether or not he had printed those books, Nouffer clearly kept a lot of them in stock, and they formed a significant part of his business. None were original editions. They were reprints of works that circulated widely through the underground trade. They might be considered as *contrefaçons*, except that no one owned exclusive rights to the texts. In his first letters to the STN, Nouffer also mentioned two books that he reprinted on his own presses, a radical political tract called *Les Vrais Principes du gouvernement français* by Pierre-Louis-Claude Gin, and *Un Chrétien contre six Juifs* (*One Christian against Six Jews*) one of the last anti-Christian broadsides by Voltaire. The

STN requested 100 of the former and 150 of the latter; but by the time Nouffer had received the order, in May 1777, he had sold out his edition of *Un Chrétien contre six Juifs* and therefore procured copies of another edition, which had appeared under a new title, *Le Vieillard du Mont Caucasse* (*The Old Man of Mount Caucasse*). Titles as well as texts got shuffled about casually in the pirating industry.

The STN's exchanges with Nouffer were similar to its dealings with several other Genevan publishers. They provided the STN with the illicit books that it needed to supply the demand of its customers, and in return it sent them shipments of the relatively innocent *contrefaçons* that it produced and that the Genevans could sell safely from their own shops. Unlike marginal Genevan publishers such as Jacques-Benjamin Téron and Jean-Samuel Cailler, Nouffer did not specialize in the "philosophical" branch of the trade. His catalogue from November 1777 contained sixty titles of which only a few were strictly forbidden in France, but he also circulated a separate catalogue, without his name and address, of *livres philosophiques*, and he printed several of those books to feed his trade in exchanges. In 1778 he swapped twenty-five copies of his edition of the works of Helvétius in five volumes, for fifty copies of the STN's edition of William Robertson's *Histoire de l'Amérique* in four volumes, noting that he had used smaller type, which made eighty-seven sheets of his book worth a hundred of the STN's. "In life's affairs, Messieurs, a reciprocal justice is necessary," he observed.

In September 1777 Nouffer and Bassompierre dissolved their association. Bassompierre continued the printing operation on his own, mainly working on the quarto edition of the *Encyclopédie*, while Nouffer took over the publishing and bookselling. In April 1778, Nouffer sent a printed circular announcing that he had taken Emmanuel Etienne Duvillard fils as a partner. He got further financial backing from another new Genevan partner, Jean Mourer, the former apprentice of Grasset in Lausanne, but they had a falling out, and Mourer left "Duvillard et Nouffer," as the firm was now known, a few weeks after he had joined it.[46]

By March 1779 Nouffer faced increasing difficulties in honoring his bills of exchange. He informed the STN that he could not pay two notes for 759 L. when they became due, because four booksellers who owed him money had gone bankrupt. He asked it to accept as reimbursement works from his stock at a reduced price of 9 sous per sheet. Ostervald turned him down cold—"We sell to make money and not to stuff our warehouse with books"— but later relented and agreed to settle for a shipment of more books, most of them "philosophical," such as Voltaire's ever-popular *La Pucelle d'Orléans* and the atheistic works of Julien Offray de La Mettrie. The STN's Geneva agent, Flournoy fils et Rainaldis, merchants who also acted as bill collectors, warned that Nouffer often fell behind in his payments. Although he had received funds from his family and could expect to come into an inheritance, he had overextended his business.[47]

In August 1779, another printed circular announced that Duvillard fils et Nouffer had turned their bookshop over to J. E. Didier, who had worked for them as a clerk, and that they would concentrate henceforth on the printing side of the business. They would begin by producing an octavo and a duodecimo edition of Raynal's *Histoire philosophique* in eight volumes. This was a supremely important work, they stressed—and one that was sure to sell: "Multiple editions, which have sold out rapidly, are sufficient proof." The *Histoire philosophique* was, in fact, such a bestseller that it touched off a boom among the pirate publishers, especially after it was condemned by the Parlement of Paris and burned by the public executioner in 1781, when Raynal fled France to escape imprisonment. Bibliographers are still working hard to identify the editions that sprang up everywhere.[48] Publishers scrambled to cash in on the demand, siphon it off, and reinforce it by all sorts of maneuvers—announcing editions they never meant to print in order to scare off rivals, pretending to include new material by compiling passages from old texts, and cutting deals on pricing behind one another's backs.

While preparing to produce the *Histoire philosophique*, Nouffer launched other speculative projects. Two involved dealing directly with authors rather than pirating. The first was a new edition of *De la philosophie de la nature* by Jean-Baptiste-Claude Delisle de Sales, which had caused a scandal in 1770 after being condemned as irreligious. In February 1780, Nouffer proposed that the STN join him in publishing a seven-volume version of the text, which would be augmented by new material furnished by the author. Although Ostervald replied that the book had long since gone out of favor, Nouffer persisted. He announced the publication and began printing but then abandoned it, because he found it impossible to deal with Delisle de Sales, who demanded endless revisions of the text.[49] The second enterprise was a translation of *Henriette de Volkmar*, a novel by Christoph Wieland, the German author best known today for his epic, *Oberon*. Nouffer, who seemed to be well informed about the literary scene in Germany, had commissioned the translation. In February 1781, he assured the STN, "This work surely merits a place among the first class of good novels." Moreover, it was so impeccable in its treatment of morals that it could be exported without difficulty into France. But the translator took forever to provide copy and held up publication for more than a year.[50]

It was better business to pirate a bestseller, despite all the competing editions produced by other pirates and the foul play involved. Nouffer chose one of the hottest works on the market in 1781, *Vie privée de Louis XV (The Private Life of Louis XV)* a scandalous, four-volume account of Louis XV's reign by Barthélemy-François-Joseph Moufle d'Angerville. By that time, however, he had fallen further behind in his payments and was still trying to amass enough money to undertake the printing of the *Histoire philosophique.* Duvillard had withdrawn from the business in October 1780 to pursue another career, and Ostervald's letters took on a dunning tone, which wounded Nouffer's pride.[51] Instead of offering his edition of the *Vie privée* as a swap, which would have balanced his account, he prepared it in secret and attempted to market it for cash without informing the STN. But the STN was tipped off by another publisher in Geneva and therefore demanded a shipment as an exchange.[52] In the end, Nouffer made peace by selling fifty copies at half his wholesale price of 10 L. with the proviso that the STN would not undercut his sales by offering it at less.[53] This obligation did not stop the STN from selling a batch at 2 L. under Nouffer's price to Johann Jakob Flick, a bookseller in Basel. Instead of keeping this deal secret, Flick wrote to Nouffer, complaining about overpricing—a matter of 110 L.—for a shipment that he had earlier ordered directly from Nouffer. Nouffer, in turn, complained to the STN. Its double dealing with Flick had forced him to cut 110 L. from the earlier sale, and, moreover, "[i]t is not on such indecent works as this that one should undercut the price." The STN responded merely by remarking that since the book had sold so well, he should do another edition of it. But he was not tempted: "I made a mistake by not printing a larger edition, but the damage is done, and there is no turning back."

Relations improved after June 1781, when Nouffer acquired yet another partner, his brother-in-law, David De Rodon, who brought more capital to the company.[54] In reply to an anxious letter from the STN, Nouffer's former partner, Emanuel-Etienne Duvillard, reassured it that they had parted on good terms and that Nouffer's finances remained solid.[55] Nouffer paid off the balance of his account in December. In April 1782 he announced that the new company planned to publish a twenty-eight-volume collection of the best English novels in translation. His printing shop had six presses, and in May he wrote that he expected to purchase five more. Nouffer De Rodon seemed to be a large and ambitious enterprise.

By the end of June 1781, Nouffer had completed the edition of the *Histoire philosophique* that he had announced in his circular of August 1, 1779. It had grown into a ten-volume, duodecimo work that he produced as a joint enterprise with other printer-booksellers, primarily Jean-Pierre Bonnant in Geneva and Heubach in Lausanne.[56] Although it was printed at a large run of 3,000 copies, it was sold out by March 1782. Nouffer had not expected to sell any to the STN, as he explained in a letter of June 6, 1781, "since you are printing it yourselves." The STN had in fact announced in a circular that it would publish its own edition, but it abandoned that plan in July, because three other publishers had already beaten it to the market—Nouffer, Clément Plomteux of Liège, and Jean-Louis Boubers of Brussels, all of them consummate pirates.

Nouffer was less cautious than the STN.[57] His edition had sold so well that he planned to do another, and in March 1782 he offered to make the STN his partner in producing it. They could reduce the number of volumes and the price in order to reach a broader public, he explained, and they would not need fear being forced off the market by yet another edition, which might feature new material provided by the author, because he had heard (wrongly) that Raynal had died.[58] The STN hesitated, however, because the *Histoire philosophique* involved an enormous investment of capital and complicated production problems, not merely to print such a large work but also to reproduce its tables, illustrations, and atlas. After a good deal of prevarication, it agreed on a tentative arrangement in early April: Nouffer and the STN would each take a half share and print half the volumes.

At the same time, however, Geneva erupted in a small-scale revolution. The city had continued to simmer with agitation after the riots of 1770 that had led to Bérenger's expulsion. On April 8, 1782, the Représentants, backed by groups of Natifs, rose in revolt, occupied the city hall, took Négatifs as hostages, and began to rule through a revolutionary committee. Nouffer, a Natif, made only passing references to the *malheureuse révolution* in his letters to Neuchâtel. At first, his main concern was the interruption of his printing operations. For a few days in May, he slipped out of Geneva in order to make sure that his paper supply would not be stalled. Troops from France, Bern, and Savoy had surrounded the city, claiming the right to intervene in its affairs by an agreement that had settled a crisis in 1738; and their siege brought all trade to a halt. On July 2, the Représentants capitulated, their leaders fled (many sought refuge in Neuchâtel), and the military forces restored the old order.

Nouffer resumed his interrupted correspondence with the STN on July 16. He was not happy: "During the miserable time we went through, no one thought about business. Everyone was discouraged about everything." He intended to make up for lost time. In fact, he planned to extend his collaboration with the STN by linking the speculation on the *Histoire philosophique* with a similar joint venture, a nine-volume edition of the works of the popular novelist, Mme Riccoboni. Instead of printing half of each of the two works, the partners would produce them separately. The STN would do the entire edition of Raynal, while he did the Riccoboni. This strategy made good sense, because it would be risky for him to print half of the notorious *Histoire philosophique* under the nose of the Négatifs, who had been restored to power by the French, along with the forces of Bern and Savoy.[59] The sentimental novels of Mme Riccoboni would offend no one. After further negotiations, the two houses decided to draw up separate contracts for the two enterprises. On September 22, they signed a contract that modified their earlier agreement by committing the STN to print all eight volumes of the new edition of the Raynal at a run of 3,000, while Nouffer handled the marketing and furnished half of the production costs. The Riccoboni was postponed, because Nouffer needed to get further information about the texts from his contacts in Paris.

Nouffer and Ostervald met in Lausanne at the beginning of October 1782 in order to iron out further details, including plans to produce a ninth volume of the *Histoire philosophique* with supplementary material. After fleeing France in 1781, Raynal was being fêted as a hero in travels through Germany and the Austrian Netherlands. If he could be persuaded to furnish some fresh manuscript, Nouffer was convinced, their edition would make a clean sweep of the market. Ostervald had gotten to know Raynal during a trip to Paris in 1775.[60] While corresponding with him since then, Ostervald had sent some information about Huguenot refugees in Switzerland for use in a book about the revocation of the edict of Nantes that Raynal planned to write. "You graciously said to me that one day or other I would be your printer," Ostervald wrote to him on March 27, 1781. In 1782 when he took up the speculation on the *Histoire philosophique*, he did everything possible to procure copy from Raynal, urged on constantly by Nouffer.[61] At a minimum, they planned to fill their ninth volume with reprints of four works, including one that documented the banning of the third reworked version of the *Histoire philosophique* in 1781—and did so in such scandalous detail as to make good reading in themselves and excellent publicity for the marketing of the pirated editions. But Raynal objected, because, as he explained in a letter to Ostervald, he wanted the book to stand on its own, and he considered it demeaning for the text to be followed by hostile criticism.[62] Ostervald consented in the hope that he could snare something more important—namely, the book on the revocation of the Edict of Nantes. In May 1783, Raynal made a visit to Lausanne, and Ostervald probably met with him to discuss this possibility. (The archives say nothing about the meeting, perhaps because Ostervald kept some of his private correspondence separate from that of the STN.) Unfortunately, Raynal never managed to write this work, which would have shown how religious persecution had deprived France of valuable talent and scattered Huguenots around the world. It belonged to the category of Enlightenment treatises that were planned but never made it into print.

Meanwhile, relations between Nouffer and the STN had grown warmer. Nouffer traveled to Neuchâtel in December 1782 to discuss business with Ostervald. Judging from his later letters, we can guess that he established a friendly rapport with Ostervald's entire family, including Ostervald's wife and his daughter, Marie-Anne-Elisabeth Bertrand, who had helped run the STN after the death in 1779 of her husband, Ostervald's partner.[63] They had a good deal in common, for Morat was close to Neuchâtel, and Nouffer belonged to the same milieu of cultivated bourgeois as the directors of the STN[64] His wife did, too, and in January her mother sent the STN news that she had just given birth to a baby. Madame Nouffer visited the Ostervald household in September while traveling to see her mother in Morat. She apparently got on well with Mme Bertrand, who was roughly her age and who later sent her a gift of some local liqueur. In return, Mme Nouffer sent material for a coat that Mme Bertrand was planning to have made. The correspondence mentioned these details only fleetingly but often enough to indicate that cordial personal relations reinforced the trade between the two firms.

Their trade, however, had ups and downs, owing to the financial troubles that continued to beset Nouffer. While continuing to swap sheets from its editions, the STN kept its eye on his firm, using its Geneva agent, Alexandre Rainaldis, who acted as its bill collector. Rainaldis had so much difficulty in exacting money from Nouffer that in July 1782 he wrote that he wanted to have nothing more to do with him.[65] On February 3, 1783, Nouffer informed the STN that he had suffered a large loss, because a shipment with five large bales of his pirated and illegal books had been confiscated in Lyon. As a result, he did not have enough capital to pay for his half of the production costs for the *Histoire philosophique*. The STN had begun printing the first volume in October, and it did not want to abandon an operation that promised to be so profitable. Therefore, it was willing to consider a proposal by Nouffer to revise the original contract. It sent its head clerk, Jean-François Favarger, to Geneva, and after a thorough inspection of Nouffer's accounts, he agreed to a new arrangement for financing the edition. "In speaking with him, I bared my heart and hid nothing," Nouffer wrote to the STN on April 1, 1783. According to the new contract, signed on February 20, the STN would finance and produce the entire edition while gradually collecting reimbursement for its advances, with 6 percent interest, as payment arrived from the customers. The text would run to ten rather than nine volumes, including the volume of new material, and Nouffer would continue to help with the marketing.[66]

The STN plugged away at the printing until the end of September, when it completed volume 10. Throughout this period, Nouffer sent news of great potential sales—Cazin in Reims planned to buy 1,500 copies, Pavie in Angers wanted 200, and it seemed certain that they could count on at least 2,000 advance orders. But slow production cut into the demand, because the retail dealers wanted to inspect the finished product before paying for it. And the competition was fierce. By September 1783 Plomteux had already produced his edition in Liège, Boubers had nearly completed his in Brussels, and Dufour was advancing rapidly with his in Maastricht.

There was also rivalry for producing supplements with fresh material. Dufour produced three additional volumes, but they merely contained extracts from an earlier Genevan edition arranged artfully to make them look new. Heubach published a supposedly new work under a different title, but when he read it, Nouffer realized it was nothing more than "pillage" of articles scattered throughout the original *Histoire philosophique*. For his part, Ostervald continued his struggle to obtain a "precious manuscript morsel" from Raynal.[67] But he never succeeded, and in the end the STN had to fill its extra volume with the polemical works connected with the suppression of the 1781 edition.

The STN also had great difficulty in procuring the atlas, having jobbed out the printing in February 1783 to Delahaye et Cie., the Brussels publisher that was heavily engaged in the illegal book trade.[68] Despite constant dunning from the STN, Delahaye delayed production for so long that by December Nouffer smelled a rat. Instead of finished work, Delahaye had sent only "a pretext that makes us suspect some tricky business and that worries us. Do you know that house very well, and do you think we can count on it?"[69] In fact, Delahaye had held back the STN's order so that it could supply a preferred customer, Dufour in Maastricht, in time for him to beat out the STN's edition.

Meanwhile, Nouffer had continued to print books and exchange them with the STN. (Among the works he sent in 1782 were 208 copies of a fast-selling *Collection complète de tous les ouvrages pour et contre M. Necker*.) Conditions remained so tense in Geneva that he was sure his mail was being opened by the authorities and did not dare publish anything illegal. "We are more threatened here than you are in Neuchâtel," he wrote on July 1, 1783. "If we risked the slightest thing that was reprehensible, we would have to pay dearly for it." Nouffer came down with a severe attack of rheumatism, which kept him in bed for three weeks in August. But he was back at work and gathering more orders for the *Histoire philosophique* in September. Prospects looked good, he wrote.

At the same time, Nouffer was involved in secret negotiations, behind the back of his partner De Rodon, to publish the works of Voltaire, probably as a knockoff of the definitive edition then being prepared in Kehl, Germany, across the river from Strasbourg; and he offered to give the STN a share in that speculation. Although it never came to anything, the offer demonstrated his determination to maintain close relations—as did an offer to help the STN smuggle its books into France, thanks to a clandestine route that he opened up in October. In November he planned to stop by Neuchâtel during a sales trip on which he would market the STN's works along with his own. He was still in Geneva on December 13, however, when he wrote about plans to sell the Raynal in Paris.

Then his correspondence suddenly stopped. Nouffer fled from Geneva in January, leaving his wife and two children. He had dissolved his partnership with De Rodon and had gone bankrupt. His creditors formed an association to sort out his affairs and squeeze everything possible from the assets that remained in his printing shop and bookstore. They eventually came to an agreement with the STN, which retained the full rights to the *Histoire philosophique*, having swallowed all the costs of producing it. The STN attempted to discover where Nouffer was hiding by writing to his mother, but she replied on January 24 that she did not know where he was and had not heard from him for three weeks.[70]

Nearly a year passed. According to the association of creditors, who had great difficulty in making sense of the confused accounts, Nouffer owed the STN over 12,000 L. plus another thousand left over from its old account with Duvillard et Nouffer—not to mention the loss it had taken on the *Histoire philosophique*, which it never sold in enough numbers to cover its expenses. Its only consolation was the handsome profit that it made by reviving the project to publish the nine-volume edition of Mme Riccoboni's works, which it completed in 1783.

On December 25, 1784, Nouffer reemerged, sending a letter to the STN from an unnamed location. He had left Geneva—and his dear wife and beloved children—he wrote, because he had been "overwhelmed by a thousand difficulties." He had been forced to do this "to escape the tyranny and domination of a cruel, greedy, and unfeeling man, who subjected me by the usurious investment he made in my business."

The man who had done him in was his brother-in-law, David De Rodon. Nouffer had not been able to seek refuge with his mother in Morat, because De Rodon's family was located there, and they, too, had turned against him. Therefore, he had decided to begin a new life in the new republic of the United States. He would leave by ship in a few months. Expecting to take up "an advantageous position" in some kind of commercial business, he would travel through all of America's "thirteen united provinces." If the STN would print a special catalogue of its stock, he would sell its books wherever he went. The catalogue should be carefully designed so that it would be easy for the Americans to read, and the prices should be twice what the STN would charge him as its middleman. It could handle this arrangement through his wife, who remained in Geneva[71] and stayed in touch with him, although separated by "a distance of 230 leagues." As an indication of his good faith, he sent the names of thirty-three booksellers who had informed him when he was in Geneva that they wanted to order the *Histoire philosophique*. The STN could dispose of its remaining volumes by contacting them.

Having nothing to lose, the STN printed a proof of the catalogue and sent it to Nouffer via his wife. He returned it on January 16, 1785, having made corrections so that his American customers would not know how to order the books directly from the STN without using him as an intermediary. He wished he could come to Neuchâtel to express his warm feelings for Ostervald in person, he wrote. But he was consoled by the thought that his honor remained intact. None of his creditors should have lost any money; and if they did, it would be the fault of De Rodon. In a letter of February 12, 1785, Nouffer asked the STN to ship 150 copies of the corrected catalogue to a friend who would have them forwarded to him in America. He was to sail from Rotterdam in mid-March. The STN mailed the catalogues but never heard from Nouffer again.

6

Underground Geneva

ALTHOUGH THEY DINED WITH Voltaire and discussed Rousseau, respectable publishers in Geneva did not produce the kind of *livres philosophiques* that had to be printed in secret and distributed through underground networks. They left the riskiest sector of the trade to marginal entrepreneurs, who played a large role in the spread of radical literature, despite the tiny size of their operations.

For a city of only 30,000 inhabitants, eighteenth-century Geneva had a great many printers and booksellers—fifteen, according to the *Almanach de la librairie* of 1781, more than Marseille, which had three times its population. Having supplied books to French Huguenots since the sixteenth century, Genevan publishers knew all the tricks of operating clandestine businesses. By mid-century, however, most of them had settled into comfortable positions within the social hierarchy. As noted, they had to be *citoyens* or bourgeois in order to engage in the trade, and some of them lived like aristocrats. At the top were the Cramer, De Tourne, Philibert, Gosse, and Barrillot families, though most of them had withdrawn from publishing by 1775. Those in the middle ranks—Barthélemy Chirol, Jean-Paul Barde, and Isaac Bardin—kept their businesses going, despite increasingly difficult times, while others—Jean-Emanuel Didier and François Dufart in addition to Nouffer—succumbed to bankruptcy. Nearly all the *libraires* functioned as publishers—that is, as explained, they invested in editions, printed them or arranged for their printing, and marketed them through networks of wholesale and retail booksellers. They produced all sorts of *contrefaçons*, but left the publication of the most illegal books to speculators at the lowest level of the trade. To understand how these books were published it is necessary to look into the lives of the men who tried to scrape together a living in the industry's underground.[1]

While on a business trip to Geneva in April 1777, Ostervald received a message from Jean-Elie Bertrand, writing from the home office in

Neuchâtel: "Until now, Geneva has been our supplier of *livres philosophiques*, which in accordance with the taste of this century have become an essential part of our stock. Cailler, Gallay, and G. Grasset have supplied us with them as exchanges at a rate of two sheets for three of ours." When it came to procuring political libels and pornography, as well as irreligious and seditious treatises, Geneva was the best place in all of Europe. The STN had learned about the danger of printing them in Neuchâtel in 1771, when it incurred the wrath of the local authorities for producing d'Holbach's *Système de la nature*. Instead of exposing itself to further sanctions, it acquired these books from Genevan publishers by means of exchanges. As Bertrand's letter indicated, it often swapped three sheets of its own works—pirated versions of books that circulated legally in France—for two sheets of *livres philosophiques*, although it sometimes had to accept the more expensive rate of two to one.

Bertrand named three of the STN's suppliers: Jean-Samuel Cailler, Pierre Gallay, and Gabriel Grasset. These, along with a fourth, Jacques-Benjamin Téron l'aîné, sent many hundreds of books to the STN, which then included them in its own shipments—hidden in the packing or larded into the sheets of ordinary books—to customers everywhere in France and in most of Europe.

Jean-Samuel Cailler

Of the dealers mentioned by Bertrand, Cailler was the most respectable, although he did not rank with the established publishers like Nouffer, who occasionally speculated on forbidden books but did not specialize in producing them. Most of Cailler's business was concentrated in the highly illegal sector.

He had spent some time in prison after the police found a cache of *livres philosophiques* when they raided his bookshop in 1783,[2] but he did not have much trouble with the Genevan authorities. He paid his bills, avoided bankruptcy, and steered his small business past political and economic disasters from 1768 until 1791, when he left Geneva for revolutionary Paris. Not that there is any whiff of revolutionary sentiment in his correspondence. He wrote polished and highly literate letters, and the books he published included a handsome edition of Montaigne, with notes in Greek. He learned his way around the trade by serving as a clerk for at least ten years in the publishing firm of Frères Martin owned by Jacob and Pierre Martin. But he was an *habitant*, thus without the right to engage in commerce. Therefore, when he bought out the Martins in 1768, he set up business with Marc Chapuis, a *citoyen* who provided him with legal cover. Chapuis also supplied some of the capital, as did Heubach from Lausanne, where Cailler stored part of his stock.[3] Cailler had close ties with publishers in Lyon, who acquired many of his forbidden books and furnished him with some of their own. His contacts extended to Rouen and Holland, and his catalogues contained nearly a hundred titles.

In a letter to the STN of August 18, 1778, Cailler wrote, "This week I will finish *Commentaire sur l'Esprit des lois*, an octavo done from the manuscript of M. de Voltaire. How many do you want?" Voltaire had died in Paris two and a half months earlier but drafted the text before his death. How did this manuscript get into the hands of Cailler, assuming it was genuine? He wasn't forthcoming on the subject and simply sent fifty copies of the printed book to the STN in December. He had published an edition of *La Pucelle d'Orléans* in July 1771, although probably without the authorization of Voltaire. The only other original manuscripts that he ever published came from the pen of a literary adventurer named Pierre Ange Goudar, who commissioned their printing.[4] Otherwise, Cailler produced reprints of standard *livres philosophiques*. Among his own editions, or at least those he mentioned in his letters, were *De l'homme*, the atheistic tract by Helvétius; *Système social*, a radical political treatise by d'Holbach; *L'Arrétin*, a scandalous libel by Henri-Joseph Du Laurens; and a new version of the pornographic classic, *Histoire de dom B*****, portier des Chartreux* (*The Story of Dom B*****, Porter of the Carthusians*), attributed to Jean-Charles Gervaise de Latouche. He probably published many more, although it is impossible to trace their origin, because the underground publishers secretly collaborated on editions and swapped their productions among themselves.[5]

Swapping was the basis of Cailler's trade with the STN. His first letters indicated what he could supply and what conditions he would accept. The STN extracted a favorable exchange rate from him: one sheet of his *livres philosophiques* against one and a half of its ordinary *contrefaçons*. Cailler amassed a large stock by striking bargains with other publishers, although they sometimes let him down. An ally in Lyon, for example, promised to furnish him with 500 copies of *De l'homme* and then reneged on the agreement, infuriating him, since he carried many Enlightenment works. His stock included a good deal of political philosophy, notably Rousseau's *Contrat social* and d'Holbach's *La Politique naturelle*. D'Holbach's *Système social* was "always in demand," Cailler noted. "All these works sell rapidly."

But he carried *livres philosophiques* of every kind—political, religious, and pornographic. An order by the STN of December 23, 1775, illustrates what it wanted and what Cailler supplied:

25 *Evangile du jour* [Voltaire, irreligion]
12 *Espion chinois* [Goudar, satirical libel]
25 *De l'homme* [Helvétius, atheism]
25 *De l'Esprit* [Helvétius, atheism]
100 *Thérèse philosophe* [de Montigny?, pornography]
50 *Compère Matthieu* [Du Laurens, libertine satire]
50 *Système social* [d'Holbach, radical political theory]
50 *Maupeouana* [Mairobert, political libel]
50 *Histoire de dom B****** [Latouche?, pornography]
50 *L'Académie des dames* [Chorier, pornography]
100 *Lettres philosophiques* [Voltaire, libertinism]
100 *Christianisme dévoilé* [d'Holbach, atheism]

In return, the STN sent him sentimental novels and works of history. It actually shipped more than it received. By August 1781, its account of exchanges had a surplus of 5,270 sheets. But Cailler restored the balance and remained on good terms with the STN through 1788, when he was offering pamphlets connected with the convocation of the Estates General in France.

Pierre Gallay

Among the other publishers of *livres philosophiques*, Pierre Gallay is the most difficult to size up. He took over his father's modest bookstore and printing shop in 1773. A sales rep of the STN reported from Geneva in 1775 that Gallay could supply "a great many *livres philosophiques*,"[6] but a Genevan merchant informed the STN soon afterward that Gallay had gone bankrupt. After cobbling together an agreement with his creditors, he offered to sell the STN large numbers of *La Fille de joie* (a translation of *Fanny Hill*, John Cleland's novel first published in 1748) and a Holbachean tract. He was then printing *La Lyre gaillarde*, an anthology of obscene poems, and he offered to produce anything of the same kind that the STN might want to commission or to procure by exchanges. When the STN's sales rep called on him again in August 1776, Gallay was printing two pornographic works.

A year later, he was destitute. He asked the STN to hire him as a worker, provided that it would pay for his travel along with that of his wife and daughter and guarantee to keep him on its work force for at least three years. The STN's informant in Geneva warned it to have nothing to do with Gallay, "a feckless drunkard."[7] He left Geneva in 1781, seeking work in Lausanne. The STN never heard from him again.

Gabriel Grasset

Gabriel Grasset also eked out a living on the fringes of the working class. On April 21, 1770, he wrote to the STN, asking it to hire him as a compositor or foreman in its printing shop. He then had a small shop of his own with two presses, which he proposed to sell. All he requested was help in settling his family and a fixed wage of 6 L. per week, because he did not want to do piece-work. The STN turned him down, despite an inducement that came with the offer: "By the way, I will tell you that M. de Voltaire was pleased to learn of my intention and that he said I would always have a claim on his kindness if I took such a step."[8] The hint was that he could procure some profitable manuscripts from Voltaire.

Although Voltaire published major, multi-volume works with Gabriel Cramer, he had his most controversial books produced on the sly by marginal publishers. He also used underground presses to turn out *rogatons* and *petits pâtés*—that is, provocative pamphlets that he used after 1762 in his campaign against *l'infâme* (the infamous thing, meaning intolerance and injustice in all its forms, particularly religious persecution). Voltaire believed that short tracts worked better than treatises in arousing public opinion. Of course, they had to be anonymous or, better yet, attributed to a doctor at the Sorbonne, an archbishop in Novgorod, or any of the more than 200 pseudonymous stooges who appeared on Voltaire's title pages. The same technique of bite-sized satire worked well in larger works, particularly the series of alphabetical books that extended from the *Dictionnaire philosophique* (1764) to *La Raison par alphabet* (1769) and *Questions sur l'Encyclopédie* (1771–1772). In these works, Voltaire scattered heresies in short entries arranged in alphabetical order in such a way that the reader could dip into the book at any point and stumble upon some outrageously funny provocation. It was too risky and inappropriate for such works to be printed on the premises of Gabriel Cramer on the Grand'Rue, although they could appear inconspicuously in his later editions of Voltaire's complete works, which would circulate only among the wealthy elite.

The foreman of Cramer's shop in 1759 was Gabriel Grasset. He and his older brother, François—who later became a publisher in Lausanne, where he had a very public quarrel with Voltaire over an edition of *La Pucelle*—had worked for Cramer since the 1740s. In 1761 Gabriel set up a shop of his own in a neighborhood known for dives and bordellos. He had no right to do so, because he was a Natif, and therefore the Genevan Conseil threatened to force him out of business. He defended himself by claiming that he was merely working for Cramer. Cramer probably lent his operation a semblance of legitimacy and even, with Voltaire's prompting, provided it with some support, for Grasset continued to operate more or less within the shadow of the law for nearly twenty years. He often got into trouble, however, mainly by producing pamphlets in favor of the Natifs, and he always had to stave off financial disaster. The STN's agent in Geneva, Louis Marcinhes, wrote him off as too poor to be trusted.[9] Yet Grasset survived—in part by his wits and in large measure by clandestine printing jobs executed for Voltaire.

In the summer of 1763, Voltaire summoned Grasset to Ferney and told him that he would make his fortune. The result was the first edition of the *Dictionnaire philosophique* and the beginning of a series of works that Grasset printed for Voltaire, whom he came to call "my good patron."[10] He might have had collaborators, because the underground printers had close ties with one another and shared their scarce resources. In 1776, for example, Grasset rented supplies from his shop to Pierre Gallay. Although such activities took place under the table, the secrets often leaked. The STN's Marcinhes notified it in August 1775 that Voltaire's *Histoire de l'établissement du christianisme* was not being printed by Cramer but rather by Grasset.[11] And when the STN's sales rep visited Geneva in 1776, he reported that Gallay, Téron, and Grasset were printing three as yet untitled works by Voltaire. "They are sure to sell well."[12]

Grasset referred regularly to his work for Voltaire in his correspondence with the STN. On April 15, 1774, he wrote that he had just finished two new books by the "number one author of this century": *Dialogue de Pégase et du vieillard* and *Le Taureau blanc*. On September 2, 1775, he shipped 54 copies of *ABC*, a short political tract. On August 26, 1776, he offered to supply 200 copies of an augmented edition of *L'Examen important de Milord Bolingbroke*. On October 3, 1776, he proposed 50 copies of *Lettre de M. Voltaire adressée à l'Académie française le jour de la Saint Louis.* On February 24, 1777, he said he was finishing *La Bible enfin expliquée par plusieurs aumôniers de S.M.L.R.D.P.* The STN ordered 100 copies, but the printing dragged on for three months. When the STN complained about the delay, Grasset replied that he could not speed up his edition, because it was being "reviewed and corrected by the author's own hand." Moreover, he had just received the manuscript for Voltaire's *Éloge et pensées de Pascal* and offered to run off an extra 1,000 copies for the STN at a rate of 14 L. per sheet. He assured them that whatever he got from his "good patron" he would make available. In mid-September he had to interrupt the printing of the *Éloge et pensées* on Voltaire's orders so that he could produce a quick edition of *Prix de la justice et de l'humanité*, a tract that Voltaire wrote to promote a prize essay contest on criminal law reform sponsored by the Société économique de Berne. Voltaire might have scattered other jobs among the underground publishers of Geneva, but Grasset was his favorite and produced at least a dozen of his works.[13]

Despite his obscurity, or because of it, Grasset therefore became an influential publisher. His letters reveal little about his operations, though they show that he did not merely function as a printer. He incorporated Voltaire's books in his general stock, informed potential retailers of their availability, and sold them (probably under the counter) along with everything else in his bookshop. In all likelihood, Voltaire dealt with him in the same way that he treated Cramer, though with less deference—that is, he probably claimed a good many copies for his own use (he sent them by various means to allies in strategic positions everywhere in Europe, taking care to deny his authorship and to express horror at their contents) and left Grasset free to sell the rest. At this stage in his life, Voltaire's main concern was to move public opinion, and he knew how to manipulate the publishing industry to get his work into the hands of readers. Grasset served him as one of many cogs in the machinery required for the triumph of a higher cause: *écraser l'infâme.*

Grasset might not have fully appreciated the part he played in what can be recognized today as a powerful force in the Age of Enlightenment. His letters show him trying to make a living in the same way as other minor players in the publishing game. He notified fellow dealers of the books he was preparing, sold as many as possible, and swapped the rest. In this manner, he built up a fairly large stock, a great portion of which were *livres philosophiques*—all kinds of them, not merely the Voltairean strain. Grasset procured some from other dealers and even was willing to pay cash for the hottest items. He slipped an unsigned note into one of his first letters to the STN, asking for information about "all the libertine and sex books, with their prices."[14] This request was exceptional, because the STN printed few *livres philosophiques*. It procured them by exchanges with specialists like Grasset, who offered them at the most common rate: one sheet for two of an ordinary book.[15]

By mid-1773, Grasset was sending the STN large assortments of illegal works, and it sent in return relatively innocent *contrefaçons*, notably the Bible. (It published two editions of the Genevan *La Sainte Bible* with commentary by the Neuchâtel pastor Jean-Frédéric Ostervald, a Protestant version of Scripture that was illegal in France.) In April 1774, he sent a printed catalogue titled "Note de livres philosophiques" without his name or any compromising information. It contained the titles of seventy-five forbidden works of all kinds, from atheism to pornography. The shipments went back and forth between Geneva and Neuchâtel for the next five years. In his letters Grasset mentioned several *livres philosophiques*, aside from Voltaire's, that he printed, including d'Holbach's *Histoire critique de Jésus Christ* and *Le Compère Mathieu* by Henri-Joseph Du Laurens. The Voltaire editions provided the foundation of his trade, however. He published so many of them that he apparently had to job out some of the printing.[16] He had only two presses and hired printers as the need arose, working alongside them at a typecase.[17] He also kept the accounts and handled paperwork—not very effectively, judging by the STN's complaints about the irregularity of his invoices and the confusion in his bookkeeping, in which he mixed up tallies kept in sheets and in currency. His correspondence gives the impression of a small-scale and rather sloppy business.

After Voltaire's death in 1778, Grasset's affairs took a downturn. In January 1780, he was implicated in the publication of some irreligious and obscene books. The Genevan Conseil condemned him to imprisonment and a fine, and he had to sell his printing shop. One of the STN's correspondents reported in February that he was impoverished and ill.[18] Yet he informed the STN in April that he had opened a *boutique littéraire*—a commercial lending library. He still had a stock of *livres philosophiques* and was eager to swap them. "I can offer you 100 *Histoire critique de Jésus Christ* in 21 sheets and 100 *Lettres philosophiques*, a beautiful edition," he wrote in August. Then his letters stopped. In March 1784 his widow sent a letter to the STN informing it that he had died on February 27, 1782, and acknowledging a debt of 123 L., 15 sous, which she could not pay.

Jacques-Benjamin Téron

The final figure among the underground publishers, and the one with the thickest dossier in the archives of the STN, was Jacques-Benjamin Téron, known as Téron l'aîné. He did business at the bottom of the publishing industry, cobbling a list together between stints as a private tutor, bankruptcies, and prison terms. Yet despite his chronic indigence and marginality, he was a real force as a publisher. He came up with ideas for books, jobbed out printing, and marketed his list to retailers, working on a small scale within the sector of *livres philosophiques*. Although he also mounted legitimate operations—a bookstore and a commercial lending library—they mainly served as fronts. What drove him is difficult to say. Téron certainly wanted to make money, but also he might have felt an affinity for the ideas in the books he sold. As a Natif, he had no right to sell anything in Geneva. He managed nevertheless to organize subscriptions for Bérenger's *Histoire de Genève*, which as we have seen defended the cause of the Natifs. As recounted in the previous chapter, when the Genevan authorities discovered what Téron was up to, they summoned him for a formal censure and had the book lacerated and burned by the public hangman.

Téron signed one of his first letters to the STN as "master of mathematics." He made no effort to hide his illegal status and maintained that he did not care about qualifying to be a bookseller. His tutoring got him in the doors of the Genevan elite and, as he put it, "I sell them everything they need in the way of books."[19] The STN often received orders from individuals who had no status as booksellers and wanted to make money by selling books on the sly. It was willing to supply them, provided they could provide assurances about payment. Téron sent a small order on June 22, 1770, reassuring the STN that it would run no risk. He promised to honor his bills of exchange and asked only that it keep their arrangement secret (except from Cailler, with whom he collaborated) to avoid provoking the hostility of the established booksellers, who were consumed by "the jealousy of the trade" (and indeed they soon learned about his activity and complained about it to the STN).[20] The shipment arrived without difficulty, and Téron sent payment on September 28. He then announced that he had established a small boutique by making a deal with "a poor bourgeois" who for a price would loan his name to the business, making it legitimate.

The bourgeois, Jacob Samson, provided cover for the bookshop that Téron set up with his younger brother, Jean-Louis, also a teacher of arithmetic who had been giving lessons in Grandson, a small town not far from Neuchâtel. Jean-Louis had recently commissioned the STN to print a treatise he had written about techniques of calculating exchange rates among various regional currencies. Its title page announced that it was available "à Genève, chez les frères Téron," as if they had established a legitimate concern. They appeared more openly in a printed circular dated July 1, 1771, which provided their correspondents with samples of their signatures, according to the conventions of commercial firms.

By this time they were boasting about carrying "a huge number of new works" in their shop. They drew some of their supplies from the STN, which sent them eleven small shipments in 1771 and 1772. The books they ordered were inoffensive reprints of the kind favored by many retail dealers—works concerning travel, history, and adventure mixed with light fiction, including sentimental novels by the ever-popular Mme Riccoboni. The orders give the impression of a modest business conducted discreetly at the margin of the main trade in Geneva.

The Téron brothers procured forbidden books from sources other than the STN. On January 10, 1772, Jacques-Benjamin was arrested for selling a notorious libel against the government and court of France, *Le Gazetier cuirassé* by Charles Théveneau de Morande. In his interrogation, Jacques-Benjamin admitted having ordered a hundred copies from Marc-Michel Rey in Amsterdam, but he claimed he had not read it and did not know the names of the persons who had bought it from him. The Genevan Council punished him with a formal censure and three days in prison. On August 22, it censured him once again, this time, as mentioned, for his involvement in the subscription campaign for Bérenger's *Histoire de Genève*.

By 1773, the Téron brothers succumbed to a practice that had led to the ruination of many book dealers who lacked capital: they ordered more books than they could sell. After they failed to honor several bills of exchange, their credit crumbled. On March 9, 1773, Daniel Argand, a merchant and agent of the STN in Geneva, warned the home office that the Téron brothers were "hunting everywhere for money." On June 15, 1773, Argand informed the STN that Jean-Louis, "harried everywhere," had gone into hiding to escape his personal creditors, while his older brother struggled to keep the business afloat. The STN later learned that Jean-Louis had abandoned his share in their trade, left his brother (and apparently his wife and children) in Geneva, and drifted from job to job. On June 21, 1775, he sent STN a defiant letter without a return address, refusing to pay the remainder of his debt for the printing of his treatise on exchange rates. He had nothing, he wrote. What furniture the family possessed belonged to his wife. If the STN sued him, it could force him into debtors' prison, but it would not collect a sou, and it would condemn his children to starvation—or even worse, slow death in a poor house (*hôpital*).[21] It never heard from him again.

Meanwhile, Jacques-Benjamin had to cope with disaster. On July 3, 1773, he tried to rescue the business by begging for clemency in a printed circular sent to his creditors. He did not mention his brother. Having fallen behind in redeeming his bills of exchange, he explained, he had been forced to suspend payments in January. Then he had developed a program to amortize his debts by forming a limited partnership (*société en commandite*) with the support of two Genevan investors who had advanced him some funds. But the demands for repayment mounted so inexorably that one investor dropped out, and Téron was forced to suspend payments and submit his balance sheet to the Genevan chancery, where financial affairs were adjudicated, once again. Nonetheless, he remained convinced that he could redeem his debts in the long run, if the main body (*masse*) of his creditors agreed to a new arrangement. He would liquidate his old business and found a new one, this time on a reduced scale with more rigorous management and bookkeeping.

After studying the balance sheet in the chancery, Argand reported to the STN that Téron had accumulated an unmanageable debt, 50,000 L., and that his assets, in the form of his stock of books, were barely worth 5,000 L. Téron himself claimed that the stock should be valued at 15,000 L. An expert's assessment later set it at 4,000 L. It was hopeless to try to exact any money from the ruins of the business, Argand wrote. The STN would be best advised to get what it could in kind—that is, *en troc*, as exchanges against written-off debt. It did so, but two years later Argand wrote that Téron continued to owe 285 L. and that it still was pointless to sue him. By then he had been formally separated from his wife—a legal maneuver known as "separation of bodies and possessions"—in order to save her personal assets from confiscation.[22]

Nonetheless, he somehow managed to revive his business. After its collapse, he had resorted to giving arithmetic lessons once again and picked up some part-time work as an accountant. He had remained determined to get back in the book trade, as he explained in a letter to Ostervald in which he wrote that he "would prefer to be employed in an occupation that has plenty of variety in itself and that provides a pleasurable variety of connections with clever persons and different kinds of characters."[23]

In the spring of 1774, Téron made a settlement with his creditors (his correspondence does not mention its terms) and resumed selling books. This time, however, he concentrated on the demand for *livres philosophiques*. On April 6, the STN wrote to him that it "would gladly stock them from you, and our business would not be insignificant." Téron immediately replied that he could supply the STN with *livres philosophiques* by swapping them at a rate of three sheets for every four that he could choose from the STN's catalogue. He soon would receive a shipment of *De l'homme*, the posthumous, atheistic treatise by Helvétius, and it would be followed by a shipment of another atheistic work. Moreover, he assured the STN that he could gradually pay off his debt by sending it 12 L.s' worth of books each month, although he would have to do so behind the backs of his other creditors, who would object to this preferential treatment.

On April 23, Téron sent his first shipment to Neuchâtel with a bill of lading indicating what he supplied and how he calculated its value (see Appendix 6.1 at the end of this chapter). The shipment contained small amounts (from two to twelve copies) of seven works, all of them in sheets. They were mainly irreligious tracts, which varied from Voltairean impiety to outright atheism of the kind produced anonymously and secretly by d'Holbach and his circle. Unlike later shipments, this bale did not include any political libels or pornographic works. As agreed, Téron swapped three sheets of his *livres philosophiques* against four ordinary *contrefaçons* from the stock of the STN and therefore asked that his exchange account be credited with a total of 711 sheets. In return, he selected four works from the STN's catalogue: *Sainte Bible*; *De l'amitié et des passions*, a moral treatise published anonymously by Marie Geneviève Charlotte Thiroux d'Arconville; *Dictionnaire des arts et métiers*; and Voltaire's *Questions sur l'Encyclopédie*. Three days earlier, Téron had ordered some novels by Mme Riccoboni and Baculard d'Arnaud. All of these books could circulate freely in Geneva. Subsequent exchanges between Téron and the STN fit into the same pattern: he procured works that he could sell safely in his shop, and it received a supply of the forbidden literature. With a few exceptions for highly desirable new works (*nouveautés*), the exchange rate remained consistent.[24] Both parties kept special accounts, calculated in sheets, which in principle were to be settled at regular intervals, the balance being attributed to a fresh account.

The exchanges continued in this fashion for five years, until 1779. The supply of forbidden books never gave out, thanks in part to Voltaire's presence close by in Ferney. On May 24, 1774, Téron wrote that Voltaire was about to publish *Éloge de Louis XV*, a new work that was certain to be much in demand, and therefore the exchange rate would have to be adjusted upward—one sheet of Voltaire for three of the STN's books. Although he did not reveal where he procured such books, he now began to indicate that he produced some of them himself. He spoke of "my *De l'homme*," which was currently being printed and said he had decided to commission the printing of *Le Christianisme dévoilé*. "I am now printing *Système de la nature* but under the greatest secrecy," he revealed in another letter. Later he referred to "my edition" of the *Système* and even applied the word *éditeur* "to himself— not *libraire* nor *libraire-imprimeur*."[25] That is the earliest use I have found of the French equivalent of "publisher." Téron had no presses and at this time did not even operate out of a bookshop, although he planned to open one in July. He was self-consciously fulfilling the role of a modern publisher— making arrangements for editions, getting them printed, and selling them to middlemen.

Téron's publishing took place clandestinely and on a small scale, yet it re-quired capital. How did a marginal entrepreneur, who had gone bankrupt a few months earlier, manage such a feat? He probably had backers such as Pons and Pestre, who had supported his limited partnership in 1773. By risking small sums, they could clear enormous profits, because *livres philosophiques* filled a sector of the trade where profitability was highest. Téron, however, did not mention any resources in his letters to the STN. They indicated only that he continued to give arithmetic lessons in the home of a wealthy banker during the summer of 1774, while he was preparing to open a bookshop "au bas de la Cité." It, too, cost money. "The demands of moving house, the masons and carpenters, have forced me to neglect my accounts," he wrote on August 26. At the same time, he had to pay his printers and fend off demands from his wife, who also needed cash. On September 9, he signed a contract with Jean Dassier, a *bourgeois* bookseller who served as a cover for the busi-ness, just as Jacob Samson had done.[26] Téron built up his stock through swaps with the STN and other publishers, and he attracted customers by installing a *magasin littéraire*, or lending library, in his shop. Instead of buying books, the members of the *magasin* could borrow them after paying a subscription fee. Booksellers often created such establishments in order to make the most of their stock and to create an atmosphere of social activity in their shops.

For its part, while the STN tried to avoid doing business with booksellers who failed to pay their bills, it needed a supply of *livres philosophiques*. Therefore, it requested its Genevan correspondent, Louis Marcinhes, to keep an eye on Téron and to make sure he reduced his debt by keeping up his side of the exchanges. In March 1775, Marcinhes informed the STN that Téron was about to ship two crates of books, and in April he recommended him as the best source of illegal works in Geneva "at the cheapest possible price." Téron had even considered publishing some original works.[27] Tiny as it was, Téron's publishing house seemed to be sustainable.

On December 9, 1774, he wrote that he was publishing a second edition of *Le Christianisme dévoilé* and that he was about to reprint one of the most powerful attacks on the French ministry led by Chancellor René-Nicolas-Charles-Augustin de Maupeou, *Journal historique de la révolution opérée dans la constitution de la monarchie française par M. de Maupeou, chancelier de France.* This work belonged to the wave of antigovernment libels that swept through France after the death of Louis XV on May 10, 1774. By then the Maupeou government had fallen, but any attacks against it were severely repressed by the new administration, because they made the entire political system look rotten. The *Journal historique* brought the "Maupeouana" (anti-Maupeou literature) together in a three-volume anthology, which sold so well that it soon would be extended to five and then seven volumes. To tap that demand, Téron had to find funds to pay for the printing. The financial pressure remained inexorable, although he could glimpse a prosperous future. His lending library was doing well, he wrote, and he hoped to hire an assistant "to deal with a greater number of other enterprises, and to undertake business trips." As his commerce expanded, he assured the STN, "I will be able to supply you with a greater number of items."

The printer began assembling the *Journal historique* at the beginning of February 1775. Téron shipped 200 copies to the STN in March and sold the rest to booksellers in Lyon and Avignon. Having followed this operation closely, Marcinhes informed the STN that Téron had pulled it off behind the backs of his other creditors, notably Dassier, who had contributed 100 louis to help set up the *magasin littéraire.* Had the creditors learned that Téron was using his new resources to cut a deal with the STN instead of paying off their debts, they would have been furious.[28] But because it took place in the form of exchanges—that is, without any payment—he managed to keep it secret.

The problem from Téron's viewpoint had to do with the exchanges themselves. After sending off the shipment of the *Journal historique,* he had made a selection of books from the STN's catalogue, as agreed. Instead of providing all the works he wanted, however, it sent him only a small number of its most recent publications. He then realized that a sizable deficit had accumulated in the STN's exchange account. It owed him 12,000 sheets and had sent him only 3,000—often sheets that he had not ordered. As a means of recovering its debt, the STN had skimmed off Téron's bestselling books and had held back its own bestsellers while at the same time allowing the balance of their exchanges to tip drastically in its favor.

In May 1775 the STN sent another shipment, which once again lacked many of the books Téron desired. At the same time, it ordered a second shipment of the *Journal historique*, which was selling briskly all over France and had now been expanded by two more volumes. Unfortunately, Téron could not obtain those volumes from the printer who had done the job for him, Gabriel Regnault in Lyon. Together with his father, Geoffroy, who had left the direction of the shop to him in 1773 but continued to be active, Regnault ran one of the most audacious publishing and pirating businesses in Lyon. He collaborated on the quarto edition of the *Encyclopédie*, on a supplementary version of the *édition encadrée*—the most handsome complete edition— of Voltaire's works, and on Nouffer's edition of the *Histoire philosophique* by Raynal. It seems likely, although there is no proof, that he printed *De l'homme* for Téron. But when it came to volumes 4 and 5 of the *Journal historique* printed at a run of 2,000 copies, he refused to ship them. Téron could not pay for them, nor had he paid the bill for volumes 1 through 3. Instead of haggling and threatening to sue, Regnault decided to keep the last two volumes for himself, to reprint the first three, and to sell the expanded set himself.

Meanwhile, Téron had to fend off the STN, which was furious. Having bought the first part of the *Journal historique*, its customers demanded the rest. In response to its protests, Téron answered that he could not supply the last two volumes and could not reprint them, because "my resources are not yet sufficient to do so many printing jobs one after the other." He had overextended himself. By way of compensation, he offered to send a new edition of the *Système de la nature*, which he had just had printed. The STN ordered fifty copies as a swap. Now fully aware of his unfavorable balance in their exchange accounts, Téron refused to send the shipment until he had received the books he wanted from the STN's stock. The STN then dispatched Marcinhes to settle the dispute, but he got nowhere and finally renounced having anything more to do with Téron, whom he wrote off as a *barbouillon*—"a lost cause."[29]

Nevertheless, negotiations resumed in November. Téron declared himself ready to provide 200 *Systèmes de la nature*. He put them aside in a pile and needed only to "tighten the ropes" to send them off, but first demanded the restoration of an equilibrium in their exchange accounts. The STN had encouraged him to publish another bestselling libel, *Anecdotes sur Mme la comtesse du Barry*,[30] and he was eager to reprint the first volumes of the *Journal historique*. By this time, however, he had learned not to undertake more than he could finance, no matter what the demand. Until he was clear of his debts, he resolved, "Neither *Anecdotes du Barry* nor any other kind of new work will tempt me."

This prudence was economic, not ideological. Téron was ready to publish pornography as well as atheism and political libel. In April 1776 he came up with another proposition involving a large number of a "salacious book," provided that the exchange of sheets would be favorable enough to him. In this manner, the STN could continue to supply its customers with forbidden literature while providing him with the standard fare that could be sold openly in Genevan bookstores. "I particularly need a great many novels, travel books, and histories."

Such was the balance of trade developed by the exchanges between an underground entrepreneur and a well-established pirate publisher in eighteenth-century Switzerland. It is impossible to follow their relations further, because Téron's dossier runs out of letters at this point. Genevan sources show that in February 1777 he replaced Dassier as a cover for his business with another bourgeois, Charles Rimon.[31] Rimon withdrew a year later, leaving Téron without a false front. The Genevan chamber of commerce threatened to close his shop, and it objected to Téron's continued attempts to remain in business under other names. At last, in September 1778, he found a third bourgeois, François Marchand, and resumed his trade under the official title of Marchand et Guerloz fils. In 1780, the chamber finally had enough of this game of hide-and-seek, and it decreed the dissolution of the firm.

There was not much left to liquidate. Téron had gone bankrupt once again in August 1779. A notary who represented the STN advised it to collect what it could in books, "because with bad debtors you have to extract whatever you can."[32] The creditors permitted Téron to continue work as a clerk in the *magasin littéraire* under the direction of his wife, from whom he remained formally separated. In his last letter to the STN, dated May 21, 1782, he reiterated that he could not pay the debt he had owed for such a long time. He was scraping together a living once more by giving arithmetic lessons, "because, as to the book trade, it hardly provides me with enough to buy bread."

Historians have often encountered authors living down and out in garrets, scribbling to stay alive. Marginal publishers inhabited a Grub Street of their own, scrambling to stay in business. There were many obscure entrepreneurs like Téron, Grasset, Gallay, and Cailler. They specialized in the most forbidden books in the literary marketplace, not only the works of the *philosophes* but also everything known as *livres philosophiques*.

Appendix 6.1

Swapping Sheets: Téron's Shipment of April 23, 1774

In his first shipment to the STN, Téron sent a bill of lading that illustrates the way exchanges were calculated. He gave the number of sheets contained in each book and the number of copies of that book contained in the bale. Then he calculated the total number of sheets, which was to be credited to his "compte de changes," the special account for him that was kept in sheets rather than in currency. The seven books in the shipment were highly illegal and mainly philosophical in content. Other shipments contained political libels and pornographic works, which Téron also carried in his stock of *livres philosophiques*.

8 Histoire critique [*A Critical History of Jesus Christ* by d'Holbach] at 21 sheets . . . 168 sheets

6 Lettres de Bolingbrocke [probably *The Political Century of Louis XIV, or Letters by Viscount Bolingbroke*] at 12½ sheets . . . 75 sheets

3 Traité des imposteurs [*Treatise on the Three Impostors*, attributed to Jan Vroesen] at 9 sheets . . . 27 sheets

6 Théologie [*Portable Theology or Abridged Dictionary of the Christian Religion* by d'Holbach] at 10½ sheets . . . 63 sheets

12 Catéchumène [*Catechumen,* translated from the Chinese, by Charles Borde] at 2 sheets . . . 24 sheets

2 Choses utiles à 3 volumes [*Useful and Agreeable Things* by Voltaire in 3 volumes] at 67½ sheets . . . 134½ sheets

Cartonnures [cardboard binding] for 6 volumes . . . 24 sheets

6 Saül [*Saül, a Tragedy Based on the Bible* by Voltaire] at 3 sheets . . . 18 sheets

[Total] . . . 533½ sheets

An additional 1/3 or 4 for 3 sheets . . . 711 sheets for which you are debited.

7

A Confederation of Pirates

PIRATE PUBLISHERS COULD NOT survive by going it alone. The risks were too great, and they occurred at every point in the cycle that ran from production to bill collecting. Depending on its size, a book often took six months to print. The paper frequently had to be ordered in advance, a large outlay of capital. While waiting for bales to arrive from paper mills and, after their arrival, for composers and pressmen to turn out sheets, a pirate often discovered that a competitor had beaten him to the market. The race to reprint was compounded by the difficulties of distribution, for shipments got delayed at border crossings, stalled in warehouses or, worst of all, confiscated by border guards and inspectors in *chambres syndicales*.

Even if they arrived on schedule, the shipments might not sell as well as expected, because of overoptimistic calculations of demand. Some became *drogues, fours,* or *garde-magasins*—publishers' colloquialisms had many ways to designate failures—gathering dust in storerooms. Many retailers failed to pay their bills on time—usually a matter of redeeming bills of exchange due to mature in twelve months from the date of reception—because they faced difficulties at the local level, whether in collecting from their own customers or in finding cash. Liquidity became increasingly rare and bankruptcies frequent, especially in the illegal sector of the trade, during the late 1770s and 1780s.

Given the difficulties, it therefore made sense to combine forces. Instead of cutting one another's throats, pirates formed ententes, nonaggression pacts, and alliances designed to share risks and profits. The simplest kind of cooperation involved swapping sheets. As in the STN's dealings with Téron, each of the partners opened up a special "exchange account" in which they kept a record of the sheets that went back and forth between them. Keeping the accounts balanced required mutual trust, and, more important, each of the two allies had to maintain transparency about the books in his stock that he was willing to swap. If he held back information about a book that sold well, he would undercut the trust that held the alliance together. Alliances were also threatened by the constant danger that partners might compete on the same local or regional market and even undersell one another, despite commitments to maintain prices. Usually, each publisher developed its own network of customers among the retail booksellers. It could count on strong sales in some cities, while its ally concentrated on others. But friction was built into piracy, which involved a constant tension between conflict and co-operation among competing publishers.

The best way to understand how the system operated is to follow the interactions of the three *sociétés typographiques* located in Neuchâtel, Lausanne, and Bern. As explained in Chapter 5, the first two developed an extensive trade in pirated books throughout the 1770s. The third, La Société typographique de Berne (STB), or Typographische Gesellschaft Bern, resembled the others, although it had a character of its own.[1] A progressive young patrician named Vinzenz Bernhard Tscharner founded STB in 1758 as a small, nonprofit publishing enterprise intended to promote Enlightenment and belles-lettres among Bern's elite. Tscharner belonged to the wealthy oligarchy that dominated the city in the eighteenth century. Like Neuchâtel and Geneva, Bern was a city-state ruled by councils restricted to the rich and powerful, but it had conquered large territories in what are now the cantons of Aargau and Vaud, and they furnished much of the city's wealth.

As envisaged by Tscharner, the STB began by producing two learned journals, which circulated among academies and universities and diffused the work of Bern's own academy, Oekonomische Gesellschaft Bern. Tscharner financed the operation and relied on Fortunato Bartolomeo de Felice (later known as Barthélemy de Félice), an Italian scholar who had settled in Bern and converted to Protestantism, to handle most of the editorial work. In 1762, Félice moved to Yverdon, where he set up another publishing house with the support of his associates in Bern. He concentrated on producing a reworked and highly Protestant version of Diderot's *Encyclopédie*, while Tscharner, along with friends and family members, continued to publish the proceedings of the Bernese academy and some treatises in agronomy. They hired another Italian man of letters, named Serini, to direct commercial affairs and later replaced him with a bookseller from Heidelberg named Pfaehler. (Although Pfaehler rose to become the director of the STB in 1774, I cannot discover his first name, or the first name of Serini.)

In 1764, Tscharner turned from publishing to politics by joining Bern's Great Council (Grosser Rat). His role was taken up by his brother, Niklaus

Emanuel, and other wealthy and well-connected patricians, who would later invest in the Société typographique de Lausanne. Under Pfaehler's direction, the STB developed commercial ties with booksellers throughout Europe, especially in Germany, where it participated actively in the book fairs of Leipzig. (It preferred Leipzig, which attracted 500 to 600 booksellers from everywhere in Europe, to Frankfurt, which it considered inadequate.) By 1769, when it began to deal with the STN, it had been transformed from a niche operation into a large publishing and bookselling business.

In July 1769, as soon as the STN began to operate, the STB sent it a letter welcoming it to the trade and proposing that they cooperate in "considerable affairs." Although the directors of both companies could speak French and German, the linguistic divide between Bern and Neuchâtel oriented their businesses in different directions. While the STN concentrated on France, Serini, writing for the STB, offered to open up the German market for large quantities of the books that were beginning to come off the presses in Neuchâtel.[2] In January 1770, he sent an order for works that he planned to sell at the spring fair in Leipzig. But the STN ran into all sorts of difficulties in its first attempts at printing and shipping. After the first shipment arrived, Serini showered the STN with complaints. The paper was substandard, the printing sloppy. He objected to charges for packing: "When one buys a horse, one usually gets the bridle free." And the transport, a mere matter of thirty-nine miles, took forever: "It is almost easier to get merchandise shipped from Constantinople than from you." Moreover, the first shipments arrived too late to make the spring fair in Leipzig. Serini needed them by February in order to take advantage of the cheaper transport costs, which would double by May, and therefore he delayed payment for a year. He even scolded the STN for its choice of what to print: "It seems to us that you are too timid in your enterprises. You want to proceed with complete surety. If that were possible, everyone would want to be a publisher."

The tone of the letters changed in 1771, when the STN had got past the breaking-in phase of its activities and was producing attractive books. The STB was particularly eager to procure works related to the Enlightenment, such as *Système de la nature*, *Questions sur l'Encyclopédie*, and *L'An deux mille quatre cent quarante*. None of them could be sold in Bern, where the censorship was strict, but they would find plenty of buyers in Germany, Serini explained.[3]

Although it operated on a smaller scale than that of the STN, the STB published enough to enter into a swapping arrangement with the STN in

1772. However, the Neuchâtelois complained that the Bernese held back some of their works while expecting the STN to make available everything it had in stock. This dispute produced a chill in the relations between the two houses during 1773. Things improved in the spring of 1774, when they resumed swapping and began to discuss producing joint editions. They considered printing an abridgment of Charles Rollin's thirteen-volume *Histoire romaine* and a translation of Cook's travels in the Pacific. Far from competing, the STB declared its determination to cooperate in "an honest and polite way," as was suitable for "neighbors and friends."

Nothing came of these plans, probably because the STB ran into financial difficulties. Having accumulated a large deficit, it was reorganized in July 1774. The Bernese patricians provided fresh capital, Serini was dismissed, and the STB concentrated on restoring its balance sheet by making the most of the German market. Meanwhile, on February 22, 1774, Jean-Pierre Heubach reorganized his company as the Société typographique de Lausanne with backing by some of the same Bernese (Samuel Kirchberger and members of the Tscharner family).[4] From this point on, the history of the three typographical societies—Bern, Lausanne, and Neuchâtel—was intertwined in ways that reveal an unfamiliar aspect of pirate publishing: diplomacy and war.

The first phase involved an alliance between the STL and the STN. Even before launching his new *société typographique*, Heubach proposed that they combine forces in order to pirate more effectively.[5] Full of optimism, he said that his new firm soon would have six presses and expected to market its books throughout much of Europe. He could meet with Ostervald to arrange joint editions, and they could begin to cooperate right away by swapping copies, informing each other about what they planned to print and announcing each other's new publications in their circular letters. The meeting took place at Payerne, near Neuchâtel on March 12–13, 1774. Soon afterward, Ostervald drafted a formal *traité*, which laid out the terms of the alliance. Heubach discussed it with his Bernese partners and returned it with comments; the alliance was ratified by signatures on April 12. It committed the two houses to collaborate on a few joint editions during a trial period of one year. Each would continue with its main line of business while keeping the other informed about its planned publications and swapping sheets at a fixed rate of 9 French deniers per sheet—that is, less than the STN's standard wholesale price of 1 sou (12 deniers). They would make joint decisions about which books to pirate and would hire an agent in Paris to keep them informed about the best prospects. Costs and profits would be shared evenly. If difficulties arose, they would resolve them by means of arbitration, not through the courts. By cooperating closely, they would attain a common goal: "greater speed, more variety, and more security . . . in our enterprises."[6]

Ostervald and Heubach had already agreed on the first book to pirate together during their discussions in Payerne: *Histoire de Maurice, comte de Saxe* by the baron d'Espagnac. A biography of France's greatest commander in the wars of Louis XV, it seemed likely to appeal to a broad public. As it had recently appeared in two volumes, each of the publishers could print one volume, and they could get to the market in half the time it would take for one of them to produce the book alone. To entice consumers, they decided to put "new, augmented edition" on the title page, even though they added nothing whatsoever to the original. Prospects for the second joint edition looked even more promising: *Relation des voyages entrepris par ordre de Sa Majesté britannique*, a four-volume account of the adventures of Cook and other English explorers in unknown parts of the world.[7] Ostervald proposed a print run of 1,500 copies, which was comparatively large. Heubach heartily agreed but thought it safer to limit the run to 1,000. A Paris correspondent sent copies of the French translation, hot off the press, and they decided that the STN would produce the first two volumes while the STL did the last two. They coordinated technical details about typography and paper so that no inconsistencies would mar the appearance of the four-volume set,[8] and by the end of the year each house was marketing joint editions with both Lausanne and Neuchâtel on their title pages.

The arrangement for a Parisian agent to supply copy and information did not work out. After some searching, they jointly hired a playwright named Harny de Guerville, but he failed to send satisfactory reports, and they decided to fall back on the Parisian correspondents who served each house separately.[9] Then they ran into difficulties with their third joint publication, a popular, nine-volume survey of history by Claude-Francois-Xavier Millot, *Éléments d'histoire générale*. Heubach had originally planned to publish it by himself in duodecimo following the original Parisian edition page by page, and to forestall competition from other pirates he sent a circular letter announcing it in this format. Meanwhile, however, the STN proposed printing it in-octavo as a joint edition and sent him a sample page to serve as a model for the design and typography. Unfortunately, Heubach was away on a business trip when the STN's proposal arrived, and the STN, eager to get to the market as quickly as possible, began work according to its plan, even though it had not concluded an agreement with the STL. When Heubach returned to Lausanne, he was furious at this violation of the Payerne pact, particularly because he had already made arrangements for the paper supply and did not want to renege on the conditions he had offered to retail dealers in his circular. To him, it seemed that the STN had preemptively appropriated a large printing job without proper consultation and lacked "the sort of delicacy that should prevail in our commitments." In the end, the STN published the entire work by itself.

The two allies also were committed to secondary alliances, which caused further conflict. The STL dealt with Samuel Fauche, the former partner of the STN who had set up a rival business of his own in Neuchâtel, and the STN traded extensively with François Grasset, the STL's main competitor in Lausanne. An additional conflict involved the STB, because the STN sold it a shipment of the *Relation des voyages*, and the STL had promised to give the Bernese bookseller, Albert Emanuel Haller, an exclusive right to market the same book in his region. By the end of 1774, so much friction had occurred that the two houses decided not to renew their *traité*.

They had learned a great deal, however, about the advantages and difficulties of confederated piracy. Far from diminishing, the need for cooperation increased after the French book-trade reforms of 1777 raised the threat of greater rigor in the suppression of pirated books. Therefore, the STL and the STN decided to make another try, this time including the STB, which had been revived under Pfaehler's direction. Heubach, who seemed to be the most enterprising of the publishers, proposed a confederation of the three *sociétés typographiques* in a letter to the STN of February 27, 1778. He had received only recently—six months after they were decreed—copies of the reform edicts of August 30, 1777, and he thought that the time had come to act.[10]

For several weeks the three publishers debated among themselves about the most effective way to organize a *Confédération typographique*. The publishing house in Yverdon could not participate, because Félice had his hands full with editing and publishing his *Encyclopédie*. The STL and STB had already become close collaborators thanks to a joint speculation on an octavo edition of the original *Encyclopédie*. At a meeting in Bern in April, they discussed ways to win the STN's adherence to a tripartite alliance and decided to request Ostervald to draft a *traité* that would provide its guidelines. He came up with a proposal that they considered excellent but unnecessarily complicated. In its place, they suggested a simplified plan. Ostervald agreed, adding further suggestions, and on May 3, Pfaehler incorporated Ostervald's ideas in a text, which they later referred to as the "Traité de Berne," that determined the basic principles of the Confederation. There were six.[11] First, the three houses would reach unanimous decisions about which books to publish, and each would print one-third of every edition. Secondly, if one house printed more than the others, it would be reimbursed for the additional costs, including items such as the wear of the type. Third, the provisioning of paper would be coordinated so as to keep a surplus on hand and to make sure that the printing of each book would be done on the same quality of paper. Fourth, each house would market the books on its own but for a common account, maintaining a standard price of 1 sou per sheet. The income would be distributed evenly among the three. At an annual or biannual settling of accounts, any associate who had collected more from his sales than the others would reimburse them with a bill of exchange to mature within six months. Fifth, if one associate had made an agreement to provide a customer with an exclusive sale of its books within a particular city or region, he would inform the other associates, and they would respect that commitment. And last, while marketing the editions of the Confederation for the benefit of its members, each associated house would continue to sell its other publications on its own as it pleased.

These principles showed a determination to avoid the difficulties that had undermined earlier attempts at cooperation.[12] The emphasis on paper, for example, reflected their unhappy experience with paper millers, who sometimes held up production by failing to supply reams on time. It was crucial to use the same paper in all three printing shops by ordering large batches, called *campagnes*, in advance. Paper varied enormously in quality at a time when each sheet was made by hand and when readers were offended by irregularities in color and texture.[13] The Traité de Berne also emphasized constant consultation and careful bookkeeping, because the associates had learned from experience how easily one partner in a consortium could assume a disproportionate share of the printing and profits. And the respect for exclusive marketing arrangements was meant to prevent turf wars of the kind that had occurred in the sales of the *Relation des voyages* in Bern. The partners agreed to sign the final version of the Traité at a meeting in Neuchâtel, where they could add further details, such as a provision to hire someone in Paris who would keep them informed about the literary scene and send books to reprint.

Heubach, Pfaehler, and Ostervald concluded the arrangements for the Confederation in Neuchâtel on May 18. In addition to the basic six provisions, they agreed that each house would reserve two of its presses for printing the joint editions and that they would create a common stock of books from the stock that each held separately. In the following weeks, each publisher submitted a list of thirty or so titles that it was willing to contribute, and the other two made the selections that they preferred.[14] Despite some squabbling (the STB suspected the STN of holding back some of its bestsellers), they were able to create a collective catalogue. Then they began marketing the books among their separate networks of customers and contributing the income from the sales to a collective account.

With six presses working full time, a common general stock, cooperative marketing, and a combined capital fund, the Confederation became a formidable power in the world of French publishing. From the beginning, however, it suffered from a nearly fatal flaw.[15] The STN had acquired a share in a venture led by the Parisian publisher Charles-Joseph Panckoucke to publish a reworked version of Diderot's *Encyclopédie*. Unlike the other members of the Paris Guild, Panckoucke speculated on a gigantic scale, won the support of key figures in the French administration, and developed France's first press empire. As we shall see in the next chapter, he played a decisive role in the publication of the works of Voltaire and Rousseau after their deaths in 1778. Two years earlier, he had engaged the most eminent *philosophes* from the generation after Diderot to prepare an *Encyclopédie* that would contain up-to-date information arranged according to subjects rather than the order of the alphabet.

In January 1777, Panckoucke had to postpone this *Encyclopédie méthodique*, as it came to be called, because a pirate from Lyon named Joseph Duplain threatened to take over the *Encyclopédie* market by producing an inexpensive quarto edition of the original text. Panckoucke possessed the rights to the original (it was a complicated transaction that involved the plates, since the *privilège* had been revoked), and he could enforce them by mobilizing his protectors in the Direction de la librairie and Versailles. But Duplain had been amazingly successful in selling subscriptions to the quarto. After much hesitation, Panckoucke decided to postpone the *Méthodique* and to join Duplain rather than to fight him. On January 14, they formed a joint venture, directed by Duplain, which turned out to be extremely lucrative. Having bought a share in Panckoucke's rights, the STN also became an associate of Duplain, although it dealt with him only indirectly, through

Panckoucke. Aside from a share in the profits, it sought to benefit from printing as many of the thirty-six volumes of text as possible. Duplain jobbed out the printing, and the STN made a large profit from every volume that he allotted to it.

Before forming the Confederation, the STL and the STB had planned to collaborate in producing their own quarto edition of the *Encyclopédie*. Duplain beat them to the market by launching his subscription campaign in December 1776. Rather than accepting defeat, they retaliated by producing a still smaller *Encyclopédie* at an even cheaper price—that is, they pirated his pirated edition and soon were collecting subscriptions throughout France and the rest of Europe for an octavo *Encyclopédie* that would follow the quarto page by page. Fierce competition between the rival editions broke out. By mobilizing his protectors in the French administration, Panckoucke engineered so many confiscations of octavo shipments that he eventually closed the border to them, despite the continuous efforts by the octavo group to reach their subscribers through smuggling operations. Hundreds of thousands of livres were at stake in these battles—Diderot's *Encyclopédie* was the most lucrative enterprise that any of the publishers had ever encountered—and the STN was caught in the middle of them. When it joined forces with the STL and the STB in the Confederation, it had already allied itself with their enemies in what was about to break out as the biggest publishing war of the century, one that lasted three years.

The STL and STB did not know of the STN's interest in the quarto speculation when they first sounded it out at a meeting of the three Swiss publishers in early November 1777.[16] After they learned that the STN was an ally of their *Encyclopédie* enemies, they nonetheless persevered in creating the Confederation the following summer. All three understood that they could still profit from cooperative pirating while the battles over the *Encyclopédies* ran their course. The STN finessed its conflict of interests as well as it could. Bérenger, a personal friend of Ostervald's, as we have seen, acted as an intermediary, smoothing over difficulties; and the Confederation held together. It lasted four years and published thirty-one pirated editions (having debated the possibilities of publishing many others). Because the three houses had to reach a unanimous decision about every project, they discussed pros and cons in a constant stream of letters that flowed around the Bern-Lausanne-Neuchâtel triangle.

The dialogue began on May 23, 1778, with a letter from Heubach, who had returned to Lausanne from the meeting in Neuchâtel, where the

Confederation had been created five days earlier. Writing in a new tone of confidentiality, he reported on the day's mail from Paris. It contained nothing very interesting, he remarked, but the STL expected soon to receive a copy of a promising work on geology, which it would forward for the STN to consider.[17] It also had a high opinion of Jérôme Lalande's *Voyage d'un Français en Italie*, which was much in demand and seemed to merit a new edition. A few days later, Pfaehler wrote from Bern that a whole slew of new books had recently arrived from Paris. Although he had not yet had time to read them, he surmised that most would not be worth reprinting and merely mentioned the titles in case the STN wanted to examine any of them. He expected more *nouveautés* to arrive soon from Holland, and he had learned that a publisher in Liège was about to put out a new edition of Jean-Baptiste-Claude Delisle de Sales's *De la philosophie de la nature*, so he advised that they cross it off the list of possible reprints that they had drawn up during their meeting in Neuchâtel.

Five days later, Pfaehler wrote that he had skimmed through the batch of books from Paris and confirmed his opinion that none warranted pirating. As to large-scale projects that could keep all three houses busy, he recommended they consider doing a translation of the works of Alexander Pope. Meanwhile, the presses in Neuchâtel and Lausanne were already turning out sheets of a new edition of Millot's nine-volume *Éléments d'histoire générale*, which they had earlier agreed to publish jointly. It soon would appear as the first of the Confederation's publications with an address on its title page that could be read as a challenge to the publishing establishment in Paris: *en Suisse: chez les libraires associés.* The STB did not yet participate in the printing, because it was then setting up a new printing shop, where two of its six presses would operate full time for the Confederation.

At this point, toward the end of May 1778, Bérenger entered the dialogue. As the STL's expert on literature, he had most to say about the literary qualities of the books proposed for pirating. He supported the idea of reprinting the *Voyage* of Lalande, and he strongly recommended a new edition of Condillac's *Cours d'étude pour l'instruction du prince de Parme* a sixteen-volume treatise full of Enlightenment philosophy. According to his information, the Lyonnais edition of it, published by Jean-Marie Barret, one of Lyon's most intrepid pirates, had sold out, leaving 250 orders unfilled, and he gave no credence to rumors that it was being reprinted in Maastricht and Liège. In response to the STN's suggestion that they publish new editions of Antoine Chamberland's *Mémoires philosophiques* and *Histoire de Miss West, ou l'heureux dénouement*, a translation of a two-volume novel by Frances Brooke, he replied that the first seemed "common" and the second "interesting" but poorly rendered into French. A few days later he wrote that *Miss West* seemed worth doing after all, provided that he reworked the text for one volume and Jean-Elie Bertrand of the STN did the same for the other. They could produce it quickly, while postponing the Condillac, which no longer looked urgent, because contrary to their earlier information they had recently learned that copies of it were still piled up in Barret's shop in Lyon. In reply, Ostervald agreed, noting that *Miss West* would add variety to the Confederation's list. But before sealing his letter, he added a P.S.: Bertrand had just read it, and "the style seemed so bad to him that it would be necessary to rewrite it completely, and the substance isn't worth the trouble." Bérenger concurred and removed it from the list. He also agreed with Ostervald's suggestion that they reprint the works of Mme Riccoboni, a better bet in the domain of light literature. The STN had published a six-volume, octavo edition in 1773, and it had sold out so rapidly that Ostervald was sure a new edition in the more portable duodecimo format would do well.

In the category of more serious and substantial literature, Ostervald recommended the four-volume *Histoire du règne de Philippe II, roi d'Espagne* by Robert Watson, translated by the comte de Mirabeau and J.-B. Durival. It covered many important events and read well, Ostervald emphasized, although unfortunately it lacked details about court intrigues and the king's private life. To test the demand, they could print a title page and mail it to booksellers as if it were already printed, asking for orders. Bérenger then gave it a careful reading and endorsed Ostervald's suggestion. He found the book "good and instructive. One reads it with pleasure, and from that point of view, I think it would be good to do a pirated edition of it." At the same time, Bérenger, full of ideas, sent Ostervald three suggestions of his own: a compendium of contemporary biographies (interesting material but presented in an inflated style); the memoirs of Jacques Fitz-James, duc de Berwick (famous as a commander in the War of the Spanish Succession); and a history of Hungary (Bérenger generally favored histories). In the end, Ostervald and Pfaehler agreed to publish only Berwick's memoirs.

By mid-August the STB's presses were mounted and it was eager for copy. Pfaehler proposed to begin with a few volumes of Riccoboni's works, and he suggested another possibility, *Voyage en Arabie et en d'autres pays de l'Orient* by Carsten Niebuhr, which they could reduce from four to three volumes by cutting the text.[18] Ostervald and Heubach agreed, and Ostervald offered to

correct the style of the translation from the German original. Travel literature had great appeal for eighteenth-century readers, who were hungry for
information about unknown parts of the world. Pfaehler also recommended
Voyages en différents pays de l'Europe by Carlo Antonio Pilati, a cosmopo-
lite and partisan of the Enlightenment in Italy. Aside from the popularity of
travel literature as a genre, the decisive factor in this case was subjective: "We
have read it with great pleasure," Pfaehler wrote, using the standard, first-
person plural of business letters. "You will read it in the same way." He was
right. Ostervald and Heubach agreed to publish the book.

Another decision taken by the Confederation as it moved into high gear
during the summer of 1778 concerned current events. Ostervald proposed
publishing an anthology of the state constitutions from the American colonies, which were then battling for their independence and had recently
entered into an alliance with France. Pfaehler hesitated at first, because he
had heard that the collection proposed by Ostervald was less comprehensive than one said to be in press in Paris. But after conferring with Heubach,
who had come to Bern to settle a court case, he changed his mind, and the
Confederation put out *Lois et constitutions d'Amérique* at a press run of
750 copies. Heubach had originally disagreed with an Ostervald-Pfaehler
proposal to reprint a standard reference work, Pierre-Joseph Macquer's
Dictionnaire de la chimie (Macquer was the most prominent opponent of the
revolution in chemistry then being led by Antoine Lavoisier), but a discussion with Pfaehler brought him around. Having debated these and other possibilities, the Confederation marketed quite a varied and well-balanced list in
1778–1779.

Unfortunately, however, the marketing campaign coincided with the most
intense period of warfare between the forces arrayed on the side of the quarto
Encyclopédie and those on the side of the octavo. The STN was working fe-
verishly to print as many volumes of the quarto as possible, for it made a
large profit from each volume that was assigned to it by Joseph Duplain. In
September 1778 Pfaehler complained to Ostervald that the STN—which had
twelve presses churning out sheets of the quarto—had not reserved two of its
presses for the work of the Confederation, as the Traité de Berne required.
The STL and the STB had scrupulously respected this commitment, he wrote.
In fact by October 1779, a year later, the STL had set up two presses dedicated to the Confederation in the printing shop of the STB. As they strengthened their ties, they suspected that the STN's connections with Panckoucke
had weakened its allegiance to the Confederation, for Panckoucke was

maneuvering to produce a gigantic new edition of Voltaire's works, and the STN seemed to have some interest in that venture. Yet all three houses continued their collaboration throughout the winter of 1778, and in March 1779 they tentatively agreed to "reinforce our ties," as the STB put it, by making a deal to market one another's *Encyclopédies* behind Panckoucke's back. In the end, the STN pulled out of this agreement, precisely because it feared alienating Panckoucke; but the negotiations demonstrated its determination to remain committed to the Confederation.

At the same time, the group had to overcome all sorts of practical problems. The STB had difficulties in setting up its printing shop. It lacked room for assembling sheets; it bungled one of its first printing jobs, the one on the American constitutions; and when the STN criticized its work, it explained that its compositors were mostly Germans who had to follow the copy line by line without being able to read it. Exact reprinting of this sort was unfeasible if, as often happened, the size of the sheets in the pirated edition did not conform to the sheets of the original.[19] All three houses had to exchange sample printed sheets in order to ensure that the separate printings of parts of the same book would be indistinguishable. They also faced the same difficulties in recruiting workers and needed to avoid raiding one another's shops. They had no qualms about sending workers packing when the supply of copy ran out, yet they needed to maintain an adequate work force to avoid delays in production. Therefore, they tried hard to calibrate decisions about what books to pirate, and they favored large-scale jobs, which would keep all the workers occupied. On September 28, 1778, Pfaehler wrote, "Winter is approaching, and we think it is necessary to choose a fairly large enterprise, which will provide work for our workers." In November he suddenly decided to print a collection of the conquistador Fernand Cortès's letters without consulting Heubach and Ostervald, because otherwise he would have had to dismiss several workers. They agreed in retrospect to accept the work as a joint edition. It was impossible to keep the workers employed if the paper supply gave out, and maintaining the right quality of paper required a great deal of advance planning along with large investments of capital. In May, Pfaehler wrote that the STB might have to dismiss four journeymen because of lack of paper.

But the most important factor was reaching common decisions in order to keep up a constant rate of production. Therefore, the proposals kept flowing through the mail. Bérenger led off the next round of negotiations by proposing a reprint of David Hume's *The History of England* in French. It was the best work on the subject and also the best selling, he asserted. True, other historians had added a good deal to the historical record since Hume, but their work could be mined for notes that would bring Hume up to date and that would make the new edition attractive. The other two publishers did not warm to that suggestion, however, so it was dropped. Pfaehler favored two frothy novels, one by Jean-François de Bourgoing and the other by Pierre-François-Cantien Baugin. Upon reflection, he decided that the second was not worth considering, but the first passed muster and was printed in 1779. Pfaehler also recommended the *Opuscules dramatiques* by the minor playwright Claude-Louis-Michel de Sacy, but Bérenger and Ostervald vetoed that idea. Ostervald favored something more solid and scientific, such as the five-volume *Précis d'histoire naturelle* by the abbé Saury. Although he had not read it, Pfaehler considered the author's reputation impressive enough to agree. But this suggestion did not make it past Bérenger, who came up with a counterproposal in the same genre: Jean-Christophe Valmont de Bomare's much-esteemed *Dictionnaire raisonné universel d'histoire naturelle* in twelve volumes. The correspondents of the STL had often requested it, he noted, and the Confederation decided to publish it, strengthening its offerings in science.

In the field of literature, the publishers spent a great deal of time in discussing various possibilities of producing the works of Voltaire and Rousseau; but in the end, they published only one of Voltaire's tragedies, *Irène* (premiered in March 1778), mainly as a part of strong-arm tactics. When the play was first published by Isaac Bardin in Geneva, the STL demanded that he furnish 200 copies as a swap. Otherwise, it threatened to pirate his edition. He refused, and the Confederation followed through with a *contrefaçon* of 1,000 copies. None of the other literary figures published by the Confederation occupies much of a place in the history of French literature, except two: Alain-René Lesage and Nicolas Edme Restif de la Bretonne. All three publishers agreed readily to do a new edition of Lesage's popular, picaresque novel, *Histoire de Gil Blas de Santillane* (1715), which Ostervald proposed and Pfaehler seconded. Pfaehler suggested Restif's *Le Nouvel Abeilard, ou lettres de deux amants qui ne se sont jamais vus.* He had received a copy of the novel immediately after its publication from a correspondent who assured him it would be "a good enterprise." Before reading it, he sent it to Ostervald, who responded with doubts about the likelihood that it would be "a good seller," but the Confederation published it, nonetheless. Pfaehler seemed to have excellent sources, because he also got a copy of Restif's *La Vie de mon père* as soon as it was published. He forwarded it to Ostervald, who determined the decision in favor of a joint edition.

On the whole, the Confederation favored nonfiction. Ostervald proposed *Relation d'un voyage fait de l'intérieur de l'Amérique méridionale* by the great explorer of the Amazon, Charles-Marie de La Condamine. Pfaehler liked the idea, because he had ordered it as a swap from its publisher in Maastricht, and it had sold well. In deference to Ostervald's opinion, Bérenger was willing to publish it, but after further consideration Ostervald decided the Maastricht edition probably had exhausted the demand. Bérenger then suggested another history book, *Histoire de la destruction des Templiers*, but he gave it only a qualified endorsement, finding it solid but "not the sort of history to make much of a splash." That argument was not strong enough to convince the other publishers, and Ostervald then came up with what he thought was a better idea: a forty-volume series of history books translated from English and published in Paris under the title *Histoire universelle*. It could keep all three printing shops busy, churning out a volume a month, and it would be very lucrative, he wrote. Bérenger agreed that it could sell well with the general public, if they made it less dry and reduced it by half. When he looked further into that possibility, however, Ostervald rejected it, probably because the abridging and rewriting would have required too much labor.[20] In the end, the partners fell back on a proposal from Ostervald to reprint more of the historical works by the prolific and popular abbé Millot, this time his three-volume *Éléments de l'histoire d'Angleterre*.

This phase of the constant dialogue about editorial decisions came to a climax in June 1779, a full year after the Confederation was formed, when the partners had scheduled the first of their annual meetings to settle their accounts. Each house prepared to claim payment for the number of sheets it had produced, and the numbers varied, because none of them had adhered strictly to the rule that bound each to produce one-third of every edition. The STN had devoted its twelve presses almost exclusively to printing its share of the quarto *Encyclopédie* and therefore had fallen behind in its printing account. But it was reaching the end of its last volume in June, while the STL and STB were increasing their output of the octavo edition. By June 12 the STN had fired half of its workers, and it needed a new printing job to occupy the other half. Therefore, it started work on all three volumes of Millot's history, and Ostervald announced a unilateral decision to pirate an economic treatise, leaving it up to the STL and STB to accept or reject

it as a collaborative publication. Ostervald also decided unilaterally to produce Antoine-Augustin Parmentier's pamphlet advocating a diet based on
potatoes.

Pfaehler objected to these seemingly arbitrary decisions and asked that
they postpone the meeting while they sorted things out. Ostervald justified the STN's behavior by noting that the STB had also monopolized some
printing, but then he backed down by agreeing that the STB and STL should
each do one volume of the Millot. He also proposed a joint edition of Anton-
Friedrich Büsching's *Introduction à la connaissance géographique et politique
des États de l'Europe* (1779), which appealed to both houses. Pfaehler, now
pacified, agreed to schedule the meeting in Lausanne on July 20. He also
had a suggestion of his own, a "spicy" political libel, *L'Observateur anglais,
ou correspondance secrète entre Milord All'Eye et Milord All'Ear*. He was sure
they could sell 1,000 copies. Meanwhile, Bérenger was proposing other
projects: an anthology of sea voyages, another of famous speeches in court
trials, and a third of various English novels. It was important, he emphasized,
to prepare several projects in advance so that they could debate them and
reach decisions at the meeting.

As no minutes were taken at the meeting on July 20, 1779, it is impossible
to know exactly what happened, other than a settling of the accounts for the
printing that had occurred during the previous year and a distribution of the
income that resulted from the sales. Bérenger had not been able to attend
the meeting, but soon afterward in a letter to Ostervald he said that he was
pleased to learn that it had gone well—"that the links among the businesses
seem to have grown closer and that nothing caused a chill that could lead
to dangerous discontent." The friendship between Bérenger and Ostervald
helped hold the Confederation together, despite the tensions created by the
trade war between the rival *Encyclopédies*.[21]

Yet conflicts of interest and a growing distrust of the STN in Lausanne and
Bern weakened the Confederation during the next months. On September
9, 1779, the STB distributed a printed circular announcing that it had been
reorganized as "La Nouvelle Société typographique." Pfaehler, who had run
the business for several years, had now become a full-fledged partner and
would continue to direct its affairs with the backing of three other partners.[22]
The old STB would continue until it had liquidated the stock in its bookshop,
and the new firm would give up retail bookselling in order to concentrate
on printing and the wholesale trade. The change represented an infusion of
new capital and a greater orientation toward the outside world of publishing.

However, it assured its partners, nothing would modify the STB's commitment to the Confederation. It also coincided with a tendency for the STB and the STL to develop increasingly close ties. One of the STB's partners, Samuel Kirchberger, a member of the Bernese elite, was also an investor in the STL. Heubach cultivated backers in Bern, and as mentioned he transferred two of his presses to the printing shop of the STB so that they could cooperate more effectively in printing for the Confederation.[23] Above all, they remained firmly allied in producing the octavo *Encyclopédie*, which was the main reason for the tension between the STN and the other two publishers during the last months of 1779.

By July, Pfaehler and Heubach fully understood and accepted the STN's commitment to the rival *Encyclopédie*, but they still hoped to reach an agreement with the quarto group, because it had nearly completed its operations. Having sold out all three of its editions, they calculated, it ought to be ready to open the French market to the octavo for a reasonable price. Heubach discussed this possibility with Ostervald at a meeting in Lausanne in October, offering to include the STN as a partner in an expanded edition of the octavo if it could persuade its partners in the quarto to make a deal. The octavo group already had 1,200 subscribers and could more than double that number by tapping the French market, he explained. By then it had reached volume 20 in its edition, printing at a run of 3,000 copies. If the STN joined it, they could double the number in printing volumes 21 through 36, and they would reprint the first twenty volumes in company with the STN, which would assume a one-third share in the entire enterprise. Bérenger followed up this suggestion with a personal appeal to Ostervald. The success of the octavo was astounding, he wrote. If given access to the French market, Heubach was sure he could sell 500 subscriptions in Paris and 750 in the provinces. And if the STN joined forces with the STL and the STB, the octavo *Encyclopédie* would become the most significant and profitable enterprise undertaken by the Confederation.[24]

This proposal put Ostervald in an awkward position, because he was being asked to mediate in the quarto-octavo war while playing on both sides. How could he shift his allegiance to the octavo while using his position as a partner in the quarto to intervene with Panckoucke? Ostervald sent an understandably equivocal response, not to Bérenger but to Pfaehler. The request brought up unhappy memories of his earlier attempt to make peace, he wrote, but he would try again if Pfaehler could provide him with precise information about the outlook for the octavo—enough, that is, for the quarto partners to decide whether negotiations would be worth their while. Pfaehler sent back an impressive account of the octavo's success: it stood to make a profit of 150,000 L. on revenue of 450,000 L. from their first edition, which was nearly sold out, and they could more than double their profit by producing a second edition at the same run of 3,000 copies. Because they would not have to reprint the last fifteen volumes, they could save 20,000 L. in production costs and offer that amount to the quarto group in exchange for receiving access to the French market.

Those were enormous sums for an industry still constrained by artisanal modes of production. Yet Ostervald refused to commit the STN and replied rather weakly that he could not make a decision before consulting the quarto partners. To Heubach, that sounded like prevarication. He needed an immediate decision, because with the passing of every day he lost money that could be saved by doubling the print run of the last volumes. Impossible, Ostervald replied on November 17. The quarto partners were to meet in a month, and he dared not commit the STN before he could win their approval. If Heubach insisted on an immediate answer, it would have to be no.

The tone of these exchanges became tenser with every letter. Thousands of livres hung in the balance, and the time pressure made it difficult for the correspondents to maintain their equanimity. Bérenger sent another personal appeal to Ostervald, reinforcing Heubach's demand for a firm and immediate commitment. When Ostervald continued to refuse, Bérenger suspected, as he later confessed, that the STN had wanted to extract information about the prospects for the octavo in order to launch an octavo of its own, keeping the French market to itself instead of selling access to it. In a letter of November 23, Bérenger poured out his feeling of betrayal. The STL and STB had treated the STN as an "ally," yet it had abused their confidence. Bérenger stood to lose a great deal personally from Ostervald's bad faith. He had been given a $\frac{1}{32}$ share in the octavo speculation, and with the doubling of the printing, he calculated that he could have earned 8,000 to 9,000 L. "I imagined in the distant future a moment when I would purchase a solitary dwelling with an orchard and a small field where I would spend time deliciously with my family. Then you blow away this dream of happiness." Ostervald, taken back, replied that he was incapable of divulging the confidential information that he had received, but he could not intervene at that moment, because in a few weeks the quarto partners would meet to wind up their affairs. Only then, after receiving a final report on their sales, would they be prepared to negotiate a peace with the octavo group. Bérenger backtracked in reply. He must have been misinformed, he wrote, and now he could appreciate Ostervald's "unhappy situation." It was worse than "unhappy," Ostervald answered. As Bérenger would appreciate once he knew all the facts, "[w]e found ourselves exactly between a hard place and a rock."

The facts finally emerged when the quarto publishers settled their accounts and dissolved their partnership at a meeting in Lyon in February 1780. Having sold out three editions of their *Encyclopédie*, they were now willing to use Panckoucke's influence with the French authorities to open France to the octavo—for a price of 24,000 L. The STL and the STB agreed and eventually marketed their second edition successfully, although without the collaboration of the STN, which had taken too much of a bruising to risk another *Encyclopédie* speculation and was beginning to sell off most of its twelve presses.

The disagreements and suspicions about the rival *Encyclopédies* had cast a pall over the operations of the Confederation in late 1779 and 1780, but the running dialogue about prospects for pirating continued, nonetheless. Of the many proposals, two stood out: *Théâtre à l'usage des jeunes personnes*, a four-volume collection of plays adapted for the education of children, by Stéphanie Félicité comtesse de Genlis; and *Dictionnaire raisonné universel d'histoire naturelle*, a twelve-volume reference work about the natural sciences, by Jacques-Christophe Valmont de Bomare. Both had the advantage of being large enough to occupy several presses, and both led to more discontent.

The plays of Mme de Genlis exerted appeal at a time when the reading public, predisposed by the success of Rousseau's *Émile*, had taken a new interest in childhood and the moral education of children. In August 1779, Pfaehler proposed publishing the Genlis collection as "a good item for a press run of 1,000." Ostervald readily agreed, and Bérenger did not object, although he preferred higher forms of drama, such as the works of Shakespeare, which he recommended, unsuccessfully, as "a good, a beautiful typographical speculation." The STB began printing the first volume at a run of 1,000, but the STN then convinced the partners that they had overestimated the potential sales, and they continued the joint printing of the next volumes at 750. The STB fell behind in its allotment of the work, because it ran into difficulties organizing its new printing shop (among other problems it discovered that it did not have enough uppercase type in the font they had agreed to use.) Its slowness earned it a scolding from the STN: "One mustn't let the customers' zeal cool off." Then by mistake, it ran off volume 3 at 1,000, which provoked the STN to remark testily that the Confederation should be compensated for the loss of 250 copies. However, advanced orders picked up in the spring of 1780. Heubach suggested they expand the edition to 1,500 by reprinting some volumes at 500 and others at 750. In the end, therefore, the Genlis proved to be a success, but it left a sense of discord.

Bomare's *Dictionnaire* ran into similar difficulties, although it looked even more promising, because as Pfaehler remarked, "The study of nature is now in fashion." The three partners agreed to publish it at their meeting in Lausanne on July 20, 1779. But they were unable to get a quick start in the printing, because they had to cope with a problem in the supply of paper, 500 reams, which Heubach arranged to have made for all three houses in a paper mill run by Widow J. J. Caproni in Divonne, a French village in the Jura foothills near Geneva. As mentioned, paper was the most expensive item in the production costs of books, and printers often ordered specially made batches of it shortly before they undertook a job, because they did not want to tie up capital by keeping a large stock on hand. Ordering involved negotiations over quality, price, and date of delivery, factors that were especially crucial in the case of joint editions. Heubach preferred Mme Caproni to a miller recommended by the STN. Her inability to deliver the paper on time added to the resentments that were brewing among the partners, and it illustrates the practical difficulties that bedeviled pirating.

Because Bomare's twelve-volume book required such an enormous output of paper, Mme Caproni had molds woven to Heubach's specifications. This was an involved process. A paper mold, which required great skill to construct, was a wire screen in a wooden frame with a deckle, or removable wooden rim. In making paper, an artisan dipped the mold into a vat filled with liquid "stuff" made from pulped rags. He let the excess liquid drain through the screen, leaving a thin film on its surface. After being covered with a felt, flipped onto a pile, pressed, and dried, the original film solidified into a sheet. Before it could be used in printing, however, it had to acquire a semi-impermeable surface by sizing, another delicate procedure, which involved dipping it into a gelatinous liquid and more pressing and drying. Unfortunately, when Heubach received a sample sheet, it turned out to be too small, and a new mold had to be made, causing a delay of several weeks. The delay extended into the winter, when the weather was too wet and cold to permit sizing. Instead of beginning work on the Bomare as planned in October 1779, the Confederation had to postpone printing until the spring of 1780.

The STN, which needed a large printing job to occupy the remainder of its work force, complained bitterly. It even considered abandoning the Bomare in January, when the Genevan publisher, Jean-Léonard Pellet, announced that he was producing an edition. If only they had published an announcement of their edition, Ostervald lamented, Pellet might have given up his. Yet Pellet's announcement could have been a bluff, intended to ward off other editions, as often happened among pirates. Ostervald recommended putting out a counter-announcement, claiming that they were far advanced in printing an edition that would be "superior to all the others by its augmentations," even though they would add little to the copy, which they planned to pirate from an edition published by Jean-Marie Bruyset in Lyon. An announcement of an "augmented" edition often served as a deterrent to competitors in the high-risk environment of pirating. The Confederation had recently given up a plan to pirate Raynal's *Histoire philosophique et politique des établissements et du commerce des Européens dans les deux Indes*, because Clément Plomteux had proclaimed that he was printing a new edition with corrections by the author.

Sure enough, the partners learned in February that Pellet was not going to publish Bomare's *Dictionnaire* after all. Therefore, they determined to push ahead with their own edition—as soon as they could get the paper. They cursed the weather, which held up the sizing through January and February. At last, on March 15, Heubach sent Ostervald a new sample sheet and a draft of the prospectus, which Ostervald returned with stylistic corrections. The STN received its allotment of paper in mid-April, and the three houses completed the first four volumes by mid-July 1781, when they had their yearly meeting to settle accounts. At one point, they even considered consulting Bomare himself in the hope of getting his endorsement of their edition, but they dropped that idea.[25] Authors did not matter much in the pirating business, except in the case of a few celebrities like abbé Raynal.

While these projects occupied most of their attention, the three publishing houses managed to put out two other works,[26] but they failed to agree on anything else. The debates in their correspondence led to an increasing number of divisive decisions. Ostervald wanted to do another edition of the works of Mme Riccoboni. Pfaehler vetoed that proposal on the grounds of inadequate demand.[27] When Pfaehler also judged that Ostervald had overestimated the sales potential of a travel book,[28] the STN went ahead and published it by itself. They had different assessments of the outlook for a new edition of Raynal's *Histoire philosophique* and another work; so they abandoned both possibilities. Bérenger killed a proposal to do a translation of the works of

Johann Kaspar Lavater, the Swiss physiognomist who was beginning to fascinate the French with his theory that character could be read from facial features. Pfaehler pushed hard to get the STN to cooperate on an edition of *Le Parfait Négociant*, a standard reference work on business practices by Jacques Savary, but Ostervald refused.

Heubach, meanwhile, liked a seven-volume history of Ireland, yet acknowledged that it was "too voluminous for a small country." Bérenger floated the idea of publishing Richardson's *Pamela*, *Clarissa*, and *The History of Charles Grandison* accompanied by Diderot's *Éloge de Richardson*, but he ran up against Pfaehler's judgment that the demand for the novels, despite their excellence, was inadequate. Bérenger later revived the proposal by raising the possibility of procuring a manuscript of *Pamela* that Richardson had corrected and that his family had refused to release after his death in 1761, owing to their discontent with previous French translations. But that, too, led nowhere, and while losing its sense of direction and cohesion, the Confederation fell apart.

Much of the bad feeling had to do with rivalry over printing jobs and the consequent claims to be compensated from the common pool of income. By 1780, the provision for printing the same work simultaneously in the three shops was no longer observed. The STN complained frequently about not receiving a fair share of the printing, and at the same time its ambivalent behavior during the *Encyclopédie* conflict eroded the trust of the other two houses. Things went badly when the publishers gathered in Neuchâtel for the annual settlement of accounts on July 20, 1780. The archives do not contain a record of the meeting, but the subsequent correspondence indicates that a quarrel broke out.

The disagreement concerned disparities in the balance of swapped sheets as well as payments for printing jobs. Apparently Pfaehler and Heubach objected to a report prepared by the STN's bookkeeper, Abram David Mercier. The Confederation's finances were recorded in many separate accounts, some kept in French *livres* and some in printed sheets, and it was fiendishly difficult to arrive at bottom lines. The meeting broke up without a settlement. At one point in the debate, Pfaehler complained that Mercier's work had been too rushed, although it actually took half a day. Ostervald retorted in a letter written after the meeting, which took Pfaehler to task for having made an uncivil observation, and Pfaehler sent back a testy reply. Personal remarks of that sort rarely appeared in commercial correspondence, which conventionally adhered to the formal use of the first-person plural. Although minor in itself, the tiff was a symptom that the goodwill underlying the Confederation had been damaged.

The three publishers did not reach an agreement on the accounts until sometime after September 1780 (the archives do not indicate when).[29] Their correspondence dropped off, and they ceased proposing new editions while winding down the production of the old ones. Although they did not formally declare the Confederation dead, the life had gone out of it. Its state can be appreciated from Bérenger's personal correspondence with Ostervald. On November 25, 1780, he wrote that he regretted he could not close the rift between the STL and the STN, and on February 9, 1781, he noted that the affairs of the Confederation had effectively ended. On September 22, he looked back on the unhappy outcome and reflected on his own incapacity as a mediator in the conflicts. He was not cut out to be a businessman: "If these rivalries and annoyances are inseparable from commerce, I will never participate in it; and if I remain attached to it by some connections, I will try to get rid of them as soon as possible."

While the Confederation went through a long period of hibernation, which lasted from July 1780 until March 1783, the three Swiss houses continued to do business with one another as occasions arose. The most significant was the publication of Jacques Necker's *Compte rendu au roi*, a report on the royal budget in February 1781, a momentous event, because for the first time a French minister (formally, Necker held the title of director-general of finance) made information about the state's finances available to the public. It was, to be sure, misleading information. Necker claimed that the Crown enjoyed a surplus of 10 million L., whereas in fact it had run up an enormous debt, largely to pay for its intervention in the American War. But whatever the accuracy of its content, the *Compte rendu* exposed a highly secret and sensitive aspect of government to public debate. Polemics broke out immediately, and publishers raced to make the most of them. The STB and the STN started setting type for their own pirate editions as soon as they could get their hands on a copy. They notified one another of their intentions, but their letters crossed in the mail during the first week of March when they had already begun work. On March 10, Pfaehler sent a page of proof to Neuchâtel as evidence of the STN's determination to strike while the iron was hot. "We are working on it day and night. . . . Drop your edition, and we will let you have as many copies as you want at the manufacturing cost." In the end, they cooperated in marketing their separate editions, and then joined forces in publishing Necker's subsequent

Mémoire de M. Necker au roi sur les administrations provinciales along with four related pamphlets.

The success of this collaboration led to further STB-STN editions in 1781–1782, leaving the STL on the sidelines. These projects included a German-French dictionary, another popular account of Cook's travels, another collection of plays by Mme de Genlis, a treatise on agronomy by Charles de Butret, and an expanded, seven-volume edition of the bestselling libel that Pfaehler had recommended three years earlier, *L'Observateur anglais, ou correspondance secrète entre Milord All'Eye et Milord All'Ear.* The demand for the latter had not slackened, if we can judge from a letter by Pfaehler that urged the STN to hurry up with the volume it was printing: "Customers are clamoring for copies."

Although these joint publications required a good deal of consultation, the letters between Bern and Neuchâtel did not convey the sense of enthusiasm for a common endeavor that had animated the earlier correspondence of the Confederation, and they thinned out considerably in 1782. On June 2, Pfaehler complained about the poor relations of the STB and the STN. "What would happen to our trade, Messieurs," he wrote, "if we ourselves set up all kinds of obstacles to it? If we wrangled among ourselves, often because of misunderstandings or the missteps of our clerks?"

Although the STL did not participate in these deals, Pfaehler and Heubach remained on good terms, and it seems likely that the STB and STL produced joint editions that left no trace in the STN's archives. In fact, they laid plans for two enterprises that promised to be as gigantic as their speculation on the octavo *Encyclopédie.* The first was a pirate edition of Buffon's *Histoire naturelle,* the monumental work on all aspects of the natural world that was then being published by Panckoucke and printed at the Imprimerie royale. (It would eventually run to forty-four volumes, but the core section, in fifteen volumes, had been completed in 1767 and the nine-volume *Histoire naturelle des oiseaux* would be completed in 1783). The second was a pirated reprint of the posthumous edition of Voltaire's complete works that was then being organized by Pierre-Augustin Caron de Beaumarchais and printed in Kehl. Both projects involved enormous commitments of capital as well as endless negotiations—so much, in fact, that in March 1783 the STB and the STL decided to enlist Neuchâtel in their speculations and to revive the Confederation.

By that time, both publishing houses were undergoing reorganization. On February 21, 1783, Heubach informed the STN that the STL was to be dissolved and replaced by an enterprise under his own name, "Jean Pierre Heubach et Cie." Having bought out Samuel Kirchberger's share in the STL, he would be the sole owner of its printing shop and would work with his former partner, Jean-Pierre Duplan, in phasing out its current affairs. Heubach expected to remain a close ally of the Bernese, who had helped fund the STL from its beginning and continued to support the STB. The operation in Bern had suffered from financial difficulties, he noted, but its backers were very wealthy and would make sure the STB survived. Bérenger, who remained as a partner in Heubach's new company, confirmed this report in a letter of March 29. The investors in the STB had held a meeting to refinance it and reorient its strategy, he explained. Instead of undertaking new publications of its own, it would limit itself to joint enterprises with the STL and STN. Therefore, like Heubach, it wanted to revive the Confederation.[30]

Pfaehler reaffirmed the eagerness of both Bern and Lausanne to have Neuchâtel as a partner once again. "All three of us," he urged, "should devote ourselves with all imaginable zeal to the two large and excellent enterprises, the Buffon and the Voltaire." He and Heubach had spent months in preparing both, he explained. They were willing to give the STN a fair share in each. However, they required a firm commitment, because the new Confederation, unlike the old one, needed to be anchored in concrete, preexisting enterprises.

Yet Ostervald still hesitated. By April 1783 the STN was having difficulty collecting payments from its debtors and honoring its own bills of exchange. To hedge his bets—and probably to avoid alienating Panckoucke, who had staked a large part of his business on the Paris edition of Buffon—Ostervald asked whether the STN could participate only in the Voltaire. Certainly not, Pfaehler replied on April 10. The STN had to invest in both projects, and he needed a definite answer without further delay: either yes or no.

By this time Bérenger had drafted a circular letter announcing that the three publishers had formed a new "solid confederation under the name of *Libraires associés en Suisse*" and inviting booksellers to place orders with any of them, as all three would be integrated in the same business. But in sending the draft to the STN, he warned that it might be a dead letter before it could be printed, because of Ostervald's prevarication. In fact, Heubach had entered into pourparlers with a Genevan publisher that could take the STN's place in both projects, and its participation could lead to other joint editions—thereby dooming the Confederation. Yet the STN's commitment need not be terribly costly. As their plans had evolved, Bérenger explained, they were now thinking of limiting the Voltaire edition to his plays, and the STN could purchase merely a quarter interest in the Buffon. It was sure to get a good return on its money, for the Buffon involved very little risk. The book was greatly in demand because it satisfied "the curiosity and amusements of readers." Indeed, Bérenter argued, it would become a "classic." "More true, more extensive, and perhaps better written than the work of Pliny, it will be at least as popular and as long-lasting as his."

Ostervald still could not bring himself to invest in the Buffon; and despite their misgivings, Pfaehler and Heubach agreed in May that the STN could join the Confederation while participating only in the much reduced edition of Voltaire. A month later, Ostervald changed his mind, backed out of the Voltaire, and raised new objections about the settlement of the old Confederation accounts. He also refused to swap some of the bestselling books in the STN's stock and to give the other confederates a friendly price on the most promising of its latest publications, *Portraits des rois de France* by Louis Sébastien Mercier.

The three publishers met in Neuchâtel in early August 1783 to see if they could prevent the Confederation from collapsing, but they got nowhere. On the way back to Lausanne, Heubach remarked, according to a letter from Bérenger to Ostervald, that the STN couldn't be counted on and that they now should feel free to pirate its works, beginning with *Portraits des rois de France*. Ostervald's erratic behavior is difficult to understand (the STN's archives do not contain copies of his letters between January 1781 and August 1784), but there was a personal aspect to it. Bérenger went on to say, "He [Heubach] knows that you speak badly about him, and he presumes that you have a low opinion of him. That does not encourage him." The patrician from Neuchâtel might have looked down his nose at the bookbinder's son from Bavaria. Ostervald had more in common with the publishers in Bern—not Pfaehler but the aristocratic partners of the STB, who had subsidized it since its origins in 1758. He corresponded with several of them. Still, Ostervald's main concern was the increasing pressure on the STN's finances. The order of June 12, 1783, by the foreign minister Vergennes that required all book imports to be inspected in Paris no matter what their destination soon would destroy most of the STN's trade in provincial France,[31] and by the end of the year the STN was facing bankruptcy.

In view of all these difficulties, it seemed in the summer of 1783 that the Confederation had died a second death. In his private correspondence with Ostervald, Bérenger bemoaned the situation with unusual frankness: "One complains that you want to profit from it [the Confederation] but not to make it profitable. . . . And one also complains about vacillations in your promises and your commerce." Yet the associates in Lausanne and Bern came up with two more projects, which they hoped would give the Confederation another lease on life.

The first, as will be explained in the next chapter, involved a new plan to pirate the Kehl Voltaire. Heubach and Pfaehler negotiated an agreement with Voltaire's secretary, Jean-Louis Wagnière, who possessed a cache of manuscripts that were not included in the Kehl edition and that could add value to a cheap reprint of the Kehl volumes. The second project was a risky venture involving a new speculation on the *Encyclopédie*, or rather on *encyclopédisme*. Having wound up the affairs of the quarto edition and reached an agreement with the octavo publishers, Panckoucke devoted most of his boundless energy to his up-to-date encyclopedia that would be arranged according to subject matter rather than the order of the alphabet. He recruited a whole new generation of Encyclopédistes to provide the copy, continuing where Diderot's collaborators had left off. The prospectus for this *Encyclopédie méthodique*, published in December 1781, promised that it would be completed in 42 quarto volumes by July 1787. However, Panckoucke kept adding new material and expanding the scale of the enterprise until it spun out of control. It would not be completed until 1832, long after his death, when its text had ballooned into 166½ volumes.[32]

The Swiss publishers had no idea of the future that awaited the *Méthodique* when its first volumes appeared in November 1782. To them, it looked like a perfect target for pirating. Heubach and Pfaehler came up with a plan to extract all the new material from the *Méthodique* and publish it as a *Supplément* to the editions of the original *Encyclopédie* that already existed in all three formats, folio, quarto, and octavo—at least 40,000 sets, according to their calculations. By subscribing to the *Supplément*, which would be printed in the same formats, the owners could bring their copies up to date while avoiding the expense of a gigantic new work. Pfaehler and Heubach even thought Panckoucke might be willing to cooperate—for a price—once he had collected all the subscriptions he needed.

The STN had owned a share in Panckoucke's rights to the *Encyclopédie* since July 1776 and continued to be a minor partner of his when he put together his speculation on the *Encyclopédie méthodique*. However, it sold its share in the *Méthodique* to Plomteux in June 1781. Having divested itself of its last stake in Panckoucke's ventures, it was ready to pirate them, despite its earlier reluctance to participate in the *contrefaçon* of Buffon. It resented the way Panckoucke had ridden roughshod over its interests during and after the *Encyclopédie* wars. Pfaehler and Heubach left the negotiations over the two pirating ventures to Bérenger. He wrote to Ostervald on September 5, 1783, emphasizing the potential profits and attaching the condition that the STN must commit itself irrevocably. Without a triple investment in large enterprises like the Voltaire and the *Encyclopédie supplément*, he insisted, the Confederation could never be revived.

A gap in the archives makes it impossible to follow Ostervald's response to this overture,[33] but it must have been positive, because the three publishers met to concert plans in early October, and the letters from Lausanne and Bern showed that they had completed preparations for both enterprises by the end of the year. On December 4, Pfaehler acknowledged the STN's signature of a preliminary contract for the Voltaire edition. At Bérenger's suggestion, Ostervald contacted Amable Le Roy, a bookseller in Lyon who had helped with the liquidation of the speculation on the quarto *Encyclopédie*, to arrange for the distribution of the *Encyclopédie supplément* within France. Le Roy replied that he dared not cooperate, for fear of antagonizing Panckoucke. Yet Heubach and Pfaehler still planned to open negotiations with Panckoucke in the hope that he could be enticed to join their speculation on the *Supplément*. Meanwhile, they concentrated on the edition of Voltaire. Heubach sent the proof for the prospectus to the STN on December 11, and at the beginning of January Pfaehler published a notice in the *Gazette de Berne* to announce that the three *sociétés typographiques* were to produce their own edition of Voltaire's works.

Once again, things began to go wrong. When Ostervald read Pfaehler's notice, he panicked, because it announced openly that the STN was a co-publisher of the Voltaire, and he feared that the authorities in Neuchâtel would take harsh action against his firm for printing the work of the notorious infidel. If they did, he warned Pfaehler, he might sue the STB for damages. Pfaehler reassured him by explaining that the censors in Bern had cleared the project after he had promised that it would contain nothing that they had found objectionable in earlier editions. Soon afterward, on January 14, 1784, Ostervald published a notice of his own in the *Gazette de Berne*. It announced that the STN would collect subscriptions to an inexpensive reprint of the entire *Encyclopédie méthodique* that was then being published at Liège.[34] Pfaehler and Heubach, who had not been informed of this new pirating venture, assumed that Ostervald had made a deal with the

Liégeois publisher behind their backs, and they wrote an indignant letter to Ostervald. His notice threatened to torpedo their ongoing negotiations with Panckoucke, who would see it as a sure sign of perfidy: "Can you at the same time be his associate and pirate him?"[35]

In fact, neither the Liégeois pirated edition nor the Confederation's *Supplément* turned out to be feasible, owing to the delays and complications that bogged down Panckoucke's operations in Paris.[36] Ostervald's latest attempt at piracy was an indication of the desperate state of the STN's finances. It had accumulated such heavy debts that it could no longer honor its bills of exchange when they became due. In December 1783 it suspended its payments and began a last-ditch effort to collect enough funds from investors in Neuchâtel to escape total bankruptcy. The refinancing required a change in its leadership. Ostervald ceased to be the STN's main partner and remained connected with it only in a peripheral capacity, which was not defined in the printed circular that announced the company's reorganization in June 1784. The STN continued to operate as normal throughout this period of transition, but it could not undertake major new ventures. On the contrary, it had to concentrate on selling off its inventory and collecting bills.

References to speculation on the Voltaire edition and the *Encyclopédie méthodique* disappeared from the correspondence of the STB and STL after January 1784. In place of plans for pirating, the partners filled their letters with angry arguments over the disputed balance of their accounts.[37] Finally, in September 1785, the three publishers made peace at a meeting to settle their financial affairs. By doing so, they wrote off the Confederation as a failure. In the beginning it had seemed full of promise, but in the end it demonstrated that honor among pirates was a dicey basis for joint ventures.

8

The Struggle to Pirate Rousseau and Voltaire

THE TWO MOST FAMOUS writers in France died within two months of each other—Voltaire on May 11, Rousseau on July 2, 1778. Their deaths marked the supreme moment in publishing during the Enlightenment. In 1778 and the following years, publishers scrambled to gather every scrap of their writings and to put out definitive editions of their works. The *Collection complète des oeuvres de J. J. Rousseau*, published by the Société typographique de Genève in 1780–1782, contained fifteen volumes in its quarto edition and thirty volumes in its octavo and duodecimo editions. The *Oeuvres complètes de Voltaire*, published in Kehl under the direction of Beaumarchais from 1784 to 1790, contained seventy volumes in its octavo edition and ninety-two volumes in its duodecimo edition. These enormous, posthumous publications included a great deal of new material, and they were accompanied by other equally large works, all of them tolerated more or less openly by the French government.

By 1778, the competition to satisfy the seemingly unlimited demand for Diderot's *Encyclopédie* had turned into the war between the quarto and octavo publishers, who produced a total of five editions, each made up of 36 volumes of text and 3 of plates. At the same time, a new generation of scientists and scholars had begun work on an even grander encyclopedia, the *Encyclopédie méthodique*, which, as we've seen, was intended to have 42 quarto volumes according to its original prospectus (1781) and in fact would eventually run to 166½ volumes. In 1778 Buffon published *Époques de la nature*, the most famous section of the most ambitious scientific work of the Enlightenment, his *Histoire naturelle*, which would reach its 36th volume at the time of his death in 1788. The Enlightenment had become a big business by 1778, involving millions of livres and reaching hundreds of thousands of readers—the beginning of what would become a mass public in the nine-teenth century.

The businessman at the heart of it all was Charles-Joseph Panckoucke.[1] He represented something new in the history of publishing: enormous enterprises put together as speculations on an international scale. Formally, Panckoucke was a member of the Guild in Paris, which he joined in 1762 after emigrating from Lille, where he had succeeded his father as a book-seller. But he got on badly with the leaders of the Guild and sided with the government during the conflict over the reforms of 1777.[2] By purchasing journals and combining them in ways that appealed to a large public, Panckoucke became France's first press baron. He used the revenue stream from the journal subscriptions to finance gigantic editions of Enlightenment works, taking care to avoid being compromised by anything highly illegal. Within the publishing industry he was known as a favorite of Le Camus de Néville, the *directeur de la librairie*, and Armand Thomas Hue de Miromesnil, Néville's superior as *garde des Sceaux* in the ministry of justice. Like other administrators during the last decades of the Ancien Régime, they favored the ideas of the moderate Enlightenment. Above all, they wanted to promote French trade, and as former administrators in Rouen, they sympathized with the plight of the provincial booksellers.

Panckoucke, a Lillois who operated independently of the Guild, served them as an ideal ally within the book industry. Yet he also had a great deal in common with the publishers outside France's borders. In putting to-gether consortiums, he juggled projects and bought and sold shares with entrepreneurs in Geneva, Neuchâtel, Liège, and other foreign centers. Beaumarchais, who matched wits with him in speculating on the works of Voltaire, disliked him intensely and disparaged him in a way peculiar to the French: "I can't say anything favorable about M. Panckoucke," he wrote to a friend. "His treatment of me has been hard, verging on dishonest. M. Panckoucke is *Belgian, Belgian* to the tenth degree."[3]

It would be a mistake, however, to understand Panckoucke's enterprises as nothing more than financial ventures. He knew Voltaire and Rousseau personally. He got on well with them, despite their well-known hatred for each other. He admired their work and wrote admiringly about it in works of his own, for he, too, was a writer of sorts and something of a *philosophe*. The difference between him and his predecessor, André-François Le Breton, the principal publisher of Diderot's *Encyclopédie*, was less a matter of temperament—both were entrepreneurs and based their businesses on journals—than a change in the environment that surrounded publishing. Le Breton barely survived the repressive measures of the French authorities in the 1750s, whereas Panckoucke enjoyed the protection of the government during the 1770s and 1780s. In the eyes of his contemporaries, Panckoucke belonged to the top rank of the power elite. The Lyonnais bookseller Amable Le Roy described him as "the favorite of all the ministers," and the eminent writer Dominique-Joseph Garat noted, "His carriage brought him to the ministers in Versailles, where he was received as if he had carried the portfolio of a councilor."[4]

Panckoucke's main concern during the year of the *philosophes'* deaths was the *Encyclopédie*, both the quarto edition, which was then being produced on a gigantic scale, and the *Encyclopédie méthodique*, which was being prepared by his team in Paris. Tempted as he was to add the works of Rousseau and Voltaire to his other enterprises, he could not finance them. In the case of Rousseau, he encouraged the STN to go after the prize, offering to back it as a hidden partner. The STN would have to court Pierre Alexandre Du Peyrou, the executor of Rousseau's will, as well as Rousseau's widow, Thérèse Levasseur, who might possess some valuable material. "You could offer up to thirty thousand livres . . . I will arrange for you to make this into a great affair. . . . Don't lose any time."[5]

In the race to capture the Rousseau, the STN had an inside track, because Du Peyrou, who possessed most of the manuscripts, knew Ostervald and lived nearby in Neuchâtel.[6] Having made a fortune from plantations in Surinam, he had retired to a palatial residence, and his main concern was to honor Rousseau's memory, provide for his widow, and oversee the best possible edition of his works. Instead of deferring to Du Peyrou's generous vision of publishing the material, however, Ostervald bargained hard. He failed to make an adequate opening bid, alienated Du Peyrou, and showed little respect for Rousseau's widow, who depended on the sale of the manuscripts for support in her old age.

Meanwhile, other publishers were already preparing editions of the works—among them Jean-Louis Boubers, who had acquired Rousseau's letters to his first love, Françoise-Louise de Warens, the "*maman*" who would be idolized in the *Confessions*; and they were being followed by a pack of pirates. In the face of these threats, Du Peyrou joined forces with two other former friends of Rousseau who also possessed deposits of his papers, René-Louis, marquis de Girardin, and Paul-Claude Moultou. The three decided to favor a publishing house that was created especially to produce the complete works in a manner that would respect their integrity instead of treating them as a commercial speculation. Unfortunately, this Société typographique de Genève (STG) was run by amateurs (only one of them, Jean-François Bassompierre, had some professional experience), and they eventually went under. By August 1782 they had finally published the *Collection complète*: a total of 10,241 sets in quarto, octavo, and duodecimo formats. But they could not exact payment for most of the copies. They were rescued from bankruptcy by a refunding operation, which strung out the liquidation of the enterprise until 1797, when the accounts were closed with a loss of at least 23,000 L.

All the profit produced by Rousseau's works fell into the hands of the pirates. Panckoucke had chided the STN for bidding so low (Ostervald had offered only 10,000 L.) in the attempt to purchase the rights to the original edition: "I would have given up to 40,000 livres. . . . This wasn't a time for haggling."[7] The STN and its allies in the Confédération typographique calculated that they could do better by reprinting whatever new material might appear, especially the *Confessions*, which was sure to be a bestseller. In July 1778, as soon as he heard of Rousseau's death, Bérenger suggested that the Confederation take steps to prepare an edition of his works and do everything possible to unearth the manuscript of the *Confessions*. Ostervald replied coolly to this proposal, because at that time he was still hoping to strike a deal with Du Peyrou. Once that hope had evaporated, the STN joined the STL and STB, which had gone ahead in planning a pirated edition of their own. They followed a common strategy of pirate publishers: leave the expensive quarto and octavo editions to the original publishers and produce a cut-rate version in duodecimo format, which would appeal to a broad public. But what text should they reprint?

The confederated *sociétés typographiques* debated this problem at a meeting in Lausanne on July 20, 1779, and in their correspondence throughout the summer. They could begin work right away, using Boubers's edition, which was already far advanced, or they could wait to see whether the texts to be printed by the new STG were preferable. A circular letter by the STG on May 1, 1779, notified booksellers that the Genevans had acquired all of Rousseau's manuscripts and would sell them by subscription in all three formats, including a duodecimo edition, which would be inexpensive enough "to prevent the brigandage of *contrefaçons*."[8] A month later, Ostervald drafted a rival prospectus for "a portable duodecimo edition," which would be cheaper than the STG edition and would follow it, volume for volume, at intervals of three months after each of the STG's shipments. As to piracy, Ostervald defended it as a way to promote competition and to prevent the monopolization of literature.[9]

In July the Confederation partners received samples of illustrations that they had commissioned for their edition; the STL had acquired a new font of type; the STN recommended circulating the prospectus to undercut the marketing of the STG; and they all were poised to publish their duodecimo edition as soon as the Genevans produced their first volumes. Ostervald assessed the situation in a letter that illustrates the way pirates worked out strategy. He argued that they should publish a prospectus quickly "in order to offset the effect of the one done by the Genevans." By underselling the Genevan duodecimo and rapidly circulating the prospectus under their common name, they could harvest plenty of subscriptions, "since it seems likely that the same booksellers who would have subscribed for the quarto and octavo editions will be happy to get the [cheaper] duodecimo in order to satisfy all tastes."[10]

At this point, when an open conflict seemed about to break out, there was a last-minute attempt to maintain peace. Bérenger favored some kind of agreement, because he was a friend of two of the directors of the STG, François d'Ivernois and Pierre Boin, who were fellow Genevans and Rousseauists committed to the Représentant cause.[11] In August 1779, Bérenger informed Ostervald that d'Ivernois soon would visit Du Peyrou in Neuchâtel. Although he professed to be "inept at typographical war," he suggested that Ostervald manage to cross paths, as if by accident, with d'Ivernois; try to discover, without seeming too curious, the intentions of the STG; and take soundings about the possibility of an "arrangement." This attempt at stage-managing did not work. Ostervald later wrote in a somewhat superior tone that it should have been up to d'Ivernois to call on him and that they had not met.

Meanwhile, Bosset, on his business trip through Germany and the Low Countries, was sending reports on rival pirating enterprises. In The Hague he was told that the Dutch booksellers were quite likely to restrict their orders to Rousseau's publisher in Amsterdam, Marc-Michel Rey. In Amsterdam, he learned that the competition over Rousseau's works came down to a struggle among three publishers (aside from the Confederation, which had not yet entered the field): the STG, supported by Gabriel Cramer as a silent partner; Boubers, protected secretly by Panckoucke, who was his brother-in-law; and Rey, who refused to deal with the Genevans, preferring to reprint their new material as a supplement to his 1772 edition of Rousseau's works.[12] In Brussels, Boubers defended the superiority of his quarto edition, which would contain a great many new documents in a forthcoming volume 8. He also said that he had threatened to undercut the Genevans by producing a duodecimo edition of his own but had renounced it after they bought him off by offering 300 copies of their duodecimo at a greatly reduced price.

In Maastricht, Dufour revealed that he, too, planned to produce a cheap duodecimo, although the STG had tried to dissuade him by warning that it could come up with a duodecimo that would undercut his. To this revelation, Bosset replied that the STN would undersell the Genevans. "I assured him emphatically that if they offered their [edition] at 30 sous per volume, we would offer ours at 25 sous, and if they offered theirs at 25, we would offer ours at 20." As to Bérenger's proposal to come to an arrangement with the Genevans, Bosset pronounced it impossible: "I don't know what propositions for an arrangement the Genevans could offer to Bérenger," he wrote, "unless it is a cash payment for abandoning the enterprise."[13]

Bérenger continued nonetheless to negotiate with his Genevan friends. In October, he reported a final proposal from d'Ivernois: if the Confederation would abandon its duodecimo edition, the STG would supply it with the STG's duodecimo at a 25 percent discount and with two free copies for every dozen purchased. It also would not oppose any editions of separate works like the *Confessions* and the *Rêveries d'un promeneur solitaire*, the autobiographical reflections that Rousseau had left unfinished at his death, provided that the Confederation delayed publishing them for two weeks after the STG launched its own separate editions. But the STG was already threatened by so many *contrefaçons* that it did not fear another: "As soon as one head is cut off," Bérenger wrote in October 1779, "a thousand others are generated."[14] Neither the STN nor the STL would bite, and therefore Bérenger abandoned the negotiations in November.[15]

By the end of 1779, the confederated *sociétés typographiques* had adopted a policy of waiting for the Genevan volumes to appear while preparing to launch a subscription campaign for their pirated duodecimo edition. However, as explained in the previous chapter, a rift had opened up within the Confederation. Bern and Lausanne suspected Neuchâtel of double-dealing in its attempt to mediate in the war between the consortia publishing the quarto and octavo *Encyclopédies*. Tempted as he was to join the STB and STL in launching a second edition of their octavo *Encyclopédie*, Ostervald needed to close ranks behind Panckoucke in order to terminate the speculation on the quarto, which had reached the last stage in the publication of its third edition. Not only did enormous sums hang in the balance at the final settlement of accounts, which took place in Lyon between January 28 and February 12, 1780, but also Ostervald and Panckoucke had discovered that Joseph Duplain, the chief entrepreneur behind the quarto, was swindling them on a gigantic scale.[16] He had manipulated the accounts to hide embezzlements worth hundreds of thousands of livres; and he wanted to exact as much as possible at the settlement, because he was about to retire. After a prosperous career as a pirate, he had left his business, along with the responsibility for liquidating the quarto, to his associate, Amable Le Roy, and he meant to enjoy the rest of his life as a gentleman, for he had spent 115,000 L. to purchase the office of *maître d'hôtel du roi*, which conferred nobility on its owner.

The meeting in Lyon turned into the dénouement of a commmercial plot that had all the makings of a *drame bourgeois*. Its cast of characters included Duplain, Panckoucke, Ostervald, Bosset, Plomteux, and the STN's banker in Lyon, Jacques-François d'Arnal. Two other figures hovered behind the scenes: Amable Le Roy and François d'Ivernois from the STG. Having secretly gained access to Duplain's accounts and gathered evidence from other sources, Duplain's partners confronted him in angry scenes that went on for two weeks. "We have already had some violent scenes about our accounts with M. Duplain," Ostervald reported to his daughter, the widow of Jean Bertrand, who had become a partner in the STN and was minding the shop in Neuchâtel.[17] "As in English cockfights, Panckoucke and Duplain have exchanged some violent blows." In the end, after raiding his office with a bailiff and threatening to drag him into court, the partners forced Duplain to compensate them with 200,000 L. in exchange for a commitment on their part to abandon legal action and to bury the affair in silence. Duplain retained enough profit to go into retirement, accompanied with a new wife. The partners then agreed to open the French market to the publishers of the octavo *Encyclopédie* for 24,000 L. They also refinanced their investment in Panckoucke's *Encyclopédie méthodique*, and they prepared for a new round of speculation on the works of Rousseau and Voltaire.

In a separate subplot during the Lyon meeting, Ostervald and Bosset entered into secret negotiations with Le Roy. They had learned that he was producing a pirated, duodecimo edition of Rousseau's works; but far from attacking the STG, he was collaborating with it, and he was having his edition printed in Geneva. Under heavy pressure and desperate for funds, the Genevans had decided to make a secret deal with Le Roy and to become a hidden partner in his speculation—that is, in effect, to pirate themselves.

Having gotten wind of this speculation, Ostervald and Bosset threatened to undercut it by publishing the duodecimo edition that they had prepared with their partners in the Confederation. However, they determined to exclude the STL and the STB from the negotiations, because they wanted to exact terms like those negotiated three months earlier by Bérenger and to keep all the gain for themselves.

On February 5, they signed a contract with Le Roy, which committed him to supply the STN with 750 sets of his edition at the rock-bottom price of 12 sous per volume. In return, they agreed to renounce any speculation, "either direct or indirect," on Rousseau's writing.[18] This affair, as they explained in a letter to Mme Bertrand, involved the approval of d'Ivernois, who was in Lyon representing the STG. They had also met with him and persuaded him that they were serious about pirating the Genevan edition. He, in turn, had impressed them with the capacity of the STG, "which is made up of active and intelligent persons and, supported by some rich houses in Geneva, is capable of pushing this undertaking very far." Therefore, d'Ivernois agreed to support their secret contract with Le Roy, who would have their 750 volumes shipped directly to them from Geneva. "It's a way of getting out of this imbroglio like Arlequin," Ostervald and Bosset wrote, meaning that their maneuver resembled the dénouement of a farce performed at the Comédie italienne.

Ostervald added a postscript: "If Bern or Lausanne bring up the subject of Rousseau," he wrote, "you should skirt around it, and it would be better to say nothing at all." Cooperation within the Confederation had then reached a low point. Had the STN's partners in Bern and Lausanne discovered its secret deal, they would have denounced it as treachery. In the end, therefore, the STN withdrew from the Confederation's plans to pirate the Genevan Rousseau; it got a cheap supply of its own; and its Swiss partners, or at least the STB, went on to produce yet another pirate edition on their own.[19] As to the STG, which had struggled for years to produce the original edition of Rousseau's works, it was a commercial disaster. The profits went to the pirates.

Self-pirating belonged to the tricks of the trade in the eighteenth century. Beaumarchais called it "farming-out pirating,"[20] and he practiced it himself while producing one of the greatest editions of Voltaire. The story of this edition involved even more plots and subplots than the speculations on the works of Rousseau. As in the case of Rousseau's works, Panckoucke participated in the early bidding and then withdrew, while the pirates attacked the original edition from every possible angle.

In June 1775, Panckoucke and his sister Amélie, the wife of the prominent author Jean-Baptiste Suard, visited Voltaire in Ferney.[21] The aged *philosophe* was charmed by the young lady and well disposed toward the publisher. Two years later, Panckoucke returned to Ferney, this time with a proposition: he would supply Voltaire with an interleaved copy of the last version of his works, the *édition encadrée* ("framed edition" known for the lines that bordered the text) produced by Gabriel Cramer in Geneva. Voltaire could make all the corrections and additions he desired on the attached sheets, and Panckoucke would then publish the perfect, complete edition that Voltaire desired to bequeath to posterity. Voltaire set to work at age eighty-three, with more energy than ever. But he interrupted his labor in the spring of 1778 for an ill-fated trip to Paris, where he died, exhausted by the general adulation, on May 11. Three months later, Panckoucke made another trip to Ferney, this time to collect material assembled by Voltaire's secretary, Jean-Louis Wagnière. Panckoucke had acquired it from Voltaire's niece and heir, Marie-Louise Denis, who had remained in Paris. Not content with accumulating the literary manuscripts, he set about retrieving Voltaire's correspondence, which eventually filled seventeen volumes of the edition. He recruited a whole team, which included two eminent authors, the philosopher Condorcet and Jean-François de La Harpe, a member of the Académie française and protégé of Voltaire, as well as Suard, to prepare the copy.

Then, however, he had to confront some hard realities. The work of the century's most notorious freethinker could not be printed in France, and it could not be distributed there, despite Panckoucke's protections, without arousing opposition from powerful enemies of the Enlightenment, especially in the Church and the parlements. Above all, it would cost a fortune, perhaps a million livres, to produce. Panckoucke was committed to so many ventures that he had nearly succumbed to bankruptcy in 1777, when he had fallen behind in his payments—by 340,000 L., a colossal sum of money. Back on his feet but still wobbly a year later, he realized that he could not finance the Voltaire along with all his other projects. He had to choose, and after a great deal of hesitation, he opted for the *Encyclopédie méthodique* and the works of Buffon. Instead of burying him in debt, the Voltaire could bring in some badly needed capital—if only he could sell it. On December 26, 1778, he dangled the possibility of a sale before Joseph Duplain, who at that time still enjoyed his confidence as a partner in the speculation on the quarto edition of the *Encyclopédie*. The tone of Panckoucke's letter reveals the turn of his mind. He was ready to sell the manuscript, but given how much he had already invested (100,000 L., he claimed), he would not part with it for less than 300,000 L. "All of Europe is waiting for a new edition. You spoke to me about a press run of 4,000. You can't be serious, my friend. You will run off 12, 15, 20 thousand copies."[22]

Duplain did not bite, and two months later, Panckoucke sold the entire enterprise to Beaumarchais.[23] This transaction, for 300,000 L., led to one of the largest and most extravagant enterprises in the history of publishing—the Kehl edition of Voltaire's complete works. Working through a general manager, Jean-François Le Tellier, Beaumarchais installed a virtual factory for making books in the fortress of Kehl, across the Rhine from Strasbourg: forty presses; facilities for producing paper, ink, and type (the fonts were to be cast from material purchased at great expense from John Baskerville's famous workshop in Birmingham, England); a bindery; offices for marketing and accounting; storerooms; and a workforce of more than 150, all housed and fed by the company known as the Société littéraire et typographique, of which Beaumarchais was the sole proprietor. His total expenditures, as he later calculated, came to about 2,400,000 L.

To mount such an operation required audacity and energy as well as capital. Beaumarchais was just the man for the job, although he understood little about the complexities of publishing. Among the greatest adventurers of the eighteenth century, he stood out for the boldness of his undertakings. He defied the government's domination of the judicial system in his famous courtroom battle with Louis Valentin Goezman in 1773–1774; then he served the government as a secret agent in England in 1775; he masterminded the supply of arms to American revolutionaries in 1776–1777; and he attracted a huge reading audience with pamphlets and plays throughout the 1770s and 1780s. *Le Mariage de Figaro*, performed in 1784 while he was organizing the Kehl Voltaire, was the greatest box-office hit in the history of the Comédie française. "And Voltaire is immortal," the refrain in its concluding song, expressed the general tenor of the play. Although Beaumarchais's devotion to Voltaire was genuine, it had a staged quality. He invited the public to admire a temple to Voltaire that he built in the garden of his Parisian town house, located opposite the Bastille. In publishing the works at Kehl, he identified himself with the great man, and he solidified his own standing in the world of letters.

Beaumarchais also hoped to make money. To be sure, numerous editions of Voltaire's works had been published, some with his complicity, some pirated, going all the way back to 1732. Voltaire had tinkered with many of them, adding and subtracting bits of copy while pretending that everything took place behind his back. This double game—making disavowals, on the one hand, and favoring distribution, on the other—continued up to the *édition encadrée* of 1775, produced by Cramer, the only publisher he trusted before he made his arrangement with Panckoucke. So many supposedly complete editions had appeared that they undercut one another, for no one wanted to buy an expensive set of volumes that would soon be outmoded by another edition full of augmentations and corrections. As Horace Walpole remarked as soon as he heard of Voltaire's death, "Now one may buy his works safely, as he cannot write them over and over again."[24] Jean Mossy, the most important bookseller in Marseille, sent a typical complaint to the STN: "The new publications of M. de Voltaire don't sell, except at the moment when they first appear, because they are reworked in edition after edition. One adds two or three pieces to them, and the original version sits unsold in a corner."[25] In fact, as already mentioned, the booksellers waited impatiently for Voltaire to die so that at last they could sell a definitive edition of his works. The Kehl edition promised to satisfy this demand. It had the makings of a great bestseller: a truly stable text augmented with posthumous writings and accompanied by thousands of unpublished letters, many to celebrities like Frederick the Great and Catherine the Great.

These features also made it a perfect target for piracy. In fact, the story of the Kehl Voltaire is particularly interesting for what it reveals about the ways of the pirates. In itself, it is a sad saga of mismanagement and missed opportunities. Although Beaumarchais trumpeted the excellence of his edition in a long and windy prospectus, the first harvest of subscriptions was a disappointment. Production became mired in technical difficulties; Le Tellier turned out to be incompetent; deliveries were delayed; the quarto version had to be dropped; and when the octavo and duodecimo sets were completed, eight years after the deadline promised in the original prospectus, they were badly blotched—certainly inferior to Cramer's *édition encadrée*, which set a standard for textual integrity unmatched until today, when the scholarly edition being published by the Voltaire Foundation at Oxford will be as definitive as possible, considering the complexity of the paper trails left behind by the Enlightenment's most prolific author. In the end, Beaumarchais recovered most of the millions he had invested in the enterprise, but he proved to be better at supplying the Americans with rifles than the French with books.

To pirate publishers, the Kehl Voltaire looked irresistible: Beaumarchais would invest heavily in preparing the copy, he would produce a deluxe text, and they would reprint it, creaming off the demand for a relatively cheap edition. Soon after his prospectus appeared, Beaumarchais learned that *contrefaçons* were being prepared in Gotha, Zweibrücken, Bern, Lausanne, and Neuchâtel. To his amazement, the pirates announced their enterprises openly and planned to pay for them by floating subscriptions even before his own volumes had appeared.[26] Of course, Beaumarchais was not naive. He knew from the beginning that his edition would be pirated; and as a consummate intriguer, he meant to outwit and outmaneuver his opponents.

Ostervald injected the STN into the speculation on Voltaire's papers even before they passed into the hands of Beaumarchais. He sounded Panckoucke about the possibilities and received a hard-sell reply very much like Panckoucke's bid to Duplain written four days later. The Voltaire manuscripts were "a very rich goldmine," Panckoucke wrote.[27] Hoping to bait a bid with an offer of further manuscripts, Ostervald informed Panckoucke on March 11, 1779, that one of their friends has "about 200 letters by Voltaire, and he will give them only to us." The STN would use the 200 unpublished letters as a bargaining point for the next two years, but by the time it dangled them before Panckoucke, he had just sold his treasure to Beaumarchais.

As soon as he learned about the sale, Ostervald wrote to Beaumarchais, asking to be his printer. Beaumarchais had not yet decided to create his own printing operation in Kehl and was looking for a safe place to produce his edition near France's borders but outside the reach of its police. Distribution within France would not be a problem, owing to an agreement with a key minister in the government, the comte de Maurepas, but it was not possible to print the book inside the kingdom. Neuchâtel would be perfect, Ostervald emphasized. The STN produced books in total liberty, thanks to the protection of the principality's sovereign, Frederick II of Prussia. Its directors were men of letters, who cared about literature and ran their affairs with less of a mercenary spirit than ordinary printers. Moreover, they could contribute those 200 Voltaire letters exclusively to the enterprise.[28]

Beaumarchais did not reply to this overture. At that time, the STN was reaching the end of the last volume of the quarto *Encyclopédie* that it was printing for Duplain. With twelve presses and a large workforce on its hands, it needed another big printing job and the income that would come with it. Rumors circulated that Beaumarchais intended to farm out the printing to presses in Geneva or Zweibrücken. Ostervald then began to think that the STN should pirate the original edition instead of attempting to win the commission to print it, and he sounded Gabriel Regnault, a bookseller and pirate publisher in Lyon, about the possibility of a joint speculation.[29] Regnault, however, had designs of his own, as Ostervald would discover a few months later. Therefore, Ostervald continued to search for Voltaire manuscripts, still hoping to use them as leverage in a deal with Beaumarchais.

The opportunity came in the spring of 1780, when Ostervald and Bosset traveled to Paris after the dramatic meeting to wrap up the quarto *Encyclopédie* enterprise in Lyon. Drawing on their contacts with two prominent authors, Jean-François Marmontel and abbé André Morellet, they met with Beaumarchais and Le Tellier in late April. By that time, Beaumarchais was committed to producing a luxurious quarto edition and several octavo editions, at different prices, of Voltaire's works at Kehl; but in the face of the inevitable *contrefaçons*, he was open to the possibility of heading off the pirates by striking a deal with one of them for the publication of a relatively cheap duodecimo edition. Ostervald and Bosset wanted to get the printing job, and they offered what they thought were attractive terms in a draft of a contract. The STN would order a new font of type; it would hire a special foreman to oversee the work; it would run off and carefully correct three sets of proofs; and it would mount enough presses to complete the job within two years. Assuming a press run of 10,000 copies, it would charge 84 L. per sheet. Moreover, it would take all sorts of measures to prevent piracy, notably through "fraud on the part of the workers," and it would collaborate in the distribution of the final product on a European scale, thanks to its warehouse capacity and its business contacts "from Moscow to Lisbon."[30] The offer sounded attractive enough for Beaumarchais to make an informal commitment that the STN would have his "preference" in the production of a duodecimo edition, although that was months away.[31]

Ostervald returned to Neuchâtel at the beginning of May, leaving Bosset to continue the negotiations in Paris while looking after some business affairs of Bosset's own. In a letter of May 11, Ostervald thanked Beaumarchais for giving the STN the "preference." It was such an important enterprise, he added, that he would gladly return to Paris to sign a contract. Meanwhile, he wanted to place orders for the paper supply before the mills would cease operations for the winter. Ostervald's letters to Bosset sounded less confident and were full of advice about how to fend off competitors. In meetings with Le Tellier, who handled most of the negotiations, Bosset should warn him about the dangers of dealing with other printers. Unlike the STN, which was known for its integrity, they sometimes secretly sold proofs to pirate publishers. Bosset should also stress that the STN's price was a bargain, because it included the cost of paper. Bosset made little headway, however. In a long session with Beaumarchais and Le Tellier in early May, he learned that Regnault, with the support of Panckoucke, was secretly negotiating with them to buy a half interest in a duodecimo edition and had sent an associate to dissuade them from jobbing out the printing to the STN on the grounds that its work "would have a Swiss odor about it."[32] Bosset indignantly defended the quality of the STN's printing but left the meeting discouraged about their prospects.

Ostervald then tried to reinforce the STN's case in a letter to Le Tellier. Despite his own (secret) attempt to make a deal with Regnault, he warned against doing business with the booksellers of Lyon, who, he claimed, were notorious for their mutual hatred and double-dealing.[33] He also tried to win Le Tellier with the offer of more Voltaire manuscripts. He had collected copies of all the edicts issued during Turgot's ministry (1774–1776), he explained, and he planned to publish them as a book. The volume required a preface by someone who could praise the *philosophe*-minister without offending anyone who had been responsible for his fall. "I dared to communicate my views to M. de Voltaire and to request him to take on such a delicate task," Ostervald wrote. "He alone could accomplish it. I have the original version of this preface, and I doubt that anyone will find a copy of it in his papers."[34] In the hope of accumulating more material, Ostervald began to woo Jean-Louis Wagnière, Voltaire's secretary, who had kept many copies of letters and several original pieces by Voltaire.[35] An unpublished essay on Turgot along with 200 letters and the prospect of many more—the STN could bring a great deal to a publication that aspired to contain all of Voltaire's works.

Bosset found Beaumarchais intrigued by the prospect of acquiring new manuscripts when they had their next meeting. Beaumarchais asked to see a sample of the Voltaire letters, and he did not exclude the possibility that the STN could have some part in the printing of the duodecimo edition—"le petit basquerville," as he called it—despite Regnault's claim to the job. In his confidential report on this negotiating session, Bosset referred to the source of the Voltaire letters that Ostervald had at his disposal: Elie Bertrand, a natural scientist, man of letters, and pastor in Yverdon, who had been a good friend of Voltaire. Bertrand was also a close friend of Ostervald and an uncle of Ostervald's son-in-law, Jean-Elie Bertrand. After the death of Jean-Elie in February 1779, Elie Bertrand replaced him as editor of the STN's enlarged edition of the *Description des arts et métiers*, which it was pirating from the edition being published for the Académie des sciences in Paris. He published several books with the STN, contributed regularly to its *Journal helvétique*, and was virtually one of its partners, having invested 12,000 L. in its capital fund. In confidential correspondence with Ostervald, Bertrand said that he would make the Voltaire letters available exclusively to the STN with the condition that he could edit out passages that would embarrass some persons if they appeared in print.[36]

Bosset's negotiations with Beaumarchais and Le Tellier continued until his departure from Paris at the end of June. They were consistently cordial and included pleasantries of the kind that seasoned table talk in Paris. Thus the anecdote, reported by Bosset, about d'Alembert's request that Frederick II have a mass said for the repose of Voltaire's soul and Frederick's reply: "Although I do not have much of a belief in eternity, I consent."[37] In the end, as Bosset concluded, the discussions amounted to little more than "a great many compliments and never anything certain."[38]

Yet Beaumarchais was encouraging. He broke off relations with Regnault[39] and indicated willingness to give the job to the STN once he had filled the subscriptions for the quarto and octavo editions. Meanwhile, he was eager to see any of the Voltaire letters that could be sent from Neuchâtel. Ostervald would not entrust the letters to Beaumarchais without a firm commitment on the duodecimo edition. He therefore sent the dates of the first 11 letters so that Beaumarchais could verify that they did not correspond to the letters already in his possession. To whet his appetite, Ostervald noted that a later letter contained a first draft of Voltaire's famous poem on the Lisbon earthquake. Others showed Voltaire at his wittiest, particularly when he ridiculed figures in Geneva, above all the clergy: "You can easily imagine how many good jokes they contain." Having now examined the letters closely, Ostervald wrote that the total number in the hands of his friend came to 162. Moreover, the cache of manuscripts also contained some observations on the plays of Corneille.[40]

Beaumarchais replied that the first volumes of the Kehl edition would be devoted to Voltaire's plays, and therefore he would like to see the Corneille material as soon as possible in order to make sure it did not duplicate texts already in his position. The correspondence would be published in the last volumes, so it was not an urgent matter. Still, Beaumarchais would check the dates, expecting that the letters would contain many "satirical passages where the humor should be abundant."[41] Meanwhile, Ostervald extended his search for more manuscripts and picked up the scent of Voltaire letters in many places: some in Bern; others in the hands of an unnamed Polish nobleman;

more (requiring redactions of sensitive passages) made available by Jacob Vernes, a Genevan pastor and a regular visitor at Ferney; and a large cache kept by another of Voltaire's close friends, Henri Rieu.[42] Wagnière would not surrender his material, because he was aligned with Gabriel Cramer, who was pursuing plans of his own for a Voltaire edition.[43] Even without him, however, Ostervald gathered enough manuscript to fill more than two printed volumes.[44]

The negotiations continued for several months, Ostervald dangling the availability of unpublished documents and Beaumarchais holding out the possibility of the STN's getting the printing job. In November 1780, Ostervald tried to lure Le Tellier, who had then set up headquarters in Kehl, to Neuchâtel, where he could appreciate the excellence of the STN's printing shop. In addition to the printing and distribution of the duodecimo edition, the STN could help with its marketing, because it would gather subscriptions for Beaumarchais. Above all, Ostervald emphasized, his sales talk getting constantly more insistent, it could be trusted, and to make his point he listed some of the wicked ways among publishers. Unlike them, the STN would be a partner who wouldn't "print a single copy in addition to the number you will have set, who won't make a deal with another publisher to split the profits on a pirated edition, who will serve you faithfully as to paper, type, etc., and who won't cheat on incidental expenses." As to the cache of letters, Ostervald's friend would not send them to Beaumarchais and would not permit them to be printed by anyone except the STN, with whom he would work to eliminate all compromising passages.[45]

Le Tellier did not visit Neuchâtel. Beaumarchais did not answer Ostervald's letters for several weeks. At last, on December 12, he resumed the correspondence; but instead of responding to the requests for a commitment on the printing, he wrote as if he had merely been offered an opportunity to buy the manuscripts. He would be happy to examine them, he said. Perhaps they could agree on a neutral party in Paris who would make the letters available for inspection and authentification. Ostervald did not pursue this possibility, because the letters would have to be redacted before they could be inspected.[46] Therefore, he had to continue to wait, his frustration building, until early February 1781, when he received the first prospectus for the Kehl edition.[47] Distressingly, it made no mention of a duodecimo edition—or the "common edition," as Ostervald now called it, as if it were a joint enterprise. Moreover, the prospectus was badly printed—poor design, faulty composition, disastrous inking—even though it was supposed to serve as a sample of the editions' quality while inviting subscriptions. Ostervald sent Beaumarchais a five-page critique of the typography, written by Jacques-Barthélemy Spineux, the STN's expert foreman, who had been trained in Liège and had run a printing shop successfully for many years in Paris.[48] The conclusion was clear: the STN could do a superior job, even for the relatively inexpensive duodecimo.

After at last receiving replies, cordial but noncommittal, Ostervald informed Le Tellier that he was ready to meet him in Strasbourg, armed with some of the manuscript letters, and settle the affair. He warned that the STN had learned about a rival edition of Voltaire's works, which was being prepared by Charles Palissot de Montenoy, a minor playwright who had ingratiated himself with Voltaire, and that the STN had an option of collaborating on it. In writing to Beaumarchais, Ostervald continued to stress the argument about his friend's letters. He had read them all and could vouch for their importance: "All of them treat interesting subjects—superstition, tolerance, the ridiculousness of system builders, the vanity of most human occupations, etc." He added that his "friend" had given him a letter from Voltaire to Rousseau after he, Voltaire, had received a copy of Rousseau's *Discours sur l'origine de l'inégalité*. "It is four pages long and is admirable in everything it contains."[49]

On March 29, Ostervald sent Beaumarchais a copy of a Voltaire letter from another source. Having now read a sample of the prose on offer, Beaumarchais sent a favorable-sounding reply. Ostervald then shot back an offer to travel to Strasbourg and settle everything with Le Tellier. Jean de Turkheim, a friend of Ostervald who was a merchant in Strasbourg, supplied him with information about the operations in Kehl. They were impressive,[50] but other reports indicated that pirate editions, notably in Gotha and Geneva, as well as Palissot's enterprise, were being prepared. There was no time to lose if Beaumarchais and the STN were to head off the pirates by publishing a prospectus for their "*common* edition" (Ostervald underscored the adjective).

By May 1781, though it seemed to Ostervald that "soon the surface of the earth will be covered by the works of the great man, just as he desired,"[51] yet Beaumarchais still had not authorized Le Tellier to sign a contract, and Le Tellier himself had stopped answering letters. On May 6, Ostervald hinted in a letter to Beaumarchais that the STN might align itself with other Swiss publishers who were planning to pirate the Kehl editions. Two weeks later, he made that veiled threat more explicit: the Société typographique de Berne had firm plans to publish an edition of Voltaire's works, and the

STN would collaborate with it if Beaumarchais did not commit himself to the "common edition." The STB had informed Ostervald that it had joined forces with Palissot, so its edition would be organized according to his plan, which would include a commentary by him and would be more thematic than Beaumarchais's. As he explained to Turkheim, Ostervald would soon have to opt for one or the other of these enterprises, "in order not to fall between two chairs."[52]

Bosset's death on August 6, 1781, interrupted the STN's activities and caused a readjustment of its finances. When Ostervald resumed his correspondence about Voltaire's works in September, he confided to a friend in Paris that he suspected Beaumarchais was stringing the STN along to gain time and prevent another *contrefaçon* while preparing things in Kehl.[53] In October, he sent Beaumarchais an ultimatum: either sign a contract for the "common edition" or the STN would become a partner in a competing edition. Beaumarchais did not answer. At last, on November 29, Ostervald wrote that he had had enough. "The time has come to end a correspondence that, flattering at first, is becoming too mortifying for my pride, even though I feel greatly honored that you consider me worthy to have been lured for such a long time, and I will carefully keep your letters in order to make use of them if the need arises."

In breaking with Beaumarchais, Ostervald added that French readers would be able to "procure your entire collection more complete and produced at half the price."[54] That meant joining forces with the STB. In fact, Ostervald was less naive than he seems in his fumbled attempts to collaborate with the Kehl Voltaire. While courting Beaumarchais during the last half of 1781, he was negotiating with Pfaehler behind Beaumarchais's back. Ostervald had known that the STB planned to pirate the Kehl Voltaire since May 1781. At that time relations between the STN and its partners in the Confederation had badly deteriorated. They no longer informed one another about their publishing plans, and the Confederation itself was virtually dead.[55] But on May 15 Pfaehler sent the STN a prospectus for a *contrefaçon* of the Kehl Voltaire with a cover letter indicating a willingness to restore good relations. A week or so later he came to Neuchâtel to propose including the STN in the speculation. As his subsequent letters explained, the *contrefaçon* was a separate enterprise divided into shares owned by a group of investors (presumably members of the Bernese patriciate who had supported the STB from its beginning). The STB would cede half of its half interest to the STN, which would have to remain in the background—that is, to have no contact with the other investors and to deal only with the STB as the head of the enterprise. Pfaehler insisted that the STN contribute its collection of Voltaire's letters to the edition. Ostervald had read one of them to him at their meeting, and Pfaehler conceded that it was "fairly interesting." However, he would not pay for the letters, and they were a condition for including the STN in the partnership, which would have to remain highly secret.[56] Secrecy mattered even more to Ostervald, because he was making the same commitment to two competing enterprises at the same time, using the manuscript letters as a bargaining tool.

The STB plan put Palissot at the heart of its venture. He had worked out a scheme for arranging all the elements of Voltaire's writing in an order that would make them easily accessible to readers, and he would add the new material from the Kehl edition to what he had already prepared, explicating each work with a commentary of his own. He promised to set up headquarters in Bern and to produce his copy within fifteen months of the publication of the Kehl volumes. In return, he would receive an enormous fee: 20,000 L. Pfaehler sent a copy of the contract with Palissot to the STN, and Palissot later sent a copy of his original prospectus, dated April 17, 1780. Taken together, they revealed an attempt to undercut the Kehl Voltaire with a cheaper and more user-friendly edition.[57]

Palissot rewrote the prospectus, and Pfaehler forwarded it to Ostervald on June 7, 1781, requesting comments. It was so inadequate, Ostervald replied, that it needed to be written again, from top to bottom. At Pfaehler's request, Ostervald provided a new draft, which they planned to publish immediately, in order to head off announcements of other *contrefaçons*, which threatened to break out everywhere.

Then suddenly Pfaehler decided to change course. On July 10 he wrote that a friend in Paris had informed him that Beaumarchais was eager to negotiate and even would travel to Bern to conclude a deal. Soon Beaumarchais—who would never set foot in Bern—had drawn Pfaehler into a lengthy correspondence, just as he had done to Ostervald. For his part, Ostervald remained hidden, hoping to cash in on the Kehl indirectly, even if he failed in his own negotiations to join it in publishing the duodecimo "common edition." He did not inform Pfaehler about the parallel negotiations that he was conducting with Beaumarchais. But at that time he was prepared to abandon them, because he now suspected they were a lure to prevent him from publishing a prospectus for a pirated edition. Therefore, he warned Pfaehler to force Beaumarchais to sign a contract as soon as possible "in order not to become the dupe of his cleverness."

Nevertheless, Pfaehler let himself be lulled into inaction. His letters to Neuchâtel repeated the same theme. July 17: "Everything will go well." August 14: they were on the verge of a settlement. August 20: he would no longer lose time in "useless negotiations." September 23: Pfaehler was ready to go to Paris to settle everything and prevent further delays. November 1: Pfaehler had sent Beaumarchais an ultimatum, demanding that he make a commitment within two weeks or they would publish their prospectus. November 22: they should take firm action soon, because there was no counting on Beaumarchais. December 4: Ostervald should touch up the prospectus in preparation for the launching of their *contrefaçon*. December 6: Ostervald's draft was excellent, and they need only wait for Palissot to sign off on it. December 30: having just visited Kehl, Pfaehler was stunned by the scale of Beaumarchais's establishment[58] and open to a new settlement with him that had been proposed by an intermediary in Paris. February 12, 1782: everything was stalled, in part because of a quarrel with Palissot, who objected to any modification of the original enterprise. At that point, Pfaehler's letters ceased to mention Beaumarchais. Drawn out and bogged down, the negotiations had led nowhere. Pfaehler abandoned them sometime in the spring of 1782. Beaumarchais had gained time, and Pfaehler had lost it, just as Ostervald had done in his own negotiations, which had run parallel to Pfaehler's and had ended in the same way a half year earlier.

Meanwhile, Pfaehler had been forced to cope with a furious Palissot. Palissot did not have much of a reputation in Paris, except as a polemicist who posed as a disciple of Voltaire while smearing Voltaire's allies among the Encyclopédistes. His pamphlet, *Petites lettres sur de grands philosophes*, and his play, *Les Philosophes,* won him no respect in Enlightenment circles. Ostervald shared the generally low opinion of him, but Pfaehler did not, insisting that he would honor the commitment to Palissot, no matter what might be arranged with Beaumarchais.[59] Palissot, however, refused to cooperate.[60] As soon as he learned about the negotiations with Beaumarchais, he sent an indignant letter to Pfaehler, who forwarded a copy to Ostervald, noting that it gave "a very bad idea of his character." Palissot would not permit any deviation from his original plan, and Pfaehler thought there might be no alternative but to cancel their contract and buy him off with 7,000 L. as compensation. That prospect seemed inevitable when an agent of Beaumarchais informed Pfaehler that any joint enterprise would have to exclude Palissot, "a feeble writer who is scorned."[61]

The Palissot problem was resolved before Pfaehler abandoned the attempt to collaborate with Beaumarchais, because Palissot accepted a payment to sever his tie with Bern and disappeared.[62] He reappeared a year later, this time with a proposal to revive his plan as a bowdlerized edition to be published by the STN. Voltaire was a great writer, no doubt about it, he explained; but women and children should not be permitted to read everything he wrote. On the contrary, his irreligious and scabrous writings should be kept under lock and key, available only to men. The rest, reduced to twenty or twenty-two volumes, could be published with suitable cuts and explanatory notes, which Palissot would provide. Readers everywhere yearned for such an edition, he wrote. It was sure to sell, not only among responsible heads of families but also to directors of schools and other institutions. He asked only for a third of what the STN would collect from selling subscriptions, "because I am much more sensitive to glory than to any other consideration."

The STN refused this proposal but did not reject it out of hand. Although the notion of a "purified Voltaire," as Palissot called it, sounds absurd today, there might well have been a demand for it in the reading public of the eighteenth century. That at least was the opinion of Palissot. "Voltaire was, to be sure, one of the rarest geniuses who ever existed," he wrote, "but his glory would be purer if he had reined in his freedom of thought, or rather his licence. To put it better, if he had written less."[63]

The greatest demand, as the Swiss pirates saw it, was still for a cheap contrefaçon of the Kehl edition. Pfaehler continued to pursue his project, first by himself, then with Heubach, and ultimately in partnership with Ostervald. In place of Palissot, he selected someone far more appropriate to give it lustre: Voltaire's loyal and conscientious secretary, Jean-Louis Wagnière. Unlike Palissot, Wagnière had no literary pretensions. He was an unsophisticated lad from a small village in the Vaud and had served Voltaire as a valet before becoming his secretary in 1756. What he could contribute to Pfaehler's enterprise was a kind of legitimacy derived from his closeness to Voltaire and a great many manuscripts that had not been swept up by Panckoucke. If they were combined with the manuscripts held by the STN, the new edition could reprint everything produced in Kehl supplemented by *augmentations* that would give it an edge in the competition to dominate the market for Voltaire.

Although Ostervald knew Wagnière quite well, he depended on someone who knew him better when he first made inquiries about material that might have escaped Panckoucke.[64] That informant was Jacques Mallet du Pan, the Genevan man of letters and journalist, who sent word on August 30, 1779, that Wagnière had just returned from Saint Petersburg, where he had overseen the installation of Voltaire's library in the Hermitage for Catherine II. "Between us, that boy is a big loud-mouth, slap-dash, and incompetent," Mallet wrote. Wagnière was unable to make any decisions without consulting Gabriel Cramer, "who cossets and directs him." Cramer, using his experience as Voltaire's principal publisher, intended to organize an edition according to a plan that Voltaire himself had favored and that differed from Beaumarchais's enterprise. Although Cramer no longer had the capacity to publish it himself, Mallet reported, he could prepare it and make a deal with another entrepreneur. Under his guidance, Wagnière was raking up every scrap of Voltaire's manuscripts, and they would not surrender anything to Beaumarchais. Cramer had to overcome the difficulty of maintaining control of Wagnière, "who drifts from project to project and will end up by doing something stupid." On December 17, 1781, Mallet reported that Wagnière was now safely "under the orders of M. Cramer," and their edition looked like a serious possibility.

Mallet's information gave out at this point, but the possibility was still alive two years later, when Pfaehler developed a new version of his old plan to publish Voltaire's works. As already explained, this project, along with a proposal to pirate the *Encyclopédie méthodique*, lay at the heart of the attempt to breathe new life into the Confederation in 1783. Ostervald recommitted the STN to the partnership with Lausanne and Bern in March, but he hesitated at first to subscribe to their speculation on Voltaire. Bérenger reported that they were also negotiating with a Genevan publisher, whom he did not name but probably was Cramer. They would pirate the Kehl volumes but might not include everything and would begin with Voltaire's plays.[65]

By May Ostervald had agreed to take out a one-third share in the Voltaire enterprise and Bérenger had drafted a prospectus to announce it. Then plans shifted, because they received word that Wagnière might be willing to collaborate. Wagnière confirmed his willingness in a letter to Heubach of November 21, 1783. He would lend his name to a prospectus and supply his manuscripts for a price to be determined later. Heubach dispatched Bérenger to Ferney to settle the terms; and Pfaehler wrote triumphantly to the STN, "To all appearances, Messieurs, this negotiation will succeed and then the enterprise will be one of the greatest that we will ever have done."[66] A draft contract, dated December 6 and probably drawn up during Bérenger's visit, specified that Wagnière would provide enough new material for two to three volumes and receive an advance of 25 louis (750 L.) plus 10 percent of the money to be raised by a subscription campaign, which he would help direct, using his network of correspondents. The STB and STL printed and circulated the prospectus in December. When it reached Paris, Beaumarchais's group replied with an "insolent note," as Heubach described it, attacking Wagnière.[67]

Unfortunately, it is impossible to reconstruct the succession of events after 1783, because most of the documentation thins out at the beginning of 1784, when the STN went through its financial crisis and reorganization. As recounted in the previous chapter, Ostervald had a brief moment of panic in early January when he saw a notice in the *Gazette de Berne* that the new edition would be produced by the three *sociétés typographiques*, because he worried about provoking the authorities in Neuchâtel. Pfaehler reassured him, and references to the edition then disappeared from the correspondence of the STB and Heubach. They could not get on with their pirating in the first months of 1784, because there was nothing to pirate. The first volumes of the Kehl edition did not appear until the end of the year or the beginning of 1785. By that time, it seems, Beaumarchais had headed off the threat by a deal with the STB[68]—or at least he had won over Wagnière. On February 2, 1785, the STN wrote to Guillaume Bergeret, a bookseller in Bordeaux, that because Wagnière had been bought off by Beaumarchais, the Voltaire project had "gone up in smoke."

The story of the struggle to pirate Voltaire ends there, although it could be continued if new documents turn up.[69] Its importance consists less in identifying the pirated editions than in demonstrating how the pirates operated. They made and unmade deals, banded together and fell out, and kept adjusting strategy and tactics in response to unforeseen circumstances. Piracy was a matter of mobilizing capital, seizing opportunities, taking risks, gaining access to reliable information, bidding, bluffing, and knowing when to cash in one's chips. The stakes were high, because the demand for Voltaire's works seemed inexhaustible. Of course, the publishers might have overestimated that demand. Beaumarchais had difficulty in collecting subscriptions, as noted earlier, and the Kehl Voltaire was a disaster, similar to the STG edition of Rousseau. Beaumarchais aimed his editions at a luxury market. The spin-off duodecimo editions satisfied a broader public, and cut-rate copies of individual works, pirated by publishers all along the Fertile

Crescent, brought Voltaire within the reach of readers everywhere in France and nearly everywhere in Europe.

The scramble to publish Voltaire included attempts to ferret out every letter and scrap of manuscript that could be discovered soon after his death. That effort continues to this day, and at the time of this writing, the Voltaire Foundation at Oxford has nearly completed a scholarly edition of the works and correspondence, consisting in all of 203 volumes.

Yet the Oxford edition does not contain the 162 letters that Ostervald had tried to use as leverage to exact a printing commission from Beaumarchais.[70] They probably still exist in an attic or a safe somewhere in Switzerland.

PART 3

INSIDE A SWISS PUBLISHING HOUSE

9

Business as Usual

THE FOUL PLAY IN the scramble to publish the works of Rousseau and Voltaire did not violate the rules of the game as they were described at the beginning of this book, because there were no rules in the pirate sector of the trade. As we have seen in case after case, pirates undercut one another as readily as they slashed into the profits of publishers in the privileged sector. Yet they could not survive if they failed to establish some kind of order in their dealings with one another, even though full-scale alliances such as the Swiss Confederation proved impossible to maintain. They also had to cope with the normal difficulties of publishing—building a list, developing a network of customers, and working out a strategy for turning a profit. To understand how a pirate publisher handled these problems in the course of its ordinary activities, it is best to take a closer look at the STN, concentrating on its everyday correspondence.

As already mentioned, information was crucial for success. Most of it came through the daily mail, as Pierre Gosse observed in his advice to Ostervald when the STN first began to operate: "Correspondence . . . is certainly the soul of commerce."[1] The STN received a dozen or so letters a day, roughly two-thirds from France and Switzerland, the rest from all the major cities of Europe. It sent off as many from Neuchâtel. Madame Bertrand said that she wrote ten to twenty letters a day while she was handling the STN's business during the first six months of 1780, when Ostervald and Bosset were on a business trip to Paris.[2]

The style of business letters adhered to certain conventions. Correspondents normally kept to a formal mode of expression, using the first-person plural, even when they knew one another personally.[3] Only a few of them adopted a casual manner and wrote as *je*.[4] Ostervald composed nearly all the STN's letters, at least until 1784, when new directors formally took over the firm and he shifted most of his activity to public administration.[5] He actually dictated them, for his handwriting was crabbed and ugly, and his principal clerk, Jean-François Favarger, had a beautiful hand. After the conventional closing phrase, "your most humble and obedient servant," he signed off in his own hand, but not with his name. He wrote "La Société typographique de Neuchâtel." This "signature" had legal force, committing the company to whatever was expressed in the letter, as we will see later.

Ordinary letters did not have separate envelopes in the eighteenth century.[6] They usually were single leaves of paper, sized in special ways so as to absorb the kind of ink used for writing, which was more fluid than printer's ink. The writer folded the leaf to form a rectangular packet, which was held together by wax impressed with a seal. Sometimes separate slips of paper called *papier volant* were included in the packet.[7] They could be lists of *livres philosophiques* or confidential messages, which sometimes ended with an order: "Tear this up right away."[8] (I have been surprised to find how many pieces of paper have survived orders for their destruction.)

More often, the devices adopted in letter writing were employed to save money on postage. Postage was normally paid by recipients of letters in the eighteenth century. (Stamps, which required payment by the person who sent the letter, were not introduced in France until 1849.) High-ranking officials had franking privileges. If a Parisian author happened to win the favor of a secretary in a ministry, the secretary would forward to him a letter placed inside a letter addressed to the minister. Jacques-Pierre Brissot received proofs of the books he published with the STN as letters within letters within letters. When the STN sent him the proofs of his *Théorie des lois criminelles*, it addressed the outer sheet (*couvert*) to Antoine-Jean Amelot de Chaillou, the secretary of state for the Maison du Roi. It addressed the inner sheet to Henique de Chevilly, an author-friend of Brissot who had contact with the minister's secretary. And it addressed the proofs, a few sheets at a time, to Brissot at his home, where Chevilly sent them. The inner packets, like the outer, had wax seals, but the seals were bulky enough to attract attention in the postal service, in which clerks felt suspicious-looking envelopes and confiscated anything not intended for the minister. Therefore, after some close calls with the wax seals, Brissot directed the STN to seal the two inside missives with wet bread, which, when dried, worked effectively as paste and had none of the telltale bulkiness of wax.[9]

Postage was an important consideration in the budgets of booksellers, who sometimes protested about the cost of the prospectuses and catalogues that the STN sent to them.[10] In order to keep its own postage expenses under control, the STN had a contract with the postmaster in Pontarlier, who paid for most of the mail it received from France and then forwarded it to Neuchâtel. In 1783, its bill from him came to 463 L., 5 sous, more than a year's wages of a skilled worker.[11] Letters traveled fairly rapidly during the last years of the Ancien Régime, especially if they were carried along the excellent roads that connected Paris with provincial cities.[12] When a letter arrived at Neuchâtel, a clerk wrote on its back an uppercase *R* followed by a dash. The *R* stood for "reçu" (received) and also for "répondu" (replied). On top of the dash the clerk wrote the date of the letter's arrival, and below it he later added the date of the STN's reply. Combining that information with the date written by the correspondent above the salutation of the letter makes it possible to measure the time expended in ordinary transactions.

The letters exchanged between Ostervald and Bosset during their stay in Paris and Mme Bertrand in Neuchâtel provide typical examples. Ostervald or Bosset would report on their activities at the end of the day and post the letter on the following day. (Letters were gathered from local letter boxes before 11:00 a.m. and dispatched from the Maison des Postes by 1:00 p.m.) It would usually arrive at the STN's office six days later, and Mme Bertrand would reply posthaste, so that the circuit of communication from sender to recipient and back to sender was completed within two weeks. That was quite rapid, fast enough for Ostervald and Bosset to receive crucial information, such as fine points of a contract while they settled accounts with Panckoucke. Letters from Moscow usually took eighteen days. The following examples illustrate the space-time relations in exchanges with French correspondents and a few non-French publishing houses.

Correspondent	Date of writing	Date of arrival	Date of reply
Bergeret, Bordeaux	22 June 1773	1 July	6 July
Sens, Toulouse	26 May 1777	15 June	17 June
Chevrier, Poitiers	20 December 1772	27 December	29 December
Rigaud, Montpellier	8 September 1777	15 September	16 September
Mossy, Marseille	8 August 1781	18 August	19 August
Revol, Lyon	9 July 1780	12 July	15 July
Charmet, Besançon	20 May 1781	22 May	29 May
Faivre, Pontarlier	24 July 1780	25 July	25 July
Cailler, Geneva	17 January 1777	18 January	20 January
Boubers, Brussels	28 January 1774	6 February	7 February

If compared with today's exchanges by email or texting, the postal service imposed a slow pace on business affairs. It was nonetheless regular and dependable. Publishers and booksellers knew when to expect a reply while they were bargaining with one another. If the reply failed to come within a normal period of time, they would suspect that something had gone wrong. After learning that recent letters between him and the STN had taken four months instead of ten days, Mossy in Marseille concluded that they had been opened by agents of the state who were looking for evidence of illegal activity. He then directed the STN to send him some *lettres ostensibles,* or fake letters, which would indicate that he served it only as a middleman, forwarding its shipments to Italy rather than selling them to his customers in Marseille.[13]

The STN's clerks wrote copies of the letters it sent in a register called *Copie de lettres.* In the margin next to a copy, they wrote another long dash, then entered on top of it the page number of the previous letter to that correspondent and below it the page number of the subsequent letter. By following this simple code, Ostervald could reconstruct the history of transactions, a critical factor when one was making an argument about disputed shipping costs or terms of a swapping agreement or obligations toward an allied house.

To read through the *Copies de lettres*—huge folios, each about 800 pages long—is to follow the simultaneous raveling and unraveling of dozens of narratives and to appreciate the complexity of running a business in which the publisher had to keep track of plots that were thickening and thinning simultaneously and at different stages of development. On the same day, Ostervald might worry about whether to order an expensive new font of *philosophie* (small pica) type from Louis Vernange in Lyon, because the old font was wearing thin; about the dirty tricks of a paper miller named Morel in the Jura hamlet of Meslières, who had a history of cheating on the weight of his reams; about ice in the Baltic, which could freeze before the STN's warehouse sent bales of books to Christian Rüdiger in Moscow (a shipment normally took four months, and the Baltic began to freeze in November); about how to extract some corrections and additions from Raynal for a new edition of the *Histoire philosophique*; about whether to accept the STB's proposal to pirate Bougainville's *Voyage autour du monde* or the STL's preference for Robertson's *Histoire de l'Amérique*; about policy changes in Versailles, where a new edict on *contrefaçons* was rumored to be in the works; about how to collect a money order for 848 L. from Jean-François Malherbe, a small-time bookseller in Loudun, whose accumulated debt was getting out of hand; and about where to find enough cash to pay off a loan of 25,000 L., for which the

STN was being dunned by Jacques-François d'Arnal, its banker in Lyon. Add to these ten or twenty other affairs, and one can get some sense of the maze through which a publisher had to find a way in the course of daily business.

All these problems were handled through the mail, and through them all ran one incessant theme: the need for information. Of course, some information traveled by word of mouth. Publishers discussed affairs with one another during trips or when they crossed paths if they lived in large cities.[14] They sent sales reps to sound the market, and they engaged in shop talk when booksellers called on them, a common occurrence. In 1783 Mme Ostervald was credited with 25 L. in the STN's account books "for various meals given to different booksellers at her house."[15] Madame Bertrand, who also received booksellers on business trips, observed that one could say more in fifteen minutes of conversation than in twenty letters.[16] Aside from person-to-person encounters, however, publishers relied on a trade grapevine operating through their commercial correspondence. Each house had a network of its own, which grew organically over time. As books were sold and bills were paid, it built up mutual trust with particular retailers and middlemen, who provided it with inside information. The ties were stronger in some places than in others, and the business patterns varied from publisher to publisher. Yet there were common nodal points, and the connections intersected so extensively that they formed a general system of relations. By following the flow of letters, we can see how the system operated.

Although every publisher faced decisions about choosing texts, the decision-making was especially high pressured among pirates, because they operated in the sector of the market where the competition was the most intense. As illustrated by the STN's dealings with other Swiss houses and with Gosse in The Hague, publishers gauged demand by culling information from colleagues and customers. Booksellers tended to be good informants, because they were usually cautious in placing orders. Returns (the possibility for booksellers to send unsold copies back to the publisher) did not exist in the eighteenth century. Rather than be stuck with unsold copies in their storerooms, booksellers preferred to order a small number of copies per title and to repeat the order if a book sold well. In a typical order, a bookseller would ask for only a few copies of each book and request enough different books to make up a bale weighing at least fifty pounds so that he could save on the cheaper rates for bulk shipments. His orders expressed his judgment of the demand among his customers, not his personal preferences. André of Versailles spoke for most in the trade when he wrote to the STN, "I do not neglect the sale of books that I would never read myself, and that is only because one must live with the multitude and because the best book for a bookseller is a book that sells."[17]

The same reasoning applied to publishers, who depended on reports from booksellers in deciding what to print. As the STN wrote to Jean Mossy, the largest bookseller in Marseille, "The choice we make for our presses is commonly that of the booksellers who send us orders and who rightly think that the best book is the one that is rapidly sold."[18] However, booksellers made scattershot recommendations for reprints, and they sometimes contradicted one another. For example, Joseph-Sulpice Grabit, a veteran bookseller in Lyon, urged the STN to pirate *Dictionnaire raisonné universel d'histoire naturelle* by Jacques-Christophe Valmont de Bomare. But Pierre Machuel, an eminent bookseller in Rouen, warned that the Bomare no longer sold well. Nicolas Gerlache in Metz advised reprinting *Analyse raisonnée de Bayle*, yet Jean-Marie Barret in Lyon wrote that its sales had dropped everywhere in France. Far from being cut off from the marketplace, the STN seemed likely to be blinded by a blizzard of inconsistent and confusing information.

At a more general level, however, it could get a clear view of the genres and authors that most appealed to the public. Booksellers emphasized their customers' interest in the life sciences (what they called "histoire naturelle"), travel (especially the round-the-world voyages of Cook and Bougainville), history (popular surveys such as the works of Claude-François-Xavier Millot), and scabrous *livres philosophiques*. Among authors, the two names that stood out in the commercial correspondence were, unsurprisingly, Voltaire and Rousseau. Before their deaths in 1778, booksellers kept asking about the next volley of tracts expected from Ferney and the likelihood that Rousseau's "mémoires" (his *Confessions*) would ever see the light. The struggle to publish the posthumous works of both writers kept the grapevine buzzing for several years after 1778. Then attention shifted to the demand for books by the current generation of authors, including several who were popular at the time but have been forgotten since. Aside from those minor figures, the booksellers devoted most of their letters to orders, queries, and gossip concerning three writers who became celebrities: Guillaume-Thomas-François Raynal, Louis-Sébastien Mercier, and Simon-Nicolas-Henri Linguet.

Booksellers everywhere clamored for new editions of Raynal's *Histoire philosophique*, especially after it was condemned and burned by the public executioner in Paris in 1781. Machuel in Rouen wrote that he had sold several thousand copies of it by June 1783 and still wanted more.[19] By 1785, the STN's agent in Paris, Jacob-François Bornand, reported that all of Europe was flooded with editions of it.[20] Similarly, Delahaye of Brussels wrote that Paris had been inundated by more than 10,000 copies of Mercier's *Tableau de Paris*, and he assured the STN that he would order anything, sight unseen, by the "famous M. Mercier."[21] The celebrity of "the too notorious Linguet"[22] derived primarily from his provocative, hard-hitting journal, *Annales politiques, civiles, et littéraires*, but his pamphlets sold well and his *Mémoires sur la Bastille*, a bestseller about his two-year detention in the Bastille, made him one of the most famous writers in Europe. Mirabeau enjoyed a similar notoriety, thanks to his *Des lettres de cachet et des prisons d'État*, but he did not figure as prominently in the shop talk of the trade as the other three.

Rumors and gossip, most of it inaccurate, filled the commercial correspondence. Was it true, Rigaud asked the STN from Montpellier, that after fleeing France, Raynal, despite his old age, had married a "young and amiable Swiss miss"? "You must understand," he explained, "that everyone in general and booksellers in particular are interested in the fate of such a celebrity."[23] Poinçot in Versailles passed on talk that Mercier had married and that Raynal had died of apoplexy. Petit in Reims reported a rumor that Mercier was the one who had died, and so did Mauvelain in Loudun, who heard that he had expired in the arms of Raynal and that Raynal had indeed had gotten married.[24] Although no author inspired a cult of personality comparable to that of Voltaire and Rousseau, Raynal, Mercier, and Linguet had become public figures, and their works were prime targets for pirating.

Yet a strategy of focusing on the big names could backfire, because other pirates were quite likely to do the same, and they might reach the market first. A pirate needed to know what his rivals planned to produce, how fast they could get their products into bookshops, and what the market would bear. His competitors tried to discover the same information about him. Sales reps were instructed to ferret out information about the operations of other houses.[25] When publishers visited one another on business trips, they kept up a front of politeness and often dined together, yet they, too, acted like spies. While Ostervald and Bosset were traveling in France in 1780, Mme Bertrand urged them to gather information that could determine whether or not they should publish the works of Samuel Richardson. They should see how Richardson's novels figured in the catalogues of the other publishers, take note of the dates of the editions, and steer the shop talk to the demand for them. "Drop a remark, with a casual air, about a new, corrected and augmented edition," she wrote. "Pretend that you have been delegated to buy it for a friend, or find out, without seeming to be concerned, whether this corrected edition (with *Pamela* reworked by the author)—which you *think* is being produced in Switzerland—will sell well. Once we have that information, we will either abandon the enterprise or we will offer it right away by subscription, determined not to begin the printing until we have sold a sufficient number."[26]

Although the pirates tried to keep their operations secret,[27] word leaked out, especially in locations like the rue des Belles Filles in Geneva, where the printing shops were clustered within a few steps of one another. Workers spread information in their favorite taverns and on the road as they tramped from shop to shop.[28] Publishers sometimes bribed journeyman in rival shops to steal the sheets of the books they were printing. The STN, which collected inside information about Beaumarchais's printing operations in Kehl, warned him "that the sheets are pilfered as soon as they are printed."[29] It received word from its Paris agent that its own workers were stealing sheets while printing its edition of the *Tableau de Paris*.[30]

Broadly speaking, pirates published two kinds of works—*nouveautés*, or books that had just appeared, and large-scale editions, which had already proved their salability. The urgency for reliable information was greatest in the case of *nouveautés*, a word that could be applied to any recent publication but was normally used to describe works that were expected to sell for only a brief period. As the booksellers used the term, *nouveautés* often referred to polemical tracts or "good, spicy, little morsels"[31] like *Lettre de M. Linguet à M. le comte de Vergennes*; works related to current events as exemplified by Necker's *Compte rendu* and the attacks against it; and light fiction such as Dorat's *Les Malheurs de l'inconstance*.[32] When it came to ordering *nouveautés*, speed was a constant theme in the booksellers' letters. Speed mattered so much to Manoury of Caen that he asked the STN to ship him, sight unseen, up to a hundred copies of any "spicy *nouveauté*."[33] For its part, the STN understood the importance of getting new works to its clients as quickly as possible. The demand for voguish works did not last long, and booksellers dreaded being stuck with works that piled up in their stockrooms after the demand had passed. Should a shipment arrived late, it might be unsellable, especially if a rival retailer had exhausted the market with a shipment from a rival pirate that had arrived earlier.

Also, retailers needed to keep a hold on their customers' business by providing an up-to-date assortment of books. They complained bitterly if they heard that the STN had sent a shipment to someone else before supplying them. Mossy expressed the general sentiment in writing from Marseille that the public was "extraordinarily impatient" and that if visitors to his store did not find a particular book, "that is enough for them to think that I am badly supplied, and the next time they won't come to me."[34] Publishers sometimes favored some retailers over others by shipping their orders first. If discovered, this kind of inside trading could lead to nasty quarrels, because time was always crucial.[35] The STN constantly urged its shipping agents to make haste. The delay of one week, it insisted, would be enough to ruin the sale of some *nouveautés*.[36]

Longer and more substantial books required a more elaborate strategy. Large publishers like the STN favored multi-volume works, which were slower and more expensive to produce yet had the advantage, if successful, of bringing in a steady stream of income. Speed continued to be an important consideration, because a publisher could lose heavily if a competitor beat him to the market with another edition of the same book. But works such as Bomare's *Dictionnaire raisonné universel d'histoire naturelle* (twelve volumes) and Millot's *Élements d'histoire générale* (nine volumes) had proved their staying power, and the market could absorb more than one re-edition of them. Large publications required costly outlays of capital, of course, particularly for paper, which, as already explained, had to be of a consistent quality and therefore ordered long in advance. Workers came and went at a rapid rate, partly because of footlooseness, especially among young journeymen on their tour de France, but mainly because most of them were hired by the job. As long as jobs held out, a printing shop could keep a workforce consistently employed. It would shed them if the income stream dried up. After printing its last volume of the *Encyclopédie* in 1780, the STN ceased using all but two of its twelve presses and fired nearly all of its workers. Then, as recounted in the previous chapter, it attempted to resume a high rate of production and profitability by producing the works of Voltaire and Rousseau. A similar strategy lay behind its decision to pirate other multi-volume editions such as Raynal's *Histoire philosophique*, despite the competition from other editions. Overall, large-scale steady sellers were a better bet than hit-or-miss *nouveautés*.

To succeed, a publisher needed to develop skill in sounding the market. He might rely on his intuition; but as Ostervald's correspondence with Gosse illustrates (see Chapter 4), he could easily miscalculate. Madame Bertrand observed that publishing required a great deal of experience. "To succeed it is necessary to have particular talent and a lengthy practice," she noted in a letter to Bosset. "It's necessary to do an apprenticeship while young."[37] Although the recommendations of booksellers provided some guidance, they were too haphazard and inconsistent to be reliable. Therefore, when the STN considered reprinting a substantial book, it often consulted its allies among the Swiss publishers and a few others such as Gosse in The Hague, Dufour in Maastricht, and Plomteux in Liège. It also took soundings among a few of its customers whose judgment it trusted—veterans like Machuel of Rouen and Mossy of Marseille. Sometimes it sent circular letters to a wider network of clients and based its decision on their response.

Although it may sound anachronistic to describe such activities as market research and marketing, those terms accurately fit the STN's way of doing business. It studied the market carefully, drawing on information from its agents in Paris and its sales reps as well as its commercial correspondence. Like other publishers, its general way of testing the waters was to issue a notice (*annonce*) of its intention to publish a book. It often published *annonces* in journals such as the *Gazette de Berne* or its own *Journal helvétique*, and it regularly sent them through the mail as an item in a circular letter.[38] An *annonce* in the widely read *Gazette de Leyde* cost only one livre a line. In 1779 the STN paid 26 L. for a half-page advertisement promoting the quarto edition of the *Encyclopédie*.[39] Sometimes it included in its letters a printed title page and a page of text, which served as a sample of the paper and type it planned to use and which also suggested that it was seriously committed to producing the book, though it might abandon the project if the response was disappointing.

A more elaborate sample took the form of a prospectus, usually a one- or two-page description of the work and the terms for purchasing it. As prospectuses were aimed primarily at booksellers, they sometimes limited themselves to typographical and commercial details, such as format, type, and provisions for discounts. For example, in June 1774, Jean-Edmé Dufour of Maastricht circulated a prospectus for his new reprint of Raynal's *Histoire philosophique*. He did not mention anything about the contents of the book, because he assumed the booksellers knew all about it. Instead, he insisted on the high quality his edition, which would exactly reproduce the latest edition—a deluxe version, augmented and corrected by Raynal himself—at a much cheaper price, including the possibility of purchasing baker's dozens— that is, a free copy for every twelve ordered.[40]

More elaborate prospectuses included a great deal of sales talk. Beaumarchais gave full play to his verve in the many prospectuses that he issued for the Kehl Voltaire, and the STN began the prospectus for its pirated edition of the *Description des arts et métiers* with a philosophic discourse on the importance of studying crafts and manufacturing. Publishers always issued prospectuses when they tried to sell books by subscription. If they failed to collect enough down payments, they abandoned the enterprise.[41] By 1770, booksellers complained so frequently about bad faith in subscription publishing that the subscription model went into a decline, and prospectuses served mainly as an enticement to make booksellers commit themselves in advance to purchasing a certain number of copies.

The STN followed up the information about its latest publications with circular letters and catalogues. In August 1776 it sent a circular to 156 booksellers, most of them in the French provinces, as part of a campaign to extend its network of customers.[42] It usually issued its catalogues once a year, listing all the works available from its stock in alphabetical order according to their titles. Rather than containing the kind of blurbs found in catalogues today, the entries merely gave the name of the author, the format of the volume, and the cost. A typical catalogue contained about 300 titles. Although some titles showed up year after year, most disappeared after a year or two, suggesting fairly rapid turnover (as is the case with catalogues today). In 1785 the STN published an elaborate catalogue of seventy-two pages including nearly 800 titles preceded by an "Avis" in which it announced an offer to supply any other books that a customer might desire. It procured most of these additional works by means of exchanges with other publishers. The STN archives contain dozens of catalogues sent by publishers who marketed their books in the same way it did. As a result of the trade in exchanges, the same titles appeared in many catalogues, giving the impression of a common stock of literature produced throughout the Fertile Crescent.

As a form of marketing, the notices in journals, prospectuses, circular letters, and catalogues belonged to age-old practices that seem straightforward—so many varieties of gaining publicity. In fact, however, they often served as weapons in the constant warfare among the pirates. By announcing a plan to publish a book, a pirate often intended merely to see whether the response was sufficient for it to go ahead with the printing. Madame Bertrand wrote to Ostervald that the STN had made so many announcements and had fulfilled so few of them that booksellers no longer took them seriously.[43] Announcements often were bluffs, and a bluff might be called by another pirate. In February 1780, the STN gave up a plan to pirate Raynal's *Histoire philosophique* when it learned that Clément Plomteux of Liège was preparing a new edition corrected by the author. It trusted Plomteux's determination to execute his enterprise. At the same time it decided against renouncing its plan to pirate Valmont de Bomare's *Dictionnaire raisonné universel d'histoire naturelle*, even though Pellet of Geneva had announced that he was publishing it, because it suspected that he had made the announcement "in order to pull a fast one on us"[44]—and sure enough, as mentioned earlier, Pellet backed off.

A pirate could also send out word that he was preparing an edition of a book that he knew was being printed by another pirate. If the latter felt sufficiently threatened, it might sue for peace—that is, agree to share the spoils by creating a joint enterprise (a publication *de compte à demi*) or by sacrificing a large proportion of its edition at a bargain price or as a swap. In a typical deal, Barret in Lyon pirated Condillac's sixteen-volume *Cours d'étude pour l'instruction du prince de Parme* at a run of 1,200 in 1776 and was forced to cede eighty copies at a cheap price in order to dissuade a Swiss publisher from producing a rival reprint.[45] When competing editions were announced, customers could play off one house against another. In 1774 Gabriel Regnault of Lyons began to market a clandestine reprint of Rousseau's works. The STN informed him that it would stock a rival reprint being produced in Neuchâtel by Samuel Fauche, unless Regnault would sell a large number of his copies at a large discount. He then agreed to part with 100 copies at a 25 percent reduction.[46]

Lyon, which had 118 active presses in 1780,[47] was a great center of piracy, despite the surveillance of the local inspector of the book trade, and its pirates perfected many tactics to dupe one another while deploring their competitors' "bickering" and "charlatanism."[48] Barret, who delighted in exposing "the wickedness of my colleagues," recounted a typical episode that took place in 1772. He had begun to produce an illegal edition of Rousseau's works, when Regnault learned about it and demanded to be given a half share. Barret reluctantly agreed, fearing that if he refused, Regnault might denounce him to the authorities in Paris. Soon before he had completed the printing, he discovered that a third Lyonnais dealer, Benoît Duplain, planned to undercut their joint edition by one of his own, which he was producing secretly in two printing shops. At that point, Regnault, who knew nothing about Duplain's plot and sensed a growing demand for Rousseau, asked to buy out Barret's other half in their speculation. Barret readily accepted, offered good terms, pocketed the money, and enjoyed the spectacle as soon as Regnault discovered the existence of

Duplain's edition: "Today these two gentlemen are quarreling with one another, and I stand back and watch them."[49]

Joseph-Sulpice Grabit, a Lyonnais publisher who was cut from the same cloth as Regnault, Barret, and Duplain, concocted a more elaborate plot concerning a *contrefaçon* of Velly's popular, twenty-two-volume *Histoire de France*.[50] Somehow, he had come into possession of 1,000 copies of volumes 17–22 of the Velly. The authorized edition was being published by Saillant et Nyon, one of the most substantial firms in Paris. Grabit persuaded the STN to write a *lettre ostensible* (fake letter) to Saillant et Nyon saying that a nearby (presumably Swiss) printer had asked it to serve as an intermediary in a deal that he proposed. The (supposed) printer had acquired the 1,000 copies of volumes 17–22, and they were exact facsimiles of the Saillant et Nyon edition. He could easily print volumes 1–16 and undersell the Parisians. However, he would magnanimously spare them if they would buy his copies, which they then could use to produce 1,000 more sets. The STN sent off the fake letter and in reply received a refusal. Grabit then concocted different variations of his scheme, which included revelations about a fake edition announced in Avignon and a faulty edition from Brussels. The STN complied with two more *lettres ostensibles*, offering better terms each time, but Saillant et Nyon continued to refuse, and in the end Grabit was stuck with an unsold rump of the pirated edition.

As mentioned in connection with the speculations on Voltaire and Rousseau, publishers even pirated themselves. If they were putting out an original edition that they expected to sell well, they knew that it would be immediately pirated. Therefore, they sometimes speculated on a cheap, knockoff edition of poorer quality, usually as a secret joint venture with another house, at a lower price. They concentrated their resources on the first edition, which they aimed at the upscale market, and calculated that its sales would not be badly undercut by the subsequent reprint, which in any case would reach the broader market before the other pirates had time to print rival editions. In 1784 the STN considered such an arrangement while planning to do an expanded edition in-octavo of Mercier's bestselling *L'An deux mille quatre cent quarante*. Grabit got wind of its plan, and instead of pirating the STN behind its back, he asked it to send him sheets as soon as it ran them off. He would willingly pay for this service, which would enable him to beat out the other pirates with a cheap *contrefaçon* in duodecimo format. In this way, the STN, whose presses would be completely occupied with its edition, could make some extra money instead of watching helplessly while other publishers profited at its expense: "Because you can expect that as soon as you have completed it in your printing shop," Grabit warned, "it will be under way in twenty others."[51] The deal never took place, because the STN abandoned its plan.

The uninhibited competition led to widespread duplicity. In Marseille, Mossy printed a fake title page to *Essai sur le commerce de l'Amérique* and sold it as a new work, *Traité général du commerce de l'Amérique*.[52] In Besançon, Lépagnez warned the STN to beware of a work entitled *Le Despotisme des Anglais*. He had printed it for the author as *Boussole morale et politique*; the author had sent the edition to be marketed in Paris; it did not sell under the original title, so "the charlatans of the book trade in Paris changed the title and sold it with a new title page."[53] In Colmar, Fontaine discovered that in one of its catalogues the STN had offered Voltaire's *Histoire du Parlement de Paris* under the title *Les Assassinats juridiques*. Encouraged by such creative marketing, he asked the STN to print new title pages for three works that he kept in stock, leaving it to choose the titles: "You will add 'reviewed, corrected, and augmented . . . .' And as I have no doubts about the ability of a company as amiable as yours, I leave the choice of the new titles entirely up to you. Thanks to that device and a bit of additional work, the books may become fashionable. Moreover, it's only a 24-hour job."[54] The STN gladly obliged.

The general conditions of the trade favored duplicity, because publishers had to deal with booksellers whom they had never met and who lived hundreds of leagues away. In 1781 the STN received a series of letters from "Bergès & Cie." in Toulouse. They included orders for large shipments of books, and they were written in the exact, professional manner of booksellers, complete with allusions to the current conditions of the trade. Although tempted to send the shipments, the STN made inquiries with a merchant in Toulouse, who informed it that no such firm existed. A clerk in a local bookshop had invented it and sent off the letters in the hope that he could induce the STN to provide merchandise that he could sell on the sly without paying the bill.[55] Booksellers' letters exposed several cases of such fraud—Grand Lefebvre in Bolbec, Joseph Le Lièvre in Belfort, and peddlars who collected shipments and paid for them with bills of exchange due to be paid from fake addresses, which were known in the trade as "domiciles en l'air."[56] Everyone used ploys—from publishers to booksellers, peddlers, and even wagon drivers, who devised fake bills of lading (*lettres de voiture*) when they faced a fine for failing to make a deadline set for their deliveries.[57]

Therefore, an important part of a publisher's job was to detect the traps that surrounded every aspect of his operations. Shipping was particularly precarious, and pirates devoted a great deal of time to constructing supply lines, rearranging them, and repairing them when they broke down. Probably a quarter of the letters received and written by the STN concerned transportation.[58] Smuggling required special attention, as it produced endless opportunities for cheating by underground agents, whether by padding expenses, taking cuts in bribes to customs officers, or covering up bungled deliveries. Even clients could not be trusted. Poinçot, the bookseller with the largest business in Versailles, was believed to be a police spy and to engineer the confiscation of bales bound for his competitors. Desauges, a dealer in Paris, was also reputed to be a spy and to arrange for the police to seize his own shipments so that he could avoid paying for them, secretly recover them from the police, and sell them *sous le manteau*.[59]

Characters as duplicitous as Desauges were nonetheless exceptional. In the normal course of its business, the STN usually received orders and fulfilled them without mishaps. Had it been swindled at every juncture, it could not have survived for two decades. Yet the write-offs in its account books for "bad debtors"—customers who ordered books and failed to pay for them—grew to such an extent that they undermined its financial solidity by 1783.[60] Despite constant efforts to collect unredeemed promissory notes, there was little the STN could do to force the payment of its bills, because the trade in pirated books took place outside the law. "The sad part about it is that affairs of this kind cannot be brought before a court," observed the STN's banker in Lyon, "and when your correspondents are cheaters, there is no way to obtain justice."[61]

Conditions deteriorated in the late 1770s, when complaints about duplicity became an increasingly important theme of the mail that arrived in Neuchâtel. They stood out especially in the correspondence of veterans of the book trade, like Pierre Machuel, the oldest bookseller with the largest business in Rouen. "The book trade has been ruined by all kinds of people," he complained, "and it has gone into such a decline that, in order to conserve what I have put aside during 25 years of work, I am determined to retire." He quit the trade in September 1783, having written it off as hopelessly corrupt: "Everything about it has turned into brigandage."[62] Other dealers, like Delahaye & Cie. in Brussels, filled their letters with lamentations about "treachery," "underhand intrigue," and "jealousy."[63] Yet Delahaye invented dubious pretexts to avoid paying his own debts. The STN's bill collector in

Brussels wrote that he had tried to get him to pay up and that taking him to court would do no good. "The path of justice is very slow, costly, and uncertain, owing to widespread chicanery."[64]

Faced with so much cheating, pirates needed to build up a network of trustworthy clients. Their trade developed organically over time and unevenly over space, strong in some places, weak in others, as circumstances changed. At its core, a pirate's business was built on reliable allies among publishers like those of the Swiss Confederation, who banded together to swap books, and among booksellers who could be counted on to send regular orders and to pay for them. For their part, the booksellers also relied on favorable relations among a core of suppliers who often offered special terms—longer credit, quicker shipments, exclusive arrangements for the sale of certain titles, and discounts such as a free thirteenth copy for every dozen ordered.

Reciprocal self-interest held networks together, but conditions were always changing. In a period of expansion, a publisher extended its trade into unfamiliar territory, taking chances on new clients. When the trade was contracting, it also faced uncertainty, because it could not simply rely on its regular customers. If debts built up, it easily succumbed to the temptation to sell books to marginal dealers, who took risks by expanding their orders beyond their ability to pay and by dealing in the dangerous sector of *livres philosophiques*. Risks, like duplicity, were inherent in the business.

Publishers summed up the principal defense against both with one word: confidence. The word—both as a noun, *confiance*, and as a verb *confier*—has appeared fairly often in the preceding pages. It expressed a common assumption: "In all trade, and especially in ours," the STN wrote to a potential customer, "it is necessary to have a great deal of confidence."[65] "Confidence" crops up constantly in the letters it received, always as a norm meant to govern the book trade.[66] It was so widely accepted as a guiding principle that it was invoked in the edicts of August 30, 1777, that were intended to destroy the trade in *contrefaçons*.[67] As book professionals employed it, the term usually described a formal relation between a publisher and a bookseller: the publisher extended his confidence to the bookseller by agreeing to supply books up to a certain value, while the bookseller committed himself to honor his notes in payment for them. The granting of confidence was similar to the extension of credit in business practices today. However, it involved much more. Credit-rating agencies did not exist in the eighteenth century, and there was little public information about the finances of firms. Before entrusting a shipment to an unknown bookseller, especially one located far away, a publisher needed to find out a great deal about him—another task performed through the daily correspondence.

The STN usually requested information from a merchant or a shipping agent who had inside knowledge about the potential customer's standing in the trade and in his local community. For example, after receiving a request for a shipment from Bruno-Ignace Sorret, a bookseller in Apt whom it did not know, the STN requested its agent in Lyon to investigate. It explained that Sorret had asked for "our confidence" and that his trade promised to be lucrative. "But we do not want to commit ourselves without assurances. That is why we are asking you to get the necessary information about his solvability and also about his moral character, up to what sum one can extend confidence to him, and whether he is loyal with his correspondents."[68] The agent replied that Sorret was unknown in Lyon and that he would seek information from others closer to Apt. He came up with nothing, and therefore, despite the temptation of a profitable sale, the STN refused to trade with Sorret.

This letter and dozens like it indicate the factors involved in extending confidence: the desire for profit, certainly, and for assurance about financial solidity, but also a concern for a customer's character and moral values. The STN instructed its sales rep, Jean-François Favarger, to gather information about the booksellers he encountered on his tour de France in 1778, and he responded with reports on their reputation and private lives as well as their history of paying bills on time.[69] If its customers failed to honor notes when they became due, the STN threatened to cease doing business with the booksellers. Then, if they caught up with their payments, it wrote that it had restored its confidence, usually up to a specific amount of money.[70] It, too, received requests for reports on its acquaintances among merchants, because the mutual need for information extended everywhere and to all sorts of trades.[71] As a result, letters of recommendation, negative and positive, occupied a large place in the STN's correspondence.

Most evaluations amounted to little more than a phrase or two, but some were character sketches, or "portraits," as the genre was known in literature. Massieu de Clerval, a friend of Ostervald's in Caen, offered to help the STN see through "Norman ruses" by portraiture with a psychological component. He reported that Le Roi, the town's principal bookseller, was "solid" but "worried, slow in making decisions, reluctant to commit himself to a transaction unless he is certain that it will provide him with a foolproof profit. He is a sharp character." And he transcribed a report from a contact in Falaise on a local bookseller named Gaillard, which reads like a mini-biography, relating whom he married, how much property she brought to the business, and his reputation among local booksellers ("they can't stand him").[72] The STN received an even more detailed report on Caldesaigues, a bookseller in Marseille; and when it began to deal with Panckoucke, it asked its Parisian banker, Jean-Frédéric Perregaux, to provide a full-scale report. He assigned two informants to the case, promising to provide information not only about Panckoucke's "faculties" or wealth but also about his "heart."[73]

Taken together, the reports reveal the qualities most desired in a bookseller worthy of confidence. He should be well off, but wealth in itself did not matter as much as personal integrity—and "heart." A military officer in Bar-le-duc sent a favorable report about Choppin, a local bookseller: good conduct, good reputation, a wife from a good family, not rich, to be sure, yet "it is not in wealth that honor consists."[74] A banker in Geneva recommended a local bookseller even though he had little capital, because "his conduct is good and he is very active in his affairs."[75] The components of "good conduct" stood out in a recommendation for a bookseller from a shipping agent in Dijon: he always acquitted his bills of exchange; he did not overextend himself; and "he resides in his own house, has funds, is known locally to be honorable, is sensible, prudent, and loves to work."[76] When the STN decided to extend its trade in Lorraine, it asked for information about the province's booksellers from several of its correspondents. C. C. Duvez, a merchant in Nancy, contacted informants of his own and sent off a series of short, blunt assessments: "Doesn't have a very solid reputation." "Never was well behaved." "A young man of good conduct."

These reports were confirmed by the STN's other correspondents.[77] Although based on information furnished by individual contacts, the reports expressed a general consensus. In cities like Nancy, Lunéville, and Metz, merchants and shopkeepers all knew one another. Word traveled when one of them failed to honor a promissory note or spent too much time in taverns. A good reputation had to be won, and it tended to stick, as in the case of Marie Audéart of Lunéville, who enjoyed general esteem even after she suspended her payments following a disastrous fire: "As to her conduct and probity, she seems to be irreproachable and has public opinion ["la voix publique"] on her side."[78] Far from being idiosyncratic and particular, therefore, the reports represented a collective judgment and a common set of values. After studying dozens of them, it is possible to distingush an ideal type. Publishers sought clients known for "solidity" (that is, a strong financial base and a record of paying bills on time), "conduct" (orderly behavior, especially hard work), and *honnêteté* (trustworthiness and integrity).[79] These qualities stood at one end of a spectrum of values shared by publishers—and probably by merchants in all other trades. At the opposite end were the vices that made business so difficult: duplicity, cheating, and treachery. Success in business depended on reading character well enough to place confidence where it would be rewarded.

That may sound simple or self-evident. In fact, publishers' strategies were complex, especially in their relations among one another. No publishing house could pursue a line of business without crossing lines with other houses. As illustrated by the STN's correspondence with Gosse and by the activities of the Swiss Confederation, publishers consulted one another, concerted plans, and formed alliances.

What especially bound them together was the exchange trade, which as we've seen provided a way for a publisher to market a large portion of an edition without incurring risks and gave him an opportunity to diversify his stock as a wholesaler without spending capital.[80] In fact, the exchange trade was fundamental to most publishing businesses, not just among the pirates. Skill in swapping books was nearly as important as expertise in selecting what books to print, for a publisher needed to know what titles to choose from another publisher's stock and how to spot a bargain.[81] If well enough informed by his correspondents, he could acquire a work in a swap and sell it for cash at a large profit.[82] Publishers frequently spent as much time in negotiating exchanges as they did in cultivating authors and in marketing. Yet the exchange trade rarely figures in studies of book history, and it deserves careful consideration, for it was a key element in developing a business strategy, and it went to the heart of publishers' efforts to defend themselves against duplicity while placing confidence in a profitable manner.

Swapping books opened up great possibilities for cheating. One party in a transaction often hid the works in his stock that he thought sold best. If he offered to make a bestseller available, he could pretend that he had exhausted his holdings of it before the deal had been completed so that he could continue to sell it himself. He also could agree on an exchange and then delay his shipment, so that he could market the books he received before his own books could be put on sale by the other party.[83] As pirate publishers often supplied the same books to the same markets, the difference of a few days could be crucial in sales. Above all, there were endless possibilities of profiting from disparities in the value of the books—not just in their selling power but in their physical qualities. In exchanges done "in the Liège way,"[84] the parties swapped sheets for sheets and kept *comptes d'échanges* in their account books calculated in sheets. An octavo volume printed on mediocre paper from the Franche-Comté and set in pica type with plenty of space between the words and spacious interlining cost much less to manufacture than an octavo with superior paper from Auvergne printed in small pica densely set. Therefore, a swap between the two was inherently unequal.

Because, as noted earlier, paper represented such a high portion of manufacturing costs, variations in the size and quality of paper mattered a great deal in exchanges.[85] Swapping accounts were often kept in "small" and "large" sheets. When they were settled, usually at the end of the year, the totals were converted into *petites feuilles* (standard small sheets) at a ratio that also was a matter of negotiation: two large sheets often counted as three small ones. Once the balance in the two accounts had been determined, the party with the surplus sheets paid off their value in notes that would become due in three, six, or twelve months—another provision that required bargaining and raised the possibility of bad faith, for unreliable swapping partners failed to honor their notes on time or found pretexts for demanding discounts: sheets were missing or misprinted or damaged by friction against the ropes during shipment—a "bad debtor" invented plenty of reasons to avoid paying in cash. These uncertainties also beset exchanges calculated according to the wholesale price of the books. The STN and some other publishers set a standard price of 1 sou per sheet, but it traded its books against books whose price had been set by publishers according to the books' potential market value, no matter how many sheets they contained. Swapping by price opened up more possibilities of disagreement than swapping by sheets, and it generally did not work out as well.[86]

Although the STN developed exchanges with a few publishers located faraway, especially in Avignon, Maastricht, Brussels, and Lyon, it did most of its swapping with fellow publishers in Switzerland. Transportation costs made it uneconomical to exchange sheets with houses in Amsterdam or Liège,[87] whereas exchanges with Swiss houses belonged to the general strategy of network building, especially during the second half of the century, when Switzerland surpassed Holland in the production of French books.[88] Cheap transport everywhere in western Switzerland made swapping inexpensive.

Equally important, contacts among relatives, friends, and business associates meant that the Swiss had an intimate knowledge of one another's affairs. They acquired information about the private lives as well as the bottom lines that determined the fate of businesses. Of course, they competed with one another and sometimes quarreled, but common interests often outweighed commercial rivalry, and they swapped books so intensively that their stock contained a great many of the same works. Their catalogues were remarkably similar—and often enormous: the catalogue of the Lausannois publisher Jules-Henri Pott ran to 128 pages in 1772. Some booksellers ordered the same book from several Swiss suppliers in order to spread out the risk of confiscations and delays. Allied publishers coordinated production so closely that they occasionally announced one another's works in their catalogues before the books had been printed. The fusion of stock and the coordination of marketing reached an extreme in the case of the Confederation, yet alliances existed everywhere, undergirded by the exchange trade.

Two examples, the STN's relations with François Grasset in Lausanne and with Jean-Edmé Dufour in Maastricht, illustrate the way alliances were formed, a gradual process of overcoming obstacles and solidifying confidence. Like his younger brother, Gabriel, Grasset served as a clerk in the Cramer house in Geneva.[89] In 1766, with the backing of some anonymous "associates," he established his own printing and bookselling business in Lausanne. His first exchanges with the STN turned out to be mutually advantageous, according to the principle, as Grasset put it, that "one hand washes the other."[90] At their initial settlement of accounts in July 1772, Grasset corrected an error to the STN's prejudice of 500 sheets. By January 1773, he had furnished the STN with 32,362½ sheets, and they continued swapping, with only occasional complaints, until 1786.[91]

As the bales shuttled back and forth between Neuchâtel and Lausanne, the confidence between the two houses grew. They kept each other informed about works they planned to pirate and sent tips about what was being pirated by their competitors. Each house placed advance orders with the other, often for 100 copies, sometimes for 500, keeping tally in the *comptes d'échanges*. When Grasset's presses were too busy for him to pirate Cornelius de Pauw's *Recherches philosophiques sur les Américains*, he suggested the STN produce it and committed himself to a swap of 100 copies. When the STN completed an edition of the Bible, it ran off 200 copies with Grasset's name and address on a falsified title page so that he could market it as if it were his own. They came to define their alliance as "houses linked by friendship." The mutual trust continued until Grasset's death in August 1789, when the STN sent a letter to his successors at François Grasset et Compagnie, expressing sorrow for the loss of "our dear old friend, M. François Grasset, whom we will miss forever."

The STN's exchanges with Dufour hit bumps at several points, because each side held back some of its bestselling books—a restriction known as a *réserve*—instead of making everything available. But after Bosset's visit in September 1779, they got on very well. They signed an agreement in August 1781 to expand their exchanges and abandon all *réserves*. They notified each other about the books they planned to pirate, sent advice about publishing possibilities and even considered collaborating on joint editions. The swapping continued without problems until 1788, when the STN had ceased most of its publishing operations. By then, the two houses had exchanged many thousands of sheets, and they, too, had become *amis*.

The word *ami* had special resonance in the publishing industry.[92] Aside from expressing a close personal relationship, it could be applied to the firms themselves. As Grasset put it, his enterprise and the STN were *maisons amies*. Friendship of this sort represented the ultimate extension of confidence. At the opposite extreme in the language of book professionals was *méfiance* (distrust), a term that excluded the possibility of commercial relations.[93] The STN's relations with Jean-Louis de Boubers of Brussels provides an example of confidence gone sour in this way.

As recounted in Chapter 3, Boubers collaborated in the STN's edition of *Système de la nature*. That speculation led to several years of exchanges, and the exchanges ended in a quarrel. When the STN protested about the quality of the books Boubers was willing to swap, he retorted, "I give you my works, which are pure gold, against your *drogues*, which will sit in the warehouse for a long time." And after falling behind in his account by 21,866½ sheets, he replied to the STN's protests, which insisted on its own straightforwardness, with insults: "It seems from your letters that you are the only honest people in the world." "I couldn't care less whether you are upstanding or not."[94] The STN never recovered the unpaid balance in sheets, because Boubers went bankrupt in 1783 for the staggering sum of 300,000 L. and fled from Brussels just in time to avoid arrest.[95]

Although Boubers's collapse was particularly dramatic, it illustrated a general trend. Bankruptcies were occurring everywhere in the book trade. Markets had already begun to clog in the mid-1770s, and by 1783 the new *sociétés typographiques* were turning out more books, and more of the same books, than the market could absorb. To a veteran publisher-bookseller like Machuel in Rouen, the trend pointed toward disaster. "As few persons can be thoroughly known in this century of ours," he wrote, "I have lost more than 50 percent in various bankruptcies—and that after 20 years of correspondence. . . . Men have changed so much over the last ten years and commerce is conducted in such different ways that one doesn't know what to make of it all."[96] Increasingly exposed to a deteriorating market, the STN often extended its confidence imprudently—to marginal bookdealers, untrustworthy peddlers, and individuals who speculated on the trade outside the law. Its correspondents warned it about taking risks with unreliable customers.[97] But it had accumulated so much debt that it could not escape the pressure to expand its sales. Nor did it recognize the extent of its exposure. Instead of modifying its business plan, it cursed the general run of booksellers. They were "a devious race," "a perverted race," everywhere, but especially in France: "Booksellers in France have no principles and no faith. They don't even know how to distinguish between what is honest and what is not."[98] The ties of confidence that had bound the network of the STN no longer held. It, too, went bankrupt at the end of 1783.

The STN's bankruptcy, to be examined later, involved factors peculiar to its own history. But it also illustrates the flaws in the confidence games at the heart of pirate publishing. The pirates struggled to build up networks that would resist the fissiparous forces of their trade. By cultivating correspondents everywhere in the world of books, they gathered information—about the supply and demand of literature, about political and economic conditions, about where to place their confidence as well as their capital. Care with correspondence could help a pirate avoid the traps set by confidence men, yet it could not prevail against the underlying forces of the trade. As the final chapter of this book will show, those forces spread disaster through much of the Fertile Crescent. The point to be emphasized here is the sapping of the spirit that drove the pirate publishers. As businesses went under, the pirates lost their drive, and they also lost illusions. Piracy at the end of the Ancien Régime had filled the marketplace with cut-rate books, yet it foundered in a world that was Balzacian before Balzac.

10

Our Man in Paris

PIRACY WAS ABOVE ALL a race to the market. To get there first, a pirate had to know what books had just appeared in print and which ones were selling best. He also had to keep up with trends in the literary world as a whole. All this information came from Paris, the center of that world. Publishers at a far remove from Paris therefore hired agents to feed them information and also to handle whatever odd jobs that might arise, for there were always bills to be collected, shipments to be rescued, and government officials to be cultivated. There were even authors to be contacted, for pirates sometimes published original works—if they could purchase a manuscript on good terms, that is.

As explained in Chapter 7, these functions were so important that the contract for the Confederation of Swiss publishers had a provision for a Parisian agent to be supported by all three members. The STN's own agent, known as its *homme de confiance*, was a crucial link in its web of correspondents. It tried for years to find the right man, considering one candidate after another, because the job required a rare combination of skills and connections. Occasionally it hired someone who could write reports that provided a running commentary on the marketplace for books and that even read like literary essays. While it held out, the information was invaluable, but something always went wrong.

One of the first Parisians that the STN tried to recruit as an agent was François de Rozier, an agronomist and member of the Académie des sciences.[1] As editor of the *Journal de physique*, he was happy to help the STN win subscribers for its *Journal helvétique*, which it was expanding under a new editor, Henri-David de Chaillet, and trying to market in France. But de Rozier did not want to take on less savory tasks, such as bribing pressmen to swipe sheets of the books they were printing so that the STN could beat its competitors to the market. In fact, he admitted, he did not follow literary affairs closely enough to recommend works for pirating. Therefore, he suggested that it hire one of his friends, the playwright Harny de Guerville, who then sent a letter proposing that he concentrate on three main functions: buy the best new works and send copies to Neuchâtel; assess each copy with a critique; and supply manuscript verse and other ephemera for publication in the *Journal helvétique*. Harny also offered to collect subscriptions for the *Journal helvétique* and to provide other services, all for 600 L. a year.

Ostervald refused the offer, probably because he found it too expensive, and tried to find recruits among the Parisian authors who sent articles for publication in the *Journal helvétique*. One, Daudet de Jossan, seemed to expect a more modest retainer and to be as well connected as Harny.[2] In fact, he claimed he could meet with Rousseau and seek his support for the STN. Ostervald encouraged Daudet to pursue that possibility, but Rousseau refused to see him. "He does not want to hear anything about literature. He does not want to have anything to do with the gentlemen of Neuchâtel," Daudet reported. While corresponding about the *Journal helvétique* and sending the occasional *nouveauté* to pirate, Daudet gradually assumed the role of a literary advisor. He urged the STN to reprint the most radical works of the Enlightenment, such as *Système de la nature*, and even to publish original manuscripts of the kind favored by Marc-Michel Rey in Amsterdam. "Look at his immense fortune. *Le Despotisme oriental* brought in more than 10,000 L. for him, and I know that he paid 50 louis [1,200 L.] for it." Although Daudet also recommended some moderate works, he favored those that caused the most scandal. There was nothing like a good book burning to promote sales, he emphasized.[3] As we've seen, however, the STN did not want to specialize in *livres philosophiques*, and Daudet's taste was too extreme for it to hire him as an agent.

Another contributor to the *Journal helvétique*, M.-A. Laus de Boissy, aspired to become the STN's "literary correspondent" in 1780. He, too, held strong views in favor of Enlightenment literature. The pious tone of the *Journal helvétique* (Chaillet was a sharp critic but a good Protestant) made it seem provincial in Paris, he wrote. "It's a great thing to believe in God, especially in Switzerland, but that doesn't make for much amusement; and your journal can only succeed if it acquires a philosophical tinge." Although he promised to recruit authors for the STN to publish, he lacked the temperament and the experience of the book trade required of a literary scout. The STN then tried out the services of Laus's secretary, an obscure writer named Thiriot. He offered to collect subscriptions for the *Journal helvétique*, sent a few books for the STN to pirate, made a brief attempt to help with its smuggling operations, and ran various errands. He shied away from anything that would get him into trouble with the police, however, and he did not have an insider's knowledge of the book trade. Ostervald thought he had found a better-qualified candidate in Vallat la Chapelle, a veteran *bouquiniste*. But after receiving a letter of inquiry from the STN, Vallat turned it over to the police, evidently as a way to win their favor for his business.[4] A bookseller named Monory provided better service for a few months in 1784. Aside from sending information about the latest publications, he had useful contacts with authors, notably abbé André Morellet and Condorcet. Yet he, too, failed to help the STN crack the Paris market. The only agent who measured up to its expectations was a highly literate and enterprising tradesman named Nicolas-Guillaume Quandet de Lachenal.

Quandet belonged to the species of *commissionnaires* who in principle received and forwarded goods for merchant houses and in practice handled any tasks that required a trusted emissary.[5] Seeking someone to smuggle books into Paris from deposits stored outside the city walls, the STN contacted him in October 1780 on the recommendation of an abbé named Le Senne. Le Senne was a protégé of Jean le Rond d'Alembert and a hack writer devoted to the cause of the *philosophes*.[6] Because Ostervald was negotiating with d'Alembert to publish his works, d'Alembert's support of Le Senne carried weight, and Le Senne's endorsement of Quandet promised to open a way into the Parisian market. In reply to Ostervald's query, Quandet explained in a letter of October 6 that he looked after shipments at a charge of 5 to 6½ percent of their value and that he had various channels for getting books into Paris. He also could act as a middleman in marketing the books to Parisian retailers. If the STN wanted to publish original works, he could steer them through the censorship. And he could keep it informed about all new publications in any genre of interest to it.

Ostervald then sent Quandet the STN's latest catalogue and asked him to select the works he thought would sell best in Paris. The STN could ship them to Versailles, where it had an agent who stored books in a clandestine entrepôt (the château had so many nooks and crannies that it operated as a warehouse for underground booksellers, who also found that courtiers were excellent customers). Quandet's job would be to get the shipment into the shops of Parisian booksellers who had placed orders with the STN. Although it had never been able to slip many of its *contrefaçons* past customs officials, the Guild, and the police, it was making a new effort to gain access to the Parisian market.

Quandet replied that he was the man for the job. He sent back a list of fifty titles from the catalogue, accompanying each title with his assessment of its sales potential. He did not mention those that he thought would not sell well, and he scored the most promising according to a graduated scale: "fairly good" (*De l'homme et de la femme dans le mariage*); "good" (*Anecdotes sur Mme la comtesse du Barry; Collection complète des oeuvres de J.-J. Rousseau*), and "excellent" (*Oeuvres de M. de Voltaire*).

Quandet assured Ostervald that he had a storage facility of his own near the city walls. Until they put together a large-scale arrangement for smuggling, he could get small quantities of books past the customs agents by hiding them in his clothing and pretending that he had taken a walk in the countryside. He made no claim to be a savant himself, he wrote, but he loved literature—and he was frank about his preferences. He abhorred religious fanaticism and admired the works of the *philosophes*: "I am one of their supporters," he wrote, "and as such I do everything I can to make their work appreciated and to make sure it sells."

Ostervald agreed to send a trial shipment with the works Quandet had recommended and, impressed with his knowledge of contemporary literature, asked him to help with the STN's pirating. A first step would be to procure a copy of Cook's *Voyage au pôle austral et autour du monde*, which soon would be published by Panckoucke. Quandet sent the book and devoted his next letters to prospects for smuggling. He knew a merchant in Orléans who could ship books directly to Paris by hiding them inside barrels of sugar. Another of his contacts, a dealer in spices from Saint Denis, could guarantee delivery to Quandet's premises inside Paris but at a steep price: 25 L. per hundredweight. There were other possibilities, and Quandet could provide other services. He had many ideas about how to open the French market to the *Journal helvétique*, but, he warned, there were obstacles to overcome. He would have to get authorization from the Keeper of the Seals—no great difficulty, as Quandet had a well-placed friend in the chancellery. Protection from the police would be crucial, and he knew where to plant a bribe. Most important of all, they had to win the agreement of the *Journal des savants*, which had an exclusive *privilège* for certain kinds of periodicals and used it to exact tribute from foreign journals. Quandet was confident that he could handle the necessary lobbying, but he did not dare collect subscriptions for an unauthorized journal. That was a sure way to join the ranks of those "who have to fear every day that they may wake up in the Bastille after having gone to sleep earlier in their beds." He clearly knew his way around the book trade.

Seduced by the flair of Quandet's letters, Ostervald began to write to him more frequently and to request more services. Could Quandet collect payment for a debt from a certain Cugnet, who peddled books from a boutique in the Louvre? (At that time the Louvre's Cour carrée was honeycombed with buildings, and Cugnet's address was "under the portal of the Cul-de-sac du coq entering from the rue Saint Honoré.") Certainly, came the answer. In fact, Quandet could set up an assortment of his own and sell the STN's works on commission. That was going too far for Ostervald, who had often lost money by confiding shipments to unknown dealers who then failed to pay their bills. Therefore, he suggested that Quandet have a meeting with Jean-Frédéric Perregaux, the STN's banker in Paris—in effect, that is, to be interviewed about his reliability and credit. Quandet wrote that he was happy to oblige, although somehow the interview with Perregaux, a wealthy financier from Neuchâtel who would be a founder of the Banque de France in 1800, never took place—nor did a similar appointment with Laus de Boissy, whose judgment Ostervald trusted.

While leaving unanswered the question of his own resources, Quandet assured Ostervald that he was on the trail of Cugnet, and he reported that Le Senne had some manuscripts for sale. "Persecuted by the clergy," the abbé had had to flee from Paris and needed money. But Ostervald wanted to pirate new books, not to publish libertine tracts of the kind that had circulated in manuscript since the beginning of the century. Ignoring the offer of manuscripts, he asked Quandet to send off posthaste two sentimental novels that had just appeared and were strong candidates for pirating: *Mémoires de Fanny Spingler* and *Les Annales de la vertu*. He also observed that he had taken up correspondence with Quandet by happenstance, on the basis of a casual remark in a letter from Le Senne. Therefore, he asked again for "some security that would justify the degree of confidence that we very much want to give to you." The STN had been duped by marginal dealers like Cugnet. It needed information about Quandet's finances. If Perregaux was not available, he could meet with Batilliot, a banker who specialized in the affairs of the book trade.

Back came an indignant letter. By seeking his advice and then sending the shipment, Quandet protested, the STN had already committed its confidence. Of course, he could understand the need for caution, because he himself had been burned—a loss of 40,000 L. from one of his many correspondents, who extended to Spain, Portugal, Denmark, and Russia. But he would not stoop to deal with someone like Batilliot, who was notorious for mistreating booksellers and would use an interview to blacken Quandet's good name and to replace him as the STN's *homme de confiance*. As to the function of collecting subscriptions for the *Journal helvétique*, he would gladly give it up and leave it to another of the STN's contacts in Paris—someone like Thiriot, a fine person, no doubt, though merely a private tutor, despite the fact that he claimed to be the secretary of an important magistrate. If the STN insisted on contacting someone about his qualifications, it could get in touch with the abbé de Villars, a grand vicar in the colonial service who employed Quandet to ship books to Canada, or Prudhomme, an eminent lawyer in the Parlement for whom Quandet had arranged the printing of his *Traité des droits des seigneurs*, or Le Tessier, a wealthy merchant in Nîmes, who had recently entrusted Quandet with a shipment of a thousand pounds of olives. Quandet mentioned his connections only because the STN's queries had offended him. Claiming to have some Swiss relatives, he replied to its letter with "a Helvetic frankness in which I take great pride."

As blarney went, this was a tour de force. Quandet had avoided an inquiry into his finances, gotten across the impression that he did business on a large scale, and discredited his rivals for handling the STN's trade. Moreover, it worked. Ostervald sent back an apologetic letter, explaining that it was "the accepted rule in commerce" to make inquiries before entrusting money, such as the fees for subscribing to the *Journal helvétique*, to an unknown intermediary. He dropped the demand for an interview, and assured Quandet that the STN's confidence would grow as he acquitted himself of further assignments.

These became more ambitious. Ostervald asked for information about the government's policies on the book trade, which, now three years after the edicts of 1777, still seemed uncertain. He wanted a confidential assessment of Pancoucke's business, and he deputized Quandet on a mission to locate one of the STN's most devious debtors, Louis Valentin de Goezman, who had commissioned it to print a book and then disappeared, leaving a debt of 1,500 L. After explaining the background to this affair (discussed in more detail in the following chapter), Ostervald assigned Quandet to the case: "Unearth M. Goezman."[7] Quandet hunted his man all over Paris, following leads that he picked up here and there: Faubourg du Temple, Faubourg Saint Martin, Faubourg Saint Denis, and finally, after a tip from a grocer in the rue des Petites écuries, a residential building near the Café de Malte. Quandet located the building, entered it, climbed a stairway to the second floor, rang a bell, and was led by a servant to the apartment of Mme Goezman, who informed him that her husband was out of town on business. Quandet poured on the charm, while Mme Goezman, warming to the subject, recounted the hardships she had endured over the past years without revealing anything that would make it possible to locate her husband. "We parted the best of all possible friends," Quandet concluded in his report, which he wrote in dialogue as if it were a scene in a play. They would stay in touch. She would write to her husband. He was never cornered.

While continuing the unsuccessful search for Goezman, Quandet busied himself with other tasks. He cultivated the secretary of the Keeper of the Seals and some employees in the office of the *Journal des savants* in the hope of clearing passage into France for the *Journal helvétique*. His hustling, as he described it, had brought down the price demanded by the *Journal des savants* to 200 L. a year (the asking price, he claimed, had been 600 L.), and he could overcome the other obstacles by well-placed bribes. Having circulated copies of the prospectus for the *Journal helvétique* among his friends in "high society" (*le grand monde*), he felt optimistic about its chances of success. By way of literary news, he reported that the bestselling works at that time, December 1780, were Raynal's *Histoire philosophique* and *Recherches philosophiques sur les Américains* by Cornelius de Pauw. He recommended a book to pirate, *Vie de Jean Bart,* and confirmed Ostervald's assessment that *Annales de la vertu* is "in great favor [*en fort bonne odeur*] in these parts." Although the demand for Voltaire's works remained strong, there was no rush to buy subscriptions to Beaumarchais's edition.

By fast footwork in the alleyways of the Louvre, Quandet had managed to track down Cugnet, who turned out to be a former cantor in a church. He currently was trying to get a place in the Opera, where he and his wife had sent their daughter "to perfect her education"—that is, to sell herself to the highest bidder. Other bouquinistes in the Louvre reported that Cugnet kept 500–600 L.'s worth of books in his stall, but that it was rarely open because he could not pay the rent and did not want to expose himself to his creditors. These activities required a great deal of tramping through the streets, waiting in antechambers, and cultivating secretaries and clerks. Quandet was pleased to promote the STN's interest, and now that he had won its confidence, would trust it to set his wages.

Ostervald replied that the STN would reward Quandet with one free subscription to the *Journal helvétique* for every five that he collected—hardly princely pay, but the beginning of a job that promised to expand. In his next reports, Quandet reversed his assessment of Le Senne and Cugnet. As to the former, he was a scoundrel, "known here as a man lacking in probity and with scandalous morals." Cugnet, on the other hand, had returned with his wife to his boutique. Quandet had called on them and found that they had fairly good credit, and were on good terms with the police, well connected, and enterprising. Cugnet looked imposing—broad-shouldered, six feet tall. His wife, "with blue eyes of the kind that Mohammed promises in paradise," was even cleverer than he. And their bookstall had promise. "The inventory of the boutique, which I did in the wink of an eye," Quandet wrote, "indicated to me that they have resources." They explained that they had bought a shipment of books from Le Senne, who had ordered them from the STN. For payment, they had given Le Senne three bills of exchange. He had sent two of them to the STN and kept the third, worth 202 L., for himself, hoping to cash it when it became due. Armed with this information, Ostervald told Quandet to head off the payment of the third note by intervening with the payer on whom it was drawn.

Quandet continued to acquit himself well. Having chatted up the secretary of Le Camus de Néville, the directeur de la librairie, he had arranged for the release of a bale of books from the STN that had been confiscated by the Parisian authorities. His most influential contact was the chief steward of the Spanish ambassador. The steward would help set up a clandestine stock room in Versailles, which would serve as a relay station for shipments to Paris. Quandet was about to go to Versailles to settle the financial details. And he had already established a depot for the bales in Paris "a place where no one, as well-connected as he may be, can stick his nose without my order." A third contact, the secretary to the Keeper of the Seals, had informed him that the government did not plan to modify its policy on repressing the trade in contrefaçons, as called for by the edicts of 1777. From another source Quandet received a tip that the government had recently dispatched spies along shipping routes to help with the confiscation of forbidden books: the STN should be on its guard. He had sent several works for the STN to pirate, including a travel book that Ostervald had requested. The reports on all these services came seasoned with bits of literary gossip.

The editorial aspect of Quandet's role became more significant after February 1781, when the STN authorized him to negotiate with authors over the publication of original books. Although they remained committed to pirating as the mainstay of their business, Ostervald and Bosset had, as noted earlier, looked into the possibility of purchasing manuscripts and of persuading authors to commission printing during the trip to Paris they had made in the spring of 1780. Ostervald instructed Quandet to follow up on the earlier *pourparlers*, stressing four points: that the STN produced books in a "country that enjoys liberty, though not licence"; that it could print them more cheaply than Parisian printers; that the quality of its work equaled that of the Parisians; and that it was run by men of letters, who could correct manuscripts and give them the care they deserved.[8]

Ostervald was especially eager to reach an agreement with one author, Jean-François Marmontel. The STN had sold large numbers of his *Contes moraux* and *Les Incas*. An edition of his collected works could be a lucrative enterprise, Ostervald wrote, and it could be marketed legally in France if the STN purchased the *privilège* held by the author. That, however, looked difficult, "because of the high price that the author puts on his scribbling." Ostervald calculated that the STN could not turn a profit unless it sold at least 3,000 copies. He thought that the STN could count on 2,000 sales in the provinces and directed Quandet to see whether an eminent Parisian bookseller such as Claude Saugrain would place an advance order for 1,000. Quandet made the rounds of the bookshops, spreading a prospectus drafted by Marmontel himself and exhausting his most eloquent sales talk: how Marmontel belonged to the inner circle of the *philosophes*; how he was permanent secretary of the Académie française; how his *Poétique* alone would bring in plenty of revenue, because it would be snapped up in all the colleges. Saugrain still would not bite. The other booksellers, who had no love for Swiss publishers, also refused to negotiate, even when Quandet offered them a monopoly of sales in greater Paris, and the project was dropped.

The best prospect among other authors was Raynal, as the first editions of his *Histoire philosophique* had caused a great stir, and the whole book trade was waiting anxiously for an expanded and even more audacious edition. Ostervald reported a rumor in a letter of March 25, 1781, that it had already been printed in Geneva and banned in France, "because the author, who claims to write in a frank manner, has put some noses out of joint—not in relation to God and the saints, about whom no one cares any more, but rather in connection with politics and the English, which is somewhat delicate." Like all the other pirates, Ostervald wanted to get his hands on a copy as soon as possible. He instructed Quandet to scour Paris for information about the new edition and even to consult Raynal himself. Ostervald had met Raynal in Paris in 1780 and had extracted from him a promise to have the STN publish his next book (the one he never wrote and planned to publish under the title *Histoire philosophique et politique de l'établissement du Protestantisme en Europe*). He gave Quandet a letter to present to Raynal with a request for information about the state of the new work. In his report on their meeting, Quandet said Raynal would keep his promise but the book would be delayed because he needed to acquire more information from sources in Germany. Although an interview with a writer as famous as Raynal could be parlayed into further contacts, it led to nothing and apparently did not go well. Quandet's only comment after leaving Raynal was that authors had "a self-love that is often very irritating."

Quandet also sent a disabused report about d'Alembert, the other *philosophe* whom Ostervald had cultivated. After a preliminary discussion in Paris about the possibility of publishing his collected works, Ostervald had corresponded with him about the cost of the manuscript. He informed Quandet that d'Alembert's expectations were excessive. Although he did not know what Ostervald had offered, Quandet recommended cutting the price in half. "Aside from his miscellaneous writings," he argued, "which aren't worth the paper they are printed on, I know from the judgment of others as well as myself, that his works on geometry, which are considered to be the best he has done, are far from demonstrating the profound genius that distinguishes those of a Kepler, a Newton, etc."

Ostervald also dispatched Quandet to discuss business with Jacques-André Naigeon, Diderot's friend and fellow Encyclopedist, who had planned to come to Neuchâtel in order to arrange for the publication of his works. Nothing came of this plan, or of other projects for producing original editions. Paris was full of authors, "devoured by ambition," Quandet wrote. Yet most belonged to the lower ranks of literature, and none of them came up with a manuscript that he could recommend. Word had spread about his access to a wealthy Swiss publisher, and he found himself under siege by writers peddling manuscripts: "They are determined, I believe, to drag me with them to the poor house [*hôpital*]." Quandet showed respect for literary talent, but his exposure to Grub Street hacks led him to feel general disdain for "the scabrous occupation of authorship."

This attitude was reinforced by negotiations with Jean-Baptiste-Claude Delisle de Sales, who had gained notoriety from the condemnation of his atheistic treatise, *De la philosophie de la nature*, by the Châtelet court in 1775. Having been drawn into correspondence with Delisle, Ostervald authorized Quandet to discuss terms for a new edition of his book but warned him that Delisle would demand extravagant conditions. "You will hear him vaunt his work and tell you that it will be epoch-making." After meeting Delisle in March 1781, Quandet sent a surprisingly favorable report. But

Ostervald insisted that the STN would not purchase the manuscript unless Delisle could arrange enough advance sales to cover its costs. Delisle then sent Quandet a memo arguing against the need for such a condition, because the new, expanded edition was certain to be a bestseller. Quandet was not impressed. "That is an author's way of reasoning," he wrote Ostervald, "and the certainty of an author is very dubious." Ostervald agreed. "It's as if any ordinary author had the wherewithal to make a fortune for all printers and booksellers, whereas sometimes and indeed often it's the other way round." He wrote that he would nonetheless sound the STN's correspondents about the demand for a new edition. If it could collect 500 advance orders, the STN would be willing to buy the manuscript.

Although he understood the requirement of nailing down advance sales, Quandet worried about testing the market through the mail, which might fall into the hands of the police. "Fanaticism has powerful partisans, even at the end of the eighteenth century," he wrote. "Fed by pride and self-interest, it is always alive in the hearts of the devout." He seemed to sympathize with Delisle's radical ideas and even with Delisle himself, for he invited the author to dinner in his apartment. Ostervald had sent some Neuchâtel cheese to Quandet as a gesture of appreciation for his service. He and Delisle devoured it together and washed it down, while toasting Ostervald, with some excellent burgundy provided by an uncle of Quandet. Meanwhile, however, Ostervald was receiving nothing but negative responses from the STN's network of booksellers. *De la philosophie de la nature* had once made a splash, they wrote, but had passed out of fashion. Ostervald offered to try again by printing and circulating a prospectus, which Delisle could help draft. Delisle responded by asking that the STN expand the edition from six to seven volumes while lowering its price. He was convinced that it would create a sensation, one every bit as great as Raynal's *Histoire philosophique*. Quandet agreed—provided it was adequately persecuted. What it needed was "a good parlementary edict that ordered it to be burned." He had already made arrangements to smuggle the shipments into Paris and had sealed the deal "with some sauerkraut and a few bottles" shared with Delisle. Food and drink were crucial to Quandet's way of doing business. (He was especially partial to Neuchâtel cheese, which was being imitated, he said, by Norman cheesemakers, who had succeeded so well that only gourmets could recognize the "contrefaçon.")

By November, Quandet had detected no evidence of interest in *De la philosophie de la nature* among Parisian booksellers. When he raised this objection in his conversations with Delisle, he received only "a few replies that would satisfy no one except an author." Having circulated 1,000 prospectuses, the STN had received very few advance orders. Ostervald finally sent a message for Quandet to transmit to Delisle. Laced with fulsome compliments, it concluded with a firm refusal to print his book unless he could get it subsidized by a Parisian bookseller. "You may laugh in reading it," Ostervald confided to Quandet, "but there is no better way to get rid of him for good. Such persons get tiresome in the end. . . . Some of them should learn how to make shoes."[9]

The mutual disparagement of second-rate authors added a tone of familiarity to the correspondence and reinforced the *confidence* that Ostervald formally extended to Quandet in the spring of 1781. On March 22, Ostervald wrote to a friend in France that at last he had found "the man that we have been seeking for a long time to take charge of the details of our business in your capital."[10] On April 3 he sent Quandet a long letter that explained the STN's relations with Panckoucke, going back to the contract they had signed for a joint venture on the *Encyclopédie* in July 1776. By 1781, following many twists and turns in *Encyclopédie* ventures, the contract gave the STN a share of $\frac{5}{24}$ in Panckoucke's latest project, the *Encyclopédie méthodique*. Delays in publishing its prospectus and evasive answers to queries about its financing made Ostervald suspect foul play. He asked Quandet to find out whether the work was being abandoned, what its print run would be if it were continued, the nature of the company that was financing it, and anything else he could discover. To help with the investigation, he sent a copy of the STN's contract with Panckoucke and a power of attorney so that Quandet could represent its interests.

Close study of the contract made Quandet suspect that the speculation, the company, the whole "shady business," was "powder thrown into the eyes." Before Quandet could begin his investigation, however (and it wasn't clear how an obscure shipping agent could penetrate the machinations of France's most powerful publisher), Ostervald called the operation off. He preferred to rely on Clément Plomteux, the veteran publisher from Liège and a fellow shareholder in Panckoucke's company, who made a special trip to Paris in order to negotiate with Panckoucke and eventually bought out the STN's stake in the enterprise.[11]

Now legally authorized by the STN as "our confidential agent," Quandet wrote that he would make its business his top priority and would leave his salary up to Ostervald. In the following months, Quandet continued to carry out the assignments that arrived pell-mell in Ostervald's letters. Most involved negotiations with government officials and Parisian publishers. Some were straightforward tasks such as arranging for a reliable censor to authorize a book about Switzerland that the STN planned to market legally in France. Ostervald was worried that an unsympathetic censor might secretly sell the manuscript to a Parisian publisher, but Quandet assured him that this danger could be avoided by giving the censor thirty free copies. He had it censored and approved without difficulty.

Other assignments required diplomatic skills and lobbying. Above all, Ostervald needed to get clearance for the STN to market its most important long-term enterprise, an expanded reprint of *Description des arts et métiers* in-quarto. The original edition, sponsored by the Académie des sciences, was issued, volume by volume, from 1761 to 1788 and eventually stretched to 113 volumes in-folio, covered with a *privilège* owned by Nicolas-Léger Moutard, a powerful member of the Parisian Guild. Jean-Elie Bertrand enriched the STN's cheaper quarto edition with a great deal of new material from German, Swiss, and English sources—so much, in fact, that the STN claimed it was producing an original work, not a *contrefaçon*. Aided by the STN's other contacts in Paris and Versailles, Quandet courted everyone he could reach—in the ministry of foreign affairs as well as the Direction de la librairie—to get permission for the STN to sell its edition in France, where it had gathered sixty-five subscriptions. He even managed to get a copy presented to the Académie des sciences by the mathematician Joseph-Jérôme Lalande. Ostervald also sent Quandet to see Friedrich Melchior Grimm, Diderot's friend and the author of *Correspondance littéraire, philosophique et critique*, a private literary newsletter addressed to princes and sovereigns. Following up on a letter that Ostervald had sent to Grimm,[12] Quandet was to persuade him to ask Catherine II of Russia to accept the dedication of the STN's edition. A dedication to a royal personage could both legitimize the book and promote its sales, but Catherine did not give it her blessing. Supported by Le Camus de Néville, Moutard kept his hold on the French market, and Quandet never managed to weaken it.

Meanwhile, Quandet continued to relay information and advice about publishing possibilities. In April 1781 he wrote that the Kehl edition of Voltaire had been denounced by "our modern Tartuffes" in the Parlement of Paris, but Beaumarchais had mobilized enough protections to prevent any damage. The main difficulty was a lack of response in the campaign to sell subscriptions. As to Palissot's proposed edition—the alternative to collaboration with Beaumarchais that Ostervald was then considering—Quandet dismissed it as unfeasible. He also noted that Palissot himself commanded little respect in literary circles. Scraps of Voltaire material could still be picked up at this time, he wrote. He had been offered a collection of supposedly new manuscripts, which would fill two printed volumes, for 480 L. Although tempted, Ostervald did not pursue this possibility. He suspected that the manuscripts were merely variations on texts that had already been published. A better prospect, he wrote, would be some Turgot manuscripts that had been offered to the STN. How would they sell, in Quandet's judgment, if accompanied by Ostervald's collection of edicts from Turgot's ministry with the manuscript introduction by Voltaire? Quandet replied that the demand would be great but the danger greater, because the government was determined to repress all publications related to financial issues. Even if Turgot's ideas did not contradict its policies, the STN's book would be "most certainly proscribed and proscribed with vigor."

Finance had become a hot topic after the dismissal of Jacques Necker as director general of finances in May 1781. Instead of reforming the system of taxation, Necker had financed France's participation in the American War with a series of expensive loans. In January 1781, when his position in the government began to be undermined by political infighting, he issued his famous *Compte rendu au roi*. Although he tried to keep the distribution of the *Compte rendu* under the control of his ministry, the pirate publishers scrambled to reprint it and then to profit from the flood of pamphlets that followed in its wake. All this agitation produced plenty of work for Quandet.[13] After dashing off 1,500 copies of the *Compte rendu* at top speed, the STN prepared a collection of the pamphlets. In order to procure more copy, Ostervald directed Quandet to send everything about Necker that he could find, except for personal libels. The first that Quandet encountered was indeed a libel, which, he reported, had aroused "universal indignation," but the second, *Lettre d'un ami à M. Necker*, was said to be excellent. Although the police had seized the manuscript, it was rumored to be so favorable to Necker's policies that Necker was having it printed, adding notes of his own.

After Necker's fall on May 19, more pamphlets poured out. The most certain to sell, in Quandet's view, was *Lettre de M. le marquis de Caraccioli à M. d'Alembert* by Louis-Antoine de Caraccioli, a prolific writer and well-known wit. Quandet promised to send it along with an anonymous tract, *Observations d'un citoyen sur les opérations de M. Necker*, and he assured Ostervald that he was trying hard to get his hands on two short pamphlets with catchy titles: *Les Pourquois* and *Les Comments* (*The Whys* and *The*

Hows). The STN did not normally publish such ephemeral literature, which it deprecated as "brochures of no importance."[14] Yet it reprinted *Les Comments*, a twenty-page pamphlet, the *Lettre de M. le marquis de Caraccioli*, and the *Lettre d'un ami à M. Necker*. And Ostervald kept calling for more. Quandet, who had pro-Necker sympathies, sent a topical poem praising the *Compte rendu* that he thought deserved publication in the *Journal helvétique*. Yet he did not come up with many new brochures. Ostervald got most of his copy from various booksellers and other publishers, such as Jean-François Bassompierre of Geneva, who supplied the STN with a three-volume *Collection complète de tous les ouvrages pour et contre M. Necker*.[15]

Quandet avoided getting his fingers burned from handling the other item creating a stir in Paris during the spring of 1781—the expanded, radical new edition of Raynal's *Histoire philosophique*. Ostervald asked him to procure a copy as soon as possible, so that the STN could produce a *contrefaçon* in time to beat the other pirates to the market. "It would truly be a great coup." Few copies had penetrated Paris, Quandet replied on May 23, and they sold for as much as 75 L. The government had issued strict orders for the confiscation of every last volume. No bookseller dared place an advance order with him for an STN edition, although 400 copies from other editions had been snapped up in the previous ten days. On May 28 he sent word that the book had been condemned and burned and that Raynal had fled from France to save himself from arrest.

Although Quandet had failed to procure a copy, the STN got one from another source and planned to reprint it in duodecimo format and sell it at the low wholesale price of 15 L. Ostervald informed Quandet that he had purposely leaked this plan to another Swiss house, which was producing an edition of its own. Worried about the danger of being undersold, the other publisher (in fact he was Jean-Abram Nouffer in Geneva) offered to supply the STN with 1,000 copies as an exchange. Therefore, Ostervald wrote triumphantly, the STN would be in a strong position to cash in on the demand. Quandet welcomed this good news, yet warned that it would be difficult to sell those copies if there was any delay. Editions were being printed everywhere. One of his contacts among the marginal dealers in Paris said that he had already been offered a shipment at 18 L. per copy. By mid-July when Paris had been "flooded" with the pamphlets about Necker, Quandet feared the same thing could happen with the *Histoire philosophique*. The first shipments began to pour in by early October, none from Neuchâtel. On November 7 Quandet wrote that several bales from Geneva had been confiscated and then secretly put up for sale by the officials who had done the confiscating. He had been offered copies by police agents but declined, smelling a trap. By the end of the year when Quandet finally had some bales in stock, overproduction had ruined the market. The STN sold most of its 1,000 copies successfully, but Quandet wrote off his small share as a failure.

In the course of these activities, Quandet got to know a writer whom Ostervald had recruited to write theater reviews for the *Journal helvétique*, Alexandre-Balthasar-Laurent Grimod de La Reynière. Celebrated today as the founder of gastronomy and France's first restaurant critic, Grimod was an obscure twenty-two-year-old in 1781. He had already begun to give dinners in the family town house during the absence of his father, a wealthy tax farmer, although the son had not yet staged the extravagant feasts that later made him famous, such as the dinner designed as a funeral (he was carried to the table in a coffin) and the dinner presided over by a formally dressed pig. Quandet, a hearty eater himself, often dined with Grimod, who introduced him to several men of letters, including Louis-Sébastien Mercier. In May 1781 Quandet mentioned Mercier's plan to come to Neuchâtel in order to produce an expanded edition of the *Tableau de Paris*, which had been published anonymously in two volumes by Samuel Fauche earlier that year. The first edition had sold very well. Its short and vivid chapters about all aspects of Parisian life could be extended indefinitely, for Mercier had an endless supply of anecdotes and observations. But he had salted his text with criticism about abuses in the social order, and the French authorities had banned it, confiscating copies whenever they could get their hands on it. In fact, the *Tableau de Paris* was far less outspoken than most of the *livres philosophiques* that circulated in the underground trade. According to Quandet, Grimod persuaded Mercier to seek out Lenoir, the lieutenant general of police, and to identify himself as the book's author. Lenoir was so impressed by this forthrightness that the police tolerated the circulation of the later editions, and for his part—or so Ostervald claimed—Mercier toned down some of his criticism in the subsequent volumes.[16]

Those later volumes of course remained to be written when Mercier left for Neuchâtel in the summer of 1781. Ostervald explained the situation to Quandet in a letter of May 8. After quarreling with Ostervald and Bertrand in 1772, Fauche had set up a business of his own, including a printing shop with three or four presses. "Greedy for lucrative wares," as Ostervald put it, Fauche specialized in forbidden literature, much of it obscene. After printing the *Tableau de Paris*, he sent his associate and son-in-law, Jérémie Witel, to Paris in order to market it and to come back with Mercier, who was to prepare a new edition expanded from two to four volumes. The Parisian police had caught Witel with a catalogue of *livres philosophiques*, trying to collect orders from booksellers, and they had detained him. Given this turn of events, Mercier might be led to reconsider his choice of publisher. "If by chance you happen to see him," Ostervald wrote to Quandet, "you could insinuate—as is true—that the reputation of his printer gives off a bad smell, whereas in the same city there is an honest firm composed of men of letters who enjoy a good repute (be it said without vanity) and who would be charmed to work with him."

Quandet did not miss his cue. When he next encountered Mercier at Grimod's house, he steered the conversation to Fauche, "whose story I sketched in a few words with some little notes added here and there at the bottom of the text, all served up with some friendly reflections about M. Mercier." This sketch seemed to produce a good effect, Quandet observed, adding that "authors are like women: they are susceptible to the same tactics." Ostervald replied that he could not court Mercier openly after he arrived in Neuchâtel without arousing Fauche's suspicions, but when the occasion arose would introduce him to "the high society of our city, something that his publisher would hardly be able to pull off."

The competition to make the most from a bestselling author produced an upheaval in the book industry of Neuchâtel. Witel was released from prison; he escorted Mercier to Neuchâtel; Mercier began reworking the text; and as soon as he discussed payment for it, a quarrel broke out. Although he had invested heavily in a new font of type and paper for a gigantic edition, Fauche had not planned to pay much for the manuscript. In fact, he proposed at first to compensate Mercier with nothing more than a Swiss clock. But Mercier, one of the first French authors to live from his pen, had modern ideas about a writer's entitlement to an income from his labor. He left Fauche's workshop, taking the copy with him. At that point, Witel and Fauche's oldest son, Jonas, also quit and formed a company of their own: Fauche Fils aîné & Compagnie. They offered to buy the manuscript from Mercier for 8,400 L. As they had no presses, they made a deal with the STN, which agreed to print the book in exchange for 750 copies run off in addition to 7,500 produced for the new publishers. Those were enormous figures for eighteenth-century publishing. Book-trade professionals expected that a fortune was to be made from an expanded *Tableau de Paris*, because the first edition had sold out rapidly and booksellers were clamoring for a new one. In fact, many more editions along with a flood of *contrefaçons*, including one by Fauche père, continued to be produced for the next eight years. In order to combat the pirates, the STN produced a cheap, two-volume version of the main, four-volume edition—a defensive move that was virtually the same as self-pirating.

There might even have been imitations. Anyone could easily cobble together anecdotes about Parisian life. In September 1781 Quandet reported that a friend of his, "a man of wit, well educated, satirical, and full of gaiety," had written a *Tableau de Paris* of his own, which he planned to publish after the demand for Mercier's had died down.[17] It never did. By 1789 the *Tableau de Paris* had grown to twelve volumes—and it still makes wonderful reading today.

Quandet played no part in the feuds among the Neuchâtelois, but he participated in the distribution of the STN's editions, taking on the role of a clandestine retailer. He had no right to sell books, yet he had access to them from his smuggling operations and got help from Grimod. Grimod also needed money, because, Quandet reported, his father was wary of his extravagant habits and allotted him little more than his living expenses. When he had the use of the family carriage, Grimod aided Quandet's efforts to transfer books to Paris from an entrepôt in Versailles kept by a garrulous widow named La Noue. Like Quandet, Grimod sold some of them on the sly.[18] Difficulties set in, because Grimod père, Quandet believed, intercepted their correspondence. Then the son disappeared for several weeks, hampering Quandet's operations. And in February 1782 he and Quandet had a falling out. "Despite all his wit, he has a screw loose," Quandet concluded, "and I would not be surprised if his family had him silenced or imprisoned."[19] A few years later Grimod's father did in fact obtain a *lettre de cachet* to have him confined for two years in a monastery near Nancy.

By September 1781, the theme of bookselling occupied an increasingly important part of Quandet's letters. He fell in with a *bouquiniste* in the Louvre named Samson, who, he assured Ostervald, was far more clever and dependable than Cugnet: "I am courting him," Quandet wrote, "so that I can operate as his supplier and split the profit." But the undercover trade was complicated. Samson, who operated without any legal authorization, drew many supplies from Robert-André Hardouin, a member of the Guild, and both of them depended on shipments from the clandestine storerooms of Versailles. Quandet and Samson agreed to split 500 copies of the new edition of the *Tableau de Paris* to be furnished by the STN, yet Hardouin had contracted to purchase 2,000 from Fauche Fils aîné & Compagnie, who had given him an exclusive right to market the book in Paris. The STN had also committed 500 copies to Poinçot, a bookseller in Versailles who had good connections with the Paris police. (As mentioned, he probably served as a police spy.)[20] The supply lines from Versailles were crucial for the Paris trade.

Although Widow La Noue stored and forwarded many shipments for the STN, she turned out to be incompetent. On one of his missions to Versailles, Quandet persuaded her to let him search through her warehouse inside the château for a missing shipment of Necker material. He looked everywhere, and then climbed into a hayloft above her establishment, and there he found a bale of STN books that had been left unclaimed for eighteen months. When the first shipments of the new *Tableau de Paris* arrived in February 1782, Widow La Noue failed to forward them as rapidly as Poinçot, and Quandet received his allotment after Hardouin began selling his. Then cheap pirated editions began arriving from at least five publishers scattered from Maastricht to Lausanne. The competition and crossed lines drove Quandet to despair. By the end of May, he said Paris had been flooded with 40,000 copies. He and Samson had been able to sell only 180 of their stock, in part because Cugnet had undercut them by peddling a cheap *contrefaçon* from Caen.[21]

Having evolved from *commissionnaire* to literary agent, Quandet effectively had become an underground bookseller. He combined all three functions in his dealings with the STN, and he now adopted a more businesslike tone in his letters. He provided services for other Swiss houses, he had written in June, although his first loyalty would always be to the STN. He kept an account of his activities but would not charge a fee for most of them, his ambition being only to acquire "an honest mediocrity." Although Quandet's letters do not describe his circumstances in detail, they indicate that he lived in a modest apartment, rue de Bourbon près des Théatins, with a woman presumed to be his wife. He might have had children but did not mention them. In December 1781, he wrote that he was still trying his best to get permission for the *Journal helvétique* to circulate in France. In January 1782 he sent a bill listing his services for the previous year and leaving a blank space for Ostervald to insert whatever fee he deemed appropriate to cover "my accounts, missions, services, and incidental expenses." But by then he owed 3,000 L. to the STN for the books he had ordered, and it had written two notes on him to cover those shipments. While acknowledging his debt, Quandet asked for an extension of the due dates on the notes and a deduction of one free copy for every thirteen he had ordered. They patched up the disagreement about his account in April. Quandet then ordered more shipments and went so far as to rent his own storage place in Versailles for 110 L. a year.

Clandestine bookselling drew Quandet into selling the most illegal varieties of clandestine books. He wrote that he was horrified by the circulation of *La Vie d'Antoinette*, a libel about the queen, which was republished in late 1781 under another title, *Supplément à l'Espion anglais*, but he requested other libels such as *Vie privée de Louis XV*. Everything in that genre sold well, he assured Ostervald.[22] He recommended that the STN reprint *L'Espion anglais*, which, he wrote, was "too delicious a morsel for you not to devote all possible attention to it." The STN need only change the date on the title page from 1779 to 1781, and he could easily dispose of 100, perhaps 200 copies.

Pamphlets about current events also sold well. Quandet urged Ostervald to publish an illegal tract about the expedition of the comte d'Estaing and the American War. He was sure the STN would make a "killing." The Parisian market also favored light literature and ephemera, "everything that appeals to our current taste and that piques our malicious curiosity." But forbidden works sold best of all. The title alone of *La Vérité rendue sensible à Louis XVI* was enough for Quandet to request a shipment. The ideal book for him was, as he put it, "a thoroughly forbidden work." The public was less interested in standard works than in "forbidden fruit, which is snapped up simply because it is forbidden."

Quandet trafficked heavily in this literature, and inevitably he got caught. In early September 1782, nine bales that the STN had shipped via Besançon were confiscated in Versailles. According to Quandet, the disaster was engineered by Poinçot, the blackest of all villains in the book trade, in collusion with the police.[23] Poinçot walked off with three of the bales, which were intended for him, and left the rest, which had been shipped to his competitors, for the authorities to impound. Three of the remaining six, full of illegal works, were for Quandet. He tried to argue that the confiscation had taken place irregularly, because Poinçot had broken the seals of the bales and had exposed their contents himself, whereas that function was reserved for an officer of the *chambre syndicale*. He appealed to the *syndic* of the Guild. He begged for support from his main contact in the police, a secretary of Lenoir named Martin. He also sent a memoir directly to Lenoir, claiming that his own role was that of a shipping agent, not a retailer.

When granted an audience, however, Quandet failed to make that argument stick. The lieutenant general had known about his activities for more than a year and was convinced that he smuggled and sold forbidden books on a large scale, a serious crime in itself and one that could have disastrous consequences for someone who lacked the authority to engage in the book trade. In recounting the events to Ostervald, Quandet concluded that he must have been denounced by other dealers who wanted to eliminate a competitor. "I believe that these scoundrels, who are scorned by all decent persons and are reviled by our good booksellers," he complained to Ostervald, "made me appear to be one of their ilk when they described me to the police." There was nothing he could do, he wrote, but wait to learn of his fate as it would be decreed by an order from the Keeper of the Seals. Yet there was some hope, for Lenoir had ended the interview by saying, "Believe me, Monsieur Lachenal, take up another trade. That is the best way to protect yourself from unfortunate eventualities."[24]

While waiting, Quandet continued to do odd jobs for the STN. He sent a bailiff to collect the debt owed by Mme Cugnet, "that chaste and modest female." She, rather than her husband, ran the boutique in the Louvre, and Quandet learned that she was one of the informers who had denounced him to the police. While taking action against her, Quandet admitted that he could not pay his own debts to the STN. He failed to acquit a bill of exchange for 1,600 L. in October and another note for 144 L. in November. He simply had no funds, he wrote, though he hoped his business would revive. He was owed money by some Dutch booksellers, but they, too, had no cash. They wanted to pay him in shipments of forbidden books, and he was now determined to stay far away from the illegal trade. He did not even dare to set foot in his storeroom in Versailles. Strangers were constantly showing up at his apartment to ask for "bad books," and he always turned them away, because he suspected they were police spies. Spies also were operating in Neuchâtel, he warned Ostervald, because Fauche and Fauche Fils aîné & Witel continued to turn out forbidden books, particularly the works of Mirabeau.

In recommending potential *contrefaçons* to the STN, Quandet now sounded horrified at the notion of anything illegal, probably because he suspected that the authorities were opening his mail.[25] He no longer sent extensive comments about literary life. The main themes of his letters were money and the danger of police action. On December 4, 1782, he wrote that he could not come up with any funds and that six more bales had just been confiscated from Widow La Noue. Spies were everywhere, and it was nearly impossible to import books, whether anodyne or forbidden, from foreign suppliers.

Ten days later he wrote that he had been banished from Paris by a *lettre de cachet*. The police had stormed into his apartment at seven in the morning, searched everything, and confiscated his papers along with a few books, including six copies of *La Vérité rendue sensible à Louis XVI*. He had been forced to leave instantly, "in the midst of a tearful family," as he told Ostervald, and was confined to a village near Chaumy, eighty miles northeast of Paris, where a curate, his friend and former schoolmaster, had taken him in. On January 12, 1783, he wrote that a young man whom he had hired as a clerk had become a spy and had denounced him to the police. Denunciations had also come from Cugnet, Poinçot, and Samson, as he had suspected, making Quandet appear as a key figure in the underground book trade at a moment when the government was undertaking new efforts to repress it. "They construed it as a crime for me to be your confidential agent." Two months later, he remained stuck in the village and had fallen ill. His morale had collapsed: "I am horribly bored here," he wrote. Having heard that Mercier had returned to Neuchâtel to prepare more books, he asked to be remembered to him. "I sincerely congratulate him for having had a whiff of the Bastille only from a safe distance. But is a *lettre de cachet* any better?"

The STN attempted to get the *lettre de cachet* revoked through the intervention of its most effective contact in Versailles, David-Alphonse de Sandoz-Rollin, the secretary to the Prussian ambassador. He arranged for Quandet's wife to have an audience with the minister of the Maison du Roi, Antoine-Jean Amelot de Chaillou, who oversaw the Paris police. Amelot informed her that Quandet did not merely run an illegal book business, but he also had furnished Swiss printers—presumably in dealing with others in addition to the STN—with the manuscripts of a great many "bad books." The government would not grant clemency. In a letter to Ostervald of August 1, 1783, Quandet wrote that the accumulation of denunciations had convinced the authorities that he had been "the central point where all bad books converged."

The STN never heard from him again. On June 23, 1784, its Paris banker, Paul de Pourtalès, wrote that Quandet had died, leaving nothing to cover his debt. In a balance sheet of May 31, 1792, when the STN had ceased all operations, it put him down as a "bad debtor," who owed it 10,145 L.[26]

11

Relations with Authors

ALTHOUGH THEY REMAINED IN touch with the world of books through their daily correspondence and their Parisian agents, publishers in the Fertile Crescent had to inspect sectors of it firsthand. They needed to negotiate directly with other publishers, government officials, shipping agents, retailers, and authors. Like businessmen today, they took business trips, and although their expense accounts covered different items, such as sessions with wigmakers and fees for postilions, the principle was the same.[1]

The directors of the STN made several journeys to Lausanne, Geneva, Lyon, and Besançon, stopping along the way to make deals with booksellers. Bosset visited bookshops and publishing houses throughout the Rhineland and the Low Countries in 1779, and Ostervald conducted business in Paris in 1775, 1777, and 1780. His letters to the home office (along with many by Bosset, who accompanied him in 1777 and 1780) reveal a great deal about the publishing industry and especially about the relations between publishers and authors, because Paris attracted talent from everywhere in France and even other countries.[2]

Ostervald discovered a new side of literary life during his trip of 1775. By then he was sixty-two and had already visited Paris. Thanks in part to his wife's family in Rouen, he knew France well and was something of a man of the world. Yet he sounded wide eyed and provincial in his first letters. After checking in to the Hôtel de Bretagne, rue Croix des Petits Champs, he began by hiring a guide in order to find his way through "this gigantic and very noisy city." First, he looked up the STN's banker in Paris, Jean-Frédéric Perregaux. Next, he contacted abbé François Rozier, the editor of the *Journal de physique* and member of the Académie des sciences, with whom he had corresponded since 1773 and wanted to recruit as a scout for the STN. Rozier welcomed Ostervald warmly in May 1775 and eventually became a good friend.[3] He and a Protestant named de Longes, a clandestine dealer who funneled books to Huguenots everywhere in the kingdom, provided inside information about Parisian booksellers.

Then Ostervald made the rounds of the bookshops, looking for allies who could open up the Parisian market for the STN's books. It was hard work. "It's a strange experience, Messieurs, to do business in this enormous city," Ostervald wrote to the home office. Parisians kept peculiar hours. "You can only see people in the morning, which goes from eight o'clock to two o'clock." Two minor booksellers, Pyre and Saugrain, and one bouquiniste in the Palais de Justice, Widow Vallat-Lachapelle, listened sympathetically to Ostervald's sales pitches. But he was in enemy territory, a good bourgeois to all appearances and yet, in the eyes of the Parisian booksellers, a pirate.

Ostervald got on better with the authors in Paris. He already knew several, including Raynal, and he looked them up, following a list of names and addresses. The first he visited was Antoine Court de Gébelin, a Protestant with Swiss connections. Although forgotten today, Gébelin was one of the best-known figures of his time. In *Le Monde primitif*, published in nine volumes from 1773 to 1784 (it was left incomplete when he died in 1784), he championed the idea of a lost universal language, which constituted the foundation of all modern languages and the possibility of penetrating beyond classical civilizations to the spiritual origins of humanity. A defender of the Huguenots, an ally of the Physiocrats, a supporter of the American revolutionaries, a Freemason, an occultist, and a mesmerist, Gébelin lived at the vortex of the cultural currents swirling through pre-Revolutionary Paris.

Although he did not publish with the STN, Gébelin was happy to help with Ostervald's affairs. One of them took an unexpected turn. While discussing the state of the book trade, Gébelin and a friend of his named Borville asked whether the STN could produce books more cheaply than the printers in Paris. If so, they could direct works to Neuchâtel, and they could then help the STN market the printed products on a large scale, bypassing the Parisian booksellers. They envisaged legal works of the kind that by then were selling openly in Paris, often with a *permission tacite*, and they also offered to assist in clearing them through the censorship. Although the STN had printed a few original manuscripts, Ostervald had not thought seriously about tapping literary output at its source. He had conceived of the STN as a pirating enterprise, like most of the other Swiss houses, whereas Gébelin raised the possibility that it could challenge the Parisian publishers on their own ground. Gébelin then took a pen and made some calculations based on the volume of

Le Monde primitif that was currently in press. An octavo printed at a run of 1,000 would cost 42 L., 14 sous per sheet for the entire edition, he reckoned. If the STN could turn out sheets at a lower cost, it could undersell everyone else.

Ostervald returned to the Hôtel de Bretagne and did some calculations of his own. The STN had recently printed *Cours de mathématiques suivant la méthode de Volff* for the author, a mathematician named de Pelt, at a press run of 1,000, and it had charged 36 L. for each of the sheets with a "decent profit" included. Costs in the eighteenth century were reckoned in sheets—that is, the paper, composition, presswork, and other expenses required to run off all the copies of one sheet printed on both sides. (A typical octavo volume of 20 sheets had 320 pages.) Ostervald worked through more calculations, including shipping costs, so that the STN could offer to deliver the bales free of transportation as far as Lyon. He noted that, in contrast to the trade in *contrefaçons*, there would be no risk. The entire operation would be legal. "In short," he concluded in writing to the home office, "it looks like good business to me."[4]

While keeping this possibility in mind as a long-term policy to be discussed back in Neuchâtel with Bosset, who had joined the STN on January 1 as its financial director, Ostervald continued on his round of visits to authors. He did not propose to buy manuscripts from them but rather to win their goodwill in general and, if possible, their willingness to collaborate in the STN's reprints of their works. As we've seen, it helped in marketing to present an edition as "corrected and augmented by the author." For a reward, the author might receive a small payment, some free copies, or simply the gratification of reaching a larger public. After meeting with Claude-Joseph Dorat, whose sentimental romances and frothy poetry were then in vogue, Ostervald reported that Dorat was eager to collaborate on an inexpensive edition of his works.[5] Ostervald also discussed publishing prospects with Raynal, Goezman, Grozier, Daudet, and Valmont de Bomare. He even tried to contact Rousseau but without success. For the most part, these visits amounted to little more than cultivating contacts, and Ostervald enjoyed their social aspect. When he returned to his room after an evening with Rozier, Lalande, and others, he wrote, "To tell the truth, I drank some Graves, some champagne, some Hermitage, some Malaga, and seated as I was between two amiable ladies, that can produce some confusion in one's ideas." He also dined with Jean-François Marmontel, Antoine-Léonard Thomas, and other writers at the country residence of Necker.

While gaining knowledge about life inside the literary circles of Paris, Ostervald pursued the seemingly endless task of getting permission for the STN's edition of the *Description des arts et métiers* and its *Journal helvétique* to circulate in France. "I was offered the opportunity of getting the sultan's favorite to intervene," he wrote, meaning apparently that he might be able to win support from the mistress of Miromesnil, the Keeper of the Seals.[6] Instead of resorting to back-room intrigue, however, he tried to argue his case directly with the authorities in Versailles—and got nowhere. Writing to the STN from Rouen, where he went to visit relatives, he had nothing good to say about the political system of France, where all foreigners are "rudely followed by spies."

Ostervald returned to Paris in February 1777, this time accompanied by Bosset. As their main purpose was to negotiate with Panckoucke about various speculations on the *Encyclopédie*, they often dined with him and sent back reports about finances. While being drawn into Panckoucke's web of enterprises, Bosset consistently cautioned that it was "better to do less business and to make more solid [enterprises]." For his part, Ostervald wrote about plans for the future *Encyclopédie méthodique*, which was being prepared by Jean-Baptiste-Antoine Suard, Panckoucke's brother-in-law. Suard got on well with the two Neuchâtelois and invited them to an "academic dinner," so they could meet some of his fellow members of the Académie française. These included d'Alembert and Condorcet, whom they later tried to recruit as authors. Ostervald and Bosset also picked up rumors about the forthcoming edicts on the book trade and discussed strategy with Clément Plomteux of Liège, who had also come to negotiate with Panckoucke. They enjoyed more dinners with worldly abbés and elegant ladies, and they tried again to gain traction in Versailles. "Today we will go to the audiences of M. de Néville and M. Boucherot [secretary to Miromesnil in the chancellery], and we must break off this letter in order to get dressed," Ostervald wrote. "It's a strange life we are leading here." Having completed their business (they agreed with Panckoucke to postpone the production of the *Encyclopédie méthodique* in order to speculate on Duplain's quarto edition of the original *Encyclopédie*), they left this alien world in early April, stopped off in Lyon to order a new font of type, and arrived back in Neuchâtel ready to participate more fully in the publishing industry as it was practiced by the leading houses in Europe.

After expanding its printing shop to twelve presses, which made it one of the largest printers in Europe, the STN concentrated for the next two years on producing the quarto *Encyclopédie*. In February 1780, as already mentioned, Ostervald and Bosset met in Lyon with Pancoucke, Plomteux, and Duplain to liquidate that enormous enterprise. Then they proceeded to Paris, looking for more projects to occupy their presses. The settlement on the quarto and contention over plans for the *Encyclopédie méthodique* led to a falling out with Panckoucke, and they were glad to sell off their remaining share in his speculations. It was at this point that they entered into negotiations with Beaumarchais, hoping to get a commission to print at least some of the Kehl Voltaire. As recounted earlier, they met with him frequently and dined with him several times in his town house, but never reached an agreement. They got further in talking business with other authors, including many they had cultivated on previous trips and through exchanges of letters. The most important of these was abbé André Morellet, a contributor to the *Encyclopédie*, partisan of the *philosophes*, and a political economist closely connected with Turgot. He had visited the STN in 1775 and had helped with its efforts to get its *Description des arts et métiers* permitted in France. Occupied with a *Dictionnaire de commerce*, which he never completed, he did not publish his own works with the STN. Nonetheless, he arranged for Ostervald and Bosset to meet some of France's most illustrious writers.[7] He was especially active as an intermediary in their negotiations with Marmontel, a close friend of his who had married his niece.

Most of the transactions took place in conversations, but their general nature can be seen from short letters that Morellet sent to Ostervald and Bosset in their hotel. One contained a list of the titles that Marmontel intended to include in a seventeen-volume edition of his complete works. He would take out a *privilège* and cede the use of it for four years. As to payment, wrote Morellet, "[h]is conditions are very simple: a thousand francs per volume." At this time, the professionalization of authorship had begun to enter a new phase, situated halfway between reliance on the market, as illustrated by Zola in the nineteenth century, and dependence on patrons, exemplified by Racine in the seventeenth century.[8] Writers like Mercier managed to live from their pens in the 1780s, but there were few of them—only thirty, according to Mercier's own estimate.[9]

Although Marmontel stood out as one of the best-known authors in France, 17,000 L. was a steep price to pay for a four-year exclusive right to publish his works. Ostervald and Bosset rejected the offer and countered it with a proposal that derived from Ostervald's discussion with Gébelin five years earlier: the STN would print Marmontel's works at a bargain price, 1 sou per sheet, far less than any Parisian printer would charge. Marmontel would pay for the printing and market the books on his own, taking advantage of the provisions in the 1777 edicts that permitted authors to sell their works directly on the market without selling their *privilège* to a member of the Guild. (In practice that would mean launching a subscription or commissioning a bookseller to work through retailers.) For his part, Morellet was skeptical about the feasibility of authors getting involved in marketing.[10] But Marmontel thought he could cover the printing costs by a subscription and responded that he found the STN's proposal "very reasonable." He agreed to draft a prospectus for the STN to print and circulate in the subscription campaign. He, Morellet, Ostervald, and Bosset had lengthy discussions over details such as arrangements for correcting the proofs and the quality of the paper.

Everything seemed settled when Ostervald left for Neuchâtel at the end of April. Bosset, who remained in Paris to tend to his own affairs as well as those of the STN, continued the negotiations until his own departure in late June. He provided samples of the paper to be used, and Marmontel explained the additions and annotations he planned to make to his best-known novels, *Bélisaire* and *Les Incas*. They agreed to postpone the publication of the prospectus until prospective customers in "high society" had returned to Paris after passing the summer in the countryside. By October, however, Marmontel was overcome with anxieties. Despite Morellet's urging, he still had not finished the draft of the prospectus. "Possible obstacles in sales, the need to come up with a rather large amount of capital, at least to pay for the first volumes, all that is tormenting him," Morellet wrote. "I am very sorry that you cannot make an arrangement with some bookseller in Paris for the payment of a flat rate and then propose to him [Marmontel] a sum for which you would have his manuscript and the use of his privilege for six to ten years, more or less." In the end, Marmontel decided he could not become an entrepreneur as well as an author. The STN never published his works.

Morellet also introduced Ostervald and Bosset to Jacques-André Naigeon, a far less famous writer than Marmonetel but a far more important philosopher. As an intimate of d'Holbach's circle, Naigeon oversaw the clandestine publication of the most audacious treatises of the radical Enlightenment. He contributed to the *Encyclopédie*, worked closely with Diderot, shared Diderot's atheistic views, and became his literary executor. Although he published only one full-scale work of his own, *Le Militaire Philosophe* (1768), he agreed to do an "essay" of some kind—the title did not appear in the correspondence—with the STN. Morellet referred to it as a firm commitment that would serve as an "example" for Marmontel. It might have been an ambitious work, because Naigeon planned to come to Neuchâtel to complete it; but it, too, never got beyond a preliminary agreement.[11]

These discussions—some in the form of table talk, some serious negotiations—included two other *philosophes* from the front ranks of Enlightenment thinkers, d'Alembert and Gabriel Bonnot de Mably, a political theorist and champion of egalitarianism. Bosset referred to Mably only briefly in his letters from Paris, but the STN published his *Du gouvernement et des lois de la Pologne* in 1781. Although the evidence is ambiguous, it seems likely that Ostervald agreed to purchase the manuscript in exchange for 200 free copies. Mably was not happy with the result. He appreciated the quality of the paper and printing but deplored changes made in the text, and he decided not to publish other works with the STN.[12]

The STN's relations with d'Alembert's can be followed more closely. Ostervald and Bosset got to know him during their trip to Paris in 1777. He received them warmly in 1780, their third trip, and even offered to solicit the support of Frederick II for their effort to get their *Description des arts et métiers* permitted in France. After a long discussion with d'Alembert about publishing original editions of his works, Bosset reported on May 17 that "he struck me as being very attached to the lucrative aspect of his publications."[13] A follow-up conversation four weeks later resulted in a concrete proposal. D'Alembert showed Bosset a manuscript of various essays that he wanted the STN to print in an octavo volume. He also proposed a three-volume edition of eulogies of members of the Académie française, a genre of belles-lettres that was fairly popular in the eighteenth century, and even proposed coming to Switzerland to complete work on them.[14] After discussing various financial arrangements, d'Alembert said he preferred that the STN print the work at its own expense and then share the profits from the sales.

Bosset was worried at that time about the STN's tendency to overextend its capital in publications that produced a slow return. It was a "hard time" for book sales, he warned in letter after letter. The STN had to find funds to repay a 50,000 L. loan that it had taken out in Lyon. "But let me say it again," he reiterated in March, "the problem is not in finding works to print—good, admirable, marvelous things—the main concern, the unique object that requires all of our attention, is before printing anything to be sure that we can make some cash from it." He therefore recommended that the STN commit itself to d'Alembert only if it could arrange enough advance sales to cover its production costs. When he left Paris at the end of June, the d'Alembert project remained unresolved. It never took place.

D'Alembert, Mably, Naigeon, Marmontel, and Condorcet[15]—the STN made attempts to publish the works of the most eminent writers in Paris. Ostervald and Bosset also entered into negotiations of various kinds with Beaumarchais, Morellet, and Suard, and they continued to court Raynal, who visited Neuchâtel in mid-June. Thanks to the good service of Morellet, they even contacted Benjamin Franklin, hoping to open up a market in the United States.[16] Judging from the letters they wrote from Paris, we can surmise that Ostervald and Bosset had a place at the table with nearly the entire last generation of the *philosophes*. For their part, they had plenty to contribute in discussions about literature, including anecdotes about the Swiss adventures of Voltaire and Rousseau and shop talk about the vicissitudes of publishing the *Encyclopédie*. Although the STN did not specialize in the works of the *philosophes*, it participated as a publisher in the general Enlightenment project of diffusing reason and combating prejudice. For a while in 1780, Ostervald and Bosset considered following the example of Marc-Michel Rey, as Daudet de Jossan had recommended—that is, they contemplated publishing original manuscripts by France's leading thinkers, exactly as Rey had done with great success in Amsterdam. By the time of their last visit to Paris, however, the climate had changed, and economic circumstances had made speculations too risky. None of their grand plans was ever realized in print.

In fact, their experience provides glimpses of Enlightenment works that reached an advanced stage of planning yet never were published—Raynal's *Histoire philosophique et politique de l'établissement du Protestantisme en Europe*, Morellet's *Dictionnaire du commerce*, Naigeon's untitled philosophical treatise, the STN's projected anthology on Turgot's ministry with a preface by Voltaire, and the 162 missing Voltaire letters. If the archives of other publishing houses had survived, we could have formed an idea of the *unpublished* Enlightenment, one that existed in the minds of writers but never came down to us in the form of books.

Aside from the occasional meetings in Paris, Ostervald and Bosset dealt with authors through the mail. The STN archives contain hundreds of letters from writers, some trying to sell manuscripts, others offering to pay for the production of their books, a few seeking a way around the censorship in France, and many looking for income of any kind, if only from correcting proof.

The fullest dossier contains the STN's correspondence with Jacques-Pierre Brissot, who would become a leader of the Girondists (the last moderate republican faction before the Terror) during the French Revolution.[17] Brissot contacted the STN in 1779 at the age of twenty-five, when he was looking for a printer to produce works that could not pass the censorship. He assured it that he could cover all costs, and in fact he promptly paid his first bill— 300 L. for an anonymous pamphlet, *Observations sur la littérature en France, sur le barreau, les journaux, etc.* In April 1780 he collected a small inheritance, following the death of his father. Then the manuscripts began to pour in—polemical pamphlets, legal tracts, philosophical treatises, multi-volume anthologies—one after another, at a rate and on a scale that demonstrated his determination to break into the ranks of the *philosophes* and win acclaim in the world of letters. Brissot explained that he had abandoned a career in the law "in order to devote myself entirely to the profession of authorship."

This "profession" had no economic base. Brissot hoped to pay for the cost of new books by selling his old ones. Sales lagged. His Parisian distributor, a shady bookseller named Desauges, did not honor the notes that Brissot wrote to cover his debts to the STN. Brissot became compromised by association with hacks and libelers. He was imprisoned in the Bastille on July 12, 1784, and when he was released, on September 10, he was ruined. "I want to finish with it all," he wrote to the STN. "I want to solemnly say good-bye to typographical speculations and to renounce a career to which I committed myself too imprudently." He owed the STN 12,301 L. and 9 sous. It recovered a small fraction of the debt by selling some of his books that remained in its warehouse, and it wrote off the rest by entering his name on the list of "bad debtors" in its account books.

Another author on the list was Louis Valentin de Goezman, the man whom Quandet was supposed to flush from his hiding place in 1782.[18] His story is worth telling in detail, because it illustrates author-publisher relations at their most baroque. Ostervald had been corresponding with Goezman since 1769, when he had settled in Paris after serving as a magistrate in the Conseil souverain d'Alsace. He had published several works on law and legal history and proposed that the STN produce a "[d]iplomatic journal about public law in Europe," which he would edit. Despite a great deal of intrigue and lobbying, that plan foundered. Goezman then came up with a proposal to publish a multi-volume treatise, *Tableau historique, politique et juridique de la monarchie française.* Ostervald agreed, provided that Goezman pay for the printing in a series of bills of exchange to be sent after he had received copies of the first volume. By the end of 1770, he had provided the first 416 pages of the manuscript, enough to make up volume 1, which the STN began to print. He suspended his work on volume 2, because he became immersed in the intrigues that eventually led to his appointment in July 1771 as a councilor in the Grand' Chambre of the Parlement that chancelier Maupeou created to replace the Parlement de Paris at the height of the political crisis during the last years of Louis XV's reign.

Goezman's letters in the first six months of 1771 give glimpses of a job-hungry political player maneuvering to profit from the crisis. He solicited protectors in Versailles, wrote anonymous pamphlets in favor of Maupeou, and asked the STN to run off 1,000 extra copies of the "Preliminary Discourse" to his *Tableau historique*, which, he claimed, had been "endorsed by the present ministry." In fact, the text of volume 1 reads like a legal and historical justification of Maupeou's political coup. Although Goezman probably began work on it long before the destruction of the old judicial system, its central theme, as Goezman wrote to Ostervald on December 27, 1770, was "entirely in accord with the present system." It refutes the claims of the Parlement de Paris to exercise constitutional authority, and it argues in favor of the theory that the king possessed undivided and unlimited sovereignty.[19]

After he won his appointment to the Maupeou parlement, Goezman gained considerable influence but little income.[20] In his early letters, he had complained about his lack of financial resources. He had even requested Ostervald to intervene with contacts in Prussia and Versailles to find him a post in an embassy. France, Italy, Germany, Holland, anywhere would do, including a sinecure that might be arranged through the papal nuncio in Basel. The tone of his letters changed after he took up his position as a magistrate. He boasted about his ability to pull strings in order to promote the STN's interests, yet he failed to include a bill of exchange for the 1,000 copies of volume 1 of the *Tableau historique*, which the STN shipped to him in May 1771. The STN demanded payment in letter after letter for the next two years, insisting that it would not print volume 2 until he had covered its costs for volume 1. A Swiss contact in Versailles managed to collect 600 L. from him in June 1772, but he continued to owe it 1,705 L.[21]

He still had not paid his debt a year later, when he was overwhelmed by a disaster: the so-called Goezman Affair. As mentioned earlier, Beaumarchais was involved in a suit that came under Goezman's jurisdiction as the court "reporter" in charge of the case. In order to gain access to Goezman, Beaumarchais paid a bribe. Goezman, however, issued an unfavorable report.

Beaumarchais then defended himself and heaped ridicule on Goezman in three memoirs published between September and December 1773 and a fourth that appeared in February 1774. The memoirs were polemical masterpieces, as witty and gripping as Beaumarchais's plays, and they did a great deal to discredit the Maupeou judiciary system in public opinion. Although Beaumarchais lost his case, Goezman was forced to resign from the parlement. Weighed down by ignominy, he sank into destitution.

The STN followed his fate through its correspondence with bill collectors and attorneys.[22] At the height of his power, they reported, he had rented a townhouse, redecorated it, and filled it with expensive furniture bought on credit. After his disgrace, he attempted to fob off his landlord and decorators by setting up a schedule of payments and assurances that he still had protectors who would come to his rescue. By May 1775 he and his wife had abandoned their house and gone into hiding, moving from one furnished room to another in order to escape creditors and bailiffs. The STN's attorney had won a suit against him, which resulted in another schedule of payments, but Goezman could not comply with it and then disappeared. Although unable to collect any money, the attorney learned that Goezman had tried to raise cash by secretly selling a copy of the manuscript of the *Tableau historique* to a Parisian publisher named Le Jay, who was having it printed in a quarto edition under a new title, *Les Trois Âges de la monarchie française*.

It was at this point—May 1775—that Ostervald arrived on his first business trip to Paris. The STN attorney informed him about the forthcoming Paris edition, which was to be anonymous but approved by a censor. With help from Beaumarchais and Le Jay, Ostervald discovered Goezman's address. And on June 7 Ostervald confronted his quarry. "At last I have unearthed M. Goetzman," he wrote to the STN. "What a man! As handsome as possible with a golden tongue and no gold in his purse." Goezman confessed that he had made a deal with Le Jay to publish the old text under the new title, having somehow persuaded a third party (he later wrote that he still had the support of a "protector in power") to advance 3,000 L. as collateral for the printing. However, contrary to Goezman's expectations, the government had refused to permit the publication, and the printing had been suspended.

In the midst of their conversation, when he learned about the problem with the Paris edition, Ostervald suddenly switched tactics. Instead of berating Goezman, he expressed sympathy and offered to print *Les Trois Âges de la monarchie française* on the STN's presses, provided that the costs of the first volume would be covered with the 3,000 L.[23] Taken by surprise, Goezman said he would reply to this proposal after consulting his financial backer. A few days later, Madame Goezman appeared at Ostervald's inn, "adorned with her natural grace" and carrying a manuscript by her husband. (She was a key character, beautiful and money hungry, in Beaumarchais's memoirs, which the STN had sold in large numbers and Ostervald must have read.) Ostervald took possession of the manuscript and parried her request for an advance of 300 L. by saying that he could not grant it without the approval of the STN's banker—who, alerted by Ostervald, later refused to consent.

The manuscript apparently was a draft prospectus for the new edition to be printed by the STN, but the printing could not take place until Goezman had overcome another obstacle, which he revealed in a letter of June 20. While arranging with Le Jay to produce an authorized edition in Paris, he had secretly contracted with the STL to publish the same text under yet another title, *Les Fastes de la monarchie française*. Unable to pay a copyist, he had recopied the manuscript himself and had sent it in batches to Lausanne, using another name, "de Thurne." The STL knew nothing about the Parisian edition. It thought it was receiving a fresh manuscript with great commercial potential. By June it had nearly finished printing the first volume of what was supposed to be a twelve-volume octavo edition printed at a run of 2,000. "De Thurne" was to pay the printing costs, using the sales of the first volumes to subsidize the rest, although the STL had held out the possibility of undertaking the enterprise itself in exchange for giving him 100 copies.

As evidence of his assertions, Goezman sent Ostervald copies of letters he had received from the STL. They exactly resembled those that the STN had sent him four and a half years earlier when it was printing the same manuscript under the title *Tableau historique, politique et juridique de la monarchie française*: complaints about delays in the arrival of the copy, disputes over printing costs, and worries about getting shipments safely into France. Like the STN, the STL thought the book had great sales potential, probably because of its relevance to the current political crisis. Goezman himself had no doubts about the book's success. "I am morally certain that the *Fastes*, especially considering the present circumstances, will be a huge success," he had assured the STL. In dealing behind its back with the STN, his only concern was to persuade the STN to take over the publication while keeping his own role and his real name secret. That, of course, was a delicate matter, because at that time the STN and the STL were allies, and it was not clear how the STL could be persuaded to give up a profitable printing job.

After Ostervald's return to Neuchâtel in the summer of 1775, Goezman wrote letter after letter pleading for a commitment. He had held back the final batch of copy from the STL so that he could settle with the STN; he had a list of subscribers who would be happy to switch to the new edition; he would dash off another prospectus replacing the STL with the STN as the publisher to whom subscribers would send payments; the payments would cover the printing costs; they would then split the profits; and the STN could use its share for the repayment of his old debt. This argument came laced with thick doses of rhetoric. He needed help, he wrote, from "persons who do not wait for the harvest in order to sustain the farmer. . . . A husbandman, destroyed by a hail storm, has no harvest to make if those who are to share the fruit of his labor do not provide him with grain to sow."

Ostervald replied that the STN would not pirate the STL, though it might be able to arrange a joint edition if Goezman could come up with an advance payment from his backer and enough subscriptions to assure the coverage of all costs. By now Ostervald had dropped the proposal to take over the Parisian quarto edition, and his offer to cooperate with the Lausanne octavo might well have been a ploy to siphon off the 3,000 L. as payment for Goezman's old debt. The money was not transferable, Goezman wrote. Any attempt to draw on the 3,000 L. would be blocked by the Parisian printer, "who despaired at having to renounce an enterprise that he had expected to be very lucrative." Goezman tried once again in a letter of October 17 to persuade the STN to make a deal behind the backs of both the Parisians and the Lausannois. Tired of this game of disguises and duplicity, Ostervald did not reply.

The correspondence ended there. The intrigues did not. Although the STN continued its efforts to collect Goezman's debt, it could no longer locate him. When he returned to Paris in 1777, Ostervald failed to discover Goezman's whereabouts and concluded, "M. Goezman is a man who has been destroyed." Quandet also failed five years later. But Goezman's text had not disappeared. In January 1778 it was published as the first volume of a work with yet another new title, its fourth: *Histoire politique du gouvernement français, ou les quatre âges de la monarchie française*, "chez Grangé, imprimeur-libraire . . . avec approbation et privilège du roi." Apparently Grangé had bought the privilege from Le Jay, cleared it with the censor, and made a deal with Goezman for the completion of the text. The first volume was to be followed by three more in a large, quarto set.

On January 13, 1778, the STL suggested that the STN join it in pirating Grangé's edition. By now Heubach, writing for the STL, knew that the actual author was Goezman, not "de Thurne." Despite the aborted attempts to publish it under three earlier titles, he still thought there was money to be made from the book. Therefore, he proposed that the two *sociétés typographiques* pirate it as a joint enterprise in an eight-volume, octavo edition printed at a run of 1,250 or 1,500. The STL would produce the first four, using its old copies of volume 1, which it had kept in its warehouse since 1775, and would complete the printing from the text of the Paris edition. The STN would do the last four volumes. Heubach included a copy of the STL volume with its old title, *Les Fastes de la monarchie française*, along with one of Grangé's new *Histoire politique du gouvernement français* so that Ostervald could compare them. But Ostervald had had enough of Goezman/de Thurne and the transmogrifications of his political treatise. He wrote that he preferred to do a joint edition of Robertson's *Histoire d'Amérique*.

It was a good decision. Not only did the Robertson sell well, but no subsequent volume of Goezman's text was ever published, and Goezman himself disappeared—at least from the bill collectors in Paris. Thanks to his remaining protections, he managed to get himself hired by the French government as a secret agent in London.[24] Disguised again as "de Thurne," an Alsatian baron, he tracked down and bought off libelous attacks on Marie-Antoinette and other members of the royal family written by French expatriates. He ran up an enormous expense account, which was paid off by the foreign ministry, along with his debts in Paris (though not what he owed to the STN). The total came to 18,296 L. Goezman and his wife returned to France in 1783. He became embroiled in more intrigues during the French Revolution and was guillotined, along with the poet André Chénier, on July 25, 1794, in the last cartload of victims to the Terror before the fall of Robespierre.

Brissot and Goezman may seem like extreme examples of literary adventurers who took advantage of a publisher eager to profit from printing jobs. They nevertheless illustrate a problem endemic to publishing in the eighteenth century. Writers often proposed manuscripts to publishers located outside France, seeking to circumvent the French censorship and to benefit from the cheaper cost of paper and printing. If they made a seemingly firm commitment to pay the production costs, a publisher was easily tempted. And if the manuscript looked promising, the publisher often helped market the book in exchange for a share in the profits. Occasionally publishers even ran off extra copies and sold them on the sly. When Brissot visited Neuchâtel in 1782, he discovered a pile of his *Théorie des lois criminelles* in the warehouse that the STN had kept for its own use after claiming that it had shipped the entire edition to him in Paris.[25] To attribute all the shady behavior in the publishing industry to authors would be misleading. Yet time and again, authors commissioned printing jobs and then failed to pay their bills.

At bottom, there was an asymmetry built into the relations between publishers and authors. Although the extent of their resources varied enormously, publishers disposed of enough capital to produce and market books (marginal entrepreneurs like Jacques-Benjamin Téron were exceptional). Authors often had little more than their wits and whatever they could cobble together in the form of patronage, sinecures, journalism, and other kinds of employment. Successful writers like Marmontel and Suard were the exception. Failures like Brissot and Goezman were far more common, and they often sank into the growing population of Grub Street hacks. When Ostervald and Bosset decided to publish original editions in addition to pirating, they naturally cultivated the most eminent authors in Paris. Yet they never concluded a contract with any of them, despite the goodwill on both sides. In the end, the original manuscripts they published came from writers in the middle ranks of the literary world, and the results were rarely successful.

The STN's greatest success came from publishing the work of Louis-Sébastien Mercier. As already recounted, Mercier traveled to Neuchâtel in July 1781 in order to prepare an expanded edition of his *Tableau de Paris*, a two-volume bestseller, which Samuel Fauche had published earlier that year.[26] After quarreling with Fauche, Mercier published the new, four-volume edition with the breakaway firm of Fauche Fils aîné & Witel, which hired the STN's presses, since it had none of its own. Young Fauche and Witel compensated the STN by an agreement for it to produce and market 750 copies for its own profit in return for printing a huge run of 7,500. In fact, the STN actually printed 1,500 copies for itself—despite its obligation to limit its share to 750—and sold them at a great profit.

Mercier returned to Neuchâtel in 1782 and made other visits during the next two years. He became a close friend of Ostervald, who introduced him to the town's elite and continued to publish his books. By 1789 the STN had produced seventeen works of Mercier, many from manuscript and more than it published by any other author. It even launched a subscription for an eight-volume edition of his *Théâtre complet*. The subscription failed, and individual editions of the plays did not sell well, according to Quandet: "The dramas of M. Mercier do not enjoy a marvelous reputation." In general, however, the STN profited greatly from its role as Mercier's principal publisher, and Mercier remained a loyal friend to Ostervald, though he occasionally dealt with other firms, such as Heubach & Compagnie in Lausanne. His few surviving letters—unfortunately only four of them can be found in his dossier in the STN archives—reveal the affective element that sometimes developed at the core of author-publisher relations. On August 27, 1782, a week after returning to Paris from Neuchâtel, Mercier informed Ostervald that he had met with some powerful officials and had defended the STN against "several calumnious accusations." He had assured them that the STN published only decent books and should not be confused with its neighbors (meaning Fauche, who was notorious for dealing in obscene and seditious works). Then he devoted the rest of the letter to his personal sentiments. "How fondly I think of Neuchâtel and of you and your amiable and brilliant family," he wrote, noting how much he missed Ostervald's grandchildren and how he felt overcome with "powerful melancholy." Even allowing for the *sensiblerie* in vogue at this time, Mercier's affection seems genuine.[27]

Other letters that the STN exchanged with authors had a different tone. They usually began on a note of optimism. After receiving a proposal to produce a book at the author's expense, the STN would assure him (no women sent proposals) that it would do an excellent job. It was run by publishers who were men of letters themselves. They would take extra care with the copy and would provide reliable services, such as procuring good-quality paper and ensuring delivery to a convenient location, often Lyon. Then problems would arise, usually about shipping and payment for the printing. The correspondence would veer off into negotiations about replacing spoiled sheets or collecting bills of exchange. It rarely ended with both parties satisfied.

The dossier of Jean-Emmanuel Gilibert, a doctor and botanist in Lyon, provides an example of the STN's relations with a rather ordinary author of an unexceptional book, although its title sounded provocative: *L'Anarchie médicinale ou la médecine considérée comme nuisible à la société* (1772), three volumes. It did not contest orthodox ideas about the state, religion, or morality, but it attacked standard practices of medicine. In the belief that his manuscript contained nothing that warranted proscription, Gilibert submitted it to the censorship in Paris, but the censor refused even to give it a *permission tacite*, because he feared it would incur the wrath of established doctors. Gilibert then sent it to the STN, saying that the lack of liberty in France forced him to have recourse to the presses in Switzerland. At his suggestion, the STN sent the manuscript to Albrecht von Haller, the Swiss physician and naturalist, who fully endorsed it. Gilibert agreed to cover the printing costs by arranging for the sale of 300 copies to booksellers in Lyon.

He asked the STN to correct the proofs and improve the style as it saw fit, because he readily acknowledged his imperfections as a writer.[28] His main concern, he emphasized, was to improve medical practices. He hoped to clear a way for the circulation of the book in France by persuading a "protector" to intervene with the authorities. He went to Paris himself, yet failed to obtain any kind of permission, even with his contacts in the Paris police. "The literary inquisition in Paris has been taken to a ridiculous extreme," he wrote. "They don't permit anyone with thoughts in his head to print his view of things on paper. They especially fear and persecute any author who is bold enough not to say that all is going well and that the abuses are an illusion."[29] Therefore, he asked the STN to market the book in France by relying on its clandestine distribution system.

When at last Gilibert received his first copies, he was disappointed again. He found so many errors that he was sure the STN had failed to do an adequate job of correcting the proofs. Therefore, he insisted on the printing of an errata, which he asked the STN to insert before sending off the shipments. As to the book's success, he had no doubts: "The work will sell, I repeat. It will sell, I am sure of it." Its proscription would actually promote sales, and he had received letters that made him certain it would make "a great sensation." Yet the STN never succeeded in marketing many copies. It even suggested that it change the title and print a new title page in order to avoid the attention of the police and revive sales. In the end, it quarreled with Gilibert over the postage cost of the letters they had exchanged, a matter of 39 L. He never paid his printing bill, and they stopped corresponding.[30]

The STN's relative freedom from censorship (the authorities in Neuchâtel rarely raised any difficulties) also made it attractive to abbé Gabriel-François Coyer, a minor man of letters known for *la noblesse commerçante*, a treatise on the right of the nobility to engage in trade; light essays, collected as *Bagatelles morales*; and *Chinki*, a Voltairean novella. When he began to correspond with Ostervald, Coyer wrote that he admired "the precious liberty of your press" and wished to take advantage of it. In his case, the main obstacle was not so much the censorship as his connections with Widow Duchesne, one of the toughest members of the Guild who owned the *privilèges* for his publications. He sent seventeen texts complete with corrections and additions, which the STN was to incorporate in an edition of his complete works. He even arranged to have his portrait engraved for the frontispiece. Still, he insisted that everything be presented as if it were a pirated edition, done without his knowledge, because he did not dare alienate Widow Duchesne.

The STN sent a printed prospectus to twenty Parisian booksellers. Fearing reprisals from Madame Duchesne, none would place an advance order. Coyer then summoned the courage to ask her whether she would cooperate with the STN if she could do so on her own terms. She proposed extravagant conditions: the STN would have to pay 2,500 L. or provide her with 400 free copies while covering all costs. It refused and went on to print a one-volume *Collection complète des oeuvres de M. l'abbé Coyer* without Coyer's collaboration. He was left with nothing but regrets and bitterness toward Duchesne for "exercising tyranny with the use of her *privilège*."

Although they sold *privilèges* to Parisian publishers, established authors sometimes cooperated with pirate editions. As in Coyer's case, their motives were unclear. They did not usually receive payment and might have wanted to reach a broader public or merely to indulge in what Quandet called "the vanity of authors." The naturalist Jacques-Christophe Valmont de Bomare refused the STN's overtures to publish an expanded version of his *Dictionnaire raisonné universel d'histoire naturelle* (1764–1768), six volumes. He explained that he had persuaded his publisher, Brunet, to produce another edition and pay him for it. Yet he indicated a willingness to send some additional material to the STN for a pirated edition, provided that it waited until Brunet's edition had been published and that it kept his complicity secret.[31]

In general, however, authors respected the system of *privilèges*. Like Marmontel and d'Alembert, they proposed new works when they negotiated with the STN, even though the negotiations rarely resulted in publications. After receiving a great many proposals, especially from second-rate writers, Ostervald wrote to Quandet that he had had enough. "Must we forever be subject to harassment by authors? Can't we get them to stop without becoming victims of their exalted self-love?"[32]

Ostervald's scorn for obscure authors meant that they often received harsh treatment from the STN. After publishing d'Holbach's *Systéme de la nature* in 1771, the STN accepted a manuscript treatise by an unknown young Protestant philosopher, Georg Jonathan Holland, who had set out to refute the *Système's* atheistic argument in a manner that would appeal to modern, secular readers. Although Holland wrote imperfect French—he was a German living as a tutor in Lausanne—Ostervald was eager to publish his work, probably because it would help the STN overcome the scandal caused by its edition of the *Système*. Holland entrusted the STN to rework his text as it judged best, and he asked only that he receive thirty copies as compensation. Although polite and deferential, his letters expressed continuous disappointment. The STN delayed the printing so much that he feared other refutations would beat his to the market; and when he received the proofs, they looked terrible—cheap paper, ugly type, typographical errors everywhere.

The finished product, *Réflexions philosophiques sur le "Système de la nature,"* two volumes, eventually sold well enough to warrant a second edition of 500 copies, which was better printed. Although Holland asked to be paid 240 L. for the new edition, he received only thirty more copies. He also had endured the frustration of seeing his work distorted in a pirated edition, which included extensive new passages that made him sound like a Catholic.[33] Meanwhile, the STN had done some pirating of its own. It had reprinted another refutation of d'Holbach's work, *Observations sur le livre intitulé "Système de la nature"* by Giovanni Francesco Salvemini da Castiglione. Castiglione protested to the authorities in Neuchâtel about the violation of his rights and the changes made to his text. Ostervald did not bother to rebut his argument, because the answer was obvious: publishers did not respect intellectual property beyond the borders of their own countries, and they felt no compunctions about modifying the copy.[34] To be rewritten, misprinted, and pirated was for an author to be subjected to the common practices of publishers in the eighteenth century. Holland and Castiglione learned this lesson the hard way, and the other authors published by the STN took it as a given in their attempts to have a literary career.

Yet they could be as nasty as the publishers when difficulties arose. Most authors commissioned the STN to print their books and to help in marketing them. In October 1779, Michel-René Hilliard d'Auberteuil, a lawyer and French official in Saint-Domingue who was then living in Paris, proposed that the STN reprint his *Considérations sur l'état présent de la colonie française de Saint-Domingue,* including all the passages that had been cut from the first edition at the censor's demand. He promised to pay one-third of the costs as soon as the bale was delivered to Paris or Versailles and the rest six months later. As permitted by the edicts of 1777, he planned to market the books himself from his residence in Paris. The STN sent him a printed page to serve as a sample of the type and printing, and he signed a contractual agreement on the back of it.[35]

Before the STN completed the printing, however, d'Auberteuil left on an unannounced journey to Saint-Domingue. He then directed STN to send the bales to an agent in Marseille, whom he had instructed to cover the costs. The agent refused to do so, and the bales were eventually confiscated, while the STN tried in vain to collect payment. A year later it sent a memorandum to the naval minister, the marquis de Castries, requesting his intervention to force d'Auberteuil to pay his bill, which came to 441 L. The minister refused. Although d'Auberteuil was back in Paris by June 1782, he still avoided paying. All the STN ever received from him was a defiant last letter, in which he proclaimed his innocence of any duplicity. It tried for the next two years to track him down, but he eluded its bailiffs and attorneys.[36]

The STN's relations with Joseph-Marie Servan de Gerbey ended on the same note, although in his case it ultimately collected its printing bill. In January 1780 when it first heard from him, he was an obscure major in an infantry regiment, far removed from a destiny that would make him war minister in the Girondist government of 1792 and a revolutionary general whose effigy would be carved into the Arc de Triomphe. He proposed that the STN print a radical treatise he had written on military reform, *Le Soldat Citoyen ou vues patriotiques sur la manière la plus avantageuse de pourvoir à la défense du royaume*. Although he hoped at first that it would buy the manuscript, Servan agreed to hire it as a printer and bargained hard over the cost. He also sent detailed specifications of what he wanted, down to the average number of letters on a line (forty) and the number of lines per page (thirty-six). The STN would have to handle smuggling arrangements as far as Versailles, and he would cover the production and transport costs in two payments, one upon receipt of the shipment and one in a note that would mature in August 1781.

Ostervald confirmed these terms at a meeting with Servan in Paris in March 1780. After receiving the manuscript, the STN sent him a complimentary letter. He replied with effusive thanks. Nothing could be more precious, he wrote, than praise from the Swiss, a people who loved liberty and spoke their minds with refreshing frankness.[37] He made only a few corrections to the proofs sent through the mail. The printed sheets arrived safely in Versailles. Servan made a first payment of 848 L. to the STN's banker in Paris and promised to pay the remainder of his bill in August 1781. When it became due, however, he said that he had no liquid funds and that his Parisian distributer, Pierre-Joseph Duplain, would cover the remaining 787 L., not in a single bill of exchange but rather in notes from other booksellers who had ordered their copies from him (for an explanation of bills of exchange and modes of payment, see the next chapter). Their notes, if they arrived, would not mature for another twelve to eighteen months; so Servan was defaulting on his debt.

The STN refused to accept this arrangement. "We are manufacturers, and payments must reach us in accordance with the agreed and current terms," it insisted. Servan would not budge. Finally, on May 20, 1781, the STN wrote a bill of exchange on Duplain to the order of one of its creditors, Meuron et Philippin, for the remainder of the debt, payable when Meuron et Philippin or one of the endorsees would present the note three months later. Instead of agreeing to accept the bill of exchange, Servan insisted that Duplain would collect payments from the provincial booksellers and endorse their notes over to the STN for collection at the future maturation dates. The STN declared this proposition unacceptable.[38] It had little confidence in Duplain, a book dealer who had cobbled together an unofficial business in Paris after an unsuccessful career in Lyon. And having run into difficulties in extracting payment from other obscure authors who had commissioned it to print their manuscripts, it was determined to collect its bill.

Servan, a military officer from a noble family, had a strong sense of honor, as he indicated in his letters and in the text of his book.[39] But it was different from the notion of honor attached to a signature on a bill of exchange. After his unremitting refusals to pay, the STN appealed to his father. By then the bill of exchange had been refused (*protesté*), because, as the STN emphasized, Servan fils, who was then forty years old, had had no scruples about causing "an affront" to its signature. Unless the father intervened, the STN threatened to resort to an extreme measure. With the help of its contacts in Versailles, it would take its case to Servan's commanding officers and ask them to cover the debt by docking his pay, a disciplinary action that, it warned, would badly damage his "honor."

The father did not reply but showed the STN's letter to his son, who then sent off a furious retort. "I am no longer a child under tutelage and still less the sort of man who succumbs to threats." After more angry exchanges in which the STN also impugned the integrity of Duplain, who had refused to cooperate, Servan finally made the payment. As a parting shot, he remarked in a letter that sounded as if he had wanted to challenge Ostervald to a duel: "I do not believe that Helvetic liberty gives one the right to be impertinent, and I know that the most important thing for a man is to be *honnête* and indulgent."[40] On the back of the letter, Ostervald wrote, "No reply as to a madman." This "madman" was to become France's minister of defense ten years later.

Nothing suggests that authors—with rare exceptions like Goezman—intended to default on their debts. They did not appreciate the complexities of marketing literature, and they had a naive confidence in the sales potential of their books. Antoine Barthès de Marmorières is another example of this literary underclass. He was a captain of a regiment of Swiss guards in Versailles and held honorific appointments in the French court. In 1780 he commissioned the STN to print his treatise on the nature of nobility, *Nouveaux Essais sur la noblesse*, which was supposed to have three volumes but never got beyond volume 1. Barthès instructed the STN to produce a handsome quarto edition with an expensive frontispiece, because he planned to distribute it among influential courtiers in the hope of winning patronage. After a great deal of lobbying, he persuaded the government to permit its sale in France. His distributor in Paris took a cut of 3 L. from the sales price—20 sous for his services and a discount of 40 sous to the retailers whom he supplied. "It's an assassination," Barthès lamented.

The book did not sell. Barthès arranged for a specially bound copy to be presented formally to the king's brother, the comte d'Artois, by Barthès's son dressed in the comte's livery. Yet no one in the court, from the royal family on down, showed the slightest interest. "In a court where authors are reviled, a book leads to nothing and isn't read," Barthès complained. He could not pay his printing bill: 2,609 L. according to the STN, 2,000 L. by his own reckoning. "I am devastated at having done a book," he wrote on May 8, 1781. He repeated this theme in later letters, insisting that he had renounced his ambition to be an author and yearned only "to live quietly in an obscure corner." He lost protections, fired his valet and his wife's maid, sold his horse, and moved into a boarding house with his large family. His wife gave birth to their seventh child in 1784. He had married her for love, he wrote, but she was a commoner, and therefore his father, who had old-fashioned ideas about nobility and evidently had not read his book, had disinherited him. "I am reduced to the most terrible poverty," he wrote on August 3, 1784. He had sold off his furniture and cut back on eating meat. In his last letter, dated May 26, 1785, and written from Narbonne, he said that he had moved to Languedoc and had abandoned the pretense that he would ever pay his printing bill.

Barthès might have exaggerated his misery in the hope of persuading the STN to forgive his debt. Dramatic stories about writers who went under can distract attention from the more prosaic cases of those who kept their heads above water. Yet the Republic of Letters suffered at this time from a tendency toward immiseration, which left its mark on works of literature set in Grub

Street, notably Voltaire's "Pauvre Diable" and Diderot's *Neveu de Rameau*. The population of French authors—an "author" being defined as someone who had published at least one book—increased enormously during the second half of the eighteenth century.[41] Authors faced a corresponding increase in the difficulties of getting published, for the book market did not expand during the last fifteen years of the Ancien Régime. On the contrary, it contracted.[42]

Yet the prestige of authorship continued to grow, fed by the cult of Voltaire and Rousseau, and in consequence, the STN was besieged by writers offering manuscripts. So many tried to sell their wares to Quandet that, as he wrote somewhat facetiously, he had to set aside visiting hours to receive them. Bosset reported a typical instance during his business trip of 1780: "An author as poor as Job came here yesterday, trying to sell me a manuscript about the Jesuits." The STN archives offer glimpses into many miserable lives: C. P. Jonval, a former journalist and friend of the *philosophes*, who offered several manuscripts for sale and would settle for a job as a proofreader; a certain de Montenay, who relied on his pen to survive after escaping from a prison where his family had had him confined by a *lettre de cachet*; Jean-Jacques Béreaud, a wigmaker, who managed to publish a five-act play but could not sell enough copies to pay for its printing; Père Martin, a clergyman-poet who had fallen into debt and was trying to write himself out of it; abbé Le Senne, who flogged manuscripts under several pseudonyms while running away from a *lettre de cachet*—the STN archives contain pleas for help from many "poor devils."[43] It usually ignored them and kept to its main business, pirating books that already existed rather than publishing new ones. More often than not, its original publications led to write-offs in its account of "profits and losses."

In fact, piracy itself required an unremitting effort to keep out of the red, as the preceding pages have shown. The economic context of this struggle for survival is the final aspect of pirating that remains to be discussed.

12

Making and Losing Money

THE SPECULATIONS, SWINDLES, AND unpaid bills described in the previous chapters raise a question about what was at the bottom of it all—what, in fact, was money. The meaning of money, like most things, differed greatly 250 years ago from what it means today. To the workers in the STN's printing shop it took the form of coins called batzen and kreuzer, which were made from copper admixed with silver and which the shop foreman paid out of a cash box on Saturday evenings.[1] At that time, he apportioned wages for the week's work at a ritual known as *faire la banque.*

Most of the compositors and pressmen, with the exception of a few veterans who received weekly salaries (working *en conscience*), collected piece rates; and as their labor varied greatly from week to week, they would leave the shop on a Saturday evening with sums that ranged from 70 to 105 batzen (10 to 15 French livres). That was good pay, more than a carpenter and as much as a locksmith would make in Paris. Some of the STN's workers owned watches, a fairly common luxury among skilled artisans, and all of them could afford food and drink—especially drink, as they sometimes went on binges that lasted from Saturday evening until Tuesday (not to show up for work on Monday was a common indulgence, known as *faire le lundi*, the equivalent of "Saint Monday" in England). The poorest, unskilled workers in Paris sometimes earned only 10 sous a day or 3 L. a week. That was barely enough to feed a family. A four-pound loaf of ordinary bread, the key element in their diet, usually cost 8 or 9 sous. If poor harvests drove up the price of bread, the working poor skipped meals, suffered from malnourishment, and often rioted in protest.

Drinking and rioting, favorite themes among social historians, serve as a reminder that for everyone in the working class money inhered in a world of concrete things—loaves of bread, jugs of wine, the occasional pocket watch. It did not belong to the abstract world of account money—that is, the livres, sous, and deniers familiar to financiers since the time of Charlemagne. The livre tournois, which was the key unit in accounting, did not correspond to an actual coin. Working people handled transactions in *monnaie de billon*, or base coins made of copper or copper with an admixture of silver, like the batzen and kreuzer paid to the workers of the STN. In France, this money came in units known as *sous* (or *sols*, coins valued at 20 to a livre), *deniers* (12 to the *sous*), *liards* (worth three *deniers*), and *écus* (worth three *sous*). Other denominations, many of them unstable or uncertain, also cropped up in everyday speech—the *pistole*, the *obole*, the *maille*, the *rond*.

Among them, the *écu* was particularly important. If a housewife managed to put aside savings, they would most likely take the form of a sack of *écus* hidden beyond the ken of the tax collector and perhaps her husband. Voltaire's anti-physiocratic novel, *L'Homme aux quarante écus*, took the *écu* as an index to misery, for his protagonist owned land that brought in an annual revenue of 40 *écus*, which, in Voltaire's calculation, was an average income and not nearly enough to keep a man alive. In fact, poor peasants did not often handle coins, except when they paid taxes. They lived in large part from subsistence farming and dealt in barter, exchanging services as well as goods. Many of them never saw a louis d'or, the coin that functioned as the ultimate measure of wealth for the wealthy and that was valued at 24 L. In his memoirs, Casanova situated that kind of coin in the social order when he spoke of receiving "a roll of a hundred louis" as down payment for participating in a plot by the Parisian high and mighty to speculate on the state's debt.[2]

Far from being an absolute, therefore, the meaning of money varied according to the ways people experienced and expressed it. To appreciate the business aspect of publishing, it is important to keep these variations in mind. Like all other publishers and merchants in general, the directors of the STN operated simultaneously in two different monetary systems. At home in Neuchâtel, they did business in a world bounded by the local coinage. They used it to pay their workers, to collect payment for the books they sold over the counter, and to cover most of their own living expenses. In the larger world, they dealt in account money (the abstract denominations of livres, sous, deniers), which tied them to credit networks extending all over Europe.

The way they kept their accounts shows how one world shaded off into the other. When he paid wages to workers, the foreman of the printing shop noted the sums in batzen and kreuzer in a notebook called *Banque des ouvriers*. Similarly, a clerk kept track of local expenditures and receipts in account books labeled *Livre de caisse* and *Petite caisse*. These sums, which corresponded to transactions made in coin, were transferred to a register, called a *Journal* (also *Brouillard* or *Main courante*). At that point, they were transformed into account money and slotted into accounts along with the STN's larger transactions, such as purchases of paper and payments from booksellers. The *Journal* recorded credits and debits chronologically according to the conventions of double-entry bookkeeping. Other account books made it possible for the directors of the STN to keep track of shipments, stock, finances, and sales of their own editions, each of which had its own account. All of this information, expressed in the basic code of livres tournois, was gathered up in a *Grand livre*, which showed the general tendency of the STN's business.[3] As they passed upward through these account books, a process known as posting (*comptabilisation*) the sums became larger and the view of them increasingly abstract. In the end, the numbers inscribed in the stately hand of an accountant stood for the success or failure of the STN as an enterprise. Between that general reckoning and a kreuzer plunked down by a pressman on the table of a tavern for a *chopine* of wine, the distance was enormous.

In principle, of course, there was an ultimate standard: a *marc d'or,* or bar of 22-carat gold, which, when worked over by *maîtres de monnaie* in France's royal mints, produced 30 louis d'or, each bearing the profile of the king but without a numerical indication of its worth. The value of the louis varied considerably until 1726, when it was fixed at 24 L. This standardization belonged to the reorganization of state finances following the collapse of the "System" of John Law, the Scottish adventurer who attempted to transform the French economy by floating a giant stock corporation, the Compagnie des Indes, and linking it to a state bank, which issued paper currency. The crash of the "System" in 1720 was so spectacular that it blocked the way for the creation of institutions that contributed so much to the power of England in the eighteenth century—that is, a central bank and legal tender in the form of paper notes backed by the credit of the state. French merchants had to do business in private notes, mainly bills of exchange, written in livres, sous, and deniers and convertible into louis d'or or other forms of specie. In 1776, the French government created a Caisse d'Escompte, which specialized in discounting notes. But it was a private stock company, not a national bank, and its chronic lack of specie led to near bankruptcies in 1779 and 1783. The state itself teetered on the brink of bankruptcy, especially after floating loans to pay for the American War—and the loans had to be paid off at ruinous rates through annuities (*rentes viagères*), because the ancient prohibition of usury made it impossible to charge interest.

Trade in France therefore suffered from a monetary and banking system that was outdated, inefficient, and saturated with values peculiar to the Ancien Régime. As Swiss Protestants, the directors of the STN were not constrained by these restrictions, and they could have bills of exchange discounted in Geneva. However, they did at least half of their business in France, and they depended on merchant bankers in Lyon—and to a lesser extent in Paris—to clear a profit from their sales.[4]

Bosset often remarked that the STN's purpose was not to publish books but to make money from them: "The problem is not in finding good things to print. It is to make money from them once they are printed."[5] To understand how publishers turned profits, it is important to consider the technical aspects of commercial exchanges in early modern France.[6] By money, Bosset meant specie, as in a favorite French phrase, *espèces sonnantes et trébuchantes*—the kind of coin whose gold or silver had not been adulterated by clipping and that gave off a reassuring sound of solidity when dropped on a hard surface. To make money, the STN needed not only to sell its books but also to collect payment for them, either in notes that could be converted into cash or directly in louis. Payment, or *recouvrement*, became a major problem for publishers, who often found it more difficult to manage than selling the books in the first place. Payment came in different kinds of notes (bills of exchange and *billets à ordre*, or promissory notes similar to modern checks). To change them into specie required a great deal of negotiation and often loss, because notes were obligations of a private sort, only as good as the credit of the individual who wrote them. The system had to function without legal tender and without banks as we know them (merchants acted as bankers by keeping deposits and discounting bills of exchange, but their resources were limited).

The bill of exchange illustrates the difficulty of making money in such a system. It involved three persons: a payer (*tireur*) who wrote it, directing a correspondent (*accepteur*) to pay a specific sum to the bearer (*porteur*) at a future date. In many cases, the correspondent was a merchant banker with whom the payer had deposited specie. The payer made out the note as payment for a debt, usually goods or services supplied by the bearer. The bearer could cash the note in for specie at the prescribed date, but he often had to make payments of his own. In that case, he would endorse the note to one of his creditors, who could do the same, and so on until the last endorsee (bearer) presented the note for payment on its date of maturity. Bills of exchange therefore circulated in a manner similar to that of paper currency, except that they were constantly being discounted, because their value at the time of an endorsement was always less than their value at the more remote date when they matured—that is, they were a form of credit. Moreover, their value varied according to the confidence enjoyed by the payer who had signed them and the correspondent who was to redeem them. If a payer was not considered sufficiently solid, the discount rate would be correspondingly greater or the note could not be negotiated at all.

The system also suffered from complications and negotiations at the time of a note's maturity. Although the note's due date might fall on any day of the calendar, aside from Sundays and holidays, it often coincided with specific, month-long periods known as *paiements*, such as the four fairs of Lyon (Rois in March, Pâques in June, Août in September, and Saints in December), which had provided financial services for much of France since the fifteenth century. During the first six days of each fair the last bearer of a note would present it for *acceptation* by the correspondent (usually a merchant banker resident in Lyon or one of the other *places* where notes were negotiated). If he accepted a note, the correspondent would have until the end of the month to come up with the specie or its equivalent in other, immediately negotiable notes (*billets à vue*), a process that normally involved settling accounts and negotiating discounts on bills with other merchant bankers. If he refused it, the bearer would have it "protested"—that is, he would add to the sum a heavy charge called a *protêt* and try to exact payment from the last endorser, who would do the same with the previous endorser until the note reverted to the payer who had originally written it. The payer would then have to find a way to pay for it. Frequently he would try to persuade his creditor to accept another note or series of notes for a higher sum and a later date of maturity— that is, to cover an old debt with a new one. But pyramiding debts could not go on indefinitely. Default on payments could lead to bankruptcy and even imprisonment (*contrainte par corps*). In order to prevent such catastrophes, payers were supposed to keep their correspondents informed about notes that were to be due and to deposit enough to cover them. If they failed to do so, they could accumulate a disastrous backlog of debt, and word about the protests could badly damage their credit. The banker-correspondent might cover a note with his own funds in order to protect the credit of the payer, but he could not do so for long. And the whole system involved something more than money. It rested on the signatures attached to the bills of exchange, a matter of *confiance*, the crucial element in commercial relations, as explained in the preceding chapters.

When a group of entrepreneurs (or an individual) established (or reorganized) a company, they commonly circulated a printed form, which announced its existence in highly stylized language. On November 12, 1773, Michel Gaude, an eminent bookseller in Nîmes, sent the STN a typical circular.

"I have the honor of informing you that I have just created a company under the appellation [*raison*] of GAUDE Father, Son, and A. Gaude. Flattered by the confidence that you have always accorded me, I dare to hope that you will be good enough to continue it and to trust [*ajouter foi à*] the legal signature as much as my own." Gaude had made his son and another relative, A. Gaude, partners in his business. At the bottom of the circular the two new partners signed the name of the firm, not their personal names, in their own handwriting. This *signature* carried legal force. It could be used as evidence in court cases and disagreements over accounts. Business letters often were written in the fine hand of a clerk but signed by a partner in conformity with the sample signature on the circular. To receive the authority to sign a company's name was an important stage in the promotion of a career and also in the evolution of the firm. In fact, the word *firm* (the French favored *raison* or *raison sociale* but also used *firme*) conveyed a concept derived from the Italian verb *firmare*, to sign.[7]

The STN often received such notices, which always used the same phraseology.[8] If, as expected, it agreed to extend its *confiance* to the new firm, it replied by affirming its commitment to "give faith" (*ajouter foi*) to the new signature. The extent of the commitment varied according to the STN's experience in collecting payment for the notes, signed with the authorized signature, that the firm sent after receiving shipments of books. According to the normal procedure, a bookseller would inspect a shipment soon after it arrived to make sure that it had no *défets* (spoiled or missing sheets) and then send a bill of exchange due to mature at a certain date, usually twelve months, after the reception of the goods. Alternatively, he might send a promissory note (usually called a *billet à ordre*) by which he committed himself, rather than his banker, to pay a sum by a date at his place of business. It, too, had to be presented for acceptance, and the STN could endorse it to its own creditors, just as in the case of a bill of exchange; but it rested entirely on the strength of the bookseller's signature and therefore might require a higher discount rate when endorsed. If a bookseller had run up a deficit in his account, the STN could write a note on him, but this kind of *billet* had less force, because the bookseller had not signed it and therefore could refuse to accept it, although he was the debtor. The only immediate consequence for him would be a loss of confidence on the part of the STN, which might hold back further shipments of books until he had redeemed the deficit. Word would spread, however, and he could suffer from a general decline in confidence that would damage the key ingredient of his business, his signature.

If a payer who had signed a bill of exchange or a promissory note failed to provide payment on the agreed date and instead let it be "protested," he had not "honored" it, and the dishonor fell on his signature. As the phrasing suggests, this notion of honor had emotional force. In 1781, the STN wrote a note on Jules-Henri Pott, a small but solid publisher in Lausanne with whom it exchanged books. Although it had fallen behind in their mutual accounts, Pott informed the STN that he had paid for the note when it was presented to him "for the honor of your signature."[9] Similarly, Matthieu, a bookseller in Nancy, paid a bill of exchange for 53 L. "for the honor of your signature," even though he actually owed the STN only 36 L.[10] After Guillaume Bergeret, a bookseller in Bordeaux, refused to pay a note that the STN had written on him in 1778 for a shipment of books, it sent him an indignant letter in which it accused him of making an "affront to our signature."[11] Similarly, the STN insisted that Servan de Gerbey "should pay honor to our signature" on its note for the payment of his debt for the printing of *Le Soldat citoyen.* As explained in the previous chapter, this demand led to a violent quarrel in which the STN's commercial concept of honor as embodied in its signature conflicted with Servan's sense of honor as a noble and a military officer.

"Confidence," "honor," "faith," "protest," "affront"—the language of commercial transactions was saturated with values and attitudes from the surrounding society. Far from being neutral and self-evident, like a dollar bill today, a bill of exchange carried an affective charge. In Diderot's *Jacques le fataliste,* the Master expressed this power when he remarked, "The word bill of exchange made me blanche."[12] The basic problem of collecting bills was therefore compounded by the nature of money itself. All the complications accompanying *billets* and *lettres de change*—signatures, endorsements, acceptances, protests—provided opportunities for debtors to postpone or escape payment. And when they were cornered, the debtors fell back on further procedures that carried the onus of bankruptcy yet often gave them a new lease on commercial life. The stages were always the same: first a default on the payment of a note; then, several defaults later, *faillite,* meaning a suspension of payments pending a possible arrangement with the creditors; and finally in some cases a full-fledged bankruptcy with a sentence by a commercial court (*cour consulaire*), which could lead to the sale of assets and the total liquidation of the business.[13]

Two cases, one from the upper ranks of booksellers, one from the bottom, illustrate the way this scenario played out in the STN's relations with its customers. Jean Manoury came from a distinguished family of booksellers in Caen and ran one of the largest businesses in Normandy.[14] In 1771, however, he spent five months in the Bastille for publishing and distributing forbidden books, most of them attacks on the controversial Maupeou ministry. Although the imprisonment badly damaged his trade, he was back on his feet—and still dealing in illegal literature along with a wide variety of permitted books—in October 1775, when he began to order shipments from the STN. The first order reached him safely; and after verifying its contents, he sent off a note for 320 L. in payment. Subsequent shipments also went well. Manoury sent a note for 621 L. in September 1776, but he attached a long maturation date to it and then began to fall behind in his payments. In order to correct the imbalance in his account, the STN wrote a note on him for 367 L. in July 1777 with a due date in September. He let it be protested, citing "unexpected circumstances," which included the postponement of a 1,200 L. debt owed to him. He also requested an extension on the 621 L. note, but he promised to pay off both notes by December 15. His finances were sound, he explained, although several of his own debtors had left him in the lurch. He did indeed honor the smaller note, but he delayed payment of the note for 621 L. until December 27, explaining, "I have experienced more misfortune than any bookseller in France."

Having cleared his account, though with some expensive delays, Manoury resumed ordering books in 1778. Then suddenly on September 27 he wrote that he had suspended all his payments—that is, his business had fallen into *faillite*. He asked the STN to accept an informal agreement, which would avoid all costs and legal entanglements. He wanted to redeem his debts by payments spread out over three years. As his accounts demonstrated, he claimed, his situation was quite strong: the credits (7,734 L. owed to him and stock worth 60,000 L.) outweighed the debits (24,654 L. in debts owed by him). By assiduously continuing his business, he would pay back everything and win back "your confidence."[15] The STN replied that it would accept three notes of 220 L. each to be paid over three years, with 5 percent interest, beginning a year from the present (October 1778)—provided that they be made payable to a solid guarantor, who would endorsed them to the STN. Impossible, Manoury answered, and also unfair, because his misfortune was not his fault:

> I entered my profession with a good heart. I expected to find uprightness in the trade, but unfortunately I confided in some persons whom I thought to be solid, who abused my excessive complaisance and who damaged my fortune by large bankruptcies. I come from a good family, my father being a bookseller and one of the most respectable citizens in Caen. My misfortunes have absorbed all my cash, but with a little time, hard work, and economizing, it will not be difficult for me to mend everything, since in truth my stock of books is the most varied and one of the largest in Normandy.

A gap in the correspondence makes it impossible to determine what agreement Manoury and the STN reached, but by mid-1781 they had resumed trading. He acquitted a note for 250 L. in October as if he had paid off his old debt. When the STN tried to settle his new account in August 1782, it claimed that he owed 1,911 L., and he acknowledged only 1,833 L., which he proposed to pay off with six notes staggered to mature at various dates up to February 1784. He needed an unusually long deadline, he explained, "in order to strictly honor everything."

Despite the long deadline, the STN accepted those conditions. But in March 1783 when the first note became due, he refused to acquit it and promised instead to make a payment three months later, "word of honor." Having attempted unsuccessfully to apply pressure on Manoury through a local merchant, the STN then resorted to a banker-bill collector in Paris, Batilliot l'aîné, who specialized in squeezing sums from recalcitrant debtors in the book trade. This plan worked, and thanks to coercion from Batilliot, Manoury also honored the next three notes, though with ill humor. "I cannot reproach myself with anything other than having extended too much confidence and therefore having suffered cruelly from my good heart." Yet he failed to acquit the fifth note, a matter of 300 L. The STN then employed a lawyer in Caen named Le Sueur to force payment by threatening legal action, and Manoury eventually covered this debt with three new notes for 100 L. each. When the sixth and final note became due, Le Sueur had to take him to court to force its payment in May 1785. By then the STN had long ago refused to send Manoury any more books, and it had notified him that it would cease to continue "a correspondence that is as tiresome as it is disagreeable."

An equally protracted process of defaulting on payments and renego-
tiating debts took place in the STN's dealings with Nicolas Gerlache, who
represented the book trade at its humblest.[16] He entered the work force as
a tanner in Thionville. Tanning led to book binding, binding to peddling
books, peddling to smuggling illegal works across the border, and smuggling
to a period in prison in 1767. After his release, he took up tanning again,
and then fortune smiled on him. He wooed and won a young woman with a
good dowry, 100 louis (2,400 L.). They decided to establish a bookstore and
bindery in Metz, drawing on all the capital they could muster: 803 L. for a
brevet de libraire (bookseller's certificate), which gave Gerlache a legal foothold in the trade; 400 L. for renting a house; 300 L. for setting up the bookshop; 600 L. for outfitting himself with tools and hides as a binder; and 300
L. for "furniture necessary for a young couple." He had hoped to stock the
shop with books sent by Jean-Louis Boubers, the publisher-wholesaler
in Brussels, but their arrangement broke down in a quarrel over shipping
and other costs. Having come into contact with the STN through Boubers,
Gerlache asked it to send supplies. His prospects were excellent, he wrote.
Although sales had been weak during the first year, 1771, his bindery had
thrived and he had set up a *cabinet littéraire,* or commercial library, which
had attracted 150 subscribers and brought in 100 écus (300 L.) a month. He
worked hard, he assured the STN; and his young wife worked alongside him,
for, as he remarked with pride, she was "born for work and for commerce."
The STN could count on his good character. He never drank alcohol, and
above all, he always paid his bills on time. "I would rather perish than to have
any of my notes protested," he declared.

Attracted by the prospect of establishing trade in Metz, where it had no
customers, the STN agreed to fill Gerlache's orders. The first shipments
arrived without mishap, and he paid for them as promised. Then in July 1772
he ran into difficulties. "I am now going through a difficult crisis," he wrote
to the STN. "My mother-in-law is about to die, my wife expects to give birth
from one moment to the other, and I fear that the death of my mother-in-law
will make her ill." In November, despite his earlier assurances, he had to ask
for an extension on one of his notes, which had been protested. By then his
mother-in-law had died, leaving 2,000 L. to his wife, though she could not
collect her inheritance for another year because she had not yet legally come
of age. In January 1773 Gerlache warned the STN that he would not be able to
acquit a second note, and he sounded desperate. If any creditor tried to crush
him, he warned, "I will set fire to everything I have in order to keep it out

of the hands of the court." He suspended his payments in February, and the STN then sent one of its trusted correspondents, C.-C. Duvez of Nancy, to investigate. Duvez reported that Gerlache should be able to pay off his debts if given enough time, for his assets came to 8,000 L. and his debits to 3,000 L. Moreover, he enjoyed a good reputation: "Many persons had nothing but good to say about him, noting that he was a young man who took great trouble with his work and had good conduct." Instead of forcing Gerlache to deposit a balance sheet and declare *faillite*, the STN accepted an arrangement whereby he would liquidate his debt by payments made every six months for three and a half years. Soon he found that he could not keep to the schedule. Having become involved in the affairs of the Société typographique de Saarbruck, he suffered a heavy loss when it went bankrupt in November. In January 1774 he confessed to his inability to continue the payments, and then he sank into silence.

The STN did not hear from him again until October, when he sent a letter pleading for another extension of his debt. He had fled to Liège, he wrote. His wife had prevented the sale of their assets by claiming sole possession of them as she was entitled from her dowry, and they still clung to the hope of continuing their business. In December Gerlache informed the STN that some of his creditors had agreed to a ten-year repayment plan, but the nego-tiations dragged on for the next seven months, while he continued to beg for indulgence in letters sent from Liège, Luxembourg, and Brussels. Finally, in July 1775, he announced that he had turned in his balance sheet and for-mally declaring *faillite*, and he asked the STN to accept the ten-year plan, which had won the approval of three-quarters of the creditors. Faced with no feasible alternative (the forced sale of Gerlache's stock would have pro-duced less than the repayments, meager as they were) it eventually agreed. By December Gerlache had resumed his business in Metz, and things were looking up, thanks to the *cabinet littéraire*, which then had 250 subscribers, most of them officers stationed in the town's garrison.

Although the subscribers mainly came to read the newspapers that Gerlache made available, they sometimes bought books. Therefore, Gerlache asked the STN to resume sending him supplies and promised to pay for them in cash while maintaining the long-term payments on his old debt. By July 1777 he had not only collected and paid for two shipments, but he also hoped to wipe out all his debts, for his *cabinet littéraire* now had 379 members, who each paid 1 L. 10 sous per month. "Voilà, Messieurs," he wrote trium-phantly, "my affairs are going better than I had hoped." In October he sent three notes, each for 131 L., which would mature in twelve, eighteen, and twenty-four months, covering the rest of his debts. In December business still looked good, and he hoped to cash in on the rush to subscribe to the quarto edition of the *Encyclopédie*. Then, however, his correspondence was interrupted by another ominous break. When he resumed it in November 1778, his business faced a new threat: the American War. France's decision to support the Americans made it likely that most of his subscribers would be transferred from their garrison in Metz. Having failed to honor a note, Gerlache had scraped up enough money to cover the *protêt*, and he hoped to honor it in full in the near future, but things had taken a turn for the worse. In June 1779 he asked for a further delay in his payments. "I am not surprised, Messieurs, that Louis XVI ordered the departure of 200 of my readers, but I have suffered badly from it, just like others who find themselves in the same circumstances." The STN fell back on the service of a bill collector from Nancy, who exacted a payment of 69 L. in February 1780 and enough in the following weeks to close the account. In the end, Gerlache repaid his debt, though at a loss to the STN, owing to the delays. By 1781 it had ceased corresponding with him, yet he was still in business, because he appeared as a "bookseller" in the *Almanach de la librairie* of 1781.

Although Manoury and Gerlache represented opposite extremes of the book trade, their financial difficulties had much in common—a matter of overextending orders, falling behind in payments, negotiating extensions of credit, accumulating additional expenses through protested notes, and *faillites*. Their experience should not be dismissed as irresponsible behavior by incorrigible bankrupts. It corresponds to the stories of many others who struggled to cope with the same problems, and it illustrates an important yet poorly understood aspect of early-modern capitalism. When booksellers went bankrupt, their creditors did not normally confiscate their assets and force them out of business. A *faillite* or suspension of payments usually led to negotiations, and the bankrupt bookseller frequently struck a deal with his creditors on terms that permitted him to resume his trade, ordering new supplies and selling them off in a continuous effort to shed the burden of debt. The system had enough flexibility to provide for fresh starts, and behind every start there was a story—usually, as the bankrupts construed it, a narrative that pitted a hard-working entrepreneur against an unfavorable turn of events.

The fate of Manoury and Gerlache, according to their own accounts, came down to a struggle of character against "circumstances,"—contingencies beyond their control. Of course they insisted on their virtue in order to gain the indulgence of their creditors. Yet their version of their experience indicates two aspects of the book business that deserve to be taken seriously: on the one hand, commercial relations were based on social relations, and character mattered as much as cash; on the other, circumstances frequently exposed individuals to forces that they could not foresee and that threatened to overwhelm them.

Both aspects stand out in one of the richest dossiers in the STN archives, that of Batilliot, the merchant banker and bill collector who squeezed a payment out of Manoury in 1783 and who handled many of the STN's financial affairs. In a printed circular dated December 1, 1776, Batilliot announced that his banking transactions came to a million livres a year, entirely in the book trade.[17] He kept accounts for publishers and wholesalers who deposited notes from their customers and drew on him for the payment of their own bills of exchange. The STN began using him to discount notes in 1777, and in March 1778 he agreed to accept everything it sent to him from provincial booksellers, up to a limit of 10,000 L. He would negotiate the notes for the STN's account and charge 1 percent of their face value for this service, although he also required the STN to back them up, if needed, with "solid paper" (easily negotiable notes). By this arrangement, the STN effectively transferred much of its bill collecting to Batilliot, because its most obscure customers paid for their shipments with *billets* that could be discounted only at a substantial loss. They tended to be small businessmen whose signatures carried relatively little weight. Batilliot knew them all, or all but the most marginal and illegal dealers. Having spent decades in the trade, he had carved out a niche, a specialized kind of banking, which involved collecting payments on notes by dunning, threats, and force. He had acquired the reputation of a bulldog. When a bookseller resisted, he would dispatch a lawyer to begin a suit, or a bailiff to impound the stock, or a police officer to haul the victim off to prison.[18]

Although he had a heavy hand, Batilliot preferred to avoid violent measures. They cost money, although the debtor always had to pay the fees. To minimize difficulties, he warned the STN to refuse to do business with anyone who might not honor notes. For example, when the STN inquired about the advisability of sending a shipment to a small bookseller in Anduze named Brotte, Batilliot replied, "I will tell you frankly that I do not know that man. And as I know pretty well all the booksellers in whom one can have confidence, I would not advise you to put yours in him."[19] Batilliot's correspondence contained a stream of similar assessments. Michel: "As to Michel in Sète, believe me, put no confidence in him. He is a peddlar given over to the sale of bad books." Bonnard: "Don't trust Bonnard. He is a man who is not known for good conduct and who often gets drunk." Prudhomme: "As to sieur Prud'homme of Meaux, he is a young man who is just beginning, undertakes a great deal, would like to print bad books, who made a fairly advantageous marriage, and in whom I have no confidence." Barrois l'aîné: "This house is one of the most solid in the book trade, outstanding in its honor and wealth. A million [invested] in this house would be as safe as a penny." Jarfaut: "Jarfaut of Melun isn't worth a damn."

Batilliot's comments resembled the recommendations that the STN received from its other correspondents (see Chapter 9): they emphasized character and confidence. What set them apart was their number, nearly three dozen, because Batilliot functioned as a one-man credit-rating agency, specializing in the book trade. This role, he explained, went with his activities as a banker. Before doing business with unknown booksellers, the STN should consult with him.[20] He had agents—"my capitalists," he called them—who supplied information and collected bills in many provincial towns; and he knew which booksellers could be trusted, because so many of their notes passed through his hands.

Dealing with marginal booksellers raised risks, of course, both for the STN, which suffered from the delays and defaults in their payments, and for Batilliot, who could not acquit the STN's own notes if it did not keep up adequate deposits in its account. He was willing to cover for it—up to the limit of 10,000 L.—if it fell behind; but that was a dangerous game, because it exposed his own resources. "My fortune isn't great, but my credit is established at a million and I must conserve it as dearly as my life," he wrote on September 14, 1778. "I am known to all the booksellers in the kingdom, and I work with three-quarters of them. . . . But as my fate is attached to my credit, I must conserve the latter until the last breath of my life so that I can leave it with honor to my children." He warned the STN against giving its confidence casually and complained when it deposited "bad paper" from marginal booksellers.[21]

By 1781 his letters began to sound anxious. In March, "for the honor of your signature," he accepted a bill of exchange that the STN wrote on him for 1,599 L. but warned it to send him some solid "paper" before that note became due. Although it then deposited two notes for 2,995 L., he paid out 6,171 L. in September for six more notes "though without funds deposited and for the honor of your signature." In October, for the first time, he refused to accept some bills of exchange that the STN wrote on him. Then suddenly on May 1, 1782, he suspended his own payments. He had gone broke, like so many of the booksellers from whom he had squeezed money, and like them he negotiated a rescue operation in the same way that he had cut deals with bankrupts while working for creditors. Thanks to his experience he got favorable terms: a write-off of a third of his debts and a three-year extension to pay off the remainder. He was back in business in August 1782, and he continued to correspond with the STN, although not to discount its notes, until 1786.[22]

At the level of banking, Batilliot's story corresponds to the tales that run through the dossiers of many booksellers at the retail level of the trade. Too much emphasis on bankruptcies can give the impression that the book trade was hopelessly mired in inadequate financing. In fact, the system, cumbersome as it was, actually worked quite well, at least in periods of prosperity. New publishing enterprises sprang up everywhere in the 1750s and 1760s, and as we have seen, the STN's trade expanded throughout the 1770s. It made a great deal of money, although the extent of its profits cannot be calculated, because of the absence of its most comprehensive accounts (*Grands livres*). It sold roughly half its books in France. The other half went to booksellers scattered all over Europe—to Antoine Adolphe Fyrberg in Stockholm, Charles Guillaume Muller in St. Petersburg, Christian Rüdiger in Moscow, J. M. Weingand in Pest, Luigi Coltellini in Naples, Antonio de Sancha in Madrid, Edward Lyde in London, Luke White in Dublin, and many others. These transactions took place on an impressive scale. Although Muller sent only one order a year from St. Petersburg, it always contained dozens of titles, enough to fill bales that weighed as much as 400 pounds. The accounts and correspondence make it possible to follow the bales down the Rhine to warehouses in Amsterdam and then on ships that sailed up the North Sea to the Baltic—unless the Gulf of Finland had frozen over and they had to go by wagon across tundra. The letters of shipping agents also reveal the itinerary of books sent over the Alps on the backs of mules, books shipped to the fair of Leipzig for distribution in German markets, books shipped down the Rhône to Marseille for storage and forwarding to ports throughout the Mediterranean. Like other large publishers, the STN worked hard to maintain a network of clients everywhere in Europe, for Europeans everywhere read French. Yet the readers were thin on the ground, a small, educated elite, and the STN did not receive enough orders from its far-flung customers for us to get a clear view of their businesses.

It was in France that the STN developed a network of customers dense enough for their correspondence to reveal the underlying conditions of the book trade.[23] Their letters do not yield anything comparable to an economic index, but they indicate a general trend: a period of expansion in the early 1770s, one of contraction at the end of the decade, and a crisis in the mid-1780s. By the time of the Revolution, the publishing industry was in disarray. The full extent of the damage cannot be measured, although the bankruptcy archives in the Archives départementales de la Seine suggest that a great many booksellers went under.[24] What the STN papers show is a prevailing sense of decline and an accumulation of bad debts and bankruptcies, beginning about 1775. Some aspects of the STN's financial difficulties were peculiar to its own business rather than to publishing in general, and the jeremiads of booksellers should be taken with a grain of salt. Yet the savviest professionals expressed well-informed judgments, and their diagnoses of their situation deserve to be taken seriously.

Pierre Machuel of Rouen, whom we met in Chapter 9, stood out as one of the most successful and experienced bookseller-publishers in France. The tone in the long line of letters that he sent to the STN changed in 1775, when he wrote that an accumulation of bankruptcies had damaged his business so badly that he saw no way to avoid further exposure to bad debts, despite his caution in extending confidence to customers. Having done business for twenty-eight years, he concluded that the risks now outweighed the profits. In March 1779, he complained that the edicts of 1777 had compounded the economic difficulties by creating uncertainty about the government's regulation of the trade. "Those who are well off are trying to withdraw [from the trade]," he wrote, "because it makes no sense to part with one's goods in exchange for lengthy credits, to have to take cutbacks, and then to watch *protêts* come in along with cumulative losses." In September he added disruptions in trade produced by the American War to his laments about the causes of the decline and announced that he was "putting my money into land, because it can't be invested safely in books; bankruptcies are too frequent, and they take place after endless extensions of debts." The war was the death knell. "The favorable moment for our trade has passed," he wrote. "It won't come back." By March 1780 his pessimism had deepened: "Sales . . . have completely collapsed." In June 1783, he concluded, "This trade is ruined." He retired from it in September.

At the other end of the kingdom, Jean Mossy, the largest bookseller-publisher in Marseille and an astute observer of the trade, came up with a similar analysis. He, too, complained about unreliable debtors, the effects of the edicts of 1777, and the American War. After the war ended, he hoped that business would pick up, but it did not; and in December 1785 he wrote that the accumulation of bankruptcies made the future look black. "We know only too well that the trade is suffering to an extraordinary degree, and we are quite sure that in ten years all retail booksellers will be ruined." As a port city, Bordeaux suffered in the same way. Guillaume Bergeret, one of its most important booksellers, cut back his orders in November 1778. "Business is so slow and has suffered so badly from the war that all sectors of trade have fallen off in this city," he wrote. Booksellers in garrison cities complained the most loudly about the war, because so many of their customers were army officers who had been sent across the sea or transferred to other locations. Christian Mondon in Verdun, like Gerlache in Metz, could no longer pay his bills. "Trade has completely fallen off," he wrote on April 9, 1780. "No business can survive without the troops, and we have been stripped of them ever since the beginning of this miserable war, which has deprived us of all resources. . . . I am unable to make any payments. Six children and few sales make me see nothing but misery in the future." Widow Charmet in Besançon cut back on her orders for the same reason. One of her competitors had sold off his stock at ruinous prices, she wrote in July 1785. That had stifled her own sales, even though an influx of soldiers had returned to the local garrison. "Our trade is in an atrocious state." Bernard of Lunéville, who catered to soldiers in a *cabinet littéraire*, ceased his payments in June 1782 after having suspended them and negotiated a deal with his creditors two years earlier. His letters repeated the same theme. Everyone was squeezing him for money, but "I have none, that is, none at all, absolutely none."[25]

The war hurt trade everywhere. Jean-François de Los Rios wrote from Lyon in September 1780, "The book trade is dead in this city. The war is the cause." Lyon especially suffered because of its importance as a financial center. In January 1779 Claudet, one of the STN's shipping agents in Lyon, reported that bills of exchange were very difficult to negotiate during the current fair, because of a wave of bankruptcies related to the war.[26] Another Lyonnais shipping agent, Jacques Revol, gave a more specific explanation two years later: the loans floated by Jacques Necker to finance the war had soaked up so much capital that there was a shortage of specie.[27] Booksellers such as Fontanel in Montpellier and Widow Charmet in Besançon made the same complaint.[28] A financial crisis occasioned by the war had produced a ripple effect that was damaging the book trade at all levels, from large publishers to small retailers.

The STN's banker in Lyon, Pomaret, Rilliet, d'Arnal et Compagnie, confirmed this view. Jacques-François d'Arnal, who was Bosset's son-in-law, reported regularly on discount rates and the availability of specie at the *paiements* of the Lyonnais fairs. After 1779, the tone of his letters became increasingly alarmed. In June 1780 he warned, "Money will be very rare in this *paiement*." In September 1781 he wrote that bills of exchange could be discounted only at a severe loss, owing to lack of specie. Things had gotten worse by September 1782, "as all notes are being offered without takers, owing to the lack of cash that we are experiencing, which makes business in general extremely difficult." The heart of the problem was located in Paris, where the Caisse d'Escompte was supposed to discount notes for the entire kingdom but lacked the specie to do so. In December 1782, May 1783, and September 1783, d'Arnal's letters registered a constant ratcheting up of the fiscal pressure; and on November 4, 1783, he announced that the crisis at the Caisse d'Escompte had produced a disaster in Lyon. "Cash is completely lacking. All business is suspended." In consequence, Pomaret, Rilliet, d'Arnal et Compagnie would not be able to accept any more long-term bills of exchange from the STN.

In fact, the crisis had resulted from a sudden drop in the value of shares in the Caisse d'Escompte, and it was solved by government intervention to withdraw some of its own notes and to recapitalize the Caisse with the help of a royal lottery. Nonetheless, the crisis hit the STN at a vulnerable moment, and its effect was compounded by other factors. Although they sometimes mentioned particular causes such as poor harvests,[29] booksellers usually blamed "bad debtors," the cumulative effects of bankruptcies, and the economic situation in general.[30] On October 27, 1783, Ignace Faivre of Pontarlier reported an outbreak of bankruptcies in Besançon that had wiped out five master ironworkers, ten merchants, and "the largest houses that deal in banking." "M. Fleur cadet drowned himself in despair. . . . Everything is desolation in this city."

Aside from the hostile economic environment, the most pervasive problem peculiar to the book trade, according to the booksellers, was overproduction. Hubert Cazin, a savvy dealer in Reims, blamed everything on "the excessive quantity of books that have been printed." Dozens of peddlers lured suppliers in Switzerland and Avignon by making cash deposits, he wrote. "Then, when they have acquired the confidence of those houses and have gradually built up credit, they stop paying. Not a single house can claim to have avoided losses from these people. All [of the peddlers] have ended up in bankruptcy, and the provinces are poisoned by books sold at half price. It must be said that the book trade is ruined."[31] His remarks corresponded closely to the experience of the STN. It tried to avoid being drawn into relations with marginal retailers, but it could not resist the pressure to expand its trade in order to pay off its own debts, and it lost a great of money from transactions with peddlers and also from retailers who supplied the peddlers in the capillary system of the book trade.

These difficulties spread throughout the Fertile Crescent. In his long tour of the Rhineland and the Low Countries in 1779, Bosset discovered that publishers were badly worried about the economic downturn. On September 19 after discussing business with Clément Plomteux, the STN's ally in Liège, he reported, "People say that a revolution in the book trade is certain to take place, because the production of books greatly exceeds their consumption." Jean-Louis de Boubers of Brussels talked boldly with Bosset about speculating on editions of Rousseau and Raynal, but it later turned out that he was teetering on the edge of catastrophe. In January 1783 another Brussels publisher, Delahaye & Compagnie, reported that Boubers had gone bankrupt for more than 300,000 L., which, as we saw earlier, was the largest loss in recent history. Delahaye himself complained bitterly about hard times. He, too, failed to pay his bills, and he went bankrupt for 100,000 L. in 1785.[32]

The two largest publishers in The Netherlands, Gosse in The Hague and Dufour in Maastricht (Rey had died in Amsterdam on June 8, 1780), remained solvent, but they ran into difficulties, both economic and political. The Dutch Patriot movement of 1781–1787 led to conflicts that verged on civil war, and the Fourth Anglo-Dutch War of 1780–1784 badly damaged Dutch commerce. On January 8, 1782, Gosse (Pierre-Fréderic, who had succeeded his father, Pierre Gosse Junior) wrote that much as he wanted to increase trade with the STN, "the sad circumstances of war and other calamities that are currently undermining the Republic, our dear fatherland, mean that we cannot think of placing any orders for the near future. All commerce has come to a halt, and the book trade is in ruins, for lack of sales." Maastrich's position in the southeast corner of The Netherlands meant that Dufour was less exposed to civil strife, but in July 1782 he wrote that his publishing business had declined so badly that he had eliminated three of the six presses in his printing shop. He sold a great many books in Germany and lost heavily, as did the STN, when Paschal Alexis Hermann, a bookseller and journal publisher in Cologne, went bankrupt in February 1787. The suspension of payments by a bookseller in Rotterdam, who had fled because of his connection with the Patriots, inflicted still more damage on Dufour's finances. "The unfortunate troubles of our Republic, which are not yet extinguished, have left the trade in a sad state," he wrote on January 8, 1788.

The Genevan revolution of 1782 resembled the Dutch Patriot uprising in many respects, and it, too, hurt the local book trade, which had already gone into decline. As explained in Chapters 6 and 8, the leading publishers retired in the 1770s, and several of those who tried to take their place—Nouffer, Didier, and Dufart—went bankrupt. Genevan speculators took the lead in investing in the loans floated by their countryman, Jacques Necker, in France. As a consequence, Genevan banks, like those in Paris and Lyon, suffered from lack of specie. In 1781 the STN's banker in Geneva, Flournoy fils & Rainaldis (formerly Argand & Rainaldis), began to have difficulty negotiating its bills of exchange, and it, too, complained about the lack of hard currency. "The new loan floated in France, makes notes on Paris and specie very rare here."[33] The STN had backers among some wealthy Neuchâtelois, who wanted to withdraw their funds so that they, too, could invest in Necker's loans.[34] Other factors added to the financial difficulties, damaging the trade throughout Switzerland. The most significant probably was overproduction. Jules-Henri Pott wrote with studied exaggeration from Lausanne, "The number of booksellers in Lausanne is almost greater than that of readers." There were too many booksellers, too many books, and therefore, as Flick wrote from Basel, far too many "bad payers."[35]

Lists of "bad payers," which publishers kept in their accounts, indicate the gravity of the payment problem.[36] The STN's list of May 31, 1785,[37] showed a staggering accumulation of debts: seventy-six individuals or companies, who owed a total of 63,366 L. in the category "debtors reputed to be bad." There were also sixty "debtors reputed to be doubtful," who owed 34,461 L., and seventy-nine "debtors reputed to be good," who owed 179,132 L. Nearly 100,000 L. of bad debts was a burden that had grown heavier and heavier over the last decade. In a series of letters that he had written during his business trip to Paris with Ostervald in the spring of 1780, Bosset warned about the danger: "The book trade here, as everywhere else, is in great decadence."[38] Yet when the STN printed an edition, it often ran off too many copies. In his view, the excess production represented misplaced capital—worthless printed paper piled up in its warehouse. They could not even calculate the extent of the loss, he complained, because they would not do a warehouse inventory until the end of the year. Bosset scolded Abram David Mercier, the STN's accountant, for sloppiness in keeping the records, which made it impossible to get a clear view of the company's finances. The STN had been forced to borrow large sums from wealthy Neuchâtelois, and Bosset worried greatly about the growing indebtedness, especially the loan of 50,000 L. owed to his son-in-law in Lyon. You had to be a merchant to appreciate the seriousness of the situation, he warned, speaking from his experience in the calico factories near Neuchâtel. Madame Bertrand, who was minding the business in Neuchâtel (as noted earlier, she had become a partner of the STN after the death of her husband in February 1779), replied that they had gotten rid of all but two of the twelve presses they had used to print the *Encyclopédie* and that they could raise capital by selling a house that they had bought in the rue des Épancheux in order to expand their productivity in 1777.[39] Bosset wrote back that he wished they had no presses at all and that they should fire all the remaining workers, but they must not sell the house, because that could damage their credit by raising doubts about their solvency. Madame Bertrand still sounded optimistic, yet she had received disquieting news. The STN's banker in Lyon had reported "that it would take only one moment of discredit, when our creditors could demand reimbursement, to crush us."[40] Bosset, however, remained unswervingly pessimistic, perhaps because his view was colored by illness. "It seems that this occupation gives one more bile than others."

What Bosset diagnosed as bile turned out to be a fatal disease, which carried him off in August 1781. The death of such a wealthy and respected partner damaged the STN's credit, although Bosset was succeeded as a partner in the STN by his son, Jean-Jacques. Despite the reduction in its presses after the great affair of the *Encyclopédie*, the STN continued to churn out books in 1782 and 1783. Yet its sales did not suffice to bring in an adequate income, and it covered its growing deficit by more borrowing. The loans included large sums from local institutions—11,714 L. from the Maison de charité, 10,857 L. from the Quatre ministraux, and 16,942 L. from the Chambre économique—in addition to the 50,000 L. owed to d'Arnal.[41] On November 4, 1783, d'Arnal had warned that the next payment in Lyon would be extremely difficult and that his bank could not receive any but the most solid notes on Lyonnais houses. Nonetheless, the STN sent him seven bills of exchange for 12,000 L. on Paris. He refused to accept them on November 30, and the STN suspended its payments sometime in the last days of December.

The correspondence does not indicate the exact date of the *faillite*, but it occurred about a month before January 28, when Flournoy fils & Rainaldi in Geneva wrote a letter acknowledging a meeting of the STN's creditors to settle its affairs.[42] On January 29 the STN sent out a circular on the financial arrangements, which stated that its signature had been transferred to two administrators named Bergeon and Gallot, who would be responsible henceforth for its management.[43] As in so many cases when it had been one of the creditors trying to get the best possible deal from a bankrupt bookseller, Ostervald and his partners, Jean-Jacques Bosset and Madame Bertrand, who now were on the side of the debtors, had to negotiate their way out of the crisis. A notarized document dated June 2, 1784, described the terms. Led by the Bosset family, a group of eleven eminent Neuchâtelois pledged 290,000 L. as security for repayment of debts that would be amortized in full but without interest over six years. As a further guarantee (*hypothèque spéciale*), three of the Bosset heirs pledged their real estate worth a total of 146,295 L. (that included their château, La Rochette, evaluated at 100,000 L.), and the three partners pledged all their goods.

In Ostervald's case, the security included vineyards, land, and his house, rue Saint Maurice (evaluated at 10,000 L.), for a total of 29,275 L. Although deprived of his managerial responsibility, Ostervald would continue to participate in the STN's affairs, which were to wind down as it sold off its stock.[44] A balance sheet drawn up in 1785 set the STN's assets at 206,732 L. and its debits at 318,795 L., showing it to be 112,063 L. in the red.[45] According to a memoire of 1823, which was kept with the STN papers in the vast attic of La Rochette, the STN's debt was paid off after a long process of liquidation, and the guarantors who had stood security lost a total of 50,000 L.[46] The estate of Ostervald, who died in 1795, probably disappeared with the other assets that he had pledged as security. The refinanced STN continued business under new management, as indicated in a letter of August 11, 1784, from Flournoy fils & Rainaldis, who acknowledged receipt of a circular announcing its new directors: "We have taken note of your new signature to accord it our trust [*pour y ajouter foi*]."

The bankruptcy of the STN exposed tendencies that had undermined publishing and the book trade in general, but it also resulted from local causes. Among them was the bad reputation that Neuchâtel had acquired from the publications of Samuel Fauche and the offshoot firm founded by his son Jonas with his son-in-law Jérémie Wittel as Fauche fils aîné, Favre & Wittel.[47] As already explained, both companies specialized in producing the most extreme kind of *livres philosophiques*, notably the seditious and pornographic works of Mirabeau. Foreign Minister Vergennes's order that all shipments from foreign publishers be inspected by the Guild in Paris was in large part an attempt to crush their business, and the STN was included in the French government's view of Neuchâtel as a source of the books it wanted most badly to keep out of the kingdom. The order was never rescinded, even after Vergennes's death in February 1787. Although aimed against strictly forbidden books, the order had the added effect of damaging the trade in all pirated works, and it afflicted all the pirating houses that had proliferated outside France since the 1750s. The route through Pontarlier was patrolled with particular severity. Fauche fils aîné, Favre & Witel went out of business, and the STN never regained a foothold in its most important market.

Among the other problems that weighed heavily on the STN was the failure of its most expensive venture, the expanded reprint of the *Description des arts et métiers* that was being published under the patronage of the Académie des sciences by the powerful Parisian bookseller Nicolas-Léger Moutard. As explained in Chapter 10, Moutard's magnificent folio volumes, accompanied by finely engraved plates, came out, one after the other, over a period of twenty-seven years, from 1761 to 1788. They were luxury items, intended for a small number of connoisseurs and collectors. The STN claimed that its relatively cheap edition, which it sold by subscription, was not a *contrefaçon*, because Bertrand, who supervised the enterprise, incorporated a great deal of new material in the text. The STN moved heaven and earth to get its volumes permitted in France. But Moutard, backed by Le Camus de Néville, the director of the book trade (and "our sworn enemy" as Ostervald reported from Paris), kept the French market tightly shut. Although the STN persevered with the project after Bertrand's death in 1779, it continued to lose subscribers, became embroiled in endless disputes, and finally suffered such a drain on its finances that it sued for peace with Moutard. In 1785 he acquired the remnants of the nineteen volumes it had produced. He paid too little too late to save the STN from a devastating blow to its finances.[48]

While hemorrhaging losses for the *Description des arts et métiers*, the STN failed to compensate for them by other initiatives. In 1775, as recounted in the previous chapter, Ostervald considered broadening the STN's business strategy by publishing original editions. But the negotiations—with Morellet, Marmontel, d'Alembert, and others—came to nothing. The only new work by a prominent *philosophe* that the STN published was Mably's *Du gouvernement et des lois de la Pologne* (1781), and it did not sell well. The

STN certainly profited by printing expanded editions of Mercier's *Tableau de Paris*, but did not publish his other bestseller, *L'An deux mille quatre cent quarante*.[49] Had the STN succeeded in launching original works, it might have developed into an influential publishing house comparable to Rey in Amsterdam and Cramer in Geneva. But it never expanded beyond the limits of the pirating industry.

The STN did print several works for hire, and it made some profit from them, as in the case of Servan. Yet its profits might have been outweighed by its losses, because so many authors failed to pay their bills. It never extracted a penny from Goetzmann, and its printing for Brissot and Barthès de Marmorières turned into disasters. The STN published few books after 1784: only three (excluding pamphlets) in 1785, two in 1786, three in 1787, two in 1788, four in 1789, and none thereafter. Essentially, it abandoned publishing and tried to retire its debt by selling off its stock.

A final factor in the STN's collapse was its tendency to sell books to untrustworthy customers. Ostervald certainly showed poor judgment in extending confidence to peddlers and marginal dealers like Lair in Blois, Malherbe in Loudun, and Bruzard de Mauvelain in Troyes.[50] The preceding account offers examples of shipments that should never have left the warehouse in Neuchâtel and of financial arrangements that should never have carried the STN's signature. Yet it is easy to criticize bad decisions in retrospect, and it is difficult to see how the STN could have escaped the economic conditions that were undermining all publishing houses in the Fertile Crescent. As its debts mounted, the STN needed to find new customers, and that meant venturing into territory where it could not be sure of safe *recouvrements*. Other publishers did the same. As Ostervald wrote to the STN from Paris on April 4, 1780, "I must explain to you that the book trade here is in great disarray. We have not met a single bookseller who does not complain about it, and as Machuel wrote to us recently from Rouen, the bad booksellers go bankrupt and the good ones don't order anything." It was impossible to restrict business to the minority of impeccably solid booksellers. Overproduction and price cutting affected publishers everywhere, pushing them to the dangerous margins of the market and triggering the bankruptcies already discussed.

In fact, the STN did better than most of its competitors. In 1780, its accountant wrote to Bosset in Paris that the STN was not suffering as much as others. "We see in the catalogues of our correspondents not only works printed 8 to 10 years ago but some that are 15, 20 years old and even older."[51] Widow Charmet, a close friend of the STN and an astute observer of the book trade, sent a sympathetic letter as soon as she heard about the STN's suspension of payments. "It was almost impossible for you to avoid being swept up in the general revolution of the trade," she wrote. "The lack of specie, your great confidence, the obstacles to transactions, all of these things together could only inflict great damage on you."[52] The Société typographique de Berne and the Société typographique de Lausanne (reorganized as Heubach & Compagnie) managed to survive the general crisis, but only with difficulty. Encumbered by 80,000 L. in debts, the Société typographique de Bouillon sold off its stock at rock-bottom prices and avoided bankruptcy in 1783 only by falling back on the journals it published.[53] The Société littéraire et typographique d'Yverdon collapsed in 1778 and the Société typographique de Genève in 1783.[54]

In short, the STN's experience illustrates the hard times that had afflicted publishing in general—certainly in Switzerland, probably throughout the Fertile Crescent, and perhaps even among the privileged houses in France. The golden age of piracy came to an end well before the French Revolution.

Yet the history of piracy cannot be reduced to economic factors. The case studies recounted in the preceding pages bear on broad issues, which deserve to be addressed in a final chapter.

Conclusion

THE BANKRUPTCY OF THE STN did not bring its affairs to a happy ending. Its new directors wrote off its losses, sold off its stock, and paid off its debts during the decade that followed the crisis of 1783. The details of its long, slow death need not be related here, because this book is not a history of the STN. It has used the archives in Neuchâtel, supplemented by those in Paris, in order to understand the ways of publishers in general and pirates in particular. Seen across a distance of two and a half centuries, what stands out in the experience of the STN and other publishing houses under the Ancien Régime are the difficulties of getting books to readers. In addition to general constraints—censorship, guild monopolies, police surveillance, and inadequate means of financial exchange—publishers had to clear a path through endless immediate problems, such as procuring copy, shipping bales past *chambres syndicales*, collecting bills, and forming alliances while fending off attacks from competitors. Yet through it all ran a positive tendency, one less visible but more fundamental than the endless obstacle course. Put abstractly, it could be characterized as the democratization of access to culture. In concrete terms, it meant bringing books within the reach of the general reading public.

From the very beginning, the STN announced its intention to supply its customers with inexpensive reprints. As it informed a customer in October 1769, it "intends principally to improve works, even good ones, as soon as they appear and to enable a larger number of persons to have access to them by eliminating the typographical luxury that weighs them down."[1] The criticism of luxury took many forms in the eighteenth century.[2] In the case of books, it referred to fine editions printed on high-quality paper with expensive type, elegant ornaments, spacious page design, and often specially engraved frontispieces and illustrations. Pirate publishers associated *luxe typographique* with the dominant members of the Parisian Guild, who sold their wares at high prices to a wealthy elite. The STN attributed this practice to the Guild's monopoly of *privilèges*,[3] and denounced it in moralistic terms: "Everything is now printed in Paris with an extravagant luxury that disgusts a great many consumers."[4]

As a pirate, the STN followed the opposite commercial strategy. Not only did it pay nothing to authors for their manuscripts, it also used cheaper paper, simpler layouts, and relatively inexpensive type.[5] It often eliminated illustrations and sometimes cut entire passages. On rare occasions, *contrefaiseurs* actually counterfeited an original edition—that is, they tried to reproduce it exactly—and they sometimes sought a competitive advantage by claiming to publish an edition with augmentations and corrections provided by the author. Yet they did not show much concern for the integrity of texts. Their main objective was to cut costs and keep prices low in order to reach a broad public. "There are always more thrifty than spendthrift customers," Ostervald reasoned.[6] This downmarket strategy was fundamental to pirate publishing. "One of the best ways to market a book that is generally considered to have a good sales potential is to make it available at a level that will appeal to most individuals," he explained. "One profits by the quantity more than one sacrifices by the price."[7] Provincial booksellers bought into his business plan. Alphonse Petit, a bookseller in Reims, wrote eagerly, "We strongly urge Messieurs of the Société typographique de Neuchâtel to continue to print books that appear in France at an exorbitant price and with a luxury that distresses true book lovers."[8] Henri in Lille put it more bluntly, "The common people want cheap prices."[9] Even some authors were attracted by the idea of publishing cheaper books for a broader public. When Ostervald discussed the possibility of producing original editions with writers in Paris, he got an enthusiastic reaction from Claude-Joseph Dorat: "Unhappy with the typographical luxury that is loaded onto his books here," Ostervald wrote to the home office, "he is enchanted that we want to reprint them more simply."[10]

It may seem surprising to associate democratization with piracy. To understand the affinity between them, it is important to recognize how fundamentally publishing in the eighteenth century differed from today. Eighteenth-century publishers operated in a world without copyright, royalties, freedom of the press, universal literacy, and a mass market. They based their business on assumptions about the rules of the game and the way it was played under conditions peculiar to the Ancien Régime. Far from setting out with high-minded ideals about free and equal access to the printed word, they tried to turn a profit. Pirate publishers, unlike the privileged members of the Parisian Guild, aimed to satisfy demand in a broad sector of the public where books had not been common articles of consumption. If democratization can be identified with opening up access to previously unavailable cultural goods, then pirates played an important part in the age of democratic revolution.

The French Revolution destroyed a social order based on privilege. For at least fifty years before 1789, pirates undercut the specific form of privilege that prevailed in literature—the *privilèges* for books. While they made a business of raiding the book market, many of the books they sold attacked privilege in principle. Hostility to privilege lay at the heart of the Enlightenment, whether in its moderate phase, as in Voltaire's pillorying of intolerance and injustice, or in its radical rejection of inequality, the central theme of Rousseau's writing. Even the least philosophical of the *livres philosophiques* undermined the hierarchy of the Ancien Régime by exposing the fatuity of the privileged elite and the abuses of *les grands* who monopolized power. Although books had challenged orthodoxies repeatedly in previous ages, the printed word in the age of Enlightenment drove the challenge home with a force unparalleled in the past, and it did so from an industrial base that operated outside the law—the law based on privileges that held the Ancien Régime together.

Although scorned in France, the pirates usually commanded respect in their home territories, where they were seen as law-abiding businessmen. The history of business deserves a place alongside the history of literature. Yet in showing how the two converged, this book does not argue that publishers were driven by nothing more than the pursuit of profit and that publishing can be reduced to economics. All those in the world of books had convictions of their own about politics, religion, and morality. Some sympathized with the principles of the philosophic books they sold, and many embraced publishing as a vocation, work that was worthwhile in itself, not merely as a source of income. Yet no one went into publishing primarily to advance an ideological cause.[11] In fact, the most enlightened publishers sometimes became entangled in activities that were incompatible with Enlightenment ideals. While publishing Voltaire, Gabriel Cramer remained aligned with his brother and partner, Philibert Cramer, who was a member of Geneva's reactionary Petit Conseil, which often burned books. Although he also published Voltaire—along with d'Holbach's atheistic *Système de la nature* (and two refutations of it)—Ostervald defended orthodox Calvinism against the heretical notion that eternal punishment in hell could not be reconciled with the concept of a merciful God. As a powerful local politician, he supported the campaign to drive Ferdinand-Olivier Petitpierre from his position as a pastor for advocating such a view, and he also defended *privilèges* in Neuchâtel while undermining them among publishers in France.

Nevertheless, as they struggled to negotiate a way through contradictions and constraints, pirate publishers contributed mightily to the Enlightenment. In fact, they made it happen. At its core, the Enlightenment was an attempt to spread light, to "change the common way of thinking," as Diderot put it.[12] In order to do so, it relied on the dominant mode of communication in the eighteenth century: the book. And to mobilize the power of books, it required the infrastructure of printing and distribution developed by the publishing houses that surrounded France. In addition to the publishers, an army of middlemen—not only booksellers but also smugglers, wagon drivers, peddlers, bill collectors, and undercover agents—kept books flowing through the channels of the trade. Quandet de Lachenal, the all-purpose agent of the STN in Paris, defined their role exactly: "I do not enlighten myself; I am content to carry the torch."[13] To appreciate the power of the Enlightenment, it is important to take into account the role of the cultural intermediaries who transmitted it and the economic forces that propelled it on the market place.

Yet the production of Enlightenment tracts was a small fraction of the books that reached the market. Most books were pirated editions of works that circulated without offending the authorities. Although it is impossible to come up with all-encompassing statistics, the surviving evidence indicates that at least half the books sold in France during the second half of the eighteenth century were pirated.[14] The predominance of *contrefaçons* inflicted so much damage on the publishing industry at the heart of the kingdom that the policies of the French authorities were driven to a great extent by economic considerations. Vergennes's coup of June 12, 1783, demonstrated that the state remained determined to repress the circulation of seditious libels and other illegal works, but after 1750 it became increasingly tolerant of books that could not receive official approbation. In legitimating the stock of pirated books currently held by booksellers, the royal edicts of 1777 acknowledged that piracy had permeated the French market.

The pirates constituted the most active and innovative sector of the publishing industry. To understand how so much entrepreneurial energy became concentrated in the borderlands of France, it is important to study piracy in relation to publishing in general and the attempts of the French state to control the printed word. Backed by the state since the time of Colbert, the members of the Parisian Guild exploited their power as a privileged corporation and supported themselves from their monopoly of book *privilèges*. With a few exceptions such as Le Breton, the main entrepreneur behind the *Encyclopédie*, Duchesne, the Parisian distributor of Rousseau's works, and Panckoucke, the powerful press baron, Parisian publishers remained content to make the most from their monopolies. They lived in a manner typical of the Ancien Régime, like rentiers, whereas the pirate publishers opened up a new market composed of consumers who would form *le grand public*, as it came to be known in the nineteenth century.

Although it is difficult to follow the diffusion of the books from retailers to readers, all the archives indicate that the demand for inexpensive *contrefaçons* came from the middle ranks of French society: from magistrates, lawyers, doctors, military officers, state officials, substantial landowners, merchants—and, no doubt, their wives, who unfortunately never appear in the documents, unlike the wives of the booksellers.

This public emerged during a transitional phase in the cultural history of France. A century earlier, the market for books—trade books as opposed to religious tracts, almanacs, and chapbooks—remained restricted to a small elite. A century later, it expanded to include the petty bourgeoisie and some workers. By bringing books within the reach of the middling segment of the population in the eighteenth century, pirate publishers helped set in motion a process that would transform French culture.

A key element in that process was the emergence of publishing itself as an activity distinct from the printing and selling of books.[15] Modern publishing had to free itself from the constraints of an archaic system of production. The members of the Guild certainly sought to make money, but they did so within the limits of an economic system based on privilege: guild capitalism. The pirate publishers took risks and pursued profits in a spirit of uninhibited entrepreneurship that can be described as booty capitalism. By destroying privilege, the French Revolution transformed the conditions of publishing. It freed the press in 1789 and abolished guilds in 1791, leaving the market open to entrepreneurs of the kind who had published books outside France during the last decades of the Ancien Régime.

Yet it would take another hundred years of false starts, intermittent repression, and economic concentration for a modern publishing industry to become established in France. The financial crisis of the 1780s had killed off many of the foreign publishers of French books before the Revolution, and the survivors could not simply pull up roots and begin all over again in a French market that opened up in 1789 only to close with the reimposition of censorship in 1793. Moreover, the material turned out by French presses shifted from books to pamphlets and newspapers in 1788, when the reading public was consumed by a passion for politics. Book publishing did not resume full throttle until the Restoration, and even then it suffered from constraints, including heavy censorship. Population growth, prosperity, increased literacy, and mass education developed unevenly and late. The *grand public* for books did not emerge until the second half of the nineteenth century. By that time inexpensive paper made from wood pulp and presses driven by steam power had transformed the technology of printing, which had remained essentially unchanged for the previous three centuries. Publishing houses could then develop on a large scale, protected by limited liability, supported by enormous distribution systems, and sustained over several generations by extensive backlists. A small firm like the STN belonged to a different world from that of a giant like Hachette. Yet the two worlds were tied together by a crucial phenomenon: the role of the publisher as an independent entrepreneur.

Viewed in retrospect over several centuries, the emergence of the publisher may look obvious or predetermined, but when studied up close it is full of surprises. Eighteenth-century practices that might appear to be identical with those of publishers today turn out to be peculiar to the Ancien Régime. Like modern publishers, the pirates conducted something that could be called market research, and they sent out agents who could be considered sales reps. But they were more worried about counter-piracy from competitors than about marketing. The books that sold best were reprinted by so many rival pirates that the demand could be sated before some editions made it to the market. Instead of being printed in large numbers by one publisher, as they are today, bestsellers were produced simultaneously by several different houses in a rush to satisfy the demand before it disappeared. Publishing decisions therefore involved calculations about what other publishers were up to, not merely what readers wanted to buy.

A pirate publisher had to take into account the inexhaustible tricks of the trade: bluffing, fake editions, false advertising, secret deals, fraudulent payments, duplicitous bankruptcies—so much bad faith that the trade seems to have respected only one imperative: dupe or be duped. By accumulating examples of foul play, the preceding chapters can make the pirate industry look like a Wild West set in the serene landscapes of the Jura and the

Rhineland. Yet piracy flourished in the Fertile Crescent because of the fundamental fact that it took place outside the law—French law, which did not inhibit Swiss and Dutch publishers and their French customers, including allied pirates and wholesalers in cities like Lyon and Rouen. Aside from border patrols and police raids, the main constraint on piracy was self-imposed: the system of *confiance* that bound partners in transactions and that protected them from the confidence games of their enemies.

To defend themselves against dupery, pirate firms made alliances. Some were improvised arrangements based on the exchange trade. Others involved joint ventures on particular editions, and the most elaborate took the form of associations that bound the partners to share investments, profits, and risks, as in the case of the Confederation formed by the *sociétés typographiques* of Bern, Lausanne, and Neuchâtel. The three houses coordinated all their activities, down to the purchase of paper and type. Because they had to agree on which books to pirate, they discussed possibilities in a constant stream of letters, which make it possible to follow the discourse on literature as it evolved among the best-informed book professionals.

Confidential relations also developed between publishers and certain wholesale dealers. The letters exchanged between Ostervald and Gosse of The Hague show a beginner taking lessons from a veteran who knew the kind of literature that appealed to ordinary customers. As Gosse observed, scholars have a lot to learn from booksellers. He was referring to Ostervald's scholarly background, but his remark applies to researchers today, who can discover a great deal about the supply and demand of literature by studying the correspondence of booksellers.

Unlike the privileged members of the Guild, the pirates scrambled to tap demand in a newly emerging consumer society, and in doing so they ran great risks. Piracy might seem to be an easy road to riches—just take a successful book and reprint it—but in an age without limited liability, adequate banking, and dependable cash, it was a constant struggle against disaster. How could a publisher entrust a shipment of books to a retailer he had never met and who lived hundreds of miles away? Transactions came down to a commitment of confidence, a theme that runs throughout the commercial correspondence. *Confiance* was extended and withdrawn in calculated doses, like credit. Yet it involved much more than a financial relationship. Before accepting an order, a publisher needed to acquire a great deal of information about the reputation and character of a bookseller. Was he known for honesty and hard work? Had he made a good marriage? Could he rely on family connections and contacts with others in the trade? Did he spend too much time in taverns? Was he burdened with too many children? Did he have a history of honoring bills of exchange? The queries went out constantly in the mail, and the answers indicated an ideal type: the *parfait négociant* described in the late seventeenth century by Jacques Savary and perpetuated in the eighteenth century with more modern traits—*honnêteté* reinforced by *solidité*, a good name accompanied by good, bourgeois morals.

To follow a chain of letters in a dossier is to appreciate the distance that separated the ideal from reality. When bills became due, booksellers frequently failed to pay them. They found plenty of excuses: the transport costs had been excessive, sheets had been damaged in the shipping, hard cash could not be found. Each dossier tells a story. There were successes, of course. "Solid" booksellers never wavered in honoring bills of exchange. Yet publishers could not restrict their sales to trusted customers from the inner circle of their commercial networks. They need to expand their businesses, and in hard times the pressure of their debts pushed them to the margins, where they exposed themselves to unreliable clients. In the 1760s retailers in the capillary system of the book trade had a good chance of riding out turbulence. In the 1780s they frequently went under. Their letters read like a catalogue of catastrophes: glutted markets, lower prices, poor sales, inadequate supplies of specie, snags in shipping, disruptions from war, the ripple effect of bankruptcies, and increased repression by the authorities charged with confiscating *contrefaçons* and libels. Taken as a whole, the correspondence of publishers and booksellers demonstrates that their trade went through a severe crisis on the eve of the Revolution—and perhaps that the crisis extended throughout the entire economy.

Economic historians have tried to find an index to measure such trends, although the paucity of statistics makes their calculations difficult.[16] I have attempted to convey the nature of the economic downturn by recounting the experience of those who suffered from it—that is, by following the succession of letters in the dossiers. The theme of bankruptcy stands out everywhere, even in the correspondence of bookseller-publishers who had strong enough businesses to survive. Bankruptcy occurred in several ways. A temporary suspension of payments could be overcome with some indulgence by key creditors and help from family and friends, because many businesses were sustained by networks of support. Serious *faillites*, on the other hand, required arduous negotiations, since the creditors, acting as a collective *masse*, had to be convinced that they would benefit more by granting terms—repayments scheduled over several years after a write-off—than by foreclosing and selling off assets. Sometimes the terms were settled by a commercial court, the *juridiction consulaire*, which was quick and efficient. Thanks to such arrangements, a surprising number of publishers and booksellers went through several suspensions of payments and managed to rescue their businesses. Yet *faillites* could turn into full-fledged *banqueroutes*, exposing the debtor to imprisonment as well as the confiscation of his property.

Faced with such a fate, bankrupts often took to the road. Many dossiers end with a letter from a neighbor, a merchant, or a bill collector. A merchant from Melun had recommended extending confidence to a local bookseller named Jarfaut in 1775 ("a good worker, tends well to his affairs"), and then, in 1783, reported, "Three years ago this bookseller disappeared, signed up for the colonies, they say. His wife and children, who are living off charity here, haven't received any news from him. Perhaps he is dead. . . . The only certain thing is that Jarfaut's wife and her five children are living in the most horrible penury."[17] So it went in letter after letter: Pascot of Bordeaux, "decamped"; Brotte of Anduze, "fugitive"; Gaillard of Falaise, "left the keys under the door"; Boyer of Marseille, "doesn't exist here any more, ran off to America"; Planquais of Saint-Maixent, "it's said that he enrolled in the army"; Blondel de Bolbec, "ran away, was summoned to justice by a bailiff beating a drum."[18]

Capitalism was unforgiving in the eighteenth century—not only for workers but also for capitalists.[19] It is cruel enough today, but now entrepreneurs are protected by limited liability, and they need not fear debtor's prison. Publishers and booksellers ran great risks while chasing profits well before the Modern Era. Their struggles to survive belonged to a *comédie humaine* played out long before Balzac, and their stories, whether successes or failures, reveal the underlying forces at work in their world—the pursuit of profit, certainly, along with a great deal of foul play, but also the spread of Enlightenment and the democratization of access to culture.

Acknowledgments

This volume is intended to be a companion to an earlier study of the book trade and the diffusion of literature, *A Literary Tour de France: The World of Books on the Eve of the French Revolution*. Although it concentrates on a separate subject, it draws on the same sources, and therefore I would like to express my thanks once more to the people who provided help and hospitality since I began work on these two projects in Neuchâtel in 1965. First, I think of the dead: friends and teachers: Harry Pitt, Robert Shackleton, and Richard Cobb; mentors: Lawrence Stone and Roland Mortier; fellow travelers in book history: Jacques Rychner, Raymond Birn, and Giles Barber; senior book historians: Henri-Jean Martin, Ralph Leigh, and Don McKenzie; and scholars who provided inspiration as well as friendship: Pierre Goubert, François Furet, Pierre Bourdieu, and Clifford Geertz. Then I think of my warm reception in the Bibliothèque publique et universitaire de Neuchâtel, its staff and its directors over several generations: Eric Berthoud, Jacques Rychner, Michel Schlup, and Thierry Chatelain.

My gratitude goes out as well to host institutions, particularly to the Radcliffe Institute for Advanced Study, where I wrote most of this book, and to those who helped improve it—Timothy Bent, my editor at the Oxford University Press; Eric Vigne, my editor at Gallimard; and Jean-François Sené, who translated it into French. Daniel Droixhe and Marc Neuenschwander helped me sort through the complexities of publishing and politics in eighteenth-century Liège and Geneva. Scott Walker composed the map of publishing sites around the borders of France. And my debts to French friends go back for many decades. Clemens Heller first welcomed me to the Maison des sciences de l'homme, and François Furet introduced me to the younger generation of the Annales School, notably Daniel Roche, Roger Chartier, and Jacques Revel, who became lifelong friends and collaborators. I cannot tot up all the years spent in Parisian archives and libraries, but I think back thankfully to long stints in the Bibliothèque de l'Arsenal, the Bibliothèque historique de la ville de Paris, the Bibliothèque nationale de

France, and the Archives nationales. The archivists and librarians were al-ways generous with help and advice. I needed it badly, especially in the early days when the card catalogues in the rue de Richelieu and the rue des Francs Bourgeois threatened to overwhelm me by their complexity. How to extract leads from them? How to construct history from trails through paper? This book is the result. I hope it has something to say to readers in the digital age.

Notes

Introduction

1. Voltaire used this phrase in the article "Livres" of his *Questions sur l'Encyclopédie* (1770), and it appeared in different versions of his *Dictionnaire philosophique*. It is quoted here from the Kehl edition of the *Oeuvres complètes de Voltaire*, 41 (1785), 428. I have translated all quotations, except in the footnotes, where they are given in the original French. In the case of book titles, I have provided a translation in parentheses after the French, but I have not translated titles whose meaning is obvious.

2. In an earlier study, *A Literary Tour de France: The World of Books on the Eve of the French Revolution* (Oxford University Press, New York, 2018), I concentrated on booksellers and the demand for literature. This book extends that investigation to the related but less familiar realm of publishing, which I found to be so rich and complex that it required a separate volume.

3. See "Le Monde des éditeurs," in *Histoire de l'édition française: Le Temps des éditeurs du romantisme à la belle époque*, vol. 3 (Promodis, Paris, 1985), 158–216; and Christine Haynes, *Lost Illusions: The Politics of Publishing in Nineteenth-Century France* (Harvard University Press, Cambridge, MA, 2010), chap. 1. In England the word "publisher" was occasionally used in the mid-eighteenth century, and the function of the publisher became differentiated from that of bookseller earlier than in France. See *The Cambridge History of the Book in Britain*, Michael F. Suarez and Michael L. Turner, eds., vol. 5 (Cambridge University Press, Cambridge, 2009), 326 and chap. 19; and John Feather, *A History of British Publishing* (Routledge, London, 1988), chap. 10. In German-speaking Europe, "Verleger" for publisher seems to have been used at an early stage in the history of printing, and publishing as distinct from bookselling can be detected, although faintly, in the early sixteenth century: Reinhard Wittmann, *Geschichte des deutschen Buchhandels: Ein Überblick* (C. H. Beck, Munich, 1991), 35. However, the German book industry remained tied to the Frankfurt and Leipzig fairs and the practice of swapping sheets until the second half of the eighteenth century. It took more than a hundred years for book production to recover from the disasters of the Thirty Years' War (1618–1648). And large publishing houses did not develop until the end of the nineteenth century: Wittmann, *Geschichte des deutschen Buchhandels*, chaps. 3 and 9.

4. *The Oxford English Dictionary*, 2nd ed. (Clarendon Press, Oxford, 1989), "To make public . . . To make publicly or generally known."

5. In his *Histoire de la langue française des origines à nos jours* 6, deuxième partie (Armand Colin, Paris, 1966), p. 1143, Ferdinand Brunot (with Alexis François) noted that the verb "éditer" was first used by Restif de la Bretonne, a famous champion of neologisms, in *Le Paysan et la paysanne pervertis* of 1784. *Le Grand Robert de la langue française* (Dictionnaires Le Robert, Paris, 2001) also gives "1784, Restif" as the first use of "éditer," and it attributes the modern usage of "éditeur" to the end of the eighteenth century, although it also cites a letter by Voltaire from 1775 that suggests the modern meaning of the word: "ces maudits éditeurs veulent imprimer tout." Émile Littré, *Dictionnaire de la langue française* (Hachette, Paris, 1883) indicates 1797 as presumably the first use of "éditer" and does not indicate the origin of "éditeur" in modern parlance. The 1762 edition of the *Dictionnaire de l'Académie française* defines "éditeur" in a way that comes fairly close to modern usage, although it does not mention the publisher's commercial function: "Éditeur. Celui qui prend soin de revoir et de faire imprimer l'ouvrage d'autrui. [Example] Cet ouvrage paraît avec une belle préface de l'éditeur." As explained in Chapter 6, this volume, I have found examples of the use of "éditeur" in the modern sense of the word going back to 1774, and I suspect that earlier examples could be discovered.

6. A trade manual from 1781, *Almanach de la librairie* (Paris, 1781, reprint edited by Jeroom Vercruysse, Aubel, Belgium, 1984), sometimes distinguished *imprimeurs-libraires* from *libraires*, but it did not use the term *éditeur*.

7. In the eighteenth century, the term for a pirated book, "contrefaçon" and sometimes "contrefaction," was used in different ways. It could refer to a work that was meant to be an exact reproduction of the original, as in the English "counterfeit." More often, it was applied to any unauthorized reprint of a work covered by a privilege, whatever the accuracy. Strictly speaking, a foreign reprint of a French book was not a "contrefaçon" unless it was sold in France, but that distinction was not widely observed. In normal usage, the term also designated a reprint of a text for which no one claimed ownership (and usually authorship), as in the case of most highly illegal books. And unauthorized editions with new material were considered pirated, unless the "augmentations" increased the text by at least 25 percent, as required by royal edicts. In my own usage, "contrefaçon" and "pirated book" refer to any unauthorized reprint, whether or not the original had a privilege.

8. In his *Lettre sur le commerce de la librairie* (written in 1763; reprint by Librairie Fontaine, Paris, 1984), p. 57, Diderot argued that an absolute property right to texts sold by authors to booksellers existed everywhere, notably England: "on ne connaît point là [in England] la différence de l'achat d'un champ ou d'une maison à l'achat d'un manuscrit, et en effet il n'y en a point, si ce n'est peut-être en faveur de l'acquéreur d'un manuscrit." (Diderot also made the comparison with property in land and in a house in an earlier passage, p. 39.) The ownership of land as an example of the natural right to property was developed by Locke and used in legal arguments by English lawyers who defended the notion of unlimited copyright. After many cases, that notion was rejected by the House of Lords in *Donaldson v. Becket*, 1774. See Mark Rose, *Authors and Owners: The Invention of Copyright* (Harvard University Press, Cambridge, MA, 1993). This issue is discussed at greater length in Chapter 1, this volume.

9. Immanuel Kant, *The Metaphysics of Morals*, Mary Gregor, ed. (Cambridge University Press, Cambridge, 1996), 71–72. An earlier version of this essay had appeared in the *Berlinische Monatsschrift*, where "What is Enlightenment?" had also been published. Kant's definition of a book and related concepts, p. 71, went as follows: "A book is a writing (it does not matter, here, whether it is written in hand or set in type, whether it has few or many pages), which represents a discourse that someone delivers to the public by visible signs. One who *speaks* to the public in his own name is called the author (autor). One who through a writing, discourses publicly in another's (the author's) name is a *publisher*." The translation gives "discourse" for "Rede" and "mandate" for "Vollmacht": Kant, *Metaphysik der Sitten in Werke in sechs Bänden*, 4 (Wissenschaftliche Buchgesellschaft Darmstadt, Darmstadt, Germany, 1998), 404. See John Christian Laursen, "Kant, Freedom of the Press, and Book Piracy," in *Kant's Political Theory: Interpretations and Applications*, Elisabeth Ellis, ed. (Pennsylvania State University Press, Philadelphia, 2012).

10. Quoted in Jean-Pierre Perret, *Les Imprimeries d'Yverdon au XVIIe et au XVIIIe siècle* (F. Roth, Lausanne, 1945), 205. For a favorable view of piracy in German-speaking Europe, see Reinhard Wittmann, "Der gerechtfertigte Nachdrucker? Nachdruck und literarisches Leben im achtzehnten Jahrhundert," in *Buchmarkt und Lektüre im 18. und 19. Jahrhundert: Beiträge zum literarischen Leben 1750–1880*, by Reinhard Wittmann (Max Niemeyer Verlag, Tübingen, Germany), 1982.

11. Rietje van Vliet, *Elie Luzac (1721–1796): Bookseller of the Enlightenment* (AfdH Publishers, Enschede, The Netherlands, 2014), 43.

12. For general accounts of piracy, see *Les Presses grises: La Contrefaçon du livre (XVIe–XIXe siècles)*, François Moureau, ed. (Aux amateurs de livres, Paris, 1988), which mainly concerns France; Adrian Johns, *Piracy: The Intellectual Property Wars from Gutenberg to Gates* (University of Chicago Press, Chicago, 2009), which concentrates on Britain and the United States; and Wittmann, *Buchmarkt und Lektüre im 18. und 19. Jahrhundert*, chap. 3, which deals with Germany and Austria.

13. Max Weber, *Essays in Sociology*, H. H. Gerth and C. Wright Mills, eds. (Oxford University Press, New York, 1958), 66–67. Max Weber, *The Protestant Ethic and the Spirit of Capitalism* (Scribner's, New York, 1958), 20–21.

14. Although systematic comparisons would reveal a great deal, I have not been able to work them into this book or to implement suggestions I made long ago: "Histoire du livre—Geschichte des Buchwesens: An Agenda for Comparative History," *Publishing History*, no. 22 (1987), 33–41. My own reading of book history in Britain and Germany owes a great deal to *The Cambridge History of the Book in Britain* (Cambridge University Press, Cambridge, 2002 and 2009), edited by John Barnard, D. F. McKenzie, Michael F. Suarez, and Michael Turner, vols. 4 and 5, which cover the period 1557–1830. In the case of Germany, I have relied heavily on the classic study by Johann Goldfriedrich, *Geschichte des deutschen Buchhandels*, vols. 2–4 (Börsenverein der Deutschen Buchhändler, Leipzig, 1886–1923); and the work of Reinhard Wittmann, especially his *Geschichte des deutschen Buchhandels* and *Buchmarkt und Lektüre im 18. und 19. Jahrhundert*. In the case of France, the best survey is *Histoire*

de l'édition française. Tome II: Le Livre triomphant 1660–1830, Roger Chartier and Henri-Jean Martin, eds. (Promodis, Paris, 1984).

Chapter 1

1. For an overview of the history of books in France, see *Histoire de l'édition française*, Roger Chartier and Henri-Jean Martin, eds., vols. 1–2 (Paris, Promodis, 1983 and 1984). David Pottinger, *The French Book Trade in the Ancien Régime, 1500–1791* (Cambridge, MA, Harvard University Press, 1958) gives an adequate account in English, although it is based only on published sources.

2. Denis Diderot, *Lettre sur le commerce de la librairie* (Paris, 1984), 57.

3. *Areopagitica: A Speech of Mr. John Milton for the Liberty of Unlicenc'd Printing, to the Parliament of England* (London, 1644), paragraph 3: "For books are not absolutely dead things, but do contain a potency of life in them to be as active as that soul was whose progeny they are; nay, they do preserve as in a vial the purest efficacy and extraction of that living intellect that bred them."

4. Jacques Proust, "Présentation" in his edition of Diderot's memoir: *Diderot: Sur la liberté de la presse* (Editions sociales, Paris, 1964), 7.

5. The memoir of the guild and the notes on it by Marin are in BnF, Fonds Français (henceforth F.F.) 22183: "Représentations et observations en forme de mémoire sur l'état ancien et actuel de la librairie et particulièrement sur la propriété des privilèges, etc. présentées à M. de Sartine par les syndic et adjoints, et en marge les observations que M. Marin a faites sur chaque article, d'après les notes instructives que je [d'Hémery] lui ai remises par ordre du magistrat," March 1764. The text of the "Représentations" was published in a collection of documents edited by Ed. Laboulaye and G. Guiffrey, *La Propriété littéraire au XVIIIᵉ siècle: Recueil de pièces et de documents* (cited henceforth as *Recueil de pieces*) (Paris, 1859), 53–121. Laboulaye and Guiffrey dug through the archives in search of material that would support their argument—namely, that copyright should be made permanent—in some polemics of the 1850s. Despite its bias, their volume provides an accurate anthology of material that is not easily accessible elsewhere. They did not know that Diderot had furnished much of the "Représentations." The extent of his contribution can easily be appreciated by comparing the text they published with modern editions of his *Lettre sur le commerce de la librairie*—for example, the text edited by Charles Bon and J. C. Maillet (Paris, 1984). Diderot scholars now generally accept the view that he wrote his *Lettre sur le commerce de la librairie*, which was not published in his lifetime, at the behest of the publishers of the *Encyclopédie*. See, for example, Jacques Proust, "Pour servir à une edition critique," *Diderot Studies* 3 (1961), 325, 334–345; and Arthur Wilson, *Diderot* (Oxford University Press, New York, 1972), 459–460. My interpretation follows that of Raymond Birn, "The Profits of Ideas: *Privilèges en librairie* in Eighteenth-Century France," *Eighteenth-Century Studies* 4 (1971), 131–168. In my view, Diderot was not naive. He knowingly wrote the memoir to promote the interest of the publisher who employed him and who at that time was *syndic* of the booksellers' guild. Diderot did

so at a critical moment, when Sartine was considering reforms that would open up the publishing industry to provincial booksellers. Yet while arguing the case for the Guild, Diderot was carried away by his personal convictions—his belief in the value of freedom of the press, both for the profit of authors and as a force that would benefit society.

6. "Représentations et observations," pp. 37–38, quoted in Birn, "The Profits of Ideas," 154.

7. An account of the Code of 1723 produced for the Paris Guild as a means of enforcing its authority is Claude-Marin Saugrain, *Code de la librairie et imprimerie de Paris, ou conférence du règlement arrêté au Conseil d'État du roi, le 28 février 1723 et rendu commun pour tout le royaume par arrêt du Conseil d'État du 24 mars 1744* (Paris, 1744).

8. The original text of the 1723 Code is in BnF, F.F., 22181, and can be consulted in *Recueil général des anciennes lois françaises*, A. J. L. Jourdan, O. O. Decrusy, and F. A. Isambert, eds. (Paris, 1821–1833), 21, 216–251.

9. *Mémoire sur les vexations qu'exercent les libraires et imprimeurs de Paris* (Paris, 1725), p. 10: "Il semble que dans les bonnes règles, le libraire est fait pour l'auteur et non pas l'auteur pour le libraire. Celui-ci est un trafiquant qui débite, l'auteur est un homme qui pense et qui invente. Ce livre qu'il fait est son ouvrage, et cet imprimeur ou ce libraire ne fait qu'en répandre des copies dans le public, pour de l'argent, s'entend." For background on Blondel and his memoir, see the edition of it by Lucien Faucou, Paris, 1879.

10. Louis d'Héricourt, "À Monseigneur le Garde des Sceaux," Bibliothèque nationale de France," F. F., 22072, nr. 62, p. 2: "Il est certain, selon les principes que l'on vient d'établir, que ce ne sont point les privilèges que le roi accorde aux libraires qui les rendent propriétaires des ouvrages qu'ils impriment, mais uniquement l'acquisition du manuscrit dont l'auteur leur transmet la propriété au moyen du prix qu'il en reçoit." This passage is quoted in Birn, "The Profits of Ideas," 145. My research in the same sources confirms the excellent work by Birn.

11. D'Héricourt, "À Monseigneur le Garde des Sceaux," BnF, F.F., 22072, nr. 40, quotations from pp. 2 and 4.

12. BnF, F.F., 22072, nr. 62; and Birn, "The Profits of Ideas," 145.

13. Pottinger, *The French Book Trade*, 231. On Luneau de Boisgermain, see Marie-Claude Felton, *Maîtres de leurs ouvrages: L'Édition à compte d'auteur au XVIIIᵉ siècle* (Voltaire Foundation, Oxford, 2014).

14. A good synthesis of work on these subjects is Pierre Goubert and Daniel Roche, *Les Français et l'Ancien Régime* (Armand Colin, Paris, 1984).

15. On the development of a consumer society in the eighteenth century, see *Consumers and Luxury: Consumer Culture in Europe, 1650–1850*, Maxine Berg and Helen Clifford, eds. (Manchester, UK, 1999); and Daniel Roche, *Histoire des choses banales: Naissance de la consommation dans les sociétés traditionnelles (XVIIᵉ–XVIIIᵉ siècle* (Paris, 1997).

16. On publishing houses aligned with the Enlightenment, see Raymond Birn, *Pierre Rousseau and the Philosophes of Bouillon* (Institut et Musée Voltaire, Geneva, 1964); and Elizabeth L. Eisenstein, *Grub Street Abroad: Aspects of the French Cosmopolitan Press from the Age of Louis XIV to the French Revolution* (Oxford University Press,

Oxford, 1992). Whether Enlightenment ideology was the driving force of these publishers seems doubtful to me, except in the case of Pierre Rousseau, who built his business on his *Journal encyclopédique*, which explicitly popularized the ideas of the Encyclopédistes. Marc-Michel Rey certainly developed a special line in the works of the philosophes, notably Rousseau and d'Holbach, but he was above all a businessman, determined to turn a profit, as explained in Chapter 3, this volume. See Jeroom Vercruysse, "Marc-Michel Rey imprimeur philosophe ou philosophique?" *Werkgroep 18ᵉ Documentatierblad* 34–35 (1977), 93–121; Max Fajn, "Marc-Michel Rey: Boekhandelaar op de Bloemmark (Amsterdam)," *Proceedings of the American Philosophical Society* 18 (1974), 260–268; and Guy Biart, "Marc-Michel Rey, libraire d'Amsterdam . . . et homme d'affaires," an unpublished paper kindly communicated to me by the author. Jean-François Bassompierre, who published daring works by Morelly and Diderot, merits the title of "imprimeur-philosophe," according to Daniel Droixhe, "Signatures clandestines et autres essais sur les contrefaçons de Liège et de Maastricht au XVIIIᵉ siècle," *Studies on Voltaire and the Eighteenth Century* 10 (2001), 57.

17. Birn, "The Profit of Ideas," 148.

18. For a scholarly account of this famous incident, see Wilson, *Diderot*, 339.

19. Malesherbes, *Mémoires sur la librairie*, Roger Chartier, ed. (Imprimerie nationale, Paris, 1994), 158.

20. Thierry Rigogne, *Between State and Market: Printing and Bookselling in Eighteenth-Century France* (Voltaire Foundation, Oxford, 2007).

21. This account is based on the documents in the BnF, F.F. 22075, nrs. 4–40. On the Machuel family in Rouen, see Jean Quéniart, *L'Imprimerie et la librairie à Rouen au XVIIIᵉ siècle* (Klincksieck, Paris, 1969), 217–221.

22. BnF, F.F. 22075, nr. 23: "Rapport sur l'affaire Ratillon."

23. Ibid., nr. 21: "Observations sur les motifs qu'on ose présumer avoir décidé Monseigneur le Chancelier à sévir contre Desventes."

24. On the creation of the fund, see ibid., nr. 41; on David's mission, ibid, nrs. 83–99. The Guild summarized its arguments for increased police action to repress *contrefaçons* in a printed *Mémoire des syndics et adjoints* dated May 12, 1759: ibid, nr. 102.

25. "Requête de Jean-Marie Bruyset, imprimeur-libraire à Lyon, contre la saisie faite sur lui, à la requête de la femme de Jean-Baptiste Garnier," May 1761, ibid., nr. 127. Wives could not become members of the Guild, but they often collaborated with their husbands, and widows of booksellers sometimes wielded great power, posthumously exercising their husbands' mastership. The role of women in the early-modern book trade deserves further study.

26. Memoir by Bruyset, undated but probably submitted in 1762, when Bruyset was involved in two court cases with Garnier and other Parisian booksellers: ibid., nr. 129. See also Bruyset's letter to an unnamed friend, dated March 12, 1762: ibid., nr. 128.

27. For example, in a memo of January 1766 about a debate within the Direction de la librairie about the modalities for inspecting shipments of books, Joseph d'Hémery noted "une discussion très vive entre les libraires de Paris et ceux de Lyon": BnF, F.F. 22081, nr. 177. He might have been referring to an argument at one of the weekly

audiences held by Malesherbes or to a discussion in a back room. In either case, the lobbying involved an oral confrontation.

28. BnF, F.F. 22075, nr. 117. In a note on the memoir, Sartine acknowledged that it contained some good ideas, and in fact it anticipated an important provision of the code that would be adopted in 1777.

29. "Mémoire à consulter pour les libraires et imprimeurs de Lyon, Rouen, Toulouse, Marseille et Nîmes, concernant les privilèges de librairie et continuations d'iceux," Lyon, October 15, 1776: BnF, F.F. 22073, nr. 144.

30. The sources for the following account are scattered through the following sections of the Anisson-Duperron collection in the BnF: F.F. 21833, 22081, 22179, 22081, 22082, and 22123.

31. The Crown levied a tax on paper in February 1784 to meet the deficit produced by the War of the Austrian Succession (1740–1748) but treated the tax as an "extraordinary" expedient and withdrew it in 1749: BnF, F.F. 22082, nr. 90.

32. "Édit du Roi portant perception de droits sur les ouvrages imprimés en caractère et en taille-douce et papiers peints" (March 1, 1771), BnF, F.F. 22123, nr. 41. See also "Déclaration du roi portant fixation d'un nouveau tarif sur les papiers et cartons," March 1, 1771, BnF, F.F. 22082, nr. 90 and on the proposed modalities for collecting the tax," Arrêt du Conseil d'État," October 16, 1771, BnF, F.F. 22082, nr. 98. The tax rate varied according to the size and quality of the paper. It came to 20 sous per ream for sheets of "carré" and "raisin," which were widely used for ordinary books. Jean-Marie Bruyset, an eminent bookseller of Lyon, referred to the rate in general as 20 sous per ream: "Observations sur la décadence et la ruine d'une des branches la plus florissante du commerce du royaume" (undated, probably written in the second half of 1783), BnF, F.F. 21833, fols. 129–130. Following Bruyset, I describe the general rate of the tax as 20 sous per ream. Bruyset also discussed the subsequent surcharges (*sous pour livre*, meaning one additional sou for every 20 sous paid in taxes). A surcharge levied in August 1781 was 2 sous per livre, and another in January 1782 replaced it with a rate of 10 sous per livre, making the amount of taxation on a ream come to 30 sous in all.

33. The figures on the comparative costs of paper come from an undated "Mémoire sur le moyen de remédier aux contrefaçons et d'empêcher l'entrée des libelles en France," BnF, F.F. 21833, fol. 87.

34. BnF, F.F. 22123, nr. 39: "Mémoire présenté au Chancelier et au Contrôleur général par les syndic et adjoints, au sujet de l'impôt projeté sur le papier."

35. "Observations sur l'édit du roi portant perception de droits sur les ouvrages imprimés" (August 1771), ibid., nr. 40.

36. *Mémoires secrets pour servir à l'histoire de la république des lettres en France*, entry for April 11, 1771. Because editions of this printed newssheet vary in numbers of volumes and pagination, I refer to its entries by date.

37. Arrêt du Conseil d'État, September 11, 1771, BnF, F.F. 22081, nr. 190. See also the copies of the edict in F.F. 22179, nrs. 202 and 205.

38. "Mémoire présenté par le corps de la librairie et imprimerie," September 24, 1771, BnF, F.F. 22070, nr. 21. The Parisian publishers also rejected the claim that they

had solicited the import duty as a way to counteract the advantage given to foreign publishers by the excessive tax on paper.

39. The texts of the arrêts du Conseil d'État are in BnF, F.F. 22179, nrs. 201 and 274.

40. Arrêt du Conseil d'État, April 23, 1775, BnF, F.F. 22179, nr. 362.

41. Pottinger, *The French Book Trade*, 135.

42. Jean-Marie Bruyset, "Observations sur la décadence et la ruine d'une des branches la plus florissante du commerce du royaume, c'est-à-dire, de la librairie, particulièrement celle de la ville de Lyon" (undated but clearly from 1784), BnF, F.F. 21833, fols. 141–153.

43. "Mémoire sur le moyen de remédier aux contrefaçons et d'empêcher les libelles en France," undated and unsigned, BnF, F.F. 21833, fol. 87.

44. Ibid.

45. The large literature on this subject is summarized in *The Cambridge History of the Book in Britain*, Michael F. Suarez and Michael L. Turner, eds., 5 (Cambridge University Press, Cambridge, 2009) . There is a strong parallel between the activities of the London Stationers' Company and the Parisian Communauté des libraires et des imprimeurs. In an attempt to enforce their monopoly against the threat of pirated editions from Scotland and Ireland, the Londoners used threats, force, and lawsuits. In 1759 they raised a fund from the Company's members and attempted to send out "riding officers" to raid provincial bookshops that carried pirated editions. See John Feather, *A History of British Publishing* (Routledge, London, 1988), 79–80; James Raven, *The Business of Books: Booksellers and the English Book Trade 1450–1850* (Yale University Press, New Haven, CT, 2007), 233; and Johns, *Piracy*, 120.

46. BnF, F.F.22073, nr 140, Letter of Benoît Duplain to an unnamed correspondent, March 30, 1774; and BnF, F.F.22073, nr. 141, *requête* signed by the lawyer Flusin: "au Roi et à nosseigneurs de son Conseil."

47. "Mémoire à consulter pour les libraires et imprimeurs de Lyon, Rouen, Toulouse, Marseille et Nîmes concernant les privilèges de librairie," October 15, 1776: BnF, F.F. 22073, nr. 144, quotation from p. 88.

48. BnF, F.F. 22073, quotations from pp. 48 and 80.

49. "Règlement du conseil pour la librairie et imprimerie de Paris," February 28, 1723, in *Recueil général des anciennes lois françaises* 21 (Paris, 1821–33), 261–251. Quotation from p. 230.

50. I have based the following discussion of the edicts of August 30, 1777, on the original manuscript in BnF, F.F., 22180, nrs. 80–87; but they can be consulted in print in *Recueil général des anciennes lois françaises*. In a speech before the Parlement of Paris delivered during three sessions on August 10, 17, and 31, 1779, the avocat général Antoine-Louis Séguier observed that the edicts of August 30, 1777, were the first to use the phrase "droit des auteurs." See Séguier, "Compte rendu," in *Recueil de pièces et de documents*, 583.

51. Siméon-Prosper Hardy, *Mes loisirs, ou journal d'événements tels qu'ils parviennent à ma connaissance (1753–1789)*, Pascal Bastien and Daniel Roche, eds. (Quebec, 2008–). The first five volumes of this edition were published by 2018. I have consulted the subsequent volumes from the digitized transcription kindly made

available by Pascal Bastien. For the sake of convenience, I refer to the entries in Hardy's journal and in the *Mémoires secrets* by date. Despite their common bias, Hardy's journal shows that he was a pious Jansenist favorable to the Parlement of Paris, whereas the authors of the *Mémoires secrets*, Mathieu-François Pidansat de Mairobert and Barthélemy-François-Joseph Moufle d'Argenville, were radical critics of the government, the court, and the general tendency that they described as ministerial despotism.

52. In his speech before the Parlement of Paris on August 10, 17, and 31, 1779, Séguier described the reaction to the edicts as follows (*Recueil de pièces*, p. 495): "La consternation s'empara des esprits; le corps de la librairie se crut entièrement perdu." Hardy also noted the "réclamation générale": entry for October 23, 1777.

53. Hardy, November 4, 1778. The symbolic message of their dress was emphasized in the protests of the Guild: see *Seconde Lettre à un ami sur les affaires actuelles de la librairie* in *Recueil de pieces*, 325.

54. Jean Quéniart, *L'Imprimerie et la librairie à Rouen au XVIIIe siècle* (Librairie C. Klincksieck, Paris, 1969), 173–188; and Jane McLeod, *Licensing Loyalty: Printers, Patrons, and the State in Early Modern France* (Pennsylvania State University Press, University Park, 2011), 93–94.

55. Hardy, October 28, October 30, and November 9, 1777. *Mémoires secrets*, November 24, December 15, and December, 21, 1777.

56. Hardy, November 28, December 18, December 20, December 22, and December 27, 1777. *Mémoires secrets*, December 21, 1777, and (on the non-enforcement of the requirement for the work permit) June 13, 1780.

57. *Mémoires secrets*, January 26, 1778. Hardy, January 23, 24, 25, and 29, 1778.

58. Documents on the Academy's meeting and the text of the edict of July 30, 1778, are in *Recueil de pièces*, 363–366 and 625–629. On the divisions within the Academy, see Charles-Guillaume Leclerc, *Lettre à M. de xxx* in *Recueil de pièces*, 386–400. Leclerc, a Parisian bookseller, attributed the role of the Academy to the machinations of Jean-Baptiste-Antoine Suard and abbé François Arnaud. They were closely connected to the powerful Parisian publisher Charles-Joseph Panckoucke, who had quarreled with the Guild and had considerable influence within the French government. See also Hardy, February 14 and July 30, 1778.

59. Hardy, quotations from the entries for March 9 and November 20, 1778.

60. *Requête au roi et consultations pour la librairie et l'imprimerie de Paris au sujet des deux arrêts du 30 août 1777* in *Recueil de pièces*, quotations from pp. 159, 185, and 192. *Mémoires secrets*, February 2 and 3, 1778. Hardy, January 12 and 14, 1778.

61. Hardy, August 5, 7, 8, 10, 11, and 19, 1778. *Mémoires secrets*, August 21 and 22, 1778. In its article of August 21, the *Mémoires secrets* wrote that the case had produced "un nouveau orage," reinforced by the violent argument of Paucton's lawyer, and in its article of August 22, it deplored the edicts as "un acte de despotisme."

62. D'Eprémesnil's speech is printed in *Recueil de pièces*, "Procès-verbal de ce qui s'est passé au Parlement touchant les six arrêts du conseil du 30 août 1777." Leclerc's *Lettre à M. de xxx*, dated December 19, 1778, is also printed in the *Recueil de pièces*, quotation from p. 427.

63. The *Mémoires secrets*, which was consistently hostile to the edicts and covered the session of the Parlement in great detail, treated Séguier's speech as a "chef d'oeuvre" in support of the guild's position: June 19, 1780. See also its entries for May 1, June 11, and June 13, 1780. Hardy, as could be expected, also reacted favorably to Séguier's oratory: entries for August 10, 27, and 31, 1780. As an example of Séguier's favorable treatment of the protests against the edicts and of the contradictory nature of his conclusion, see his "Compte rendu" in *Recueil de pièces,* 509 and 592–593.

64. Hardy chronicled the decline of support in the Parlement for taking a strong stand against the edicts in entries of September 6 and July 6, 1779; July 25, 1780; and December 23, 1781. The quotation comes from "Mémoire des libraires au Garde des sceaux," 1787, in *Recueil de pièces,* 601. An account of the polemics following the publication of the edicts of May 30, 1777, can be found in the French version of this book, translated by Jean-François Sené and published by Gallimard. I have eliminated it from the English version in order to avoid overburdening the English reader with detail.

Chapter 2

1. In 1781, the *Almanach de la librairie* by Antoine Perrin (Paris, 1781, reprinted by P. M. Gason, Aubel, Belgium, 1984, and edited by Jeroom Vercruysse) listed thirty-six Parisian master printers, including four widows, who appeared in a separate list entitled "Mesdames les veuves"; and it listed 146 Parisian booksellers, including thirty-six widows, also listed separately. Perrin probably calculated the population of professionals in Paris accurately, but he made many mistakes in listing the masters in the provinces. See the introduction to the reprint of the *Almanach* by Vercruysse, vii–xi, and Robert Darnton, *A Literary Tour de France: The World of Books on the Eve of the French Revolution* (Oxford University Press, New York, 2018), 47–48, 154, and 164.

2. These requirements were spelled out in great detail by the general book Code of February 28, 1723, published in *Recueil général des anciennes lois françaises,* Jourdan, Decrusy, and Isambert, eds., 21 (Paris, 1830), 216–251.

3. On the restriction of masterships in Paris and the provinces, see Thierry Rigogne, *Between State and Market: Printing and Bookselling in Eighteenth-Century France* (Voltaire Foundation, Oxford, 2007), especially chaps. 4 and 5; and Jane McLeod, *Licensing Loyalty: Printers, Patrons, and the State in Early Modern France* (Pennsylvania State University Press, University Park, PA, 2011), which stresses the complicity of printers in the reinforcement of their monopoly by the state.

4. *La Police des métiers du livre à Paris au siècle des Lumières: Historique des libraires et imprimeurs de Paris existans en 1752 de l'inspecteur Joseph d'Hémery,* Jean-Dominique Mellot, Marie-Claude Felton, and Elisabeth Queval, eds., with the collaboration of Nathalie Aguirre (Bibliothèque nationale de France, Paris, 2017). This superb edition of d'Hémery's reports, supplemented by information compiled from a wide variety of sources, makes it possible to form a complete picture of the book trade in eighteenth-century Paris. The editors have also added biographical sketches of twenty-four book

professionals, most of them obscure, who did not figure in d'Hémery's files. I have published d'Hémery's survey of authors, along with extensive annotation, on my website, robertdarnton.org.

5. For a balanced account of this famous episode, see Arthur Wilson, *Diderot* (Oxford University Press, New York, 1972), 468–491.

6. On Le Breton and his three associates in the *Encyclopédie* enterprise, see Frank A. Kafker and Jeff Loveland, "André-François Le Breton, initiateur et libraire en chef de l'*Encyclopédie*," *Recherches sur Diderot et sur "l'Encyclopédie*," nr. 51 (2016), 107–125. As this article points out, Le Breton was sent to the Bastille for eight days in April 1766, but this punishment was merely a slap on the wrist for refusing to obey an order not to ship copies of the *Encyclopédie* to customers in Versailles at a time when the General Assembly of the Clergy was holding a meeting there. On Durand, see Frank A. Kafker and Jeff Loveland, "Diderot et Laurent Durand, son éditeur principal," *Recherches sur Diderot et sur "l'Encyclopédie*," nr. 39 (2005), 29–40; and Frank A. Kafker and Jeff Loveland, "The Elusive Laurent Durand, a Leading Publisher of the French Enlightenment," *Studies on Voltaire and the Eighteenth Century* 12 (2005), 223–258.

7. Augustin Martin Lottin, *Catalogue chronologique des libraires et des libraires-imprimeurs de Paris* (Paris, 1789, reprinted by B. R. Grüner, Amsterdam, 1969), xiv. In a preface to his book, Lottin stressed, p. 1, "Il aura de quoi satisfaire toutes les familles de la librairie et imprimerie de Paris qui aimeront à y trouver la suite de leurs ayeux et les différentes branches de leurs généalogies."

8. BnF France, F.F., 22081, nr. 188. The entries were dashed off in a way that makes many of the books difficult to identify. Rather than making educated guesses, I have placed the ambiguous entries in the category "unidentified" in Table 2.1.

9. The growing use of *permissions tacites* is a common theme in studies of the book trade in eighteenth-century France. See, for example, François Furet, "La 'Librairie' du royaume de France au 18e siècle," in Furet et al., *Livre et société dans la France du XVIII* *siècle* (Mouton & Co., Paris, 1965).

10. I should add, however, that I am puzzled by the report on the books being printed in the shop of G. Desprez. It mentioned two books, "un volume de Nicole" and "L'Esprit de Nicole" (evidently *L'Esprit de M. Nicole, ou Instructions sur les vérités de la religion* first published by Desprez in 1765), which were works of the eminent seventeenth-century Jansenist, Pierre Nicole. Both had *privilèges* and therefore had been cleared by censors, who had a sharp eye for heresies. Jansenism had been declared a heresy (notably by the bull Unigenitus in 1713), and therefore it would be surprising to find openly Jansenist works listed in the inspection reports. Desprez, "imprimeur du roi et du clergé," ran a large printing shop in the rue Saint Jacques, and he also printed several orthodox religious works, including "Le Nouveau Testament de Sacy," "Les Lois ecclésiastiques," and "Missel de Noyen." In his reports, d'Hémery had noted that some of the most eminent publishers— Jean Desaint, Charles Saillant, Jacques Vincent, and Philippe-Nicolas Lottin—had dealt in Jansenist books.

11. On the signs and the "shaving" of Paris, see Louis Sébastien Mercier, *Tableau de Paris*, Jean-Claude Bonnet, ed., vol. 1 (Mercure de France reprint, Paris, 1994), 177: "La

ville, qui n'est plus hérissée de ces appendices grossiers, offre, pour ainsi dire, un visage poli, net et rasé."

12. This figure includes all master booksellers and printers, along with widows, listed in *Tableau des libraires et des imprimeurs jurés de l'Université de Paris* for 1768, BnF, F.F. 22106, nr. 8. It strikes me as low. The number listed under Paris in the *Almanach de la librairie* was 221 for 1777, 199 for 1778, and 184 for 1781: Antoine Perrin, *Almanach de la librairie*, Jeroom Vercruysse, ed. (Paris, 1781; reprint, Paris, 1984), viii.

13. As far as I can tell, the Compagnie des libraires associés has never been studied. Information about it can be found in the catalogue of the Bibliothèque nationale de France and at the BnF's website data.bnf.fr. It included several members of the Saugrain dynasty, whose history was traced by Joseph Saugrain: "Généalogie de la famille des Saugrain, libraires, depuis 1518 jusqu'à présent" (1736), BnF, F.F. 22106, nr. 15.

14. A more thorough picture of book production in Paris could be produced by further research on manuscript F.F. 22081, nr. 188, along with the documents covering the inspection of printing shops in 1770 and 1771: F.F. 22081, nrs. 188 bis and 189. I should add that one unexpected result of the study of the inspections in 1769 is the large number of editions, sixteen, that were printed with *privilèges* "pour le compte de l'auteur." Authors were not permitted to sell their own works at this time. Many of them evidently acquired *privilèges* and arranged for the printing of their works, which they then sold to booksellers. On self-publishing, see Marie-Claude Felton, *Maîtres de leurs ouvrages: L'Édition à compte d'auteur à Paris au XVIIIᵉ siècle* (Voltaire Foundation, Oxford, 2014).

Chapter 3

1. Diderot, *Lettre sur le commerce de la librairie* (Librairie Fontaine, Paris, 1984), 115.

2. For an overview of the publishing of French books from outside France, see *Histoire de l'édition française* 2 (Promodis, Paris, 1984), 302–359. Among studies of the subject from a pan-European viewpoint, see Giles Barber, *Studies in the Booktrade of the European Enlightenment* (Pindar Press, London, 1994). On pirating, see *Les Presses grises: La Contrefaçon du livre (XVIᵉ–XIXᵉ siècles)*, François Moureau, ed. (Aux Amateurs du Livre, Paris, 1988).

3. Of course Europeans who read French were a small elite, but the French language imposed itself everywhere among the upper strata as the medium of a desirable way of life: Marc Fumaroli, *Quand l'Europe parlait français* (Éditions de Fallois, Paris, 2001). In their petitions to the government asking for support, the booksellers stressed the importance of their industry, in view of the fact that "la langue française est devenue aujourd'hui celle de toutes les nations": "Observations sur la décadence et la ruine d'une des branches la plus florissante du commerce du royaume, c'est-à-dire, de la librairie, particulièrement de celle de la ville de Lyon," BnF, papers of the Chambre syndicale de la Communauté des libraires et des imprimeurs de Paris, ms. F.F. 21833, fol. 141.

4. When Émeric David, a printer-bookseller in Aix-en-Provence, visited Lyon in 1787, he jotted in his notebook under the rubric Lyon, "12 imprimeries—les 3 quarts ne s'occupent qu'aux contrefaçons." Bibliothèque de l'Arsenal, Paris, ms. 5947.

5. See the excellent account of Mettra's career in Jeffrey Freedman, *Books without Borders in Enlightenment Europe: French Cosmopolitanism and German Literary Markets* (University of Pennsylvania Press, Philadelphia, 2012), 62–75.

6. The following discussion draws on the dossiers in the STN archives of three Liégeois publishers: Clément Plomteux, J. J. Tutot, and C. J. Renoz, and Demazeau (first name unknown) along with the extensive research of Liégeois scholars, particularly *Guide bibliographique pour l'histoire de la principauté de Liège au 18ᵉ siècle*, Daniel Droixhe, ed., in *Annuaire d'histoire liégeoise* (Liège, 1995); Daniel Droixhe, *Une histoire des Lumières au pays de Liège* (Les Éditions de l'Université de Liège, Liège, 2007); and *Livres et Lumières au pays de Liège (1730–1830)*, Daniel Droixhe, P.-P. Gossiaux, Hervé Hasquin, and Michèle Mat-Hasquin, eds. (Desoer Editions, Liège, 1980).

7. Joseph Brassine, "L'Imprimerie à Liège jusqu'à la fin de l'Ancien Régime," in *Histoire du livre et de l'imprimerie en Belgique des origines à nos jours* 5, "Première partie" (Musée du livre, Brussels, 1929), 41. The *Almanach de la librairie* of 1781 lists ten booksellers without giving the number of printers and presses. However, Daniel Droixhe, the greatest expert on publishing in Liège, is convinced that Liège had at least fifteen booksellers at this time—more than those in Namur, Mechelen (Malines), and Tournai: information kindly communicated in a private letter dated April 13, 2019.

8. Diderot, *Lettre sur le commerce de la librairie* (Librairie Fontaine, Paris, 1984), 102.

9. Jean-François Marmontel, *Mémoires de Marmontel*, M. F. Barrière, ed. (Firmin-Didot, Paris, 1891), 355. This passage has been quoted by several historians, beginning with Joseph Brassine, "L'Imprimerie à Liège jusqu'à la fin de l'Ancien Régime."

10. Plomteux described his edition of the *Histoire philosophique* to the STN in a letter of June 26, 1781: "J'aurai moi-même achevé le mois prochain une édition en 10 volumes octavo avec les planches, tableaux, et atlas. Je puis me flatter qu'elle sera plus belle et plus exacte que l'édition originale . . . J'ai eu le bonheur de posséder chez moi M. l'abbé Raynal depuis le moment de son départ de Paris, et je viens d'établir cet illustre proscrit à Spa, où il prend les eaux." Plomteux along with Jean-Edmé Dufour of Maastricht led the pack in the race to reprint Raynal's *Histoire philosophique*, a great bestseller.

11. Demazeau to STN, April 11, 1774.

12. Droixhe, *Une histoire des Lumières au pays de Liège*, 91.

13. In addition to the sources cited above, this account is based on the outstanding monograph by Raymond Birn, *Pierre Rousseau and the Philosophes of Bouillon* (Institut et Musée Voltaire, Geneva, 1964).

14. The following account draws on Droixhe, *Une histoire des Lumières*, chaps. 6 and 8 and *Livres et Lumières au pays de Liège*, especially chap. 7.

15. Auguste Vincent, "La Typographie bruxelloise au XVIIᵉ et XVIIIᵉ siècle," in *Histoire du livre et de l'imprimerie en Belgique* 5, "Quatrième partie," 32–33.

16. This summary of the complex relations between the STN and Boubers is based on Boubers's dossier in the STN papers, which I have discussed at length in "The

Life Cycle of a Book: A Publishing History of d'Holbach's *Système de la nature*," in *Publishing and Readership in Revolutionary France and America*, Carol Armbruster, ed. (Greenwood Press, Westport, CT, 1993), 15–43. On the STN edition of the *Système de la nature*, see also Charly Guyot, "Imprimeurs et passeurs neuchâtelois: L'Affaire du *Système de la nature* (1771)," *Musée neuchâtelois* 33 (1946), 74–81 and 108–116; and Jeroom Vercruysse, "L'Édition neuchâteloise du *Système de la nature* et la librairie bruxelloise," in *Aspects du livre neuchâtelois*, Jacques Rychner and Michel Schlup, eds. (Neuchâtel, 1986), 77–88.

17. STN to Charles Triponetty, a merchant in Brussels who acted as its bill collector, January 6, 1772. In a letter to the STN of February 25, 1774, Triponetty reported that, once again, Boubers had refused to pay his debts: "Il me répondit vaguement et je prévois qu'il cherchera des chicanes dont il n'est pas mal endoctriné." Triponnety found nothing but "mauvaise volonté" in Boubers's behavior.

18. On the plotting, see Chapter 8, this volume. On the speculations to produce Rousseau's works after his death in 1778, see Raymond Birn, *Forging Rousseau: Print, Commerce and Cultural Manipulation in the Late Enlightenment* (Voltaire Foundation, Oxford, 2001); and Ralph Leigh, "Rousseau, His Publishers and the *Contrat Social*," *Bulletin of the John Rylands University Library of Manchester* 66, nr. 2 (1984), 204–227.

19. Delahaye to STN, January 2, 1783. In a letter to the STN of April 18, 1783, Pierre-Joseph Duplain also referred to Boubers's bankruptcy. Boubers married the sister of Charles-Joseph Panckoucke, and Panckoucke loaned him 38,000 L. in September 1783: Suzanne Tucoo-Chala, *Charles-Joseph Panckoucke & la librairie française 1736–1798* (Editions Marrimpouey Jeune and Librairie Jean Touzot, Pau and Paris, 1977), 404. Given Panckoucke's support, it seems likely that Boubers resumed some activity in the book trade, but I have not found any evidence to bear out that supposition.

20. *La Vie culturelle dans nos provinces (Pays-Bas autrichiens, principauté de Liège et duché de Bouillon)*, Hervé Hasquin, ed. (Brussels, 1983), 17; and *Almanach de la librairie*, 89. In Pascal Durand and Tanguy Habrand, *Histoire de l'édition en Belgique XVᵉ–XXIᵉ siècle* (Les Impressions nouvelles, 2018, no place of publication given), it is argued (pp. 73–74), although without evidence, that there was a great deal of piracy in Brussels.

21. Overman frères to STN, August 31, 1785.

22. Delahaye & Compagnie to STN, April 5, 1787. The correspondent, who merely signed "Delahaye & Compagnie," made similar remarks in letters of June 8, 1787, and October 1, 1788.

23. Overman frères to STN, August 31, 1785: "La société des libraires Delahaye et Compagnie de notre ville est tout à fait [dissoute]. La femme de Delahaye et le principal associé sont condamnés à la maison de force. Lui, qui n'était pour rien dans cette affaire, a obtenu sa liberté. Il ne lui reste aucune ressource." In a letter of February 17, 1784, Overman had warned the STN that the Delahaye were "des chicaneurs et des gens qui par des détours tendent à s'appoprier ce qu'il ne leur appartient pas."

24. Villebon's dossier in the STN archives contains only eleven letters, but they indicate the general character of his trade. He mentioned his detention in the Bastille in a letter of June 25, 1782, which included his latest catalogue. It contained more than 200 titles

covering a large variety of literature, with entries about *livres philosophiques* added in hand. The STN's shipping agent in Ostend, Frédéric Romberg & fils, mentioned Villebon's arrest in a letter of January 24, 1782, which concluded, "Ces gens, ayant été arrêtés pour cause capitale, perdront selon toute apparence au moins la liberté."

25. On conditions in the Netherlands, see Ivo Schöffer, *A Short History of The Netherlands* (De Lange, Amsterdam, 1973); and Simon Schama, *Patriots and Liberators: Revolution in the Netherlands 1780–1813* (Alfred A. Knopf, New York, 1977).

26. The dominance of these three is implicit in many of the letters that the STN received from the Netherlands. Louis de Joncourt, the librarian of the Stadholder in The Hague and a brother-in-law of Frédéric-Samuel Ostervald, one of the founders of the STN, discussed them with Ostervald in a letter of September 22, 1775, which concluded, "Je vous indique ces Messieurs comme les seuls qui fassent le vrai commerce de la librairie étrangère et qui entendent leur profession." For an overview of publishing and the international book trade in the Netherlands, see Y. Z. Dubosq, *Le Livre français et son commerce en Hollande de 1750 à 1780* (Amsterdam, 1925); and *Le Magasin de l'univers: The Dutch Republic as the Centre of the European Book Trade*, C. Berkvens-Stevelinck, H. Bots, P.G. Hoftijzer, and O. S. Lankhorst, eds. (Brill, Leiden, 1992).

27. Unfortunately, there still is no full-scale biography of Rey. Among the biographical and bibliographical studies, see Max Fajn, "Marc-Michel Rey: Boekhandelaar op de Bloemmark (Amsterdam)," *Proceedings of the American Philosophical Society* 118 (1974), 260–268; and Jeroom Vercruysse, "Marc-Michel Rey imprimeur philosophe ou philosophique?," in *Werkgroep Achttiende Eeuw* (Nymegen, 1977), 93–121.

28. Details of their relationship can be followed in *Correspondance complète de Jean-Jacques Rousseau* (Voltaire Foundation, Oxford, 1965–1998), 52 vols., superbly edited and annotated by R. A. Leigh. See also Leigh's essay, "Rousseau, His Publishers and the *Contrat Social*," and the excellent monograph by Birn, *Forging Rousseau*.

29. Leigh, "Rousseau, His Publishers and the *Contrat Social*," 211.

30. Ibid., 222–223.

31. Jeroom Vercruysse, "Typologie de Marc-Michel Rey," *Wolfenbütteler Schriften zur Geschichte des Buchwesens* 4 (1981), 167–185. In this article, Vercruysse identified and listed 106 books published by Rey.

32. Raymond Birn, "Michel Rey's Enlightenment," in *Le Magasin de l'univers*, 26.

33. Gosse to STN, December 8, 1769.

34. Gosse to STN, July 16, 1779. Gosse had subscribed for 200 copies of the *Description des arts et métiers*, which the STN reprinted from the Paris edition in nineteen volumes, but after the STN failed to provide the volumes on time, he wanted to cancel his subscription. After an attempt to resolve the dispute "à l'amiable" in 1779, it was eventually settled to the STN's advantage in court. Gosse's son, Pierre-Frédéric, took over the firm on January 1, 1774. At that time Pierre Gosse and his partner, Daniel Pinet, both retired.

35. David. W. Smith, "A Preliminary Bibliographical List of Editions of Helvétius's Works," *Australian Journal of French Studies* 7 (1970), 299–347; and Daniel Droixhe and Nadine Vanwelkenhuyzen, "Ce que tromper veut dire: À propos des éditions

maestrichtoises d'Helvétius (1744–1777)," *Studies on Voltaire and the Eighteenth Century* 329 (1995), 197–206.

36. Bosset to STN, September 17, 1779. In a letter to the STN of January 19, 1778, Dufour wrote that he had difficulty keeping up with his extensive correspondence and was working flat out with two of his sons. In a letter of August 2, 1780, he said that he had visited his family in Paris for the first time in twenty-two years. And in a letter of February 7, 1787, he notified the STN that his partner, Philippe Roux, had just died and had been replaced by a brother of Roux. Although Dufour's dossier is quite large, fifty-one letters, it contains no other details about his personal life.

37. Dufour to STN, July 8, 1777.

38. STN to Dufour, December 16, 1776.

39. Dufour to STN, December 25, 1787.

40. Dufour to STN, September 28, 1776.

41. In a letter to the STN from Amsterdam of August 30, 1779, Bosset wrote, "On imprime dans ce pays à 25% plus cher . . . qu'en Suisse."

42. P. J. Hoftijzer, "The Leiden Bookseller Pieter van der Aa (1659–1733) and the International Book Trade," *Le Magasin de l'univers*, 169–184. On connections between the French book trade and The Hague, see Christiane Berkvens-Stevelinck, *Prosper Marchand: La Vie et l'oeuvre (1678–1756)* (Brill, Leiden, 1987).

43. For example, Elie Luzac specialized in the works of the French Enlightenment and published the first edition of *L'Homme machine*, the materialist treatise by Julien Offray de La Mettrie, but by 1760 neglected publishing in order to devote himself to law and political activism. See Rietje van Vliet, *Elie Luzac (1721–1796), Bookseller of the Enlightenment* (AfdH Publishers, Enschede, The Netherlands, 2014).

44. Bosset's letters to the home office in Neuchâtel (ms 1125 of the STN archives) extend from July 12 to September 23. He stayed nearly three weeks in his brother's château at Huth near Cleves in early August. In addition to seeking opportunities for the STN, he may have pursued business interests of his own, because he also was involved in banking and calico manufacturing. He stopped off at book stores and printing shops along the following route: Basel, Strasbourg, Rastatt, Mannheim, Karlsruhe, Darmstadt, Frankfurt, Hanau, Mainz, Coblenz, Bonn, Cologne, Düsseldorf, Duisburg, Wesel, Cleves, Arnheim, Utrecht, Leiden, Haarlem, Amsterdam, The Hague, Rotterdam, Antwerp, Brussels, Louvain, Maastricht, Liège, Mons, Valenciennes, Cambrai, and Saint Quentin.

45. Bosset to STN, August 30, 1779: "J'ai beaucoup de peine à le faire revenir de sa prévention contre la Société typographique ayant cru que Fauche [Samuel Fauche, the rival publisher of the STN in Neuchâtel] et nous étaient la même chose et que nous avions imprimé Bonnet [Charles Bonnet, the naturalist, whose *Oeuvres d'histoire naturelle et de philosophie* was pirated by Fauche] et Rousseau dont il a le privilège en Hollande." The STN had sounded Rey about doing business soon after it began operating. He turned it down bluntly in a letter of September 4, 1769. Rather than buying books from the STN, he said, he preferred to print his own, even though production costs were greater in Amsterdam: "Je conviens qu'il m'en coûte encore plus ici, mais je donne du pain à mes compatriotes, et je préfère ce moyen quoique plus dispendieux."

46. Bosset to STN, September 7, 1779: "J'ai appris à être fort circonspect sur les livres que j'ai offerts aux différents libraires, qui tous du plus au moins [sic] impriment les mêmes ouvrages que nous et qui en général voient avec jalousie la quantité de livres qui sortent de la Suisse."

47. This observation is based on the study of dozens of catalogues, but I have not done any statistical analysis. A systematic study of catalogues along with advertisements in journals could reveal a great deal about the international trade.

48. Pierre-Frédéric Gosse to STN, July 26, 1776: "Je ne m'attendais pas de votre part, Messieurs, des réimpressions de mes propres éditions, et je suis très surpris que vous jugez encore à propos de me les annoncer."

49. D. J. Changuion to STN, December 24, 1781.

50. Widow Charmet to STN, September 3, 1783.

51. C. A. Serini to STN, May 25, 1774. In a letter of October 28, 1781, to François Pilâtre de Rozier, Ostervald wrote, "Mes liaisons avec toutes les typographies de la Suisse me mettent à même de vous fournir ce qui sort de leurs presses comme de celle que je dirige. Je pourrai même vous annoncer à l'avance toutes nos diverses nouveautés."

52. On the enormous production of *contrefaçons* in Avignon, see René Moulinas, *L'Imprimerie, la librairie, et la presse à Avignon au XVIIIe siècle* (Presses universitaires de Grenoble, Grenoble, 1974); and on the exchange trade between Avignon and Switzerland, see Darnton, *A Literary Tour de France*, 93–108.

53. Quoted in Thierry Rigogne, *Between State and Market: Printing and Bookselling in Eighteenth-Century France* (Voltaire Foundation, Oxford, 2007), 178.

54. Quoted in Dominique Varry, "Le Livre clandestin à Lyon au XVIIIe siècle," *La Lettre clandestine* 6 (1997), 244.

55. Jeanne Veyrin-Forrer, "Livres arrêtés, livres estampillés, traces parisiennes de la contrefaction," in *Les Presses grises,* Moureau, 108.

56. Jean Baptiste Antoine Suard, *Discours impartial sur les affaires actuelles de la librairie* (1778), 26–27. *Lettre à un ami sur les arrêts du conseil du 30 août 1777* reprinted in *Recueil de pièces,* 289.

57. *Requête au Roi et consultations pour la librairie et l'imprimerie de Paris au sujet des deux arrêts du 30 août 1777,* BnF, ms. F.F. 22075, pièce 189; *Lettre à un ami sur les arrêts du conseil du 30 août 1777,* reprinted in *Recueil de pièces,* 289; and *Lettre d'un libraire de Lyon à un libraire de Paris* (1779), 4. The reactions to the edicts of August 30, 1777, and the polemics surrounding them can be followed closely in the journal of Siméon-Prosper Hardy, *Mes loisirs, ou journal d'événements tels qu'ils parviennent à ma connaissance (1753–1789),* currently being edited by Pascal Bastien (Quebec, 2008). I have consulted the subsequent volumes from the digitized transcription of the manuscript kindly made available by Pascal Bastien.

58. "Mémoire des syndics et adjoints représentants le corps de la librairie et imprimerie de Paris," May 12, 1759, BnF, ms. F.F. 22075, pièce 102. See the similar argument from a memoir of 1754: "Mémoire de la Communauté de Paris au Chancelier contre les contrefaçons d'Avignon," BnF, ms. F.F. 22075, pièce 119.

59. "Précis d'un mémoire pour le bien de la librairie de Paris, même du royaume et de l'État," August 20, 1763, BnF, ms. F.F. 22068, pièce 47.

60. "Mémoire sur la librairie de France," February 8, 1767, BnF, ms. F.F. 22123, fols. 60–61. Guy wrote that pirating had taken off as an industry around 1744: "C'est depuis ce temps-là qu'on a vu croître cette multitude de libraires-imprimeurs dans les républiques de Genève, Lausanne, Avignon, Liège, etc." Yet few of these entrepreneurs made large fortunes, he noted, "parce qu'il arrive souvent qu'un même ouvrage se contrefait en même temps chez plusieurs d'eux."

61. Pierre Bruyset-Ponthus, "Mémoire sur les contrefaçons," September 16, 1769, BnF, ms., F.F. 22075, fol. 327.

62. The sixth edict authorized any owner of a <u>privilège</u>, duly accompanied by a police official, to inspect a shop where he suspected that a pirated edition of his book was being sold. If he found one, he could collect substantial damages, but the bookseller could also collect damages if no *contrefaçon* was discovered. The raids by the Parisians in Lyon before 1777 had demonstrated the unfeasibility of such self-appointed policing, which was roundly criticized in the attacks on the edict. See, for example, *Lettre à un ami*, 303–304.

63. Machuel to STN, September 20, 1779. In a letter to the STN from Nancy of June 1784 (no exact date), Matthieu, one of the city's most important booksellers, described the local chambre syndicale, created by the edicts of 1777, as "la plus dure de tout le royaume."

64. I have traced this issue through the archives of the ministry of foreign affairs and discussed it in *The Devil in the Holy Water or the Art of Slander from Louis XIV to Napoleon* (Philadelphia, 2010), chap. 14.

65. D'Hémery summarized these events in notes that he used to keep a record of his activities: BnF, F.F. 21864, entries for February 13 and May 22, 1783. The STN was not implicated in this affair, but it used the same routes as the other Neuchâtelois publishers, notably the border crossing near Pontarlier, where, according to d'Hémery's informants, inspections were particularly lax.

66. I have not been able to find the original text of Vergennes's order, but its key provision was quoted in a "Mémoire relativement à un ordre envoyé par MM. les fermiers généraux" by Jean-André Périsse-Duluc, the *syndic* of the booksellers' guild in Lyon, dated July 29, 1783: BnF, F.F. 21833, fol. 107: "Que la multitude des libelles imprimés dans l'étranger et introduits dans le royaume paraît au gouvernement mériter l'attention la plus particulière; que son intention est que tout ce qui entrera à l'avenir d'imprimé par les bureaux des frontières soit arrêté sans restriction, qu'il en soit donné un acte qui exprime l'ordre du roi, et que ces imprimés soient expédiés sous plomb et par acquit à caution pour la douane de Paris, d'où ils seront envoyés à la chambre syndicale afin d'y être soumis à l'inspection de M. le lieutenant général de police."

67. Mallet's confession provides the most detailed account of an underground publishing venture that I have found in any archive in France. I have published its text along with an essay about the activities of Fauche fils aîné, Favre et Vitel under the section "Middlemen and Smugglers" in my open-access website: robertdarnton.org. After Vergennes issued his order, the officials concerned with the book trade discussed the problem of suppressing the circulation of forbidden books, and, influenced in part by

the information provided by Mallet, they decided that the order was such an effective measure of controlling foreign shipments that it should be made permanent. See an undated and unsigned "Mémoire" in BnF, F.F., 21833, fols. 99–104 and a similar "Mémoire" dated July 1783 in ms. 22063, nr. 71.

68. D'Hémery mentioned the protests from Rouen in a note dated June 27, 1783; and from French Flanders in a note dated August 31, 1783: BnF, F.F. 21864. The *chambre syndicale* of Lille protested in a letter dated February 1, 1784: BnF, F.F. 21864 fol. 108 verso. References to other protests are scattered through BnF, F.F., ms. 21833. The "Mémoire relativement à un ordre envoyé par MM. les fermiers généraux" by Périsse-Duluc is in ms. 21833, fols. 96–110, and Jean-Marie Bruyset's "Observations sur la décadence et la ruine d'une des branches la plus florissante du commerce du royaume," dated February 28, 1784, is in ms. 21833, fols. 141–153. See also Bruyset's letter to Miromesnil of March 22, 1784, in which he again complained bitterly about Vergennes's order, which he described as an example of the government's bias in favor of the Parisian booksellers. In a note of October 31, 1784, d'Hémery observed that Miromesnil had refused requests to rescind Vergennes's order, because "[i]l avait de fortes raisons à laisser subsister cet ordre": BnF, F.F. 21865, fol. 167.

69. Among the many letters from French booksellers to the STN about Vergennes's order, see Rosset of Lyon, September 4, 1783, and May 14, 1784; Bruyset of Lyon, July 26, 1783; Grabit of Lyon, May 20, 1784, and September 15, 1785; Cazin of Reims, November 17, 1783; Poinçot of Versailles July 8, 1783, and February 21, 1784; Matthieu of Nancy June 1784 (exact date not given); Rameau of Dijon, December 13, 1787. Evidence from other publishers and shipping agents is in letters to the STN from Daniel Argand of Geneva, December 13, 1783, and September 3, 1785; Chirol of Geneva, September 26, 1783; and Meuron of Saint Sulpice, July 21, 1783, and May 23, 1785.

Chapter 4

1. Abram Bosset de Luze, one of the directors of the Société typographique de Neuchâtel (STN), to the STN's home office, writing during a business trip to Paris, February 15, 1780: Papers of the STN, Bibliothèque publique et universitaire de Neuchâtel. These papers will be referred to henceforth simply as STN. The names of the correspondent are adequate to locate the dossiers within the STN archive.

2. STN to Gosse, October 4, 1770.

3. Gosse to STN, October 16, 1770.

4. STN to Gosse, April 9, 1770.

5. Gosse to STN, May 4, 1770.

6. STN to Gosse, July 10, 1770.

7. STN to Gosse, August 2, 1770.

8. Gosse to STN, August 17, 1770.

9. Gosse to STN, August 31, 1770.

10. Gosse to STN, November 22, 1771.

11. Gosse to STN, February 25, 1772.
12. Gosse to STN, July 3, 1772.
13. STN to Gosse, January 31, 1771.
14. Gosse to STN, October 2, 1770.
15. Part of this correspondence has been printed by Theodore Besterman in *The Complete Works of Voltaire*, vols. 120–122 (Voltaire Foundation, Banbury, 1975), , but I am citing it from the manuscripts in Neuchâtel.
16. Gosse to STN, March 9, 1770.
17. STN to Gosse, April 19, 1770.
18. STN to Gosse, April 19, 1770.
19. Gosse to STN, May 4, 1770.
20. Jean-Marie Bruyset to STN, September 9, 1770.
21. STN to Gosse, August 20, 1770.
22. Gosse to STN, August 31, 1770.
23. STN to Gosse, September 10, 1770.
24. Gosse to STN, January 18, 1771.
25. Gosse to STN, October 2, 1770.
26. Voltaire to Cramer, c. February 15, 1771, in Besterman, *The Complete Works of Voltaire*, vol. 121, p. 263. See also the similar remarks in an undated letter from Voltaire to Cramer, vol. 120, p. 295. The documents relating to the censuring by the consistory are in vol. 122, pp. 484–486.
27. Voltaire to Cramer, February 19, 1770, Besterman, *The Complete Works of Voltaire*, vol. 120, p. 40.
28. STN to Gosse, March 29, 1771.
29. Widow Réguilliat et fils to STN, June 17, 1771.
30. These intrigues can be followed in detail through the correspondence published in *The Complete Works of Voltaire*, vols. 120–122. See especially Antoine Adam to Elie Bertrand, June 11, 1770, vol. 120, pp. 247–248; Marie-Louise Denis to Elie Bertrand, June 12, 1770, vol. 120, p. 250; Voltaire to Cramer, September 15, 1770, vol. 120, p. 438; STN to Voltaire, September 15, 1770, vol. 120, p. 446; and Voltaire to Elie Bertrand, September 25, 1770, vol. 120, p. 457.
31. The STN's copies of the letters that it sent to its correspondents, a huge register entitled "Copie de lettres," ms. 1095, does not contain all the correspondence concerning this affair and sometimes provides only short summaries. Thus a synopsis of a letter sent to Père Adam on 13 March 1771: "On lui écrit pour le prier de nous procurer par le moyen de Mme Denis les 4, 5, et 6 volumes des *Questions*." But most of the details can be reconstructed from the letters printed in *The Complete Works of Voltaire*. See especially Antoine Adam to Ostervald, March 17, 1771, vol. 121, p. 321; STN to Wagnière, April 3, 1771, vol. 121, pp. 342–343; Wagnière to STN, c. April 29, 1771, vol. 121, p. 367; STN to Voltaire, April 29, 1771, vol. 121, p. 375; STN to Wagnière, June, 27, 1771, vol. 121, p. 453; STN to Cramer, September 4, 1771, vol. 122, p. 68; STN to Wagnière, Sept. 6, 1771, vol. 122, pp. 68–69; STN to Durey de Morsan, September 17, 1771, vol. 122, pp. 82–83; Durey de Morsan to Elie

Bertrand, December 3,1771, vol. 122, pp. 169–171; and Voltaire to Elie Bertrand, December 10, 1771, vol. 122, p. 182.

32. STN to Gosse, January 31, 1771.

33. Gosse to STN, November 5, 1771.

34. Gosse to STN, February 25, 1771.

35. Gosse to STN, May 29, 1772.

36. Ibid.

Chapter 5

1. See Philippe Henri, *Histoire du canton de Neuchâtel, tome 2: Le temps de la monarchie politique, religion et société de la Réforme à la révolution de 1848* (Éditions Alphil-Presses universitaires suisses, Neuchâtel, 2011).

2. There is a biographical sketch of Ostervald by Jacques Rychner and Michel Schlup in *Biographies neuchâteloises, tome I: De Saint Guillaume à la fin des Lumières*, Michel Schlup, ed. (Editions Gillers Attinger, Neuchâtel, 1996), 197–201. Notarial archives in the Archives de l'État de Neuchâtel contain several documents indicating Ostervald's wealth and status. According to the registers of Claude-François Bovet, B652, entry for April 10, 1771, Ostervald had acquired three horses and a carriage worth 1,296 Swiss livres. After the STN suspended payments on its debts and was reorganized under new management, a group of wealthy Neuchâtelois agreed to guarantee the repayments to its creditors over a period of six years. The agreement, recorded in an entry for June 2, 1784, in Bovet's register B656, specified that Ostervald's assets had been evaluated at 47,681 L., including thirteen portions of vineyards and a house and garden worth 10,000 L. That evaluation indicated that Ostervald was quite well off, although his fortune did not approach that of Abram Bosset de Luze, his recently deceased partner, which amounted to 100,000 L.

3. *Mémoires pour servir de réfutation à la brochure intitulée "Considérations pour les peuples de l'État": Imprimés par ordre et avec l'approbation des cinq corps de l'État de la Souveraineté de Neuchâtel & Valangin* (Neuchâtel, 1761), 56. Writing in his quality as Neuchâtel's former maître bourgeois en chef, or chief executive of the municipal government, Ostervald also defended the authorities' prohibition of a pamphlet in favor of Petitpierre.

4. Ostervald, *Devoirs généraux et particuliers du Maître Bourgeois en Chef pendant sa préfecture. Rédigés en 1763*, Bibliothèque publique et universitaire de Neuchâtel, ms. 1592, p. 2.

5. Ibid., p. 5.

6. Ostervald to STN from Paris, May 21, 1780.

7. Ostervald to STN from Lyon, March 13, 1772.

8. Ostervald to STN from Lausanne, March 20, 1772.

9. Ostervald to STN from Monlezy, Switzerland, August 15, 1769.

10. *Description des montagnes et des vallées qui font partie de la Principauté de Neuchâtel et Valangin*, reprint edited by Michel Schlup (Neuchâtel, 1986), 44–45. In describing

the village of Môtiers (p. 23), Ostervald generally kept to topographical subjects, but he included a disparaging remark about Rousseau, who claimed to have been persecuted when he sought refuge there in 1762–1763.

11. *Cours élémentaire de géographie ancienne et moderne et de sphère par demandes et réponses: Avec des remarques historiques et politiques* (Neuchâtel, 1757), 5.

12. Abbé François Rozier to Ostervald, July 19, 1775. During a trip to Paris in 1777, Ostervald bought two prints for 16 L. each, which suggests that he might have shared the sentimental *sensiblerie* that was then in vogue. According to his personal account (ms. 1189), they were "1 estampe de la mère bien aimée" and "une estampe de la dame bienfaisante."

13. Ostervald from Paris to STN, February 20, 1780.

14. Bosset to STN, June 2, 1780. A detailed account of Ostervald's and Bosset's trips to Paris appears in Chapter 11, this volume.

15. Bosset referred to his reading and writing in various undated notes to Ostervald in ms. 1125, fols. 41–80. In one note, he described a visit from a French "princesse" who went with him to call on Rousseau's protector in Neuchâtel, Pierre-Alexandre Du Peyrou: "L'abbé Raynal et Diderot sont ses favoris. Elle me fit grand plaisir de dire pis que pendre de Rousseau hier à M. Du Peyrou."

16. Bosset to STN July 2, 1778.

17. Bosset to STN, September 3, 1779: "Je vous demande la grâce d'être exact pour les payements; le crédit du public est la base de tous les commerces."

18. Bosset to STN, May 26 and June 14, 1780.

19. Bosset to STN, March 31, 1780. In a letter of September 3, 1779, Bosset warned against the STN's tendency to advance too much money for its paper supplies: "Ce n'est pas le tout que d'imprimer. Il faut payer, et cela en bel argent, le papier que nous achetons."

20. The following account of Bérenger's early life is based on Claudius Fontaine-Borgel, "Jean-Pierre Bérenger, historien, ancient syndic de la République de Genève 1737-1807," *Bulletin de l'Institut National Genevois* 27 (1885), 1–140. There are also short articles on Bérenger in the *Dictionnaire des journalists 1600-1789*, Jean Sgard, ed., vol. 1 (Voltaire Foundation, Oxford, 1999), 75–76; and *Dictionnaire historique et biographique de la Suisse* 2 (Neuchâtel, 1924), 63–64. For a useful survey of Genevan publishing houses, see John R. Kleinschmidt, *Les Imprimeurs et les libraires de la république de Genève, 1700-1798* (A. Jullien, Geneva, 1948). I am grateful to Marc Neuenschwander for guidance in the complicated history of Geneva, although he should not be held responsible for any errors in my account.

21. Among the many studies of this subject, two of the oldest have stood up best: Robert R. Palmer, *The Age of the Democratic Revolution: A Political History of Europe and America, 1760-1800* (Princeton University Press, Princeton, NJ, 1959-1964); and Robert Derathé, *Jean-Jacques Rousseau et la science politique de son temps* (Presses universitaires de France, Paris, 1950).

22. The term comes up frequently in Bérenger's works: for example, in *Histoire de Genève depuis son origine jusqu'à nos jours* 6 (1772), 107.

23. In his exhaustive *Bibliographie historique de Genève* (J. Jullien Georg, Geneva, 1897), 2 vols., Émile Rivoire has identified several dozen pamphlets written by Bérenger and against him. See especially vol. 1, pp. 153–155, 157–159, 193, and 196–197.

24. Bérenger justified his conduct during the uprising in a pamphlet written from Versoix, his place of exile, *Lettre de M. Bérenger à M. Cramer, premier syndic de la République de Genève* (1770). The authorities also burned it.

25. Quoted in Fontaine-Borgel, "Jean-Pierre Bérenger," 25.

26. The following account is based on Bérenger's dossier and his publications. Because Ostervald kept his private correspondence in his own papers, most of his replies to Bérenger were not entered in the STN's "Copies de lettres."

27. Bérenger to Ostervald, December 14, 1771. In a letter of October 14, 1772, he discussed further details about the publishing arrangement: "Vous voyez donc, Monsieur, qu'il s'agit pour moi d'en tirer le plus grand profit possible."

28. Both Cailler and Téron have fascinating dossiers in the STN archives, which provide the material for the following chapter.

29. In a letter of August 19, 1775, Bérenger informed Ostervald about this arrangement: "Je ne suis pas nommément de la Société, mais M. Heubach m'a cédé une demie action et a fait une convention avec moi qui me rend participant de tous les avantages de ce commerce et m'assure un fixe d'environ 50 louis par an comme homme de lettres et pour faire en cette qualité tout ce qui sera utile à la Société."

30. *Les Amants républicains ou lettres de Nicias et Cynire* ("Paris," 1782), 9.

31. *Rousseau justifié envers sa patrie* ("Londres," 1775), quotations from pp. 59 and 69.

32. Bérenger to Ostervald, December 30, 1774.

33. Jean-Pierre Bérenger, *Histoire de Genève*, quotations from vol. 1, pp. 22 and 238, and vol. 6, pp. 108 and 179. In describing this patriotic festival, Bérenger asked himself rhetorically (p. 109), "Pourquoi ne puis-je finir ici . . . ?" Then, in fact, he did end there, noting, "Il est doux de détourner les yeux du spectacle affligeant des dissensions civiles et de la misère publique, du tableau d'aussi tristes passions que la haine et la fureur, pour les fixer sur celui du triomphe de l'amitié. . . ." Bérenger intended to continue his history, but never published any subsequent volumes. Although the *Histoire de Genève* was his most ambitious work, the text appears misshapen and cobbled together, and there are errors in the pagination. In an "Avis" at the end of volume 1, Bérenger gave notice that the printing had been done hurriedly in two separate places and that he had not been able to correct all the proofs. An actual festival, similar to the one described by Bérenger, took place in Geneva in 1761. A Genevan sent an enthusiastic account of it to Rousseau, who was deeply touched. See Jean-Louis Mollet to Rousseau, June 10, 1761, and Rousseau to Mollet, June 26, 1761, in *Correspondance complète de Jean-Jacques Rousseau*, R. A. Leigh, ed., vol. 9 (Institut et Musée Voltaire, Geneva, 1969), 9–14 and 33–34.

34. The following account is based on Heubach's dossier in the archives of the STN and Madeleine Bovard-Schmidt, "Jean-Pierre Heubach, un imprimeur lausannois du XVIIIe siècle," *Revue historique vaudoise* (1966), 1–56. There is further information in Silvio Corsini, *La Preuve par les fleurons? Analyse comparée du matériel ornemental des imprimeurs suisses romands 1775–1785* (Centre international d'études du XVIIIe

siècle, Ferney-Voltaire, France, 1994); and Jean-Daniel Candaux, *Voltaire imprimé tout vif: Un choix d'éditions suisses 1723–1778* (Bibliothèque publique et universitaire de Genève, Geneva, 1994).

35. Heubach provided information about his wealth in a printed circular dated December 22, 1785, which was intended to refute rumors spread by his enemies with the intention to "détruire notre commerce au moment où il devenait le plus florissant."

36. Mallet du Pan to Ostervald, October 1, 1779, in the STN archives, ms. 1178.

37. For these scant details on Heubach's private life, see Bovard-Schmidt, "Jean-Pierre Heubach."

38. Grasset to STN, January 29, 1773. Heubach informed the STN of their feud in a letter of February 10, 1773. The following account is based on the dossiers of Gabriel Décombaz (131 letters), Jean Mourer (138 letters), and François Lacombe (134 letters), in addition to the still larger dossiers of François Grasset, Heubach, and the STL. Some of this material has been used to good effect by Silvio Corsini in bibliographical studies, notably "L'Édition française hors des frontières du royaume: Les Presses lausannoises sous la loupe," *Revue française d'histoire du livre*, nrs. 62–63 (1989), 94–119. See also Corsini's general sketch in *Le Livre à Lausanne: Cinq siècles d'édition et d'imprimerie 1493–1993* (Payot, Lausanne, 1993), chap. 4.

39. Décombaz described his situation in a letter to the STN of June 12, 1787. According to an advertisement in the *Journal général de Saint-Domingue* for October 16, 1790 (kindly provided to me by James McClellan, an authority on colonial Saint-Domingue), he had established his "cabinet littéraire" in Port-au-Prince. McClellan determined that at some point after the revolution of 1791, Décombaz emigrated to the United States and became a clerk in the bookstore founded in Philadelphia by Médéric Louis Elie Moreau de Saint-Méry, the apologist for slavery in the Constituent Assembly, who emigrated from France in 1793.

40. Mourer to STN, August 14, 1781.

41. Lacombe to STN, July 10, 1781.

42. Among the other booksellers in Lausanne, Marc-Michel Martin quarreled with Heubach and maintained good relations, reinforced by family ties, with Grasset. Gabriel Dufournet also had strong links with Grasset, having worked for him as a clerk and married his daughter. Neither he nor Martin speculated in publishing ventures. Jules-Henri Pott, a distinguished publisher and printer, specialized in Latin works and kept out of the local feuds, although he had been an associate of Grasset in the early 1770s.

43. On the importance of the STN's foreman, see the masterful study by Jacques Rychner, *Jacques-Barthélémy Spineux (1738–1806), prote de la Société typographique de Neuchâtel: De Liège à Carouge en passant par Paris, Neuchâtel et La Neuveville* (Alphil, Neuchâtel, 2013).

44. In February 1783, the STN sent its most trusted clerk and sales rep, Jean-François Favarger, to investigate the state of Nouffer's affairs in Geneva. Favarger reported in a letter of March 15 that Nouffer had a wealthy mother and uncle in Morat and that they favored his plan to move his printing shop (a large enterprise with six presses) there.

45. STN to Nouffer, June 15, 1776.

46. In a letter to the STN of June 29, 1779, Nouffer attributed the firm's increasing financial difficulty to Mourer: "Sa fureur d'acheter et d'entasser livre sur livre m'aurait gêné si je n'avais ouvert les yeux à temps."

47. Flournoy fils et Rainaldis sent a report on Nouffer to the STN on March 6, 1779: "Quant aux facultés de sa maison avec M. Duvillard, nous ne les connaissons pas trop. Tout ce qu'il y a de certain, c'est qu'ils sont toujours très gênés dans leurs payements, ce que nous attribuons aux entreprises qu'ils peuvent faire qui surpassent les fonds que chacun d'eux a eu de ses parents. L'un et l'autre ont cependant des prétentions à attendre, qui seront dans le cas de les mettre un jour plus à l'aise qu'ils ne sont. Nous pensons que jusqu'alors on doit modérer la confiance qu'on est dans le cas de leur faire."

48. A group of experts led by Cecil Patrick Courtney have recently completed a monumental effort to identify all the editions of Raynal's works and to trace their history: *Bibliographie des éditions de Guillaume-Thomas Raynal (1747–1826)*. I would like to thank Cecil Courtney for permitting me to study a final draft of their book, which at the time of this writing has not yet been published. See also Cecil Patrick Courtney, "Les Métamorphoses d'un best-seller, *l'Histoire des deux Indes* de 1770 à 1820," *Studies on Voltaire and the Eighteenth Century* (2000), nr. 12, 109–120; and Claudette Fortuny, "La Troisième Édition de *l'Histoire des deux Indes* et ses contrefaçons: Les Contributions de Genève et Neuchâtel," *Studies on Voltaire and the Eighteenth Century* (2001), nr. 12, 269–297, which makes good use of the STN archives.

49. In a letter to the STN of October 26, 1780, Nouffer explained, "Les prétentions exorbitantes de M. Delisle pour ses retouches et une trentaine de cartons qu'il voulait faire à une quinzaine de feuilles déjà imprimées de la Philosophie de la nature m'ont fait renoncer totalement à cette entreprise. J'ai préféré sacrifier ce qui se trouvait fait des deux éditions que de courir risque de perdre gros sur l'édition entière par les faux frais considérables auxquels je m'exposais par les caprices continuels de l'auteur."

50. On September 23, 1781, Nouffer informed the STN, "L'auteur est souvent absent et demeure en campagne. Il ne me donne le manuscrit que par petits cahiers, et veut revoir les épreuves. Cela me retarde beaucoup, et je n'ose m'en plaindre."

51. In a letter of February 2, 1781, Nouffer said he was "vivement affecté" by the STN's attempt to collect payment by using another Genevan publisher, Barthélemy Chirol, as an agent: "Je suis incapable d'abuser de la confiance de personne, et je n'aurai jamais à rougir de ma conduite." The STN also sought assurance about Nouffer's solvency in letters to his former partner Duvillard, who replied in a letter of June 12, 1781, that Nouffer was able to meet his obligations.

52. Barthélemy Chirol to STN, March 30, 1781: "C'est M. Nouffer qui imprime la *Vie de Louis XV*, in-12, 4 volumes, et comme il est votre débiteur, je crois que vous feriez bien de lui en demander, mais sans lui faire mention de moi."

53. In a letter of May 10, 1781, Nouffer explained that he would sell it to the STN for half the wholesale price rather than supply it as an exchange, because the print was much denser than that of the STN's volumes and the paper was superior. His reasoning provides a good example of the factors involved in the exchange trade: "Je le vend

au libraire 10 livres. De tout côté on me le demande sans mot dire au prix. Veuillez je vous prie le maintenir. Je ne puis vous le céder à la feuille, car trois feuilles de votre Molière n'en valent pas une de celui-ci, imprimé sur grand bâtard, d'un format in-12, d'une grandeur extraordinaire, sur petit romain, petit texte mignonne."

54. Kleinschmidt, *Les Imprimeurs et les libraires de la République de Genève*, 148, dates the partnership from June 10, 1781, but this might have been a preliminary agreement, because Nouffer did not send a printed circular announcing its existence until April 25, 1782.

55. Duvillard to ST, June 12, 1781.

56. For a detailed account of Nouffer's role in the publishing of the *Histoire philosophique*, see Fortuny, "La Troisième Édition de l'*Histoire des deux Indes* et ses contrefaçons."

57. Barthélemy Chirol, a solid and respectable Genevan publisher who had close ties to the STN, noted in a letter of February 13, 1782, "M. Nouffer est encore en prison, mais il ne tardera pas à en sortir. Son affaire n'est pas aussi grave qu'on l'avait d'abord pensé. On lui a rendu ses livres." I cannot find any other reference to this incident, which might have involved a brief detention for failure to pay bills of exchange.

58. Nouffer first broached this possibility in March 1782 when he met with the STN's clerk, Jean-François Favarger, in Geneva. They were on good terms, and Nouffer expanded on his idea in a letter to Favarger of March 21, 1782: "Tous les jours on me demande ce livre, et plusieurs de mes correspondants m'ont conseillé déjà depuis longtemps d'en faire une édition sur plus petit caractère, en moins de volumes, afin de pouvoir la donner bon marché." See also Fortuny, "La Troisième Edition de l'*Histoire des deux Indes*," 273.

59. On July 23, 1782, Nouffer wrote that he was eager to conclude a contract for both works and that he wanted to print the entire Riccoboni: "Vous le seriez de l'*Histoire philosophique* que nous n'oserions dans ce moment faire ici. Les deux entreprises se feraient à la fois, et cela serait plus avantageux pour nos deux maisons."

60. In a letter from Paris to the STN on June 5, 1775, Ostervald mentioned Raynal as someone he knew and needed to see, but he did not report on their meeting in later letters.

61. For example, on October 16, 1782, Nouffer wrote, "Il est réellement essentiel de faire des adjonctions [i.e. augmentations] pour donner du mérite à notre édition. Les amateurs prévenus par le prospectus s'empresseront à en faire l'acquisition. Vous le sentez comme nous, Messieurs, et il serait inutile de vous presser de faire les instances les plus vives auprès de l'auteur, parce que vous le ferez."

62. Raynal's dossier in the STN archives contains only two letters, which are quoted in Fortuny, "La Troisième Édition de l'*Histoire des deux Indes*," 275–278. Ostervald might have retained others in his private collection of correspondence. The STN's "Copie de lettres" has copies of letters that he sent to Raynal on June 19, 1780; December 31, 1780; and March 27, 1781.

63. Nouffer to STN, December 7, 1782, and January 3, 1783.

64. In a letter from Geneva of February 14, 1783, the STN's clerk, Jean-François Favarger, reported that Nouffer was considering setting up shop with six presses in Morat, where his wealthy mother and uncle wanted him to return.

65. Rainaldis to STN, July 24, 1782: "Deux à trois affaires à traiter avec un homme de sa trempe occuperaient, mais très désagréablement, toutes les personnes de notre comptoir. . . . Nous bénirons le moment où nous n'aurons plus rien à faire avec lui dans aucun genre."

66. Favarger reported on his negotiations with Nouffer in letters to the STN of February 14 and 16, 1783, and Nouffer described his discussion with Favarger in a letter to the STN of April 1, 1783.

67. Nouffer to STN, July 1, 1783.

68. The dossier of Delahaye et Cie. in the STN archives reveals some dubious maneuvering in the illegal sector of the book trade. The three partners in the firm were arrested for dealing in forbidden books in February 1785. By the time of their release in 1787, they had lost 100,000 L. and had failed to provide the STN with the atlases it needed. When it threatened to sue, Delahaye replied on October 1, 1788, in a style adopted by many bankrupt houses: "On nous a poursuivi injustement. D'après ceci, et connaissant l'humanité et la sensibilité que donne l'éducation à des coeurs bien nés, au lieu de chercher à anéantir une activité reconnue en nous, vous vous porterez au contraire à la seconder et à relever une maison que la calomnie et la jalousie la plus insigne ont voulu vainement détruire jusqu'à la dernière pierre des fondements."

69. Nouffer to STN, December 5, 1783. Delahaye did not begin to ship copies of the atlas until February 1784 and never provided a full supply. The STN finally had to have the illustrations engraved in Paris and did not receive shipments of them until August 1784. These complications and delays meant that the STN never completed the full edition of 3,000 copies envisaged by its contract with Nouffer and lost heavily on the speculation. The details of that story can be followed in its correspondence with Delahaye and with its Brussels agent, Frères Overman, which is discussed in Fortuny, "La Troisième Édition de *l'Histoire des deux Indes*," 278–282.

70. The STN also wrote to its agent in Geneva, Alexandre Rainaldis, trying to discover more about Nouffer. He replied on January 28, 1784, that Nouffer was rumored to have fled to Basel, although no one knew his address. "On est après [sic] à dresser un état de ses affaires, où il y a beaucoup de désordre." Nouffer's dossier contains several letters from the "masse," or group of his creditors, who negotiated with the STN over his debt and the disposition of the *Histoire philosophique*.

71. In letters of January 28, February 3, February 11, and November 23, 1784, Rainaldis reported on the attempts to settle Nouffer's affairs, which were in great disorder, in Geneva. He said that Mme Nouffer had remained there and that no one had been able to locate Nouffer himself, although he had sent a letter to his wife from Basel.

Chapter 6

1. The following argument, which associates socioeconomic marginality with the publishing of dangerous books, may not hold for other cities such as Amsterdam, where Marc-Michel Rey produced many *livres philosophiques* in addition to the works of Rousseau, and Brussels, where Jean-Louis Boubers speculated on the *Système de la*

nature and similar books. Of course, many of Voltaire's works offended the French authorities, particularly those in the Church, and as mentioned in Chapter 2, this volume, Gabriel Cramer was censured by the Genevan clergy for publishing *Questions sur l'Encyclopédie*. But that was merely a slap on the wrist, and he was protected by his brother, Philibert, in the Petit Conseil. The collected works of Voltaire circulated freely in France during the 1770s and 1780s. His polemical and anticlerical writings did not. He had them printed by marginal entrepreneurs like Gabriel Grasset rather than by Cramer.

2. On January 8, 1783, Barthélemy Chirol informed the STN, "Notre gouvernement plus rigoureux sur la typographie qu'auparavant fait dans ce moment des perquisitions sévères sur je ne sais quel écrit. Déjà M. Cailler vient d'être mis en prison et tient compagnie dans cette demeure sombre à deux imprimeurs établis."

3. Kleinschmidt, *Les Imprimeurs et les libraires de la république de Genève, 1700–1798*, 83–85.

4. Cailler to STN, April 9, 1778: "M. le chevalier Goudar m'a bien fait passer des manuscrits, mais pour les imprimer pour son compte, tels que les *Remarques sur les Anecdotes de Mme la comtesse du Barry*, in-12, 6 feuilles, qu'il m'a chargé de vendre à l'argent."

5. For example, in a letter of September 21, 1773, Cailler listed among the works he could supply "*Recherches [philosophiques] sur les Égyptiens et les Chinois*, in-12, deux volumes que j'ai fait à compte à demi à Lausanne."

6. Jean-François Favarger to STN, September 5, 1775.

7. Louis Marcinhes to STN, July 11, 1777. Marcinhes added, "La fausse honte le retient, dit-il, ne voulant pas 'd'évêque venir [*sic*] meunier' et craignant que les autres ouvriers se moquent de le voir à leur niveau qui est lui maître imprimeur." This account of Gallay's career is based on his dossier in the STN archives, references in Marcinhes's letters to the STN, and Favarger's letters to the STN of September 5, 1775, and August 7, 1776. Gallay had only one press in his shop and, as a Natif, had no right to operate it as a business. He probably disguised his publishing activities by claiming to be a worker in the employ of legally established printers.

8. Gabriel Grasset to STN April 21, 1770. Like Gallay, Grasset sought a steady job, which would support his family. He, too, was a Natif, yet managed to operate a printing business, despite run-ins with the Genevan authorities: Kleinschmidt, *Les Imprimeurs et les libraires de la république de Genève*, 131–132. In addition to his dossier in the STN papers, the following account draws on the correspondence of the STN's agents in Geneva, Louis Marcinhes and Daniel Argand.

9. Daniel Argand, a Genevan merchant who assessed the credit of booksellers for the STN, warned it to beware of Grasset in a letter of August 31, 1773: "Je dois vous dire en confidence qu'il y a peu ou point de fond à faire sur lui. Si vous ne prenez pas des livres en troc, vous aurez bien de la peine à être payé."

10. Grasset to STN, June 15, 1777. On October 5, 1777, Voltaire wrote to Panckoucke, "Je vous recommande le Grasset de Genève [as opposed to Gabriel's brother, François, a bookseller in Lausanne whom Voltaire detested]. Celui-là est un honnête homme." *Correspondence and Related Documents*, Theodore Besterman,

ed., vol. 45 (Voltaire Foundation, Oxford, 1976), 43 (D20825). On the following day, Voltaire wrote another letter to Panckoucke, indicating that he was using Gabriel Grasset as his printer and, for the latest work (probably *Prix de la justice*), asked only to receive fifty copies to send to friends: "Il [Voltaire] a choisi depuis longtemps ce Grasset de Genève, pour le servir, et il l'a cru un honnête homme." *Correspondence and Related Documents*, p. 48 (D20830). On the first edition of the *Dictionnaire philosophique* and Grasset's relations with Voltaire, see, in addition to the preceding sources, Andrew Brown, "Gabriel Grasset, éditeur de Voltaire" in *Voltaire et le livre*, François Bessire and Françoise Tilkin, eds. (Centre international d'étude du XVIIIᵉ siècle, Ferney-Voltaire, France, 2009), 67–105. It is difficult to identify the works Grasset printed for Voltaire, although some can be determined from typographical ornaments. See, for example, Andrew Brown and Ulla Kölving, "Voltaire and Cramer?," in *Le Siècle de Voltaire: Hommage à René Pomeau* 1 (Voltaire Foundation, Oxford, 1987), 149–183. Such arguments sometimes run into the difficulty that printers often collaborated and shared their materials.

11. Marcinhes to STN, August 15, 1775. On October 18, 1775, Marcinhes wrote that Grasset "allait à Ferney où il était demandé *toutes affaires cessantes*. Peut-être est-ce pour continuer l'*Histoire du christianisme* suspendue par ces ordres."

12. Jean-François Favarger, "carnet de voyage," 1776, ms. 1150.

13. References to Grasset's work for Voltaire appear often in the standard biography by René Pomeau, *Voltaire en son temps* 2 (Fayard, Paris, 1995), 168, 174, 193, 205, 224, 278, 280, 303, and 548.

14. Grasset to STN, June 11, 1771. Evidently Grasset had gotten wind of the STN's edition of *Système de la nature*. After its unhappy experience with this speculation, the STN rarely printed *livres philosophiques* and Grasset no longer requested such illegal literature in his letters.

15. For example, in a letter of June 19, 1772, Grasset wrote, "Comme tous les libraires me donnent deux feuilles contre une de la partie philosophique, je vous propose le même change." At times he expressed the exchange rate in money, using the STN's standard price of one sou per sheet. Thus his letter of July 31, 1772: "Pour accélérer un change qui pourrait être avantageux des deux parts, je crois que tout ce qui est de la partie philosophique prohibée doit être mis réciproquement à deux sols de France la feuille et la partie permise à un sol."

16. Grasset implied that he had jobbed out the printing of Voltaire's *Tocsin des rois* in a letter to the STN of January 29, 1773: "Le *Tocsin des rois* me manque, mais ils seront faits la semaine prochaine, et je les remettrai à qui vous l'ordonnez."

17. Grasset's letter to the STN of April 21, 1770, refers to his two presses and printing materials, and it indicates his competence by describing in marvelous detail his work as a foreman of Cramer's shop.

18. Flournoy fils et Rainaldis, shipping agents, to STN, February 13, 1772: "Cet homme-là est malade depuis longtemps et peu moyenné."

19. Téron to STN, June 22, 1770. Téron's dossier in the STN archives is the main source of the following account, along with supplementary information from the many

hundreds of other letters that the STN received from Geneva. The dossier also contains letters, scattered through it, from Jacques-Benjamin's younger brother Jean-Louis.

20. On September 19, 1770, Barthélemy Chirol denounced Téron to the STN: "Cet homme n'est ni libraire ni relieur. Il n'a point de boutique et n'a aucun droit de commercer. Il donne seulement des leçons d'arithmétique. D'ailleurs les libraires lui empêcheront bien de faire ce commerce auquel il n'entend rien, et ceux qui lui confieraient ne pourraient manquer d'en être la dupe."

21. Jean-Louis Téron to STN, June 21, 1775: "Je n'ai d'autre ressource que mes talents, car le peu d'effets mobiliers que je puis avoir ne sont pas à moi mais à mon épouse ... de sorte que si vous vous obstiniez à me poursuivre je ne pourrais vous payer que de ma personne, et mes enfants seraient alors réduits à mourir de faim ou à se prévaloir de la ressource avilissante des hôpitaux, et ce dernier moyen est plus terrible que la mort même ... Je ne suis pas fait pour languir toujours dans l'indigence, et sans doute un moment favorable viendra où j'en sortirai, et alors soyez convaincus que je me ferai une loi de vous satisfaire." On May 17, 1777, Argand informed the STN that Jean-Louis had finally found employment in the "bureau des coches" in Bern. He never paid the 242 livres that he still owed for his printing bill.

22. Argand to STN, August 31, 1773, and October 11, 1775.

23. Téron to Ostervald, December 7, 1773. Téron had gotten to know Ostervald during a visit to Neuchâtel in the summer of 1772.

24. Téron committed himself to a consistent rate in a letter of April 14, 1774: "Je vous donnerai 3 feuilles de livres philosophiques que vous m'aurez demandés contre 4 des vôtres à choisir indistincement."

25. On May 6, 1774, Téron informed the STN that he had sent it three brochures, adding, "Je n'en suis pas l'éditeur. Celui qui les a imprimées ne veut me les fournir qu'à des conditions qui ne me permettent que de vous donner une feuille contre trois des vôtres." Another example of the use of the word in this sense occurs in a letter from Charles-Frédéric Perlet, a Genevan bookseller, to the STN of June 27, 1780. Speaking of an edition of Montaigne's *Essais*, he wrote, "Il n'en reste plus chez M. Cailler, qui en est l'éditeur."

26. In a letter to the STN of October 25, 1774, Téron wrote, "Je vais mettre en train ma partie philosophique à présent qu'ayant ouvert ma boutique je pourrai me livrer d'avantage à mes occupations de librairie." His address now was "au Magasin littéraire, au bas de la Cité." The associations he formed and the stages of his career are outlined in Kleinschmidt, *Les Imprimeurs et libraires de la république de Genève*, 172–174.

27. In a letter to the STN of June 1, 1774, Téron wrote, "On me propose trois manuscrits. Je vous donne ci-jointe copie des titres. C'est quelque chose de bien profond et bien médité. Dites-moi, je vous prie, Messieurs, l'opinion que vous en avez pour le débit."

28. Marcinhes to STN, April 24, 1775.

29. Marcinhes to STN, August 15, 1775.

30. STN to Téron, November 22, 1775: "Vous pouvez spéculer sur cet article."

31. Kleinschmidt, *Les Imprimeurs et libraires de la république de Genève*, 173–174.

32. Bernier, "notaire et procureur," to STN, August 18, 1779: "Ses biens ont été mis sous la garde d'un curateur que la justice a établi pour la sûreté de ses créanciers; et comme le vide de son bilan n'était pas petit, que le peu qu'il restait a été discuté en faveur de créanciers hypothécaires ou privilégiés, je ne vois pas, Messieurs, que vous y puissiez prétendre [à] quelque chose." Bernier expected Téron to continue to work as "le commis ou la personne salariée du cabinet littéraire."

Chapter 7

1. See Stephan Bösiger, "Aufklärung also Geschäft: Die Typographische Gesellschaft Bern," *Berner Zeitschrift für Geschichte* 73 (2011), 3–46, which makes some use of the STN archives.

2. The STN's trade in Germany has been studied exhaustively by Jeffrey Freedman: *Books without Borders in Enlightenment Europe: French Cosmopolitanism and German Literary Markets* (University of Pennsylvania Press, Philadelphia, 2012). All quotations in the following account are taken from the STN's archives and can be identified by the names of the correspondents.

3. Serini promised to keep the STN's printing of the *Système de la nature* top secret. In September 1771 he recommended that it reprint a Dutch edition of *L'An deux mille quatre cent quarante*, a work "d'un débit assuré, très bien écrit, mais fort cher." In January 1772 he recommended a notorious libel: "N'imprimez-vous pas le *Gazetier cuirassé*, ouvrage qui fait beaucoup de bruit et qui se vendra très bien?" He also requested more standard bestsellers such as Bougainville's *Voyage autour du monde*: "Le *Voyage* de M. Bougainville sera sûrement d'un grand debit."

4. In a letter to the STN included in the printed circular dated February 22, 1774, that formally announced the existence of the STL, Heubach wrote that "nos associés de Berne" were eager to promote cooperation between the STL and the STN. Earlier, in a letter of November 22, 1773, he said that he had just returned from a meeting in Bern, where he had concluded the agreement to transform his business into the STL and that he hoped the new firm would cooperate closely with the STN. From this point on, the complex relations among the three *sociétés typographiques* must be studied in five dossiers from the STN archives: those of Heubach; of Bérenger, who handled much of the STL's correspondence with the STN, because of his friendship with Ostervald; of the STB; and of the "Confédération typographique" (ms. 1235), which was created in January 1778 as an alliance of all three. Rich as they are, the dossiers contain only letters addressed to the STN. Unfortunately, there are many gaps in its "Copies de lettres," where it recorded copies of the letters it sent to its correspondents.

5. Heubach to STN, August 18, 1773: "C'est à présent le temps à faire quelques bonnes entreprises et de former un établissement stable et lucratif."

6. The text is in the STL's letter to the STN of April 6, 1774. The article concerning the Paris agent went as follows: "On se procurera [et] l'on entretiendra à frais égaux et communs à Paris un correspondant homme de lettres afin d'être diligemment avisé de tout ce qui paraîtra de nouveau et des entreprises à former."

7. The full title was *Relation des voyages entrepris par ordre de Sa Majesté britannique pour faire des découvertes dans l'hémisphère méridional et successivement exécutés par le commodore Byron, le capitaine Carteret, le capitaine Wallis & le capitaine Cook dans les vaisseaux le Dauphin, le Swallow & l'Endeavour rédigé d'après les journaux tenus par les différents commandants & les papiers de M. Banks par J. Hawkesworth.*

8. Joint editions required careful planning, because eighteenth-century readers objected to irregularities in printing and paper, and every aspect of eighteenth-century books required highly skilled artisanship. The STL's letter to the STN of April 22, 1774, about the arrangements for printing these four volumes illustrates the care that had to be taken: "Comme notre St. Augustin [a type font known as "english" in English] n'est pas le même que le vôtre, pour faire cet ouvrage uniforme, on pourrait se server du Cicéro ["pica" in English] avec lequel vous avez imprimé votre Bible, ayant le même dans notre imprimerie. Il présente le même coup d'oeil que le St. Augustin et fera moins de feuilles. Nous vous laissons le choix de la qualité du papier, sur celui de Reboul [a paper miller] à 40 batz [the price per ream in the currency of Lausanne] ou de Cignat [another miller] à 36, qui se trouve quelquefois aussi blanc et aussi net, sans le mélange qu'il fait quelquefois des papiers de ses deux fabriques, ce qui est fort désagréable."

9. They originally agreed to hire the STN's main Paris correspondent, abbé François Rozier. He was a member of the Académie des sciences and editor of the *Journal de physique*, but he turned down the offer, saying that he was too busy with his scientific activities. In a letter of July 1, 1774, he recommended Harny, who indicated his willingness to accept the task in a letter of July 14. But in a letter to the STN of August 31, 1774, the STL complained that Harny's correspondence "ne remplit point le but auquel nous souhaitions." That purpose was to supply material for pirating and even to bribe workers in Parisian printing shops to steal proof of promising books. On December 14, 1774, the STL wrote that it was pleased that the STN had discharged Harny.

10. According to a letter from Bérenger to Ostervald of November 21, 1777, the three publishers had discussed the possibility of a "confédération" at a recent meeting in Lausanne, but Ostervald had reacted coolly to the suggestion. The rivalry of the quarto and octavo Encyclopédies, discussed in the following, probably explains his reaction, and the French legislation against *contrefaçons* might have made him change his mind.

11. The final text of the *traité*, or collective agreement, does not appear in the STN archives, but the correspondence of the three publishers shows that it conformed closely to the text proposed in Pfaehler's letter to the STN of May 3, 1778. That text is a rewritten version of Pfaehler's earlier proposal included in his letter to the STN of April 28, 1778. I have published the full text from Pfaehler's letter of May 3 in "La Science de la contrefaçon," in *Le Rayonnement d'une maison d'édition dans l'Europe des Lumières: La Société typographique de Neuchâtel 1769–1789*, Robert Darnton and Michel Schlup, eds. (Editions Gilles Attinger, Neuchâtel, 2005), 88–113. See also Silvio Corsini, "Un pour tous . . . et chacun pour soi? Petite histoire d'une alliance entre les Sociétés typographiques de Lausanne, Berne et Neuchâtel" in the same volume, pp. 115–137.

12. On April 28, 1778, the STB informed the STN that it had accepted Heubach's proposal for a confederation "avec d'autant plus d'empressement que nous souhaitions souvent une liaison aussi étroite que possible pour que l'intérêt particulier ne pût plus prévaloir et faire naître des difficultés haïssables."

13. The importance of paper for marketing books in the eighteenth century is difficult to appreciate today, when readers pay little attention to the material basis of literature, but it stands out everywhere in the correspondence of eighteenth-century booksellers. In a letter to the STN of December 19, 1778, for example, Jean-Guillaume Virchaux, a dealer in Hamburg, wrote, "Je vous avoue que j'aimerais bien que vous prissiez de plus beau papier pour vos éditions. Celui dont vous vous servez est jaune. Voyez, je vous prie, les éditions de M. de Félice.... C'est en partie ce qui fait vendre."

14. The titles of the thirty-one books published by the Confederation along with the size of their press runs (usually 1,000 copies) and other valuable information is in the dossier "Confédération typographique" in the STN archives, ms. 1235. The lists of books that the three publishers offered to contribute to the common stock can be found in their respective dossiers. See especially STL to STN, May 23, 1778; STB to STN, May 24, 1778; and STB to STN, June 7,1778. These lists provide a revealing view of the stock held by each publisher and deserve detailed study.

15. The following account summarizes the research that I have discussed at length in *The Business of Enlightenment: A Publishing History of the Encyclopédie 1775–1800* (Harvard University Press, Cambridge, MA, 1979).

16. The position of Ostervald and the first stages of the conflict over rival editions of the *Encyclopédie* can be followed in Bérenger's letters to Ostervald of November 21, December 15, and December 23, 1777, and in the STL's letters to the STN of November 20 and December 23, 1777, as well as in the STN's reply to the STL of January 8, 1778.

17. Because the publishers made only brief and sometimes inconsistent references to book titles, it is difficult to identify many of them. In this case, later letters confirmed that this work was Deluc's *Lettres physiques et morales* and not his *Relation de différents voyages dans les Alpes du Faucigny,* as it seemed when it was first mentioned.

18. In a letter to the STN of August 18, 1778, the STB recommended Niebuhr's *Voyage* as "une entreprise qui ne pourra qu'être fort bonne. Tout y concourt au moins à nous le persuader.... L'ouvrage a été reçu avec empressement, et il l'aurait été davantage si son [prix] exorbitant ne l'eût empêché."

19. In a letter to the STN of November 16, 1778, the STB explained, "Ci-jointe une page du format, etc. du dictionnaire [Macquer's *Dictionnaire de chimie*]. Le papier que nous devons recevoir étant un peu court, nous sommes obligés de retrancher deux lignes, ce qui donne en même temps un meilleur coup d'oeil au format, qui page sur page aurait été un peu trop grand pour ce papier."

20. The factors involved in the decision-making show up clearly in the correspondence about the *Histoire universelle*. On May 15, 1779, Ostervald wrote, "Je désirerais de trouver une bonne et forte entreprise qui pût occuper agréablement et surtout lucrativement les trois sociétés confédérées. En voici une que je couche en joue et qui pourrait être notre fait. Vous connaissez de réputation au moins la grande *Histoire universelle* traduite de l'anglais d'une société de gens de lettres dont il a paru trente et

quelques volumes in-quarto. On convient généralement que la traduction a été mal faite. Aussi quelques littérateurs français qui disent posséder la langue de l'original viennent-ils d'en proposer une nouvelle édition revue et corrigée en une suite de volumes in-octavo. . . . Vous savez que l'ouvrage est très bon et forme une véritable encyclopédie historique." On May 21, Bérenger replied that he had already considered the possibility of pirating the original edition but had rejected it, because it was so unpleasant to read: "Les savants, les riches, en prendront peut-être, mais ceux-là ne forment pas le commun des lecteurs. La plupart ont déjà cet ouvrage. En le réduisant à la moitié, il perdrait peu et se vendrait mieux, parce qu'il deviendrait d'un usage plus général." On June 21, however, Ostervald explained that he had learned more about "l'histoire de l'*Histoire universelle*." François-Henri Turpin, the editor of the new translation, had abandoned it after publishing two volumes, and a pirated edition now seemed to be unfeasible. Bérenger accepted this judgment in a letter of June 27.

21. Unlike most of the STN's other correspondents, Bérenger sometimes included personal observations in his letters to Ostervald. On April 9, 1779, he offered some remarks about the American Revolution: "J'aurais quelque intérêt à désirer que les Américains devinssent indépendants. Cependant les suites de cette indépendance dans un gouvernement fédératif, qui unit des républiques si diverses par le pouvoir, les intérêts, l'étendue, le commerce, me fait [*sic*] pencher à croire que s'ils obtiennent les mêmes privilèges que les Anglais, conservent leur gouvernement, leur commerce libre, et ne forment avec les premiers qu'un même empire, ils en seront plus heureux, plus paisibles—et c'est gagner à perdre."

22. As in all such formal notices, the circular named the partners—Emanuel Friedrich Fischer, Amedé Fischer, and Samuel Kirchberger, as well as Pfaehler—and asked everyone doing business with the new firm "de n'ajouter foi qu'à nos signatures ci-dessous." The four then signed the name "La Nouvelle Société Typographique," each in his own hand, so that future correspondence would commit the firm to be responsible for the information communicated by letters bearing those signatures. The circular also noted, "Nous avons donné intérêt dans notre nouvelle Société au sieur Pfaehler, qui a géré nombre d'années à notre satisfaction les affaires de l'ancienne." In fact, Pfaehler had signed letters as "La Nouvelle Société Typographique" since the beginning of August. Emanuel Friedrich Fischer and Samuel Kirchberger belonged to the wealthy elite that had supported the "Typographische Gesellschaft Bern" from its beginning in 1758. It is clear from the STB's correspondence that Pfaehler wrote or dictated the letters that went out in its name, except when he was traveling and a clerk handled the letter writing without being empowered to make important decisions: see, for example, STB to STN, June 15, 1779.

23. Although the correspondence does not mention details about the printing operation in Berne, the STB and STL seemed to have worked closely together. In a letter to the STN of August 4, 1779, Heubach referred to "notre imprimerie commune avec Messieurs la Société typographique de Berne." In a letter of May 21, 1779, Bérenger had informed Ostervald of the STB's reasons for concentrating on printing rather than retail bookselling: "Elle a pensé que ses opérations en devenant plus faciles,

plus promptes, le gain plus assuré, les pertes moins à craindre, qu'elle aurait moins de dépenses à faire, moins de commis fripons à soudoyer."

24. In his letter, dated October 15, 1779, Bérenger did not refer specifically to the Confederation, because the octavo, like the quarto, required such an enormous outlay of capital that it was organized as a separate speculation, probably with several investors.

25. The STN had considered reprinting an earlier edition of Bomare's *Dictionnaire* in 1773 and had sounded him out about his willingness to supply supplementary material for it. His reply, dated February 22, 1773, illustrates the attitude of an established author—he was a well-known botanist—toward foreign pirating. He said he felt obligated to honor his commitment to his Parisian publisher, who had paid him for the purchase of the *privilège* and would pay him more for subsequent editions. Bomare planned to expand the *Dictionnaire* considerably in a forthcoming edition; and, far from objecting to a Swiss *contrefaçon*, he advised the STN to wait for its publication: "Alors vous aurez mes corrections et augmentations et le public lecteur sera mieux servi." He even offered to send the STN some additional new material behind the back of his Parisian publisher, provided it kept his collusion secret. At the same time, he indicated a desire to make money. He was preparing some new books, he wrote, and he would consider publishing the first editions of them outside France: "Je les vendrai à l'éditeur qui exécutera le mieux la partie typographique et me fera le meilleur compte . . . Il y aura des figures, ce qui empêchera la contrefaction."

26. *Mémoires de M. le comte de St. Germain* and *Voyage dans les mers de l'Inde, fait par ordre du Roi, à l'occasion du passage de Venus sur le disque du soleil le 6 juin 1761 et le 3 du même mois 1769* by Guillaume-Joseph-Hyacinthe Le Gentil de La Galaisière.

27. A letter of September 9, 1779, from the STB to the STN is a good example of how publishers could disagree about demand: "Nous sommes fâchés, Messieurs, de ne pouvoir accepter votre proposition pour Riccoboni. Cet ouvrage ne nous paraît plus assez recherché pour faire une nouvelle édition. Il y a longtemps qu'il en était question et que nous l'avons refusé. Nos amis de Lausanne penseront comme nous."

28. *Voyage de Vienne à Belgrade et à Kilianova, dans le pays des Tartares Budziacs et Nogais dans la Crimée et de Kaffa à Constantinople au travers de la mer Noire, avec le retour à Vienne par Trieste.*

29. The dossier "Confédération typographique," ms. 1235, contains detailed information about the accounts, but it does not indicate how the publishers resolved their differences after the rancorous meeting of July 20, 1780.

30. In his letter to Ostervald of March 29, 1783, Bérenger described the situation of the STB as follows: "Ses membres ont donné des sommes considérables pour remplir les vides, mais non point pour se dissoudre. Il est vrai qu'elle ne fera de longtemps d'entreprises particulières, mais son but est de continuer en confédération, parce que de cette manière elle peut écouler ce qui la charge sans faire de grandes avances, sans risquer de grandes pertes et avec moins d'hommes que par le passé. Elle se bornera aux objets de la Confédération." The separate folder of letters from Pfaehler in the STN archives, ms. 1194, includes a letter to the STN of January 16, 1783, in which he

said he had conferred with Heubach about establishing a "nouvelle Confédération," which they thought would be acceptable to the STN.

31. As explained in Chapter 1, this volume, Vergennes's order was a disaster for all Swiss publishers, including Heubach. On July 11, 1783, he wrote to Ostervald that he was cutting back on all his enterprises, because of the "ordre inouï pour la librairie étrangère."

32. If one includes its plates and supplements, a complete set of the *Encyclopédie méthodique* might run to 200 volumes, but the final figure is difficult to estimate, and the number of volumes vary greatly according to the catalogues of research libraries. I have traced its history through the French Revolution in *The Business of Enlightenment*, 395–519.

33. The registers of "copies de lettres" in which the STN recorded copies of its outgoing mail are missing from January 1782 to August 1784. By consulting the dossiers of the STL, STB, and Bérenger, we can make inferences about the STN's responses to the constantly shifting circumstances, but the documentation thins out by 1784.

34. The *annonce* in the *Gazette de Berne* contained the sales talk typical of pirated editions: "Cette édition sera faite scrupuleusement sur celle de Paris et n'en différera que par la supériorité de l'exécution et la modicité du prix."

35. The letter, dated January 17, 1784, and sent jointly by the STB and the STL, was unusually strong: "Il [Pancoucke] y verra de la fausseté ou de la perfidie, et cependant nous avons fait cette offre avec sincérité. Il sera irrité; au lieu de favoriser l'entrée du *Supplément* en France, il nous l'interdira, et il n'y aura pas d'espérance de succès."

36. On February 10, 1784, Heubach informed Ostervald that the negotiations on the *Supplément* had been dropped: "M. Panckoucke nous a répondu qu'il ne peut entrer pour rien dans le *Supplément* de l'*Encyclopédie* tant que l'*Encyclopédie par ordre des matières* ne sera pas achevée."

37. The STB had run into financial difficulties of its own. In a letter to the STN of March 2, 1784, Pfaehler said it had sold its printing shop and would continue with its enterprises by jobbing out the printing. The financial pressure added to the acrimony of the disputes, which was indicated by a letter from Pfaehler to the STN of May 3, 1784: "Vous préférez la guerre à la paix."

Chapter 8

1. The following account is based on Panckoucke's dossier in the STN archives, which I used extensively in *The Business of Enlightenment: A Publishing History of the Encyclopédie 1775–1800* (Harvard University Press, Cambridge, MA, 1979); on Suzanne Tucoo-Chala, *Charles-Joseph Panckoucke et la librairie française 1736–1798* (Marrimpouey Jeune, Pau, France, 1977); and George B. Watts, "Charles Joseph Panckoucke, 'l'Atlas de la librairie française,'" *Studies on Voltaire and the Eighteenth Century* 68 (1969), 67–205.

2. Siméon Prosper Hardy, a loyal Guild member who was hostile to the government, described Panckoucke as "reconnu pour traître à son corps": *Mes loisirs, ou journal*

d'événements tels qu'ils parviennent à ma connaissance (1753–1789), Pascal Bastien and Daniel Roche, eds. (Quebec, 2008–), entry for February 16, 1778.

3. Beaumarchais to Jacques-Joseph-Marie Decroix, August 16, 1780, Bodleian Library, Oxford, ms. Fr. d.31 (the emphasis is Beaumarchais's). See Darnton, *The Business of Enlightenment*, 392–394.

4. Amable Le Roy to STN, December 17, 1783; and Dominique-Joseph Garat, *Mémoires historiques sur la vie de M. Suard, sur ses écrits, et sur le XVIIIᵉ siècle* 1 (Paris, 1820), 274. In a pamphlet to promote his unsuccessful candidacy to the Legislative Assembly in 1791, *Lettre de M. Panckoucke à Messieurs le président et électeurs de 1791* (Paris, dated September 9, 1791), 9, Panckoucke wrote that, thanks to his influence in Versailles before the Revolution, he had cleared a way for the circulation of the works of Voltaire, Rousseau, and Raynal: "Je sus si bien manier les ministres du roi que je les ai fait librement circuler dans le royaume."

5. Panckoucke to STN, June 1, 1779. The following account is based on research I did long ago in the STN archives, especially in the dossier "Pièces relatives au projet de publication des oeuvres de J.-J. Rousseau, 1778–1779" (ms. 1220) and in the dossiers of Pierre-Alexandre Du Peyrou (ms. 1144); René-Louis, marquis de Girardin (ms. 1157); and Société typographique de Genève (ms 1219). Since then, Raymond Birn has drawn on this and other material to provide a masterful account of the publishing of Rousseau's works: *Forging Rousseau: Print, Commerce, and Cultural Manipulation in the Late Enlightenment* (Voltaire Foundation, Oxford, 2001). In his great edition of Rousseau's correspondence, Ralph A. Leigh reconstructed most of the publishing history of Rousseau's works: *Correspondance complète de Jean-Jacques Rousseau* (Voltaire Foundation, Geneva and Oxford, 1965–1998), 52 vols.; see especially vols. 44 and 45.

6. On the STN's role in the competition to publish Rousseau's works, see Ralph A. Leigh, "Une balle qu'il eût fallu saisir au bond: Frédéric-Samuel Ostervald et l'édition des Oeuvres de Rousseau (1778–1779)" in *Aspects du livre neuchâtelois*, eds. Jacques Rychner and Michel Schlup (Bibliothèque publique et universitaire de Neuchâtel, Neuchâtel, 1986), 89–96.

7. Panckoucke to STN, June 1, 1779.

8. Société typographique de Genève to STN, May 1, 1779. The circular announced that the STG would print the quarto and octavo editions, and it referred rather ambiguously to a duodecimo edition, which it would make available. Its intention probably was to head off *contrefaçons* in duodecimo format while it considered making a separate deal for a duodecimo speculation with another publisher. In the end, it published its own duodecimo edition and then made an agreement with Amable Le Roy of Lyon to do yet another duodecimo—that is, it speculated on a pirated edition of its own work.

9. The draft, dated June 1, 1779, appears in the folder "STN. Pièces relatives au projet de publication des oeuvres de J. J. Rousseau" (ms. 1220). In defending piracy, it argued, "Le monopole des détailleurs qui seraient seuls possesseurs d'un livre ou d'un ouvrage quelconque n'aurait pas de bornes s'il n'était arrêté par la concurrence et par les contrefaçons." Apparently it was never published.

10. STN to STL, July 31, 1779.

11. In a letter to Ostervald, undated but written in April 1779, Bérenger explained that he had persuaded d'Ivernois and Boin to go into the Rousseau venture and that he dreaded making "ennemis éternels" if their rivalry with the Confederation turned into a commercial war. He originally tried to negotiate a deal in which the STN would receive a large number of discounted STG copies instead of producing its own edition.

12. In a letter from Amsterdam of August 30, 1779, Bosset described how he had to keep the STN's plans secret while talking with Rey: "Et à l'occasion de Rousseau, je me suis bien gardé de lui dire que nous allions l'imprimer in-12, m'ayant fait confidence que M. Bassompierre [Jean-François Bassompierre, one of the three directors of the STG, who had recently traveled through the Low Countries, drumming up business for the Genevan Rousseau] a été chez lui il y a trois semaines, qu'il n'a absolument pas voulu lui permettre l'entrée de l'in-octavo, mais qu'il a pris des arrangements avec lui pour l'in-quarto, et qu'il est résolu d'imprimer ce qu'il y aura de neuf à la suite de son édition in-octavo. Je n'oserais donc, comme vous voyez, Messieurs, parler de Rousseau en Hollande qu'avec la plus grande prudence."

13. Bosset to STN, September 3, 1779. Ostervald had informed Bosset that the marquis de Girardin was expected in Neuchâtel, where he would discuss the STG's publishing plans with Du Peyrou.

14. Bérenger explained this offer in a letter of October 9, 1779. He added further details in a letter of October 15, which stressed that the directors of the STG were motivated by "le désir véritable de ne pas vivre en ennemis . . . Leurs propositions leur paraissent honnêtes, vû les prix des manuscrits."

15. The STN explained its objections to the STG's propositions, which it considered inadequate and "entortillées" in a letter to Bérenger of October 18, 1779, and he replied in a letter of November 5 that the negotiations had been abandoned.

16. The following account draws on the detailed study of the Lyon meeting that I published in *The Business of Enlightenment*, chap. 7.

17. Mme Bertrand's succession to her husband as a partner in the STN is attested by the notarial archives in the Archives de l'État of Neuchâtel, B655, p. 224, "procuration donnée par la Société typographique à M. Quandet de la Chenal," February 10, 1781.

18. The contract is in Le Roy's dossier, ms. 1175, in the STN archives. The STN had been corresponding with Le Roy since April 1779, when he had established himself as a bookseller in his own right, not merely as an associate of Duplain. He appears as a bookseller in the *Almanach de la librairie* of 1781, and he continued to correspond with the STN until November 1788. On July 14, 1780, the STG informed the STN that it was awaiting an order from Le Roy so that it could ship the first delivery of the 750 copies "qu'il vous a cédés."

19. The STN archives contain little information about the subsequent *contrefaçon* in duodecimo format of the STG's Rousseau. It probably was produced by the STB alone. On January 13, 1780, the STG wrote to the STN, "On nous assure que la Société typographique de Berne nous contrefait." It is impossible to calculate all the pirated editions of Rousseau's individual and collected works. This study is meant to show how the pirates operated in one of the few cases that can be investigated in detail.

20. Quoted in Giles Barber, "The Financial History of the Kehl Voltaire," in *The Age of the Enlightenment: Studies Presented to Theodore Besterman* (London, 1967), 157.

21. The following account draws on the extensive research on the Kehl edition of Voltaire, notably Barber, "The Financial History of the Kehl Voltaire," 152–170; Jeroom Vercruysse, "Voltaire, Sisyphe en Jermanie: Vers la meilleure des éditions possibles," *Studies on Voltaire and the Eighteenth Century* 179 (1979), 143–157; Vercruysse, "L'Imprimerie de la Société littéraire et typographique de Kehl en 1782: La Relation d'Anisson-Duperron; Beaumarchais éditeur de Voltaire," *LIAS: Sources and Documents Relating to the Early Modern History of Ideas* 13 (1986), 165–233; George B. Watts, "Panckoucke, Beaumarchais, and Voltaire's First Complete Edition," *Tennessee Studies in Literature* 4 (1959), 91–97; George B. Watts, "Catherine II, Charles-Joseph Pancoucke, and the Kehl Edition of Voltaire's *Oeuvres*," *Modern Language Quarterly* 17 (1956), 59–62; and Brian N. Morton, "Beaumarchais et le prospectus de l'édition de Kehl," *Studies on Voltaire and the Eighteenth Century* 81 (1971), 133–149. Among other primary sources, I have consulted Panckoucke's dossier in the STN archives (ms. 1189, ninety-two letters); in the Bibliothèque publique et universitaire de Genève (ms. suppl. 148); in the Bodleian Library of Oxford University (ms. French d.31) and Panckoucke's *Lettre de M. Panckoucke à Messieurs le président et électeurs de 1791* (Paris, 1791). Some of the complex story is related in the standard biographies of the main players: Tucoo-Chala, *Charles-Joseph Panckoucke et la librairie française 1736–1798*; and Louis de Loménie, *Beaumarchais et son temps: Étude sur la société en France au XVIIIe siècle d'après des documents inédits* (M. Lévy, Paris, 1873). After this chapter was written, a major study of the Kehl edition was published: Linda Gil, *L'Édition Kehl de Voltaire: Une aventure éditoriale et littéraire au tournant des Lumières* (Honoré Champion, Paris, 2018), 2 vols. In vol. 1, pp. 192–217, it discusses the pirate editions and comes to the same conclusions as in the preceding account. I am happy to acknowledge the thoroughness of the research throughout that book.

22. Panckoucke to Duplain, December 26, 1778, quoted in Watts, "Panckoucke, Beaumarchais, and Voltaire's First Complete Edition," 94–95. In the spring of 1779, a rumor circulated that Panckoucke was on the verge of bankruptcy: *Mémoires secrets pour servir à l'histoire de la république des lettres en France* (London, 1777–1789), entry for May 20, 1779.

23. Panckoucke held on to the hope that he could publish the Voltaire edition himself, provided he could get funding from Catherine II through the intermediary of her Parisian correspondent, Frédéric Melchior Grimm. She eventually agreed, but the bill of exchange arrived too late. Staggering under the accumulated pressure of his debts, the "Atlas" of the French book trade therefore sold the Voltaire to Beaumarchais. One can form some idea of the state of his mind from letters he sent to the STN in the spring of 1779. On March 18 he wrote, "J'ai vendu mon manuscrit de Voltaire à une compagnie, et M. de Beaumarchais est à la tête." On April 25, he said he was overwhelmed with the preparations for the *Encyclopédie méthodique*: "Je suis accablé de besognes et d'affaires difficiles." And on June 1, he noted that it was past midnight and he was still at his desk, exhausted while laboring to defend his encyclopedias, the quarto as well as the *Méthodique*. He later described the crisis in his finances of

1777 and the sale of the Voltaire in *Lettre de M. Panckoucke à Messieurs le président et électeurs de 1791*, 17–18.

24. Quoted in Barber, "The Financial History of the Kehl Voltaire," 152.

25. Mossy to STN, October 30, 1776.

26. In an *Avis de la Société littéraire typographique sur les oeuvres de Voltaire*, Beaumarchais observed, "Jusqu'à présent les contrefaçons ont été entreprises après que les éditions originales ont été publiées; mais anticiper la livraison d'une édition, ouvrir la souscription pour une contrefaçon avant qu'un seul volume en ait paru, c'est ou s'accuser soi-même d'avoir fait voler les propriétaires pendant le cours de l'impression, ou promettre ce que l'on n'a pas." Quoted in Morton, "Beaumarchais et le prospectus de l'édition de Kehl."

27. Panckoucke to Ostervald, December 22, 1778. Panckoucke used some of the same phrasing as in his letter to Duplain of December 26: "Toute l'Europe attend une nouvelle édition. . . . Le manuscrit me revient à cent mille livres. Je veux doubler mon argent et 500 exemplaires. Vous n'avez point d'idée de ce que j'ai acquis. J'ai tout réuni et il y a telle correspondance qui m'a coûté deux mille écus."

28. STN to Beaumarchais, March 23, 1779. Ostervald included this letter in a letter to Panckoucke written on the same date. He asked Pancoucke to recommend the STN in delivering its letter to Beaumarchais. In a letter of April 25, Panckoucke said he had performed this service but that Beaumarchais was intent on buying the Baskerville typecasting materials, which indicated that he meant to do the printing himself.

29. STN to Regnault, May 26, 1779. In a letter to Panckoucke of May 2, 1779, Ostervald said he had heard a rumor that Beaumarchais would print the edition in Geneva "et à nous la partie scabreuse, ce qui ne pourrait pas nous convenir."

30. "Copie des propositions faites à M. de Beaumarchais, faites par nos sieurs Ostervald et Bosset pendant leur séjour à Paris, 1780," in Copie de lettres, ms. 1109, p. 300.

31. Beaumarchais probably made this remark during a meeting with Ostervald and Bosset in Beaumarchais's residence on April 24, 1780. He confirmed it, though without making a firm commitment, in a letter to Ostervald of April 30, 1780 (written in the formal, third-person voice): "S'il ne dépend que de la voix de M. de Beaumarchais et de M. Le Tellier, la Société de Neuchâtel aura la préférence."

32. Bosset to Ostervald, May 22, 1780. Regnault was an important publisher in Lyon, who speculated on pirated and hidden editions with Genevans, notably Gabriel Cramer. See Dominique Varry, "L'Édition encadrée des oeuvres de Voltaire: Une collaboration entre imprimeurs-libraires genevois et lyonnais?," in *Voltaire et le livre*, eds. François Bessire and Françoise Tilkin (Centre international d'étude du XVIIIᵉ siècle, Ferney-Voltaire, France, 2009), 107–116.

33. In a letter to Le Tellier of June 6, 1780, Ostervald referred to the Lyonnais booksellers as follows: "Rien ne ferait mieux le jeu de ceux qui aspirent à contrefaire votre édition par [sic] l'effet de la haine et de la jalousie dont chacun sait que sont animés les uns contre les autres tous ceux qui dans cette ville-là font le même commerce."

34. Ostervald to Le Tellier, June 6, 1780. Voltaire's introduction to the edicts of Turgot was first published in the Kehl Voltaire and not republished until recently: *Les Édits de Sa Majesé Louis XVI pendant l'administration de Monsieur Turgot*, in *Oeuvres complètes*

de Voltaire, Helga Bergmann, ed., vol. 77b (Voltaire Foundation, Oxford, 2014), 273–287. I am grateful to Nicholas Cronk for this information,.

35. Ostervald knew Wagnière but tried to deal with him through their close mutual friend, Jacques Mallet du Pan. In a letter to Ostervald of August 30, 1780, Mallet wrote that Wagnière was assembling all sorts of Voltaire material and would not dispose of it with Beaumarchais, because he was being guided and dominated by Gabriel Cramer. Cramer could not afford to undertake a new enterprise and therefore might be willing to negotiate. As to Wagnière, he had expected to receive some payment from Panckoucke when Panckoucke purchased the bulk of the Voltaire manuscripts and bore a grudge because he had received nothing.

36. Elie Bertrand probably discussed his plans for the letters with Ostervald in face-to-face meetings. His dossier in the STN archives, ms. 1120, has a gap for most of 1779 and all of 1780, but in a letter to Ostervald of March 10, 1781, he made a clear reference to his cache of Voltaire letters along with a warning about the dangers of an "édition commune" with Beaumarchais: "Si vous ne prenez pas de précautions, mon bon ami, pour l'édition commune de Voltaire et que la vôtre ne précède pas toutes les contrefaçons, l'entreprise sera mauvaise et l'attache des éditeurs de la grande ne vous servira rien [*sic*]. Il y a plus de 10 projets pareils en divers lieux et deux projets en Suisse pour tirer les additions et les imprimer à part pour les éditions de Genève et de Lausanne. Je ne me résoudrai à donner un choix de mes lettres que pour votre édition, si elle a lieu."

37. Bosset to Ostervald, June 16 and June 23, 1780.

38. Bosset to Ostervald, June 9, 1780.

39. Beaumarchais's letters do not indicate the reason for his rejection of Regnault's proposal to collaborate on a duodecimo edition, but it could have been related to Beaumarchais's recent disenchantment with Panckoucke, who was a backer of Regnault's speculations.

40. Ostervald to Beaumarchais, October 26, 1780. On the same day, Ostervald wrote to a Parisian friend, Girardot de Martigny, "Je continue de travailler pour le Voltaire de M. de Beaumarchais, et je viens de faire encore à cet égard une découverte intéressante."

41. Beaumarchais to Ostervald, November 3, 1780.

42. References to the quest for Voltaire letters occur in Ostervald's correspondence with Jacques Mallet du Pan, who helped him locate many of them. On September 21, 1779, Mallet wrote, "Songez-vous toujours à glaner les correspondances du Nestor? Le Pasteur Vernes m'a offert, comme je vous l'ai dit, ce qu'il a, avec les retranchements qui pourraient compromettre beaucoup de gens." Mallet mentioned Ostervald's connection with Rieu in a letter of November 4, 1780. And, as explained in the following text, he discussed Wagnière's cache of manuscripts in several letters beginning on August 30, 1780. Further references are scattered through the STN's "copies de lettres" for the last half of 1780, notably in letters of October 26 to Girardot de Martigny, October 29 to Claude-Vincent Cantini, November 2 to Beaumarchais, November 16 to Beaumarchais, and November 21 to Beaumarchais. In the last of these, Ostervald described his unsuccessful attempt to retrieve Voltaire's famous letters to the marquise

du Deffand from the family of Horace Walpole, who had inherited them. That attempt is also mentioned in an undated note from Bosset to Ostervald, ms. 1125, which said they might be in the possession of one of Walpole's relatives in Lisbon whom the STN could contact. In fact, they were obtained by Beaumarchais.

43. Mallet du Pan described Cramer's project in a letter to Ostervald of December 17, 1781, noting that Wagnière "est aux ordres de Cramer."

44. Ostervald to Beaumarchais, May 22, 1781.

45. Ostervald to Beaumarchais, November 21, 1780.

46. Beaumarchais to Ostervald, December 12, 1780, and Ostervald to Beaumarchais, December 19, 1780.

47. Ostervald vented his frustration in letters to Girardot de Marigny, a Parisian who had contact with Beaumarchais, and to a certain Cantini, who handled some of the Kehl accounts and whom Ostervald hoped to recruit as a spy. See especially Ostervald to Girardot, February 4, 1781.

48. Ostervald to Beaumarchais, February 18, 1781. On Spineux, see Jacques Rychner, *Jacques-Barthélemy Spineux (1738–1806), prote de la Société typographique de Neuchâtel: De Liège à Carouge en passant par Paris, Neuchâtel, et La Neuveville* (Neuchâtel, 2013). On the disastrous prospectus, see Vercruysse, "L'Imprimerie de la Société littéraire et typographique de Kehl en 1782."

49. Ostervald to Beaumarchais, March 8, 1781. Beaumarchais was interested enough by Ostervald's description of the letters to ask to inspect them under the supervision of a representative of the STN. In an undated letter to Ostervald, ms. 1125, Bosset wrote, "Rien de mieux, Monsieur, que la proposition de M. de Beaumarchais de vérifier devant un tiers les papiers et manuscrits de Voltaire," and he proposed someone who could be trusted to do the supervising.

50. Jean de Turkheim to STN, May 16, 1781: "Elle [Beaumarchais's enterprise] marche grand train. On fait des dépenses considérables. Il y a près de 100 ouvriers par jour qui nivellent le terrain à Kehl et font des constructions intéressantes. Les fontes de caractères sont arrivées vendredi passé, et les ouvriers vont les suivre incessamment. Il y aura 24 presses."

51. Ostervald to Turkheim, May 3, 1781.

52. Ostervald to Turkheim, June 28, 1781.

53. Ostervald to Mailly, September 23, 1780.

54. Ostervald to Beaumarchais, November 29, 1781. Beaumarchais did not answer this letter, but on February 16, 1782, he acknowledged receipt of some subscriptions the STN had collected for him long ago and added, "Si ce que notre société avait projeté de faire avec la vôtre, Monsieur, n'a point eu lieu, ne croyez pas que ce soit par les raisons que vous avez voulu nous faire pressentir. Vous avez dû voir par tout ce que nous vous avons écrit que nous sommes entièrement étrangers au commerce de la librairie. S'il ne s'agissait que d'imprimer, nous n'aurions cherché à nous associer avec personne pour consommer cette affaire."

55. In a letter to Ostervald from Paris on May 17, 1780, Bosset had written that he opposed renewing the contract for the Confederation on the grounds that it ate up too much of the STN's capital.

56. In a letter to the STN written on June 2, 1781, after his return to Bern, Pfaehler insisted on this point: "Les manuscrits que vous possédez, Messieurs, ont été une raison, outre celle que nous ayons de vous obliger, à [sic] vous céder une part dans cette entreprise, et nous n'en pouvons rien payer. Il est vrai que la lettre que vous eûtes la complaisance de lire à notre sieur Pfaehler a été assez intéressante; mais cependant pas tant pour que le public y perde considérablement s'il ne [la] recevait [pas], car sûrement il y en aura d'autres dans le même genre, puisqu'il est impossible que M. de Voltaire ne se soit point répété souvent et très fort dans sa correspondance."

57. Pfaehler explained these details in letters to the STN of May 15, May 26, and June 3, 1780. In a letter of June 21, Pfaehler said he planned to charge 3 L. per volume, thereby undercutting Beaumarchais's price of 3 L. 10 sous for his octavo edition. Three years later the STN entered into its own correspondence with Palissot, who included a copy of his original prospectus in a letter of June 22, 1783.

58. In reporting his impressions to Ostervald in a letter of December 31, 1781, Pfaehler indicated that he had found a possibility of procuring stolen proofs in order to facilitate their pirating: "L'établissement de Kehl est une chose à voir par son arrangement. C'est une ancienne caserne du temps de Louis XIV qui est entièrement occupée. Il y a 17 ou 18 presses entièrement montées et 4 volumes de Voltaire faits. Il y aura encore 6 presses en peu de temps. L'impression en est réellement belle. C'est tout ce que nous avons pu apprendre, mais nous espérons d'y avoir fait une connaissance qui pourrait peut-être nous procurer les volumes à mesure qu'ils sortent de presse."

59. Pfaehler to Ostervald, July 15, 1781: "M. Palissot a ses ennemis, mais il a aussi ses amis, et nous mettons plus d'importance que vous à son travail. . . . Nous sommes entr'autres fermement résolus que M. Palissot ne souffre en rien de cette affaire [that is, a possible arrangement with Beaumarchais]."

60. Pfaehler to Ostervald, July 19, 1781: "Le plus difficile à notre avis est de concilier ensemble Beaumarchais et Palissot. Le premier est du parti opposé, et le dernier est trop fier pour départir de son plan."

61. In a letter to Ostervald of December 30, 1781, Pfaehler included a copy of the letter he had received from the agent, whom he did not name (it might have been Le Tellier). While insisting on the elimination of Palissot, the agent proposed new terms for collaborating on an "édition commune" of the complete works along with a separate "Supplément" composed of unpublished manuscripts and a separate edition of Voltaire's correspondence, which would include more than 12,000 letters. The proposal stressed the strength of Beaumarchais's ability to fend off pirates: "Il est le maître de son manuscrit. Il peut faire ou faire faire des éditions communes. Il peut s'arranger à cet égard comme il lui plaira, les publier tout à la fois ou par livraisons de douze volumes. Il ne peut craindre aucune espèce de concurrence. Il pourra même établir cette édition commune à tel prix que personne ne serait tentée de la contrefaire et s'en trouverait même dans l'impossibilité."

62. It is not clear when Palissot and the Bern group abandoned their planned edition, but in a letter to Ostervald of March 25, 1783, Pfaehler mentioned that the cancellation of the Palissot enterprise meant that the STN's hidden partnership in it had become null,

although it still owed payment for its share of 2,000 L. that had been used to buy off Palissot.

63. Palissot to STN, May 7, 1783. He proposed this edition as "une des meilleures spéculations de typographie qu'on puisse faire." It was a trimmed-down version of the edition he had planned to do for the STB, which, he said had strung him along for nearly a year and then dropped him while it was being strung along itself by Beaumarchais. Palissot had rejected the STB's offers to renew their ties, because, he said rather grandly, "ma confiance une fois trompée ne revient jamais."

64. The following account is based on Mallet's rich dossier in the STN papers, especially his letters of August 30, 1780; November 4, 1780; June 2, 1781; and December 17, 1781. On Mallet, see the biography by Frances Acomb, who used some of the STN material: *Mallet du Pan: A Career in Political Journalism* (Duke University Press, Durham, NC, 1973).

65. Bérenger to STN, April 23, 1783: "On n'annonce pas une édition plus complète que M. de Beaumarchais, du moins d'une manière positive, parce qu'il était incertain si ce qu'on croit avoir méritera d'être imprimé ou du moins sera bien reçu en l'annonçant. On est si accoutumé à voir grossir des oeuvres complètes d'un auteur avec les balayures de son cabinet que cette annonce n'est plus encourageante."

66. STB to STN, December 4, 1783. Information about Bérenger's mission to Ferney and a copy of Wagnière's letter of November 21 are in a letter from Heubach to Ostervald of December 2, 1783. A copy of the proposed contract with Wagnières is in a letter that Heubach wrote to the STN on December 6.

67. Heubach to STN, February 10, 1784. The *Avis de la Société littéraire typographique, sur les ouvres de Voltaire*, published by Brian Morton in "Beaumarchais et le prospectus d l'édition de Kehl," p. 145, took note of the prospectus published by "des contrefacteurs associés de Berne, Lausanne et Neuchâtel unis au sieur *Wagnière*," and held Wagnière up to mockery as the "ci-devant copiste chez M. de Voltaire," who had made some furtive copies of Voltaire's letters, the originals of which would be published in the Kehl edition.

68. This is Barber's conclusion in "The Financial History of the Kehl Voltaire," p. 159, but Barber gives no source for it.

69. After the Confederation's edition folded, the main *contrefaçon* of the Kehl Voltaire was an octavo reprint by Jean-Jacques Tourneisen of Basel, who cooperated with Charles-Guillaume Ettinger of Gotha. For a general overview of the editions, see Georges Bengesco, *Voltaire: Bibliographie de ses oeuvres* 4 (Perrin, Paris, 1882–1890).

70. In a letter to Beaumarchais of October 26, 1780, Ostervald gave the dates of the first 11 of the 162 letters so that Beaumarchais could verify that they were not copies of those in his possession. The dates were December 28, 1754; January 3, 4, 9, 14, 22, 28, and 31, 1755; and February 12, 18, and 28, 1755. In the Oxford edition of Voltaire's correspondence, there is no letter written by him on January 22, 1755. His letters on the other dates were written to many different persons, and those mentioned by Ostervald were all addressed to the same person, Elie Bertrand. Therefore, I believe that Bertrand's cache of letters was never published. Because they were considered so valuable in 1780, it seems unlikely that they would have been lost or destroyed.

Chapter 9

1. Gosse to STN, February 25, 1772. On Gosse's relations with the STN, see Chapter 4, this volume.

2. Mme Bertrand to Ostervald and Bosset, March 5, 1780, in a dossier labeled "Ostervald et Bosset de Luze en voyage," ms. 1189.

3. Jean-Marie Bruyset of Lyon was one of the few eminent bookseller-printers who used the first-person singular in his letters, which contained an unusual number of personal observations, perhaps because he knew Ostervald. See, for example, his letter to the STN of September 9, 1770, in which he expressed his opinion about Voltaire's works.

4. In a letter of November 23, 1769, Jean-Christophe Heilmann, a publisher in nearby Bienne who was planning to do a joint edition with the STN, objected to the formal tone of its letters: "Vos Messieurs depuis quelques temps se sont servis d'un style réservé, du barreau, qui n'est point du tout celui du commerce, point du tout ce style ouvert, franc, amical, qui caractérise des associés liés du même intérêt." In a letter to the STN of December 12, 1784, Poinçot, a particularly tough bookseller of Versailles, reported a rumor that Ostervald or Bosset had said in a Paris bookshop that "vous f. . . de la police et du gouvernement de France." Ostervald replied in the first-person plural on December 19, 1784, that he abhorred such "propos indécents": "Nous ne connaissons point ce style méprisable."

5. On March 12, 1786, the STN wrote to Chantran of Besançon that Ostervald had become much less involved in running the business, as he had become "chef de notre magistrature."

6. On the history of the mail in France, see Eugène Vaillé, *Histoire générale des Postes françaises*, 1–7 (Presses universitaires de France, Paris, 1947–1955)—and, for a more recent but less detailed survey, Yves Lecouturier, *Histoire de la Poste en France* (Éditions Ouest-France, Rennes, 2011).

7. For example, in a letter of June 3, 1772, Jean-Marie Barret of Lyon asked the STN to send him a list of its latest *livres philosophiques*: "Mais ne m'écrivez de cela que sur un papier volant et non sur vos lettres, et dans les factures il faut mettre ces ouvrages sous un nom différent."

8. Gabriel Regnault of Lyon to Manoury of Caen, January 11, 1775, Bibliothèque de l'Arsenal, ms. 12446.

9. Brissot to STN, July 14, 1780: "Pour l'envoi des premières épreuves, je vous prie de me le faire comme je vous l'ai marqué à l'adresse de M. Amelot. Mais *il faut avoir soin de bien envelopper et serrer le tout* [Brissot's emphasis] afin qu'à la poste on ne s'aperçoive point que c'est de l'imprimé. Ainsi ne *ménagez point les enveloppes*. Mettez-en une pour M. Amelot, une pour M. Henique de Chevilly, une troisième pour moi." Brissot explained the use of bread as a seal in a letter to the STN of September 16, 1780. He also used other intermediaries, including M.-C. Pahin de La Blancherie, the head of the Musée de Paris, a literary association, who had won the favor of a secretary to Amelot.

10. Waroquier, a relatively small bookseller of Soissons, complained in a letter to the STN of April 5, 1783, "Vos frais de lettres et de paquets absorbent tout le bénéfice."

11. Entry in the account titled Journal C for December 31, 1783, ms. 1028.

12. For a cartographical account of the postal service, roads, and communications, see *Atlas de la Révolution française: Routes et communications*, Guy Arbellot and Bernard Lepetit, eds. (Éditions de l'École des hautes études en science sociales, Paris, 1987), 38–43.

13. Mossy to STN, February 6, 1782; November 6, 1782; and April 1, 1783.

14. Ostervald often mentioned dining with other publishers and offering them hospitality in Neuchâtel. He and Bosset were entertained by Beaumarchais and others during their trip to Paris in 1780, and Bosset dined with Marc-Michel Rey in Amsterdam during his tour of 1779. See their letters to the STN gathered in separate dossiers, mss. 1125 and 1189.

15. Journal C (ms. 1028).

16. Mme Bertrand to STB, March 25, 1780.

17. André to STN, August 22, 1784. For a detailed discussion of calculating demand and the character of the book trade, see Darnton, *A Literary Tour de France*, especially chap. 13.

18. STN to Mossy, May 1, 1773.

19. Machuel to STN, June 4, 1783.

20. Bornand to STN, September 15, 1785.

21. Delahaye to STN, March 30, 1783

22. Mossy to STN June 29, 1778.

23. Rigaud to STN, February 18, 1784, and July 30, 1783.

24. For examples of these rumors, all of them false, see the letters to the STN from Poinçot of March 28 and August 27, 1782; from Petit of March 30, 1784; and from Mauvelain of March 15, 1784.

25. For a detailed discussion of the activities of sales reps, see Darnton, *A Literary Tour de France*, especially chap. 7.

26. Mme Bertrand to Ostervald and Bosset, February 20, 1780.

27. In a letter of September 13, 1769, Jean-Frédéric Perregaux, the STN's banker in Paris, wrote that he was trying to recruit an agent who could furnish it with *nouveautés* as soon as they appeared in Paris, but that task was difficult, because "le secret est une loi imposée à tous les imprimeurs . . . La plupart des libraires ne connaissent les ouvrages de leurs confrères que 2 ou 3 jours avant qu'ils paraissent."

28. The STN mentioned instances of inside information transmitted by workers, in letters to François Grasset of Lausanne on December 1, 1773, and to Panckoucke in Paris on February 22, 1778.

29. STN to Beaumarchais, February 27, 1781. In a "Copie des propositions faites à M. de Beaumarchais, faites par nos sieurs Ostervald et Bosset pendant leur séjour à Paris, 1780" (undated but entered in the Copie de lettres between February 13 and 15, 1781), the STN guaranteed that it would take great precautions to prevent "fraude de la part des ouvriers" and "fraude de la part des marchands ou fabricants." On the plans of the Swiss Confédération typographique to spy on the printing operation in Kehl and to steal sheets from it, see STB to STN, December 30, 1781.

30. Quandet de Lachenal to STN, December 3, 1781. In a letter of July 2, 1781, Quandet also warned about spies working for the police: "Notre police a des espions

dans toutes les villes de Suisse où il y a des imprimeries un peu considérables, et d'après ce que j'ai appris là-dessus je suis moralement sûr qu'elle est déjà instruite, ou peu s'en faut, de vos dessins."

31. Manoury to STN, February 5, 1777.

32. On April 6, 1780, Mme Bertrand observed in a letter to Ostervald and Bosset, who were then in Paris, that Dorat's novel had sold well: "Ces nouveautés données promptement se vendent ordinairement très bien."

33. Manoury to STN, September 18, 1776: "NB, Quand vous aurez quelque bonne nouveauté piquante, vous pouvez hardiment m'en envoyer un cent." Manoury sent similar instructions in letters of December 17, 1775; March 13, 1776; and December 27, 1777.

34. Mossy to STN, September 19, 1777, writing in this case about shipments of the *Encyclopédie*. On August 8, 1781, Mossy canceled an order for *Tableau de Paris*, because the STN could not get it to him on time: "Comme toutes nos boutiques en ont, les vôtres venant trop tard me seraient à charge. . . . Il est des cas où le moment manqué, tout est dit."

35. In a letter to the STN of August 30, 1780, Jacques Mallet du Pan described a quarrel, which threatened to degenerate into a law suit, between Amable Le Roy of Lyon and the Société typographique de Genève over "mauvaise foi" in the timing of shipments.

36. STN to its Pion, its shipping agent in Pontarlier, April 13, 1777: "Un retard de 8 jours peut souvent empêcher pour toujours la vente de quelques livres qui ne sont bons que dans leurs premières nouveautés."

37. Mme Bertrand to Bosset in Paris, May 21, 1780.

38. The *Almanach de la librairie* of 1781, pp. 16–18, listed twenty-two general periodicals and twenty-four local "affiches" that carried notices of new books.

39. Darnton, *The Business of Enlightenment*, 258. The bankruptcy papers concerning Anne Françoise Desmarais, Archives de la Seine, Registre B6 1153, lists some minor expenses, including 16 L. "pour avoir fait mettre des annonces dans la gazette," presumably a reference to the *Gazette de France*.

40. The prospectus, dated June 15, 1774, in Dufour's dossier in the STN archives, gave a flattering description of the edition Dufour had pirated (without mentioning where it could be procured) and then added his sales pitch: "Le désir d'augmenter notre correspondance, me porte à vous offrir cette même édition, grand octavo, 7 volumes, caractère neuf, interligné, très bien imprimé, avec les cartes et estampes gravées par les meilleurs artistes et sans nulle épargne pour les frais, au prix modique de 15 livres argent de France." I have reproduced it and several other documents related to the commercial activities of publishers as illustrations in "La Société typographique de Neuchâtel et la librairie française: Un survol des documents," *L'Édition neuchâteloise au siècle des Lumières*, 210–231.

41. In 1771 the STN considered purchasing a manuscript by J.-H. Bernardin de Saint-Pierre, but hesitated because of the cost, the risk of poor sales, and the certainty of being pirated. In a letter to him of January 13, 1771, it suggested that they split the cost of publishing a prospectus for a subscription. If the response was inadequate, they would abandon the project: "En un mot, il ne s'agit que de sonder le goût du public."

In a typical remark denigrating subscriptions, Machuel of Rouen wrote in a letter of March 31, 1780, "L'homme qui réfléchit un peu ne doit jamais souscrire, parce qu'il est toujours dupe."

42. The circular letter with some additional material adapted to the trade of certain booksellers appears in the Copie de lettres for 1776 under various dates from mid-August.

43. Mme Bertrand in Paris to Ostervald, October 16, 1785: "La Société a si souvent annoncé des ouvrages qu'elle n'a point faits, entre autres L'An 2440, que les libraires ne croient plus à ses offres."

44. STN to STB, February 10, 1780.

45. Barret to STN, January 18, 1777.

46. Regnault to STN, February 10, 1774. Regnault published his edition clandestinely as a joint venture with another Lyonnais pirate, Benoît Duplain, and Fauche produced his independently of the STN.

47. Los Rios, a Lyonnais dealer who specialized in antiquarian books, to STN, April 6, 1780: "Vous sentez bien que nous sommes ici dans une ville de ressources, de 118 presses bien montées et à tout instant du jour prêtes à rouler."

48. These expressions, which recur frequently in letters by and about pirates, come from Barret's letters to the STN of June 17, 1781, and December 28, 1772. Emeric David, an important bookseller from Aix-en-Provence, did a tour of bookshops and recorded his impressions in a journal, "Mon voyage de 1787": Bibliothèque de l'Arsenal, Paris, ms. 5947. When he arrived in Lyon, he noted, "12 imprimeries, les 3 quarts ne s'occupent qu'aux contrefaçons . . . Point d'imprimeur qui cherche à bien faire, routine, amour de l'argent."

49. Barret to STN, December 28, 1772.

50. The following account is based on the dossiers of Grabit (letters to the STN between December 17, 1773, and May 30, 1774) and Saillant et Nyon (letters from January 4 to May 8, 1774) along with the STN's replies in its Copies de lettres.

51. Grabit to STN, May 20, 1784.

52. Mossy sent fifty copies of the purportedly new book to the STN. When its customers discovered the fraud, they protested, and the STN complained. After attempting to deny his duplicity, Mossy finally admitted it and gave the STN a large discount in their swapping account as compensation, while complaining for his part about the "tripotages" of Swiss publishers: Mossy to STN, March 8 and June 18, 1784.

53. Lépagnez to STN, March 30, 1781.

54. Fontaine to STN, April 23, 1773, and November 31, 1775.

55. Bergès & Cie. to STN, May 26, June 18, June 23, August 5, September 1, and October 3, 1781. While replying favorably to these letters, the STN asked for information about Bergès in a letter to a merchant in Toulouse named Chaurou. He reported on October 24, 1781, that the affair was a scam.

56. For examples, see Grand Lefebvre to STN, December 30, 1780; February 19, 1781; and June 4, 1781—all about a fraud exposed in a letter of Machuel to STN, July 11, 1781; and Le Lièvre to STN, December 31, 1776, and January 3, 1777—both about a confidence trick exposed in a letter of Sombert to STN, January 11, 1777.

57. Barret to STN, October 19, 1781: "Les frères Martin, qui chargent le plus pour cette route, accaparent toutes les marchandises qu'ils trouvent, les déposent dans une auberge, où ils les laissent quelque fois cinq à six semaines; et quand ils les chargent, ils refont eux-mêmes de nouvelles lettres de voiture." J. B. Laisney of Beauvais accused the STN of sending a fake notice of a shipment (*lettre d'avis*) that it had never sent as a ruse to induce him to pay a bill for an earlier shipment, which had been confiscated. Laisney to STN, January 19, 1778: "Vous poussez l'audace, je pourrais dire la fourberie, jusqu'à m'annoncer une expédition que je devrais avoir reçue il y a plus d'un mois, si elle avait été effectivement effectuée."

58. For a detailed discussion of transport and smuggling, see Darnton, *A Literary Tour de France*, chap. 2.

59. In a letter to the STN of December 12, 1782, Jacques-François d'Arnal, its banker in Lyon, reported that its Lyonnais agent, Jacques Revol, had told him that Poinçot, "un fripon reconnu," had engineered the confiscation of a shipment from the STN as a pretext to avoid paying for it. "Il [Revol] m'a fait voir deux lettres de Versailles dans lesquelles ce Poinçot était clairement désigné pour un espion dont il fallait se défier. . . . Je vous plains, Messieurs, d'avoir à faire à pareille canaille." Quandet de Lachenal, the STN's agent in Paris, wrote on April 12, 1782, that Desauges, an "âme damnée de notre police," had done the same thing and then recovered the books from the police so that he could sell them.

60. There is an enormous list of "débiteurs réputés mauvais" in the accounts drawn up on May 31, 1785: ms. 1042.

61. D'Arnal to STN, December 12, 1782.

62. Quotations from Machuel's letters to the STN of September 30, 1773; April 21, 1780; and April 2, 1781.

63. Delahaye to STN, March 30, 1783; April 5, 1787; and October 1, 1788.

64. Overman frères, shipping agents in Brussels, to STN, February 17, 1784.

65. STN to Bergès, November 4, 1781. In a letter to Machuel of March 11, 1773, the STN described "la confiance réciproque" as "l'âme" of commerce. Following the work of Georg Simmel, sociologists have developed a theoretical approach to confidence ("Vertrauen"). See Guido Möllering, "The Nature of Trust: From Georg Simmel to a Theory of Expectation, Interpretation and Suspension," *Sociology* 35 (2001), 403–420. However, the use of "confiance" by publishers was more closely tied to commercial relations than the Simmelian concept of trust, which applies to human relations in general, and there is much conceptual slippage between "Vertrauen" in German, "trust" in English, and "confiance" in French.

66. For example, Jean-Marie Bruyset to STN, February 13, 1775: "Il est sans doute dans le commerce peu de marchés qui puissent se passer d'une confiance réciproque, et la sécurité qu'elle donne est le premier principe qui puisse assurer une suite d'affaires et les rendre considérables."

67. *Arrêt du Conseil d'État du Roi concernant les contrefaçons des livres*, preamble, reprinted in *Almanach de la librairie*, 1781, p. 172, referring to "la confiance qui est le lien du commerce."

68. STN to Jacques Revol, February 27, 1781. Evidently the STN had forgotten a report on Sorret by it sales rep, Jean-François Favarger, who wrote in a letter of August 8, 1778, that while in Avignon he had met a merchant from Apt "qui dit n'y avoir dans sa ville de libraire qu'un nommé Sorret à qui l'on ne confie pas pour 6 livres qu'il n'en dispute la moitié, soit de mauvaise foi, soit faute de pouvoir payer."

69. Darnton, *A Literary Tour de France*, 47–52.

70. See, for example, STN to Nicolas Gerlache, January 18, 1776; to Jean-François Malherbe, June 8, 1777; and to Jean Ranson, May 8, 1777. Gerlache's dossier in the STN papers shows how a marginal dealer built up a career in Metz. Through it all his correspondence with the STN illustrates how confidence was extended and retracted in the minor branches of the book trade.

71. In a letter of July 24, 1776, C.-C. Duvez, a merchant in Nancy, who sent reports to the STN about a half-dozen booksellers in Lorraine, requested information about a merchant in Geneva with whom he contemplated doing business.

72. Clerval to STN, September 5, 1777, and December 17, 1780.

73. Perregaux to STN, February 19, 1777. In a letter of February 28, Perregaux said he had communicated the result of his investigation orally to Ostervald and Bosset, who were then in Paris. In referring to Panckoucke's "facultés," Perregaux meant his possessions and general wealth. According to the 1762 edition of the *Dictionnaire de l'Académie française*, "facultés" in the plural meant "les biens de chaque particulier." The long report on Caldesaigues appears in a letter of June 27, 1777, from Claudet, the STN's shipping agent in Lyon. On Caldesaigues's checkered career, see Darnton, *A Literary Tour de France*, 147–151.

74. Volland to STN, July 23, 1780.

75. Daniel Argand to STN, September 15, 1779.

76. Veuve Rameau et fils to STN, August 12, 1784.

77. See especially the dossiers of Louis Antoine, a shipping agent in Nancy, and C. P. Hugard, a lawyer in Lunéville.

78. C. P. Hugard to STN, March 31, 1778. During the fashionable season at the spa of Plombières, Mme Audéart sold books from a boutique, which was destroyed by a fire. Her dossier in the STN papers is full of information about the capillary system of the book trade.

79. The prototype of the "honnête homme" emerged in seventeenth-century literature, invoking qualities of politeness and refinement developed in aristocratic salons. See John Lough, *An Introduction to Seventeenth Century France* (New York, 1966), 225–229. In the STN's commercial correspondence the use of "honnête homme" also applied to persons of modest standing who were reliable and upright. The *Dictionnaire de l'Académie française*, edition of 1762, indicated that "honnêteté" had multiple meanings, including "toutes les qualités sociales et agréables qu'un homme peut avoir dans la vie civile."

80. For example, in discussing swapping arrangements with the Lyonnais publisher Jean-André Périsse in a letter of April 5, 1774, the STN emphasized "l'avantage d'avoir mis beaucoup de variété dans les objets et d'avoir contribué à l'écoulement plus rapide des éditions un peu fortes." In its instructions to Jacob-François Bornand, one of its sales

reps, it wrote on March 8, 1783, "Les échanges donc ne peuvent nous être onéreux; au contraire, ils nous facilitent un écoulement plus prompt en nous assortissant et nous procurent un bénéfice que nous ne pourrions nous flatter d'acquérir sans cette manière d'opérer." In a letter to the Société typographique de Neuwied of May 23, 1789, it expressed pride in the stock of books it had accumulated by skillful swapping.

81. Clever swapping could lead to profitable coups. In July 1773 Isaac-Pierre Rigaud, the most important bookseller in Montpellier, ordered twenty copies of Raynal's *Histoire philosophique* from the STN, thinking it could provide them from its stock. The STN had none, but it knew that Joseph Grabit kept a supply of them in his shop in Lyon. Therefore, it arranged an exchange with him and directed its Lyonnais shipping agent, Claudet frères, to collect the books and to ship them to Rigaud. It then charged Rigaud the full wholesale price and even the supposed shipping cost from Neuchâtel to Lyon. For an example of a similar coup, see Darnton, *A Literary Tour de France*, 96–99. In a letter of June 10, 1773, to Joseph Duplain, a wily publisher in Lyon, the STN complained about his delay in sending books as his part of an exchange: "Ce retard nous cause du dommage, et nous avons quelque raison de nous plaindre de cette espèce de défiance qui vous a fait différer l'expédition jusqu'à ce que vous ayez été nanti de nos articles."

82. In September 1772 the STN acquired as a swap fifty copies of *Recherches sur les Américains,* valued at 180 L., from Baerstecher of Cleves, and it sold them to Chénoux of Lunéville for 257 L., 3 sous: entry in the account book labeled Brouillard A, ms. 1033, 290.

83. When the STN arranged its first exchange with Jacques Garrigan of Avignon, it worried that he would damage its sales by delaying his shipment. Its shipping agent in Lyon, Jacques Revol, warned that Garrigan was capable of such foul play and therefore held back the STN's shipment to Garrigan until he had received Garrigan's shipment to the STN: STN to Revol, November 29, 1780, and Revol to STN, December 19, 1780. On the "méfiance" aroused by delays in delivering exchanges, see Gabriel Regnault to STN, September 24, 1773.

84. Jean-Marie Bruyset to STN, May 20, 1774. In a letter to the STN of February 20, 1777, Jean-François de Los Rios remarked that in swapping by sheets, "vous suivez exactement la manière et l'usage du prudent Bassompierre de Liège."

85. On sheet sizes, see Philip Gaskell, *A New Introduction to Bibliography* (Oxford University Press, New York, 1972), 66–77. When Jean Mossy, the largest publisher in Marseille, opened negotiations over swapping with the STN, he worried about its tendency to use too much *St. Augustin* ("english" in English) type, which took up a great deal of the page, and he was especially concerned about paper: "Votre papier, est-il grand? Est-ce du papier bâtard de la grandeur de celui d'Auvergne, ou bien est-ce du papier messel ou couronne? Est-ce blanc et collé?" Mossy to STN, June 30, 1773. See also the similar remarks in Mossy's letters of July 24, 1775, and September 5, 1782.

86. The difficulties in swapping by price are illustrated by the STN's relations with Jean-Marie Bruyset, a leading bookseller-publisher in Lyon. Both parties were eager to develop relations based on exchanges. But Bruyset explained that he could not swap "à la manière de Liège," because his manufacturing costs were a third more expensive than

the STN's, thanks to the higher price of paper in France and the payments he made to authors for original editions. Moreover, the type on his pages was usually denser: he often used *petit romain*, or long primer, while the STN favored *St. Augustin*, or english. And he set prices "relatif à la consommation." The STN agreed to swap books according to wholesale prices, but to avoid incurring losses it subtly adjusted its own prices upward. Although they exchanged a few shipments, the arrangement broke down, because each side suspected the other of overcharging. "L'un des deux contractants est toujours la dupe de l'autre," Bruyset concluded in a letter of March 21, 1776.

87. Liège was too far from Switzerland to make swapping arrangements feasible, according to Clément Plomteux, Liège's most important publisher, in a letter of August 18, 1780: "Les frais de voiture absorberaient tous les bénéfices que pourrait offrir l'échange de nos livres."

88. On the rise of publishing in Switzerland relative to that of Holland, see *Histoire de l'édition française* 2 (Promodis, Paris, 1984), 302. There are no solid, comparative statistics on book production. According to the *Almanach de la librairie* of 1781 (Librairie Pierre-M. Gason reprint, Aubel, Belgium, 1984, Jeroom Vercruysse, ed.), Amsterdam had 16 booksellers and Geneva 19, but there were 109 booksellers scattered throughout thirty-four cities in The Netherlands and only 61 in twelve cities in Switzerland, which had a much smaller population. In discussing these figures in his introduction to the *Almanach*, pp. xix–xxvii, Vercruysse rightly stresses their conjectural nature. See also Giles Barber, "Pendred Abroad: A View of the Late Eighteenth-Century Book Trade in Europe," *Studies in the Book Trade in Honour of Graham Pollard* (Oxford Bibliographical Society, Oxford, 1975), 231–277; and Giles Barber, "The Cramers of Geneva and Their Trade in Europe between 1755 and 1766," *Studies on Voltaire and the Eighteenth Century* 30 (1964), 377–413.

89. The following account is based primarily on Grasset's dossier, one of the largest (421 letters) in the STN archives. On Grasset's career, see *Dictionnaire des journalistes 1600–1789*, Jean Sgard, ed., vol. 1 (Voltaire Foundation, Oxford, 1999), 358–359; and Silvio Corsini, "Imprimeurs, libraires, et éditeurs à Lausanne au siècle des Lumières," *Le Livre à Lausanne: Cinq siècles d'édition et d'imprimerie 1493–1993*, Silvio Corsini, ed. (Payot, Lausanne, 1993), 51–53 and 61.

90. Grasset to STN, October 11, 1771.

91. On November 7, 1783, Grasset complained that the STN had refused to swap its edition of *Cécilia ou Mémoires d'une héritière*, and on March 16, 1784, he objected that the STN had inflated its count of the sheets in Mercier's *Mon bonnet de nuit*. They soon patched up these minor conflicts, whereas Grasset wrote in a letter of December 21, 1781, that his exchanges with Fauche had degenerated into a nasty quarrel: "[Fauche] nous a bassement trompés, dupés et fait turlupiner par son gendre."

92. For example, on June 25, 1770, Meuron frères assured the STN, "Avec des amis on fait tout."

93. In a letter of September 23, 1773, Gabriel Regnault, a shady publisher in Lyon, assured the STN that he did not want to "rendre méfiance pour méfiance." It had complained about foul play in swapping sheets and eventually stopped dealing with him.

94. Boubers to STN October 4, 1771; December 20, 1772; and May 17, 1776. Charles Triponetti, a merchant in Brussels who attempted to collect Boubers's debt, warned the STN in a letter of February 25, 1774, "Je prévois qu'il cherchera des chicanes dont il n'est pas mal endoctriné."

95. Boubers published one of the many editions of Raynal's *Histoire philosophique* and speculated with Delahaye & Cie. of Brussels on printing the atlas that was to accompany it. See Delahaye to STN, January 2, 1783.

96. Machuel to STN, November 6, 1775.

97. Pierre Godefroy, a merchant in Lyon and a confident of Ostervald's, passed on some advice he had received from Machuel, Rouen's leading bookseller: "Il me paraît n'être pas d'avis que vous étendiez votre confiance sur les libraires de bourgs et petites villes tels que Les Andelys et Forges. Tous ces gens-là, qui sont de vrais colporteurs, ne sont nullement bons; et on court avec eux les plus grands risques. Je suis aussi de cette opinion.... En général depuis dix ans, tout colporteur est devenu très douteux."

98. STN to Don Alphonse, marquis de Longhi, February 12, 1787; Ostervald and Bosset to STN, February 15, 1780.

Chapter 10

1. The following remarks about the STN's Paris correspondents are based on their dossiers in the STN archives, which can be identified according to their names.

2. Daudet sometimes used a pseudonym, comte de Lambergen, and therefore his extensive correspondence with the STN was filed under both names in ms. 1139 and ms. 1173.

3. Daudet to STN, August 28, 1770: "Vous savez que la prohibition est un furieux attrait dans notre capitale et qu'un livre qui vaut 3 L. chez vous en vaut 6 et 9 ici. On vient de décerner les honneurs du fagot à quelques uns; cela a augmenté sur le champ d'un tiers leur valeur numérique." In a letter of February 15, 1771, Daudet recommended that the STN make the *Journal helvétique* more radical: "Tâchez de rendre vos articles bien intéressants; rendez compte de tous les livres défendus."

4. The STN's letter with a covering note by Vallat is in the BnF, Collection Anisson Duperron, ms. fr. 22109.

5. In a letter to the STN of April 2, 1781, Quandet formally described himself as a "négociant-commissionnaire," and in other letters, he insisted on the importance of "négociant" as part of his professional self-description. The following account is based on Quandet's rich dossier of 137 letters in the STN archives, which has already been the subject of an article by Charly Guyot: "Un correspondant parisien de la Société typographique de Neuchâtel: Quandet de Lachenal," *Musée neuchâtelois* 23, nrs. 1 and 2 (1936), 20–28 and 64–74. In going over the same material, this chapter is intended to explain Quandet's role in relation to the pirating activities of the STN.

6. I have described Le Senne's attempt to survive as a hack writer in "The Life of a "Poor Devil" in the Republic of Letters," in *Essays on the Age of Enlightenment in Honor of Ira O. Wade*, Jean Macary, ed. (Geneva and Paris, 1977), 39–92.

7. Ostervald to Quandet, February 4, 1781. In a letter of February 25, 1781, Ostervald described Goezman as "un homme d'une belle figure, parlant d'or, jadis conseiller dans la Grand'Chambre, très savant publiciste, du reste ne valant pas un clou à soufflet, qui nous doit 4,500 L. au moins."

8. STN to Quandet, March 12, 1781.

9. In a later letter, dated November 25, 1781, Ostervald modified the message slightly by saying the STN would publish the book if Delisle could get a firm commitment from a Parisian bookseller to buy 600 copies.

10. Ostervald to David-Alphonse de Sandoz-Rollin, March 22, 1781.

11. Ostervald explained the STN's suspicions about Panckoucke in letters to Plomteux of March 10 and April 3, 1781. Having enlisted Plomteux to look into the speculation on the *Méthodique*, he instructed Quandet, in a letter of April 29, 1781, to cease the investigation of Panckoucke.

12. STN to Grimm, April 22, 1781. Ostervald wrote on the recommendation of a Russian princess who had visited Neuchâtel. Grimm replied in a letter of April 30, 1781, that he only received orders from Catherine II and did not take initiatives of his own. Nevertheless, he agreed to mention the STN's request. If, as he expected, Catherine did not reply to it, the STN should conclude that she had refused.

13. On the pamphleteering and the background to it, see Léonard Burnand, *Les Pamphlets contre Necker: Médias et imaginaire politique au XVIIIe siècle* (Garnier, Paris, 2009).

14. STN to Frantin, a bookseller in Dijon, September 27, 1781.

15. In a letter of October 9, 1781, Ostervald explained the background to the publication of the *Collection complète* to Charles-Antoine Charmet, a bookseller in Besançon.

16. In letters of June 4 and 15, 1781, Quandet recounted his conversations with Mercier and Mercier's activities. In a letter to Quandet of May 13, Ostervald reported that Mercier had avowed his authorship to Lenoir, and in a letter of September 11 he wrote that Mercier had toned down the text because he wanted to be allowed back in France. According to one version of Mercier's meeting with Lenoir, Mercier appeared before the *lieutenant général de la police* with a copy of the *Tableau* and said, "Voici en même temps le livre et l'auteur": Jean-Claude Bonnet, "Introduction," *Tableau de Paris* 1 (Mercure de France, Paris, 1994), xxix. The following account draws on research by Michel Schlup, which should lead to an important book about Samuel Fauche. See Michel Schlup, "Les querelles et les intrigues autour de l'édition du *Tableau de Paris* de Louis-Sébastien Mercier (1781–1783)," in *L'Édition neuchâteloise au siècle des Lumières: La Société typographique de Neuchâtel (1769–1789)*, Michel Schlup, ed. (Bibliothèque publique et universitaire, Neuchâtel, 2002), 131–141.

17. Quandet to Ostervald, September 3, 1781. On September 25 Ostervald replied that he had hidden this information from Mercier and that the STN would be happy to publish the rival *Tableau de Paris*: "Il faut tâcher d'obtenir que ce second peintre nous fasse gagner de l'argent comme le premier et souhaiter à ce prix que la providence en multiplie l'espèce."

18. Quandet to Ostervald, June 4, 1781: "Ce Monsieur est plein de génie et d'adresse. La portion congrue que lui donne M. son père l'a rendu un intrigant, honnêtement

s'entend. . . . Il fait un peu de commerce, soit dit entre nous, et je compte infiniment sur lui pour un de nos meilleurs débitants moyennant certaine remise."

19. Quandet to STN, February 20, 1782. By this time Grimod had ceased to write for the *Journal helvétique*.

20. This is my impression from reading Poinçot's dossier of 157 letters in the STN archives. It is a rich source about the bookselling operations in Versailles and deserves a monograph of its own.

21. On March 22, 1782, Quandet reported that the price of the *Tableau de Paris* had dropped by 30 percent, owing to the influx of pirated editions. He also claimed that Mercier had alienated the public by padding the two new volumes and cutting parts of the two old ones: "Je doute que l'auteur puisse se laver devant le même public de la supercherie évidente qui règne d'un bout à l'autre de cet ouvrage." Quandet made several negative remarks about Mercier after the arrival of the new edition in Paris. His criticism reached Mercier in Neuchâtel, who replied, according to a report transmitted by Ostervald and repeated in a letter by Quandet to Ostervald of April 15, 1782, "Il [Quandet] a manqué d'honnêteté à mon égard et même de justice, car il devrait savoir que ce n'est pas à lui qu'il appartient de juger l'intention et l'oeuvre de l'auteur, qui en sait plus que lui sur la forme et la publication. . . . Qu'il fasse son métier sans juger autrui, et qu'il me laisse faire le mien."

22. Quandet to Ostervald, June 20, 1781: "Je serais enchanté, et pour vous et pour moi, que nous ayons des *Vie privée de Louis XV* et autres articles de ce genre que vous m'annoncez. Ils seraient sans doute de grand debit." Quandet's remark on the libel about Marie-Antoinette, in a letter of January 14, 1782, would seem to disprove the claim of some historians that no such works were published before the Revolution: "Les justes et légitimes recherches que l'on fait d'un ouvrage infâme sur le compte de la reine intitulé en premier *La Vie d'Antoinette* et depuis *Supplément à l'Espion anglais*, pour le faire passer plus aisément sous ce titre moins scabreux en apparence, occasionnent les plus rigoureuses perquisitions et feront saisir encore bien des balles." However, Quandet might have reported only a rumor, because the *Supplément à l'Espion anglais, ou lettres intéressantes sur la retraite de M. Necker, sur le sort de la France et de l'Angleterre, et sur la détention de M. Linguet à la Bastille: Adressées à Milord All'Eye; Par l'auteur de l'Espion anglais* ("Londres," 1782), attributed to Joseph Lanjuinais, was not an attack on the queen: see Hervé Guénot, "Lanjuinais, Joseph" in *Dictionnaire des journalistes*, Jean Sgard, ed., vol. 2 (Voltaire Foundation, Oxford, 1999), 563.

23. Quandet's account was confirmed by Widow La Noue in a letter to the STN of September 8, 1782.

24. Quandet to Ostervald, September 16, 1782. Quandet might also have acted as a police informer, perhaps to ingratiate himself with Martin, because he attributed the denunciations that had ruined him to "les gens du métier et surtout la basse jalousie de quelques uns d'eux dont j'ai eu plus d'une fois occasion de démasquer les turpitudes et les friponneries."

25. Quandet to Ostervald, October 17, 1782: "Je vous assure que vos démarches sont éclairées de près de chez vous par des espions de notre police. . . . Les *Fastes de Louis*

XV dont vous me parlez font avec les *Lettres de cachet* et cette autre infamie intitulée je crois *L'Espion cuirassé* ou *dévalisé* un bruit affreux. Ce sont ces ouvages avec un autre encore plus infâme écrit contre notre auguste et respectable souveraine qui ont occasionné toutes les recherches et toutes les saisies qui ont été faites." Despite the new note of horror about forbidden books in his letters, Quandet favored Ostervald's intention to reprint *Vie privée de Louis XV*. His other recommendations at this time were minimal. He advised against reprinting a genealogical treatise related to Germany and a life of Cardinal Dubois, and he favored a tract on contemporary Turkey and two works concerning the theater.

26. The "Registre de la librairie pour l'année 1782" in BnF, Collection Anisson Duperron, ms. fr. 21863, noted two petitions in favor of Quandet, one from his wife and one from Antoine Barthès de Marmorières, maréchal des Gardes Suisses and a correspondent of the STN in Versailles. In letters to Ostervald of January 16 and February 10, 1783, Barthès described his fruitless efforts to persuade the authorities to end Quandet's exile. In a letter of November 12, 1783, he wrote that Quandet's wife had gained access to Quandet's secret depot of books in Versailles and had sold them off. Moreover, she was not his wife at all, he claimed, but "une odieuse et perfide concubine." The STN also received negative reports about Quandet from one of its other confidential correspondents in Paris, David Alphonse de Sandoz Rollin (letter of February 24, 1783), and from an underground dealer named Thiriot, who wrote on August 28, 1783, "Son nom révolte à la police, et c'est indisposer contre soi-même que d'y parler de lui." Despite Quandet's unsuccessful intervention with Cugnet and his wife, the STN also failed to recover their debt, which eventually amounted to 830 L. 11 sous. Their extensive dossier in the STN archives reveals a great deal about the struggle for survival in the underground book trade of Paris. The STN's banker in Paris, Paul de Pourtalès, wrote on June 23, 1784, "Cugné [sic] et sa femme sont des bandits sans moeurs et sans pudeur. Lui, sa femme, et sa fille [sont] réprouvés d'un chacun. On ne leur confierait pas un sol. Il y a six mois qu'ils ont vendu leur misérable boutique."

Chapter 11

1. Records for the travel expenses of Ostervald and Bosset have disappeared along with their personal papers. But Bertrand kept a careful account of expenditures during a business trip to Lyon in 1773: Bertrand, "Carnet de voyage," ms. 1058. They included "Perruquier 4-4-0" [that is, 4 livres, 4 sous, 0 deniers]; "Guide 2-2-0"; "Pipe 0-14-0"; "Ruban pour moi 0-7-0"; "Gazette 0-2-9"; "Comédie 2-2-0"; and "Coiffures 7-14-0".

2. The letters from Ostervald and Bosset are in two, overlapping dossiers of the STN papers: mss. 1189 and 1125. There is also information about Ostervald's travels in his "carnet de voyage" of 1774, ms. 1056.

3. In a letter to the STN of July 13, 1773, Rozier said that he did not participate in the mundane side of intellectual life in Paris: "Les gens de lettres sont faits pour s'aider mutuellement, vérité dont sont bien peu convaincus ceux de Paris qui se déchirent de la manière la plus honteuse; aussi je n'en connais que très peu." Later letters indicated

that he had close ties with Malesherbes and d'Alembert. On January 23, 1774, he expressed sympathy with the Swiss in general: "Quoique habitant de Paris, j'aime mieux la bonne franchise des Suisses. Je n'ai pas encore perdu dans cette ville celle que j'ai apportée du fond de ma province." After he got to know Ostervald personally, his letters—for example, one written on July 19, 1775—became especially warm and friendly.

4. Because Ostervald's calculations are relevant for the history of printing and publishing, his letter to the home office of the STN, dated June 5, 1775, is worth quoting at some length. "M. de Gébelin prit la plume et se dirigeant par l'ouvrage qu'il fait imprimer actuellement, supposant que l'on tirât à mille, calcula comme suit:

La composition et tirage coûte par feuille de 1,000	22 livres
Papier, 2 rames à 10 livres, à cause de l'impôt	20
Correction par feuilles	10 [sous]
Assemblage	4
En tout	42-14

He then calculated the cost of the *Cours de mathématiques* as follows: "la composition 6 livres, le tirage 4 livres 10 sous, papier 2 rames 15 livres, [fraix] 2 livres 10 sous." Therefore, its total cost per sheet came to 28 L. If the STN charged the author 36 L. per sheet, it made a profit of 8 L. per sheet. Assuming the book contained 20 sheets, the charge to the author would have been 720 L. and the production cost 560 L, leaving the STN a profit of 160 L., or 22 percent of the cost. After working through this calculation, Ostervald wrote, "Il me paraît que je puis traiter sur ce pied là . . . , d'autant plus qu'il n'y a nul risque à courir suivant M.de Gébelin et qu'il se charge d'introduire, d'obtenir des permissions et [de] nous indiquer les meilleurs livres à mettre sous presse pour le goût non des frivolistes mais des gens comme il faut d'ici." In a letter to Gébelin written on July 18, 1775, three days after their discussion, Ostervald said that the STN could print books for 25 percent less than the rate charged by Parisian printers. As a rough indicator, he said that the STN would charge 9 deniers per sheet for each copy of an ordinary book printed at a run of 1,000 copies.

5. However, after calling on him for a second time, Ostervald wrote that Dorat planned to have a new edition of his works published in Paris and did not want it to be undercut by a STN *contrefaçon*. Furthermore, "On le dit attaché à la matière et rançonnant un peu ceux qui l'impriment." The STN published a great deal of his writing, notably *Les Malheurs de l'inconstance* (1773) and *Collection complète des oeuvres de M. Dorat* (1776–1780) in nine volumes. The STN put its name on the title pages of these works, but there is no evidence that it paid Dorat for his cooperation in their reprinting.

6. After leaving Paris, Ostervald wrote to the STN from Rouen, where Miromesnil had been *premier président* of the parlement, on June 20, 1775: "On m'avait offert à Paris de mettre en jeu la sultane favorite, mais on est ici d'avis différent, fondé sur ce que le Garde des Sceaux, extrêmement jalousé par tous ceux qui l'environnent et homme

d'esprit, est très attentif à ne pas se montrer trop accessible par ce canal, d'autant plus qu'on sait qu'il est très galant."

7. In a letter to Bosset dated June 2, 1780, after Ostervald had returned to Neuchâtel, Morellet wrote that he was pleased "de vous avoir mis en liaison avec nos gens de lettres." The following account is based on Morellet's dossier in the STN archives, which is now available online at www.e-enlightenment.com/coffeehouse/project/ morellet 2011.

8. Among the many studies of the social and economic position of writers in the eighteenth century, the work of Maurice Pellisson still provides the best overview: *Les Hommes de lettres au XVIIIe siècle* (Armand Colin, Paris, 1911).

9. Mercier, *De la littérature et des littérateurs* (Yverdon, Switzerland, 1778), 38.

10. Morellet had commented on the edicts of May 30, 1777, in a letter to Ostervald of December 17, 1777, "Les règlements de la librairie dont vous me parlez sont désapprouvés de presque tous les gens de lettres. On blâme surtout le Conseil d'avoir donné un effet rétrospectif à sa loi et de détruire des privilèges anciens qui ont été regardés par ceux qui les possédaient comme autant de propriétés commerçables entrant dans des partages de famille, etc. La loi bornée seulement aux privilèges à vendre n'aurait pas été désapprouvée si généralement, quoiqu'il faille convenir qu'elle est contraire aux intérêts des gens de lettres indivisibles d'avec ceux des libraires avec lesquels ils traitent. Quant à ceux qui garderaient pour eux leurs ouvrages, ce cas où la loi favorise les lettres est trop rare. Presque aucun auteur ne peut faire d'avances et profiter des droits que la loi lui laisse."

11. Morellet referred to the plans for Naigeon's work in an undated note written in April 1780 and in letters of June 2 and October 20, 1780. Bosset mentioned it in letters to the home office of May 12 and June 19, 1780.

12. In a letter to the STN of May 12, 1780, Bosset reported that Mably was "fort incertain" that the authorities would permit his book to circulate in France. Bosset also mentioned it in two undated notes in his dossier, ms. 1125. In the first, addressed to Ostervald, he sounded skeptical about the financial aspect of publishing Mably: "À propos de l'abbé Mably, si vous imprimez son manuscrit, à plus forte raison ses oeuvres, vous avez sans doute, Monsieur, trouvé à les placer." In the second, to Mme Bertrand, Bosset wrote, "J'ai été présent en effet que M. votre père a demandé à M. l'abbé Mably le manuscrit et qu'il lui a promis 200 exemplaires qu'il lui a demandés." The STN dealt with Mably through the intermediary of David Alphonse de Sandoz Rollin, the Swiss secretary to the Prussian ambassador in Versailles. In a letter to the STN of February 16, Sandoz Rollin wrote that Mably expected to send other manuscripts to the STN if he was pleased with its printing of *Du gouvernement et des lois de la Pologne*. On April 18, he reported on Mably's reaction to the first copies he received: "Il se loue du caractère de l'impression et du papier, mais il se plaint amèrement des fautes qui s'y trouvent en grand nombre: des mots substitués, des phrases entières oubliées, des contre sens."

13. Jean-Marie Bruyset, a major publisher-bookseller in Lyon who published d'Alembert's *Mélanges de littérature, d'histoire et de philosophie*, informed the STN in a letter of January 26, 1775, that he had paid d'Alembert handsomely for the manuscript: "Nous

avons payé 1,200 livres pour le tome 5 seul des Mélanges de d'Alembert." In a letter of April 20, 1774, Bruysset referred to "des honoraires que nous payons quelque fois à raison de quarante francs la feuille d'impression."

14. In a letter of June 14, 1780, Bosset reported on d'Alembert's proposal to publish "un volume d'opuscules octavo" and "trois volumes environ d'éloges." The latter probably corresponded to d'Alembert's *Histoire des membres de l'Académie française* (1785), which was published as a sequel to his *Éloges lus dans les séances publiques de l'Académie française* (1779). Despite the mutual goodwill, the STN never published anything by d'Alembert, who died in 1783 at the age of sixty-five.

15. Ostervald and Bosset did not mention Condorcet in their letters of 1780, but they probably ran into him at one of their meetings and dinners, and they met him during their trip to Paris in 1777. In 1780 he was collaborating actively with d'Alembert and Suard on the preparation of the *Encyclopédie méthodique*, and in 1781 the STN published his antislavery tract, *Réflexions sur l'esclavage des nègres* "par M. Schwartz, pasteur du Saint-Evangile à Bienne." Bienne was a Swiss city located close to Neuchâtel.

16. On April 14, 1780, Ostervald and Bosset informed the STN that they had not received a reply to a letter they had written to Franklin. In an undated letter to the STN (probably from February 1783), Morellet wrote, "Je ferai votre commission auprès de M. Franklin. J'ai cependant peine à croire qu'il y ait rien à faire en ce genre en Amérique. On n'y lit guère de français, et tout ce qui peut s'imprimer en anglais se fera ou en Amérique ou à Londres—plutôt même à Londres qu'en Amérique, parce que les prix de main d'oeuvre seront encore bien longtemps infiniment trop haut en Amérique pour soutenir la concurrence des Européens." But on March 23, 1783, Morellet wrote that he now believed that the STN could profitably set up a deposit of its books to be sold on commission in America, and he said he would discuss this possibility with Franklin. In a letter of May 31, 1783, he said that Franklin, though terribly busy negotiating the treaty to end the American war, would reply to an inquiry on this subject from the STN. Nothing ever came of the STN's plan to expand its business to the new republic.

17. I have made all of Brissot's letters available on my website, robertdarnton.org. The following account summarizes the study of Brissot's prerevolutionary career that I published online as J. P. Brissot, *His Career and Correspondence 1779–1787* (The Voltaire Foundation, Oxford, 2001), http://www.voltaire.ox.ac.uk/vf-etc.

18. The following account is based on Goezman's dossier (forty-four letters) in the STN archives, ms. 1158, and the STN's correspondence with its contacts and representatives in Paris and Versailles: Quandet, its general agent; Perregaux, its banker; Bailleux, its attorney; and Du Terraux, a Swiss employee in the department of the Maison du Roi who knew Goezman and sent reports about him while trying to get him to pay his debt to the STN.

19. As will be explained, Goezman's text went through several incarnations and never got beyond volume 1. I have consulted the version in the Bibliothèque nationale de France published anonymously under the title *Histoire politique du gouvernement français, ou Les quatre âges de la monarchie française* ("chez Grangé," Paris, 1777).

The text rejects the notion, favored by the Parlement, that the authority of the Crown derived from a primitive contract with the nation, such as a supposed pact created in an assembly at the Champ de mars, and that the Parlement or its predecessor in the Estates General was therefore coeval with the monarchy. It grounds this argument in a historical and juridical account of the evolution of royal power, which it supports with elaborate documentary evidence. It also eliminates any role for the Church in political affairs—a position that would justify an attempt by the Maupeou ministry to overcome the Church's exemption from taxation.

20. A friend of Ostervald named Du Terraux, who was employed in the department of the Maison du Roi, tried to collect payment for the STN from Goezman in 1772 but noted in a letter of February 10, 1772, "Ces Messieurs de ce nouveau parlement sont très mal payés des appointements attachés à leurs places." Du Terraux was also a friend of Goezman's and originally put him in contact with the STN.

21. The intermediary, Du Terraux, made repeated attempts to collect Goezman's debt until November 1783, when he gave up and advised the STN to begin legal proceedings. His letters appear both in his dossier in the STN archives and in Goezman's.

22. While applying pressure to get Goezman to pay his debt, the STN threatened to denounce him before the public in a memoir that would reinforce Beaumarchais's memoirs. In a letter to him of November 16, 1773, it warned that it would take its case to the public and concluded, "Il est clair que nous allons par là donner le plus beau jeu à ceux de vos compatriotes qui ont sujet de ne pas vous vouloir du bien. . . . Vous n'avez qu'un seul moyen de prévenir cet orage dont vous devez redouter les effets dans la conjoncture critique où vous vous trouvez. C'est d'aller au reçu de notre lettre payer à Perregaux la somme que vous nous devez."

23. In a letter to the home office of June 7, 1775, Ostervald made his reasoning clear, although he did not go into detail: "Mon homme a été frappé de ma proposition. . . . Ses associés et lui dans l'entreprise ne peuvent se tirer d'affaire et éviter une perte certaine qu'à l'aide de cet expédient. Il m'a demandé le temps de le leur communiquer. Vous devinez mes vues. Si je ne me trompe, voilà l'occasion d'être payé et de gagner encore, bien entendu qu'on y mettra toutes les herbes de la St. Jean."

24. Goezman's career as a spy can be followed in the archives of the French ministry of foreign affairs. I have drawn on them to recount his relations with the expatriate French libelers in London during the 1780s. See Darnton, *The Devil in the Holy Water or the Art of Slander from Louis XIV to Napoleon* (W. W. Norton, New York, 2009), chaps. 2, 3, 11, and 12.

25. In a letter to the STN of February 3, 1784, Brissot protested against this fraud and used it as an argument to get better terms for the repayment of his debt after his release from the Bastille. See the section on Brissot in my website, robertdarnton.org.

26. The following account is based on Mercier's correspondence with the STN, which has already been studied by Charly Guyot: *De Rousseau à Mirabeau: Pélerins de Môtiers et prophètes de 1789* (Éditions Victor Attinger, Neuchâtel, 1936), 81–126. On the *Tableau de Paris*, see Michel Schlup, "Les Querelles et les intrigues autour de l'édition du *Tableau de Paris* de Louis-Sébastien Mercier (1781–1783)" in *L'Édition neuchâteloise au siècle des Lumière: La Société typographique de Neuchâtel (1769–1789)*, Michel

Schlup, ed. (Bibliothèque publique et universitaire de Neuchâtel, Neuchâtel, 2002), 130–141.

27. In "Les Querelles et les intrigues autour de l'édition du *Tableau de Paris*," p. 140, Michel Schlup quotes a letter by Mercier of December 16, 1784, in which he makes a disparaging remark about the directors of the STN. I believe Mercier was not referring to Ostervald but rather to the directors who took over after the financial collapse of the STN at the end of 1783. Mercier published the first two volumes of *Mon bonnet de nuit* (1784) with the STN and the last two with Heubach. The STN did not publish Mercier's other great bestseller, *L'An deux mille quatre cent quarante*, which went through at least twenty-five editions between 1771 and 1787.

28. On August 16, 1771, he wrote to the STN, "Depuis deux ans que mon ouvrage est fini, l'amour paternel s'est assez ralenti pour en connaître les défauts. . . . En général, j'y aperçois chaque jour des mots peu corrects, des phrases louches, des métaphores peu exactes. Comme je ne doute pas que vous ne soyez très en état de rectifier tous ces défauts, non seulement je le permets, mais je vous en prie."

29. Gilibert to STN, June 15, 1773. The following account is based on Gilibert's dossier in the STN papers supplemented by letters from some of its correspondents in Lyon, notably Schodelli, Schaub, and Widow Reguilliat. On January 3, 1775, in a letter to Schaub, who was then a shipping agent of the STN, Ostervald described Gilibert as "un homme en place, qui tient un état honorable dans la société." During the Revolution, Gilibert sympathized with the Girondists and was elected mayor of Lyon in 1793.

30. On November 6, 1775, André Schodelli, the STN's shipping agent in Lyon, informed it that Gilibert had left the city four months ago and was rumored to have gone to Russia.

31. Valmont de Bomare to STN, February 22, 1773. Apparently Bomare did not expect any compensation for this service: "S'il m'arrivait pendant le courant de cette édition [of Brunet] des observations remarquables qui n'auraient pas été insérées dans l'édition de Paris, et que vous en fassiez ensuite la vôtre à Neuchâtel, vous pourriez m'écrire dans le temps et m'indiquer par quelle voie je pourrais vous les faire passer, pour le bien du lecteur, mais à la condition que vous ne me nommerez pas, ne voulant absolument ne me jamais donner aucun mauvais vernis."

32. Ostervald to Quandet, November 25, 1781.

33. Holland's dossier of twenty-nine letters and the STN's replies provide a detailed record of relations between an author and his publisher. In a letter of November 6, 1771, he left payment entirely up to the STN: "Je m'en remets entièrement à la discrétion de la Société typographique, qui déterminera le mieux la proportion qui doit se trouver entre l'honoraire de l'auteur et le profit qu'elle tire de son travail." The poor quality of the printing resulted from the STN's difficulties in setting up its shop during its first two first years. Looking backward on its dealings with Holland, Ostervald observed in a letter to him of September 3, 1773, "Nous sommes fort fâchés, Monsieur, d'avoir un peu exercé votre patience. La nôtre a été quelque fois à l'épreuve aussi. C'est là le train de la vie."

34. The STN published Castiglione's *Observations sur le livre intitulé "Système de la nature*," 2 vols., in 1772. His memoir, addressed "Au Magistrat," dated March 14, 1772, and accompanied by a note by Ostervald, appears in his dossier in the STN papers.

35. The agreement, included in a letter from d'Auberteuil to the STN of November 10, 1779, read, "Pour tirer in-12. Accepté à 35 livres la feuille tirée sur 1000 tout compris, même assemblage." The letter confirmed this arrangement in greater detail. Although d'Auberteuil's dossier in the STN papers has some gaps that make his story difficult to reconstruct, he clearly belonged to the category of "mauvais débiteurs" who failed to pay their bills. Apparently the STN published a short work, *Mémoires pour et contre les "Considérations sur Saint-Domingue"* rather than the full text of the *Considérations*.

36. Antoine Barthès de Marmorières, a trusted correspondent of the STN in Versailles, wrote on Octobre 2, 1781, "M. d'Auberteuil est sans ressource, mais il vous faut écraser le ministre de la marine de lettres, en écrire même à M. de Vergennes." On July 25, 1784, he wrote that d'Auberteuil had accumulated many other debts and could not be located. David-Alphonse de Sandoz Rollin, another confidant of the STN in Versailles, reported on d'Auberteuil in a letter of March 12, 1781: "L'ouvrage dont il est question a été prohibé sévèrement (si je suis bien instruit) et son entrée en France défendue. L'auteur a été destitué de son office de procureur général à La Grenade et rappelé, ce qui n'annonce pas une conduite sage et réglée."

37. Servan's reply to the STN, dated March 17, 1780, expressed a view of the Swiss that was widely held at that time: "Je suis infiniment sensible, Messieurs, aux louanges que vous voulez bien donner à des rêveries qui ne peuvent être excusés que par l'amour de la patrie et de l'humanité qui les a dictés et qui doit les faire supporter. Je serais trop enorgueilli si des Suisses, si des hommes libres, si des êtres autant intéressants par leur manière de vivre que par leur façon de penser m'assuraient avec la franchise helvétique que quelques unes de mes idées ont véritablement mérité leur attention et leur approbation."

38. STN to Servan, June 14, 1781.

39. *Le Soldat Citoyen, ou vues patriotiques sur la manière la plus avantageuse de pourvoir à la défense du royaume* (1780). The title page gave no place of publication other than "Dans le pays de la liberté." Writing anonymously, Servan expressed respect for Louis XVI and avoided criticism of the Church, but he advanced radical proposals for reforms on all fronts, including taxation. He argued for the creation of a new kind of army or "milice nationale" inspired by "l'amour de la patrie et de l'humanité" (p. 456), and he adopted a Rousseauistic argument about national sovereignty and the social contract (pp. 79 and 86). Although he opposed aristocratic privilege in the officer corps, he acknowledged the aristocracy as "un état dont l'honneur doit faire la base" (p. 51), and he invoked "l'honneur, cette divinité de notre ancienne chevalerie" (p. 50).

40. Servan to STN, February 27, 1782.

41. Estimates involve some guesswork, because they must be based on imperfect sources. But I believe that a conservative estimate of the number of authors in France in 1789 is at least 3,000. See my essay, "The Facts of Literary Life in Eighteenth-Century France,"

in *The Political Culture of the Old Regime*, Keith Baker, ed. (Oxford University Press, Oxford, 1987), 261–291.

42. The following chapter discusses the evidence for the decline of sales and the increase of bankruptcies among booksellers after 1775.

43. Each of these authors has a dossier under his name in the archives of the STN. I have discussed the career of Le Senne at length: "A Pamphleteer on the Run," in *The Literary Underground of the Old Regime* (Harvard University Press, Cambridge, MA., 1982), 71–121. In the case of Béraud, the STN received reports from two of its correspondents in Geneva. On March 23, 1775, Louis Marcinhes, a merchant, wrote, "Le fait est que la misère l'a forcé à fuir, qu'il est absorbé de dettes et chargé d'enfants." And on June 6, 1775, Léonard Bourdillon, *directeur des coches de France*, wrote that Béraud had decided to "décamper, après avoir écrit à Monsieur le syndic de l'hôpital pour lui recommander sa femme et ses enfants." On February 22, 1774, Béraud had informed the STN that he could not pay his printing debt: "J'avais composé et fait imprimé cette comédie dans l'espérance que son produit me tirerait de l'indigence, et j'ai été cruellement trompé . . . Il m'est douleureux, dis-je, de me voir forcé d'être fripon avec tous les sentiments d'un honnête homme."

Chapter 12

1. There were 4 kreutzer to 1 batz and 10 batzen to 1 Neuchâtel livre. Seven Neuchâtel livres equaled 10 standard French livres tournois. On these sums and finance in general, see Samuel Ricard, *Traité général du commerce* (Amsterdam, 1781), which is the main source for the following discussion. Among other eighteenth-century treatises on money and commercial practices, the best known is *Le Parfait Négociant* by Jacques Savary, available in an excellent edition by Edouard Richard (Droz, Geneva, 2011), 2 vols. However, *Le Parfait Négociant*, first published in 1675, was out of date in some respects by 1770, despite frequent revised editions published throughout the eighteenth century. The *Encyclopédie* of Diderot and d'Alembert contains several articles on money and finances, but they lack details about actual practices. See, for example, "Lettre de change," "Commerce," "Banque," and "Monnoie." For a detailed discussion of wages and work in the STN's printing shop, see Rychner, "Le travail de l'atelier," 275–287; and Darnton, *The Business of Enlightenment*, 212–227. On wages and earning power in France, see C.-E. Labrousse, *Esquisse du mouvement des prix et des revenus en France au XVIIIᵉ siècle* (Paris, 1932), 447–456; Pierre Léon's contribution to *Histoire économique et sociale de la France*, C.-E. Labrousse, ed., 2 (Paris, 1970), 651–693; and George Rudé, *The Crowd in the French Revolution* (Oxford University Press, Oxford, 1959), 21–22. The price of bread, which varied enormously according to quality and grain yields, is discussed in Steven Laurence Kaplan, *The Bakers of Paris and the Bread Question 1700–1775* (Duke University Press, Durham, NC, 1996), chap. 18. Among the many works on money, two provide general, contrasting views: Marie-Laure Legay, *Histoire de l'argent à l'époque moderne: De la renaissance à la Révolution* (Armand

Colin, Paris, 2014); and William M. Reddy, *Money and Liberty in Modern Europe: A Critique of Historical Understanding* (Cambridge University Press, Cambridge, 1987).

2. Giacomo Casanova, *Histoire de ma vie*, Jean M. Goulemot, ed. (Librairie générale française, Paris, 2014), 214.

3. Unfortunately, the STN's *Grands livres* have disappeared, but its archives contain a rich array of account books in which one can follow the posting of transactions from the concrete to the abstract.

4. On the Caisse d'Escompte, see Léon Say, *Histoire de la Caisse d'Escompte, 1776 à 1793* (P. Regnier, Reims, France, 1848); and on the connections between finance and attitudes toward usury and money, see the fundamental work of Herbert Luethy, *La Banque Protestante en France, de la Révocation de l'Édit de Nantes à la Révolution* 1–2 (S.E.V.P.E.N., Paris, 1959–1961).

5. Bosset to STN, February 13, 1780.

6. Among the many works on credit, banking, accounting, and legal constraints, I have found the following to be especially useful: Romuald Szramkiewicz, *Histoire du droit des affaires* (Montchrestien, Paris, 1989); and Pierre Gervais, "Crédit et filières marchandes au XVIIIe siècle," *Annales: Histoire, Sciences Sociales* 67 (2012), 1011–1048.

7. I do not know of any study of the signature as an element in commercial exchange, but there is an important work on the signature as a cultural phenomenon: Béatrice Fraenkel, *La Signature: Genèse d'un signe* (Gallimard, Paris, 1992).

8. Another example of a printed circular came from Jean-François Pion of Pontarlier, who announced on November 12, 1787, that he had created a new company by making his son a partner: "La Société sera sous la raison de JEAN-FRANÇOIS PION ET FILS. Vous avez ci-bas nos signatures respectives auxquelles seules vous voudrez bien ajouter foi. J'ose me flatter, Messieurs, que vous daignerez continuer votre confiance à la nouvelle raison." Companies could also withdraw the formal right to make a signature. When Heubach reorganized his company as the Société typographique de Lausanne, he took as a partner Louis Scanavan, who also continued a separate line of business. In 1775 that business collapsed and Scanavan fled. Heubach wrote to the STN on June 7, 1775, "Le public vous aura sans doute appris l'évasion de notre ci-devant sieur Scanavin et la faillite qu'il vient de faire. Nous vous prions en conséquence de ne plus reconnaître sa signature pour bonne." On June 13, 1775, Heubach sent a printed circular about the reorganized Société typographique de Lausanne with the sample signatures of its two partners, Heubach himself and Jean-Pierre Duplan, "auxquelles il vous plaira d'ajouter foi et en prendre note, pour n'avoir désormais de confiance qu'en ces deux seulement."

9. Pott to STN, December 28, 1781.

10. Matthieu to STN, July 4, 1782.

11. STN to Bergeret, January 23, 1777.

12. Diderot, *Jacques le fataliste* in Diderot, *Oeuvres* (Gallimard, Paris, 1951), 665. Unlike many notes, a bill of exchange bound the correspondent (payer) to make an immediate payment and could not be delayed under any pretext, such as the objection that the correspondent had not received adequate notification in advance.

13. On early modern bankruptcy, see *The History of Bankruptcy: Economic, Social and Cultural Implication in Early Modern Europe*, Thomas Max Safley, ed. (Routledge, London, 2013), especially the chapters by Jérôme Sgard and Natacha Coquery. *Faillite* can be translated as "bankruptcy" and sometimes was used as a synonym for *banqueroute*, but in fact it was very different from the kind of bankruptcy that took place in England, which was judged in common law courts and frequently led to the liquidation of a firm, although legislation of 1705 opened up some possibility for a fresh start. In France, the debtors often initiated a *faillite* by deposing a balance sheet with a notary or other authorized person, making their accounts available for verification, and negotiating a schedule for the repayment of the debt with the creditors. Although the creditors would suffer losses, they would gain more than they could get by forcing the liquidation of the business, for the debtor could continue his trade and pay them off according to an agreed schedule. By entering into private negotiations, sometimes even from a hiding place, the debtor would try to persuade the creditors to grant favorable terms. If they agreed, the case could be resolved without legal action. If only a majority of them agreed, it could go before a *cour consulaire,* or commercial court, an efficient institution composed of merchants who acted outside the state's judicial system. The court would then decide on a final settlement, which would be binding on all parties. The STN archives contain several references to this procedure and also correspondence indicating settlements arrived at privately, without resort to *juridiction consulaire*. In addition to the STN archives, this account is based on a reading of all the bankruptcy cases concerning booksellers in the Archives de la Seine (now renamed as the Archives de Paris), 4B6 and 5B6.

14. The following account is based on Manoury's dossier of sixty-five letters in the STN papers and the supplementary dossiers of two of the STN's contacts in Caen: Massieu de Clerval, a merchant, and Le Sueur, a lawyer. I have written an extended account of Manoury and his trade in *Édition et sédition*, 87–104.

15. Manoury's declaration took the form of a circular letter addressed to his creditors, copied out by a scribe and dated September 27, 1778. In the copy sent to the STN, he added a note indicating that he would make his accounts available for inspection by its representative in Caen, Massieu de Clerval.

16. The following account is based on Gerlache's dossier of fifty-nine letters in the STN papers and the complementary dossiers of Jean-Louis de Boubers of Brussels and C.-C. Duvez of Nancy. There are scraps of information about Gerlache's early career as a peddler and smuggler in a report from the police inspector Joseph d'Hémery to A.-R.-J.-G. Gabriel de Sartine, lieutenant general of police, July 11, 1765, and a letter from Bonin, a peddler, to d'Hémery of June 28, 1767, in BnF, F.F., ms. 22096.

17. Batilliot to STN, December 1, 1776. The circular described Batilliot's functions as follows: "Mon état particulier est celui de la banque, principalement avec tout le corps de la libairie, tant de Paris que de province, avec lequel je fais pour plus d'un million d'affaires par an. Je vous offre mes services à ce sujet, soit pour la négociation de vos billets, soit pour leur paiement à mon domicile, soit pour les acceptations que vous seriez dans le cas de faire ici."

18. Batilliot's ferocious bill collecting appears in several dossiers of the STN's debtors. For example, Jean-François Malherbe, an illegal dealer in Loudun, was driven desperate by Batilliot in 1784. After threatening to drag him to court, Batilliot sent a bailiff who confiscated 1,559 L. worth of books. The STN had let Malherbe run up debts for many years. On June 10, 1781, Batilliot notified it that he had handled a "remise sur Malherbe à Loudun protestée de 1,319 L. . . . Je l'ai envoyée à mon correspondant avec ordre de faire les poursuites nécessaires. . . . Si vous voulez en être payé, n'accordez aucune grâce audit sieur." On February 18, 1778, he had sent another warning: "Malherbe ne vaut rien du tout: méfiez-vous en."

19. Batilliot to STN, March 13, 1788. The following discussion comes from Batilliot's dossier of 101 letters in the STN papers.

20. Batilliot to STN, June 12, 1777: "Toutes fois que vous serez dans le moins de doute de la solidité de Messieurs nos libraires de province, je me ferai toujours un vrai plaisir de vous en rendre un fidel compte. La position de mes affaires me met à même de connaître la solidité de ces Messieurs, ne faisant autre commerce que celui de la banque, sur le papier de Messieurs nos libraires de Paris et de province seulement."

21. For example, on April 24, 1778, he wrote that Sombert, a small bookseller in Châlons-sur-Marne, could not honor a note: "Ledit sieur est un fripon, et je suis fâché que dans le temps vous ne m'en ayez point demandé information." And on January 9, 1781, he criticized the STN for dealing with Malherbe of Loudun: "Vous avez été un peu trop facile à faire crédit à des libraires aussi minces."

22. Batilliot might have received help from Panckoucke, who had saved him from bankruptcy in November 1778. See Darnton, *The Business of Enlightenment*, 326.

23. In *A Literary Tour de France*, I provide case studies of eighteen of the STN's regular customers. Rather than repeating that information, the following account is meant to show how financial conditions led to a crisis in the 1780s. It is based on a reading of virtually all the letters that the STN received from France. There is no valid statistical index to the state of the book trade during the last years of the Ancien Régime, but the number of *privilèges* and *permissions tacites* granted for books went into a steep decline in 1775. The number recovered, however, after 1782: François Furet, "La 'Librairie' du royaume de France au 18e siècle," in *Livre et société dans la France du XVIIIe siècle* (Mouton & Co., Paris, 1965), 8–9. See also Robert Estivals, *La Statistique bibliographique de la France sous la monarchie au XVIIIe siècle* (Mouton & Co., Paris, 1965), 247–248 and 296.

24. Archives départementales de la Seine, 4B6 and 5B6, contain thirty-nine dossiers and registers of booksellers from the period 1769 to 1789. In studying them, I found a great many references among the creditors and debtors of bankrupts to correspondents of the STN. A systematic study of these archives probably would reveal many overlapping commercial networks. Contrary to the previous remarks about chronology, most of the bankruptcies occurred in the 1770s rather than the 1780s.

25. Bernard to STN, October 25, 1779.

26. Claudet to STN, January 8, 1779: "La guerre fait sans doute un tort considérable à tout le royaume. Mais cette ville s'en sent particulièrement. Ce paiement a été on ne peut pas plus rude à raison de la quantité des banqueroutes."

27. Revol to STN, March 20, 1781: "L'espèce est très rare dans Lyon en égard aux emprunts qui se sont faits par l'État."

28. Fontanel to STN, August 28, 1782; Widow Charmet to STN, December 28, 1783.

29. Jean-Joseph Guichard of Avignon to STN, July 7, 1775.

30. In a letter of May 4, 1778, Buchet of Nîmes said that he could not pay two notes to the STN, owing to "l'inaction totale où se trouve notre commerce et celui de notre ville, inaction qui influe si fort sur tous les autres états."

31. Cazin to STN, January 1, 1780. As early as January 22, 1774, Chappuis frères of Bordeaux attributed "la dureté du présent temps" to the "surabondance des livres"—and went bankrupt ten months later. In a letter of May 3, 1777, de Gaulle of Joinville complained, "Le commerce est bien désavantageux dans la librairie. Il y a présentement trop de personnes qui s'en mêlent." In a letter of November 3, 1783, Joseph-Sulpice Grabit of Lyon expressed concern about "le public qui regorge de livres."

32. On Boubers's bankruptcy, see Chapter 2, this volume. The Delahaye dossier in the STN papers indicates that the company was directed by three associates and that all three were sent to prison in Brussels for dealing in forbidden books. After his release, in a letter to the STN of April 5, 1787, one of the three said they hoped to reach a settlement with their creditors, but Overman frères, the STN's representative in Brussels, had warned in a letter of August 31, 1785, that they were "ruinés totalement."

33. Flournois fils et Rainaldis to STN, March 10, 1781.

34. STN to Barthez de Marmorières, June 21, 1781, "Nous avons grand besoin de fonds, ayant été obligés de rembourser quelques dépôts à des personnes qui les ont placés dans les emprunts de Louis XVI, où tous les capitalistes se sont considérablement intéressés, ce qui rend l'argent d'une rareté étonnante."

35. Pott to STN, September 28, 1781; Flick to STN, August 7, 1783.

36. Several lists in the bankruptcy papers of booksellers (Archives départementales de la Seine, 4B6 and 5B6) illustrate the pervasive difficulty of collecting debts and of losses produced by the domino effect of *faillites*. Good examples of long lists of debtors can be found in the dossiers of Costard, Brunet, and Bailly.

37. Ms. 1042.

38. The first letters from Paris were written by Bosset and Ostervald together and addressed to Madame Bertrand.

39. A document in the notarial archives in the Archives de l'État de Neuchâtel, B654, p. 348, dated November 7, 1777, shows that the STN had purchased the house of Anne-Marie Brun in the rue des Épancheux near Madame Bertrand's house for 1,100 L. plus 336 L. in "étrennes."

40. Madame Bertrand to Bosset, May 7, 1780. Despite this danger, she emphasized, "Il est certain que la réputation de notre maison est bien établie, que notre commerce est très bon s'il est bien conduit et bien fait."

41. The loans were entered in the STN's journals, mss. 1027 and 1028, and also in its balance sheets, ms. 1042.

42. On December 28, 1783, Widow Charmet, who had close relations with the STN, wrote that she had heard of the "crise" in its affairs and reaffirmed her confidence in

it. Her letter suggests that the STN probably had suspended its payments a few days earlier.

43. Unfortunately, gaps in the correspondence and accounts make it impossible to acquire exact information on the STN's collapse, but the dossiers of Pomaret, Rilliet, d'Arnal & Compagnie and of Flournoy fils & Rainaldis provide a rough chronology.

44. Archives d'État, notarial papers B656, p. 59, "Cautionnement de divers concernant la Société typographique," June 2, 1784. The document noted that the "assemblée" of creditors had named *syndics* to evaluate the STN's assets and draw up a balance sheet. Most of the eleven guarantors pledged 36,000 L. in security. The largest pledge, 48,000 L., was made by Jacques Louis Pourtalès, a merchant from a wealthy family of merchant bankers.

45. Ms. 1042.

46. "Mémoire de J. J. Meuron sur la liquidation de la Société typographique de Neuchâtel," May 22, 1823, ms. 1220. In it, Meuron stated that he got this information from "le grand livre que j'ai sauvé d'un galetas de La Rochette où il était enterré dans un tas de paperasses qui y étaient déposés dans un grand désordre."

47. For an account of the following events and full documentation, see the section on Jacques Mallet in my website, robertdarnton.org. Vergennes's order of June 12, 1783, and the surrounding context is discussed in Chapter 1, this volume. The scandal produced by Mirabeau's works and its effect on the book trade was mentioned in several letters to the STN. On August 17, 1783, for example, Mercier wrote to Ostervald from Lyon: "On a saisi au sieur Fauche père des horreurs qu'il voulait introduire avec le *Tableau de Paris*. Ce nom fait grand tort à Neuchâtel. Comme on connaît le sieur Fauche sans délicatesse, on surveille ce qui vient de ce côté-là, et cet homme a nui à votre établissement."

48. On July 21, 1785, the STN noted in its Journal C (ms. 1028, p. 424) a settlement with Moutard for 26,643 L. That sum was reduced to 24,522 L. on December 6, 1785 (ms. 1028, pp. 453–454), and Moutard was to pay it in installments stretching from December 1786 to September 1790. Tractations over the *Description des arts et métiers* appear everywhere in the STN's Copies de lettres and in the letters it received from many of its correspondents. The story of Bertrand's contribution, made in the spirit of eighteenth-century *encyclopédisme*, has been put together by Alain Cernuschi: "'Notre Grande Entreprise des arts': Aspects encyclopédiques de l'édition neuchâteloise de la *Description des arts et métiers*," in *Le Rayonnement d'une maison d'édition dans l'Europe des Lumières*, 184–218.

49. Mercier commissioned the STN to print his *Portraits des rois de France* (he paid for the printing by allotting it 500 copies), and it bought the manuscripts for two of his minor works: *Mon bonnet de nuit* (at a cost of 1,410 L.; it sold well but suffered from the competition of pirated editions printed from copy secretly supplied by the STN's workers) and four of his plays (for 2,000 L.; they did badly on the marketplace, as on the stage).

50. On Lair and Malherbe, see *A Literary Tour de France*, chaps. 10 and 11. On Mauvelain, see "A Clandestine Bookseller in the Provinces," in Darnton, *The Literary Underground of the Old Regime* (Harvard University Press, Cambridge, MA, 1982).

51. Abram David Mercier in a note added to a letter from Ostervald to Bosset of May 21, 1780.

52. Widow Charmet to STN, December 28, 178.

53. Raymond Birn, *Pierre Rousseau and the Philosophes of Bouillon* (Institut et musée Voltaire, Geneva, 1964), 156–161.

54. Jean-Pierre Perret, *Les Imprimeries d'Yverdon au XVIIe et au XVIIIe siècles* (Slatkine, Geneva, 1981), 140; and Raymond Birn, *Forging Rousseau: Print, Commerce and Cultural Manipulation in the Late Enlightenment* (Voltaire Foundation, Oxford, 2001), 193.

Conclusion

1. STN to abbé Reynard, October 14, 1769.

2. See *Luxury in the Eighteenth Century: Debates, Desires and Delectable Goods*, Maxine Berg and Elizabeth Eger, eds. (Palgrave, New York, 2003).

3. In a letter to comte Batthyani in Vienna of May 17, 1777, the STN described itself as "aspirant, par la modicité de nos prix à soustraire le public aux suites du monopole que les privilèges exclusifs occasionnent nécessairement chez les Parisiens."

4. STN to comte Carli-Rubbi in Milan, April 15, 1773.

5. While avoiding *luxe typographique*, the STN prided itself on the quality of its printing. As Mme Bertrand wrote to Ostervald on April 6, 1780, when he was in Paris, "Nous nous sommes toujours picqués de donner ces sortes de contrefaçons mieux imprimées et sur beau papier."

6. STN to J. G. Virchaux in Hamburg, April 13, 1780.

7. STN to Gosse, November 20, 1769.

8. Petit to STN, May 10, 1783. He added: "Ils [the directors of the STN] peuvent être sûrs du débit et de la reconnaissance de ceux qui, plus curieux de la chose que des ornements, ne veulent point être dupes de tout le luxe typographique."

9. Henri to STN, August 21, 1770.

10. Ostervald to STN from Paris, June 8, 1775.

11. The most likely exception to this general statement is Pierre Rousseau, the founder of the Société typographique de Bouillon. His publishing activity developed from his *Journal encyclopédique*, which defended the cause of the Encyclopédistes. Yet two-thirds of the books he published were "innocuous," and he concentrated heavily on the business aspect of his enterprise. See Birn, *Pierre Rousseau*, 201–202.

12. *Oeuvres complètes de Diderot*, Jules Assézat and Maurice Tourneux, eds., vol. 14 (Garnier, Paris, 1876), 463.

13. Quandet de Lachenal to STN, December 4, 1780.

14. Although we lack general statistics about book sales during the last two decades of the Ancien Régime, I have summarized the qualitative and quantitative data about the demand for literature in *A Literary Tour de France*, chap. 13.

15. The following remarks are meant only to put the discussion of publishing during the pre-Revolutionary years into a larger context. They are based on Carla Hesse,

Publishing and Cultural Politics in Revolutionary Paris (University of California Press, Berkeley, 1991); Christine Haynes, *Lost Illusions: The Politics of Publishing in Nineteenth-Century France* (Harvard University Press, Cambridge, MA, 2010); Jean-Yves Mollier, *L'Argent et les lettres: Histoire du capitalisme d'édition, 1880–1920* (Fayard, Paris, 1988); and Jean-Yves Mollier, *Édition, presse et pouvoir en France au XXe siècle* (Fayard, Paris, 2008).

16. The best example is still the work of Ernest Labrousse, *Esquisse du mouvement des prix et des revenus en France au XVIIIe siècle* (Dalloz, Paris, 1932), 2 vols.

17. Perrenod to STN, March 2, 1777, and April 21, 1783. Jarfaut's dossier shows that he ran up a bill for 907 L. for shipments sent from 1776 to 1778.

18. The quotations come in the order at which they appear from the following letters to the STN: Roques, July 24, 1779; Revol, February 16, 1782; Favarger, August 15, 1778; and Grand Lefebvre, June 4, 1781. I have included this material in *Édition et sédition: L'Univers de la littérature clandestine au XVIIIe siècle* (Gallimard, Paris, 1991), 124–125.

19. This book has not dealt with the workers employed by publishers; but when publishers operated printing shops, they did not treat their compositors and pressmen with paternalistic sympathy. The STN eliminated ten of its twelve presses after completing work on the *Encyclopédie*. Ostervald and Bosset, writing from Paris, directed Mme Bertrand in Neuchâtel to dismiss nearly the entire work force. She objected in a letter of February 12, 1780: "On ne saurait mettre sur la rue du jour au lendemain des gens qui ont femme et enfants." But Ostervald and Bosset insisted, and the men were fired.

Index

For the benefit of digital users, indexed terms that span two pages (e.g., 52–53) may, on occasion, appear on only one of those pages.